# Handbook of Current English  **4**

Fourth Edition

Porter G. Perrin

Jim W. Corder
Texas Christian University

**Scott, Foresman and Company**  Glenview, Illinois

Dallas, Tex.  Oakland, N.J.  Palo Alto, Cal.  Tucker, Ga.  Brighton, England

Library of Congress Catalog Card Number: 74-84277
ISBN: 0-673-07922-8
Copyright © 1975, 1968 Scott, Foresman and Company.
Philippines Copyright 1975 Scott, Foresman and Company.
This book was previously published under the title The Perrin-Smith
Handbook of Current English, Copyright © 1962, 1955 by Scott, Foresman and
Company.

Acknowledgments
The sources of quotations used for illustrative purposes are indicated in the
text. Special acknowledgment is due for permission to reprint the following
selections:
From "In Time of Trial" by Barbara Ward from The Atlantic Monthly (February,
1962). Copyright © 1962, by The Atlantic Monthly Company, Boston, Mass. Reprinted by permission of The Atlantic Monthly and the author. From "The Eye
of the Beholder" by Joseph Wood Krutch from The American West (May 1967).
Reprinted by permission of Mrs. Joseph Wood Krutch. From "Coronary Thrombosis" by William A. R. Thompson, M.D., from Today's Health (September 1952),
published by the American Medical Association. Reprinted by permission. From
"A Pontifical Splendor" by Sean O'Faolain from Holiday Magazine (April 1960).
Copyright © 1960, Curtis Publishing Co. Reprinted by permission of Curtis
Brown, Ltd. From I Have a Dream by Martin Luther King, Jr. Copyright © 1963,
by Martin Luther King, Jr. Reprinted by permission of Joan Daves. Entry "ad-
vance." Reprinted by permission of Collins + World Publishing Company from
Webster's New World Dictionary, College Edition. Copyright © 1968 by the
World Publishing Company. From "Onward and Upward with the Arts" by
Jacob Brackman from The New Yorker, June 24, 1967. Reprinted by permission
of David J. Cogan Management Co. From Word, Self, Reality by James E.
Miller, Jr. New York: Dodd, Mead & Co., 1972. From "The Lottery" by Shirley
Jackson. Reprinted with the permission of Farrar, Straus & Giroux, Inc., and
Brandt & Brandt from The Lottery by Shirley Jackson, copyright 1948, 1949 by
Shirley Jackson. "The Lottery" originally appeared in The New Yorker. Entry
"advance." From Funk & Wagnalls Standard College Dictionary. Copyright ©
1973, 1968, 1966, 1963 by Funk & Wagnalls Publishing Company, Inc., with per-
mission of the publisher. From The Angry Decade by Leo Gurko. Copyright
1947 by Leo Gurko. Published by Dodd, Mead & Company. Reprinted by permis-
sion of the author. From Abraham Lincoln: The Prairie Years by Carl Sandburg.
Reprinted by permission of Harcourt Brace Jovanovich, Inc. From "Such, Such
Were the Joys" by George Orwell. Reprinted by permission of Harcourt, Brace,
Jovanovich, Inc., Mrs. Sonia Brownell Orwell and Secker & Warburg, Ltd. Se-
lections from pp. 249–250, 231–232 in Only Yesterday by Frederick Lewis Allen.
Copyright 1931 by Frederick Lewis Allen; renewed 1959 by Agnes Rogers Allen.
By permission of Harper & Row, Publishers, Inc. From "Crossing the Atlantic in
a 13-Foot Sailboat" adapted from Chapter 1 of Tinkerbelle by Robert Manry.
Copyright © 1966 by Robert Manry. Reprinted by permission of Harper & Row,
Publishers, Inc., and Brandt & Brandt. From The Second Tree from the Corner
by E. B. White. Copyright 1954 by E. B. White. Reprinted by permission of Harper
& Row, Publishers, Inc. From Dissenter in a Great Society by William String-
fellow. Copyright © 1966 by William Stringfellow. Reprinted by permission of
Holt, Rinehart and Winston, Inc. From "The Portable Phonograph" by Walter
Van Tilburg Clark from The Watchful Gods and Other Stories. Published by
Random House. Reprinted by permission of International Famous Agency. Copy-
right © 1941, 1969, by Walter Van Tilburg Clark. From "Unnameable Objects,
Unspeakable Crimes" (originally titled: "White Man's Guilt") by James Baldwin
from Ebony (August 1965). Copyright © 1965 by James Baldwin. Reprinted by
permission of the author. From "Nuptials at Tipasa" by Albert Camus from
Lyrical and Critical Essays, translated by Ellen Conroy Kennedy. Copyright ©
1968 by Alfred A. Knopf, Inc., and reprinted with their permission. From Word
Play: What Happens When People Talk by Peter Farb. Copyright © 1973 by Peter

# Preface

*Handbook of Current English* has, from the first edition, been based on Porter G. Perrin's pioneering philosophy of appropriateness in language usage, a principle now almost universally accepted. Recognizing that "good English" need not always be a formal language — contemporary writers and speakers use language in many ways, and to good effect — the *Handbook* shows the importance of being selective in language use. It is designed to show students how and why some forms of expression are more effective and, for college writing, more appropriate than others, and to help them learn to make the best choices. Finally, the *Handbook* is based on the principle that a "good" language is a language decently suited to its speaker or writer, to the subject at hand, and to the audiences that receive the language.

## Content and organization of the *Handbook*

This revision of the *Handbook of Current English* contains new material on writing, and it has been reorganized for the special uses of students in beginning composition courses. It still preserves, however, much of Perrin's plan and most of his philosophy, with some modest and logical extensions and amplifications, and with some alterations made in the light of recent studies of language. None of the changes is fundamentally inconsistent with Professor Perrin's conception of appropriateness in language use. The Introduction, new in this revision, is a discussion of the English language that retains some features from Section 1 of the Third Edition. The discussion includes an account of distinctions between speaking and writing and of some varieties of English and ways they might be used. The Introduction also suggests some ways of moving among varieties of English according to the principle of appropriateness. Some recommendations made throughout the text may be clearer if students read this material at the start of the course. The first parts of the *Handbook* summarize and illustrate the basic principles of current grammar and usage and the various conventions of writing. Whether or not these sections are taught systematically, their content and format make the *Handbook* a reference tool that students can use on their own:

Sections 1–9 review the grammar of English sentences and the functions and uses of various kinds of words and word groups.

Sections 11–17 discuss and illustrate the principles governing the use of punctuation, mechanics, and other conventions, including the use of end stops, commas, and semicolons, as well as various customs for using capital letters, apostrophes, abbreviations, and numbers. The sections on internal punctuation suggest ways in which the choice of punctuation can relate to meaning and effect; the section on spelling suggests ways to overcome various spelling problems.

The sections in this first half of the *Handbook* treat single, definite topics. Grammatical definitions are included where they are relevant and necessary to the discussion rather than in a separate glossary. Similarly, particular matters of usage are discussed at the point where they relate to general principles. In cases of divided usage, suggestions are offered that may be helpful to students as they decide on forms and constructions appropriate to their writing.

The second half of the *Handbook* serves both as a brief rhetoric and as a practical guide to college writing tasks:

Part Two: Practices in Composition

Sections 18–20 include material that in former editions of the *Handbook* was reserved for a later portion of the rhetoric section. Since it is likely that many students will need to start writing early in many of their courses, this material is put at the outset of the rhetoric portion of the *Handbook* for the early and continuing help it may offer. Section 18 discusses ways of exploring the potential of a subject in order to find a real purpose in writing and to find useful connections among the writer, the subject, and the possible audiences; this section also discusses and illustrates some ways of arranging ideas and information in writing. Section 19, on writing the first draft, draws on the rhetoric of sentences and paragraphs to show the practical use of these elements in directing the development of an essay.

Section 20, on revising, suggests ways of altering emphasis, mood, tone, and direction to suit the needs of student writing.

Sections 21–23, on diction, deal with appropriate and effective uses of words.

Sections 24–26, on sentences and paragraphs, discuss means by which these elements of composition can be managed and controlled to shape meaning. These sections show ways of using various sentence patterns and various patterns of paragraph development to develop ideas.

Sections 27–28 return to problems and practices in longer compositions and writing done in certain situations. Section 27 discusses and illustrates some of the possibilities and problems in particular kinds of writing, including exposition, argumentation, description, narration, answers to essay examinations, reports, critiques, literary analyses, and letters. The final section is devoted to the special problems of research writing.

## Exercises

The exercises in this revision of the *Handbook* have been altered considerably. As in earlier editions, exercises at the end of each section reinforce and further develop the points made in the text by giving the students practice in applying what they have learned and by encouraging them to analyze particular writing practices and to use particular methods. Many of the exercises are new; of the older exercises that have been retained, some have been slightly modified. Most of the exercises now call for the students to do some writing themselves, rather than to respond to another person's writing.

For the exercises I am grateful to Professor Robert H. Bentley, of the English faculty at University of Michigan—Flint. With the pressure of a deadline, but with great energy and insight, Professor Bentley prepared most of the exercises for this edition of the *Handbook*. He is co-author of *Black Language Reader* (Scott, Foresman: 1973). He teaches linguistics and is Director of the Writing Laboratory at Flint. He has brought to the exercises a keen understanding of modern practices in composition and of the needs of students. The exercises are both useful complements to the text and valuable instruction in their own right.

## Index and correction chart

A full index provides a quick means of referring to both general and particular points of discussion, and students should find it useful if they use if regularly when they write and revise their papers. The marginal tabs on the text pages, giving both correction symbol and section number, are designed to increase the *Handbook's* usefulness as a reference tool.

Themes can be marked by using either the correction symbols or the section numbers; the two are coordinated in the correction chart at the end of the book as well as on the marginal tabs. In the text itself, correction symbols are printed on color bars together with specific suggestions for revision. Students should study the text that follows each suggestion whenever they are not sure why revision is necessary.

## Design of the book

In this edition, the color used on the marginal tabs has been carried over into the text and is used for all the headings within each section. These color headings will help to make plain the organization of each section, and will make rapid reference easier.

The work of more scholars and teachers than I can name has filtered into this edition of the *Handbook*. I am particularly indebted to the work of E. P. J. Corbett, W. Ross Winterowd, Richard Larson, James Kinneavy, Richard E. Young, Alton L. Becker, and Kenneth L. Pike.

I also wish to thank many of the *Handbook*'s users for valuable suggestions on the revision of the text. I am especially grateful to Robert Bain, Robert H. Bentley, George R. Bramer, Charlotte K. Brooks, Terry Everett, and Vincent A. Lopresti. Ronald Newman, J. Karl Nicholas, Joyce S. Steward, and Gilbert F. Tierney were most helpful in commenting on the revised manuscript. Amanda Clark of Scott, Foresman and Company has been unflagging in her help and unfailing in her patience. I am especially grateful to Richard Welna of Scott, Foresman for his good friendship, wise counsel, and fruitful conversation. His easy but pointed direction has from the first been both happy and necessary. My first gratitude, in this and all other enterprises, is to Patsy Corder.

Jim W. Corder

# Contents

Part One
Resources for Composition: Grammar, Usage, Punctuation, and Some Conventions

**Grammar and Usage**

Grammar
and
usage

Punctuation
and
other
conventions

Composition

Diction

Sentences
and
paragraphs

The
writer's
work

Part Two
Practices in Composition

**Composition**

**Diction**

## The effect of words 23

## Sentences and Paragraphs

## Sentence Length and Economy 24

## Sentence variety, control, and emphasis 25

## Paragraphs 26

## The Writer's Work

# Introduction: The languages we use

*In reading and writing, there are none of those helpful accompaniments we count on in the actual practice of conversing, such as vocal intonation, facial expression, gesture. One of the writer's principal problems is to compensate for these losses, for most people are more convincing in person than on paper. That is why writing has to be learned; that is why books like this one are offered as helps for writers. Somehow the writer has to evoke, out of mere ink marks on paper, a character whose language the reader will trust, enjoy, profit from. — Walker Gibson,* Persona

The title of this book is *Handbook of Current English.* Everyone who uses the book speaks English. But when we speak, we don't all sound alike, and when we write, what we write doesn't always seem similar. Each of us can speak in several different ways. Few of us speak in exactly the same way to a little three-year-old girl who has just fallen down, to a friend our own age, and to a forty-four-year-old English teacher, and yet in each instance we would still claim to be speaking English. Each of us can speak in several ways. In the talk that we hear every day we understand more ways of speaking, and we can read and understand still other ways of speaking in print.

What this seems to suggest is that English isn't one thing, but many things. It is varied; it changes; it is alive and shifting. Some forms of speaking are controversial; some are not. Words such as *whitey, honky, jig, stud, spic,* and *greaser* may create conflict and controversy just by being uttered because they seem to carry heavily weighted value judgments. In any given circle of a society the minority dialects may not easily win approval and may often be viewed with open disapproval, while the majority dialect, since it is associated with school, books, and management, will easily win approval. The verb sequence *she go, she be go, she been go* may among particular hearers be an accurate and systematic accounting of a sequence of actions, but outside that group it may be thought simply another instance of poor usage. What one person says seems strange to another — different in vocabulary, in sound, in tempo, in construction from what he would say. Both, perhaps, sound different from a television announcer whom both of them hear. Yet all three speak English. English comes in many shapes and in many sounds.

We know it long before we study it. Well before school starts we can usually understand sentences that other people utter, even though we may never have heard words in precisely those combinations before. By the time older people will admit that we have learned to talk, we can say sentences that we have never said before and never heard before. We can say sentences long before we know that there are such things as sentences. But even if we know English before we study it, there is ample reason to study it in school and all our lives. It is an agency, a medium, by which we live with ourselves and with each other, by which we can conduct our affairs, whether trivial or important. We need to know what we can about the language and work toward using it wisely and well.

Using a language well is something more than writing "complete" sentences, using correct verb forms, making verbs agree with their subjects and pronouns with their antecedents. Beyond these forms and conventions, using a language well is a matter of choosing from the broad range of our language the words and constructions that will best convey our ideas to a particular audience in a particular situation, that will best enable us to present ourselves fully and honestly to another. But no one can make choices unless choices are available; no one can choose among beans, corn, and broccoli unless beans, corn, and broccoli are on the table for the choosing. To make good choices in language, we must understand something about the versions of English and become sensitive to the various ways English is used in contemporary writing and speaking.

## The elements of language

Basically a language consists of a system of sounds, a collection of words, some changes in word forms, and some patterns into which the words fit to convey meaning. It may or may not have a system of writing and printing.

### Sounds

English has between forty and fifty sounds (about twenty of them vowel sounds and the rest consonant) and variations in pause, pitch, and stress. Each sound is used with slight modifications in actual speech; for example, some people have a full *r* and others a very slight indication of the sound. The pronunciation of words varies considerably among the different regions in which English is used, so that we can easily identify some people as Englishmen, others as Southerners, others as New Englanders.

## Words

Counting everything from slang and local words to rarely used words and limited scientific terms, English has a vocabulary of well over two million words. Many of these are used in several different senses—one dictionary gives forty different meanings for the word *check.* An unabridged dictionary has about 500,000 entries; a college dictionary has about 150,000 entries; a college student probably uses or recognizes over 50,000 basic words, not including derivatives made by adding syllables like *-ed* and *-ly.* English forms many new words by adding prefixes *(in-, anti-, re-, super-)* and suffixes *(-er, -ish, -ship, -teria),* and it makes compounds freely by putting two or more words together *(bookcase, streamlined).*

## Word forms

Some languages are *inflected;* that is, their words change form to express grammatical relations in case, number, gender, person, tense, and the like. Latin and German, for example, are highly inflected. English uses very few changes in word forms: only a few endings, like the *-s* or *-es* of nouns *(boys, churches),* the *-s, -ed, -ing* of verbs *(asks, asked, asking),* -er and -est for comparing adverbs and adjectives *(hotter, hottest; nearer, nearest),* and a few internal changes, like the changes in vowels in *man-men, sing-sang.* These changes in form are one basis for grouping words into parts of speech.

## Constructions

English has two basic ways of combining words into groups: by phrases centered on nouns or their equivalents *(in the morning; crossing the street)* and by clauses centered on verbs *(he runs the forty-yard dash; when she saw the results).* We interpret the meaning of these familiar patterns very largely from the order in which the words stand, an order that we pick up naturally as children and follow almost instinctively. Out of these simple word groups we build sentences of varying length and complexity. The study of the relationships between words and word groups in sentences is *syntax,* the principal division of *grammar.*

## Writing practices

English, which like other languages first developed in speech, is represented in writing and printing by the twenty-six letters of the alphabet, a dozen or so punctuation marks, and devices like capitals and italics. The conventions of spelling, punctuation, capitalization, and the like were developed mostly by printers and serve chiefly to represent the spoken language.

These are the *materials* of language. What we do with them is another matter. This book is about current English, which appears in many forms. It seems clear enough that it is not possible to make a handbook about every one of the ways in which English is used, or even about several ways of using English. The book by and large uses—and from time to time recommends—a kind of standard English, that is, a kind of English you might expect a person to use who has spoken, heard, written, read, and examined English enough to begin to know some of its traditional characteristics and some of the ways it is habitually used in many books, magazines, classrooms, and some public meetings. English doesn't belong to any single speaker or writer, or to any single nation. It has been used elsewhere longer than it has been used in North America, and Australians no doubt make some claim upon it as their language. Another way to describe the standard English referred to above is to say that if you use a standard English, that means you will generally accept the judgments on usage made by many people in many places over a long period of time.

There is good reason to do so. When you talk to other people, you are with them; they can watch your face and your hands and whether you lean toward them or turn coolly away from them and they can know instantly whether you speak softly or boldly. But this book is chiefly about *writing.* When someone else reads what you have written, you can't count on being there. More often than not, you are *not* there. That may mean that you will want or need to give your readers a language whose characteristics you can expect them to understand. You and your readers may not ever be together unless you hold a language in community property. Qualities that a language accumulates in many places over a period of some time are likely to be clearer to readers, more accessible to them, than qualities that belong only to you or to you and a close circle of friends. We'll return a little later to the question of what it means to know that you are not there when a reader reads what you have written.

This book, again, by and large uses and often recommends a kind of standard English. It describes some of the qualities of English words, language patterns, and conventions, and it discusses some of the choices open to us as we try to express our hopes and needs in the language. The remainder of this introductory section is about the range of possibilities available in the English language and about the processes of choosing from among them in your writing.

## Varieties of English usage

Living languages undergo continual growth and change. Ordinarily the changes are slow and barely noticeable — slightly different pronunciations, new shadings in the meaning of words, and gradual shifts in grammatical constructions — but their cumulative effect can be dramatic. The works of Shakespeare, written four centuries ago, present difficulties to the modern reader: many of the words are unfamiliar and the grammar often seems strange. The writings of Chaucer, who lived a few centuries earlier, are hard to read without a large glossary and a grammar guide. Still earlier works, like *Beowulf,* can be understood only by specialists who have studied Old English much as they would study a foreign language. Yet all these works are written in a language that can claim to be called English and have been admired by many generations of readers of English.

Obviously our language has passed through many changes in the course of its history, and it will go on changing from generation to generation. But the language doesn't just change as time passes; at any given moment in its history, it also shows many internal variations. The work and worry and play of everyday life include all kinds of activities and situations, and language, both spoken and written, must serve them all. There are differences in the words and constructions typically used in different kinds of publications, even within a range no wider than that from newspapers to textbooks, and we use different language in writing or speaking to different people and in writing papers for different purposes. If in your writing you needed to say something about an object presented as something that it is not, you might use any one of the following words: *simulated, spurious, fraudulent, counterfeit, imitation, false, sham, pseudo, phony, bogus,* perhaps *put-on.* Which you use depends on a number of things. When you use one of the words, you may not think of it as an act of choice, and it may not be. You may simply use the word that comes as you speak or write, the word you are most accustomed to using, or to hearing. If you do make a deliberate choice, however, the choice depends on many things—who you are, where you live, the people you spend most time with, the audience that will receive what you say or write, how much of your own personal language you are willing to use, and other factors. But you do have some choice among the words in this series, and in most other instances, especially when you write.

Since choices in vocabulary and construction are often available, it seems foolish to place a thoughtless trust in what we already know about language and assume that the way in which we use words is always going to be sufficient. There is no one "right" kind of choice to make; no language should be forced into or kept in a neat mold. Until fairly recently, it was common for students of language to assume that "good" English was fixed, that departure from an inflexible set of rules governing its use was automatically "bad" English. This highly *prescriptive* approach to language study reflected the belief that there was some ideal form of English, orderly and uniform. Students had merely to learn the laws and apply them, just as they would in studying physics or chemistry. Although the prescriptive approach often produced good results, both practical experience and modern linguistic scholarship—called *descriptive* because it studies and describes the language as it *is*—have shown it to be unsound. No single system of conventions and rules can accurately describe a complex, changing language. Whether we like it or not, our language is changing and varied, and because it is, it offers choices.

Understanding and making choices means knowing what some of the varieties are from which to choose. There is no perfect way of describing or listing available and useable languages. *One* way to catch the variety of language is to start with highly personal language, and then see what happens to personal language in groups, in special times, in special places.

## Idiolects

Everyone has a personal language. It may be remarkably different from the language of someone who lives two hundred miles away, or even next door; it may be scarcely distinguishable from another person's language. This personal language can be called an *idiolect.* The word is formed by a combination of two terms, the first of which *(idio)* originally meant something like *personal, separate,* or *one's own;* the second originally comes from a word meaning *to converse.* An idiolect is distinguishable in some way, even if the speaker only occasionally uses words that those around him do not habitually use, or uses words in ways that others do not employ. An idiolect grows out of your own life, and it may change as your life changes. Each of the speakers in the passage that follows begins to be recognizable, even in a few lines. The second speaker's language, in particular, tells something about his age, his location, the manner of life he has led:

Potter looked at his enemy. "I ain't got a gun on me, Scratchy," he said. "Honest, I ain't." He was stiffening and steadying, but yet somewhere at the back of his mind a vision of the Pullman floated: the seagreen figured velvet, the shining brass, silver, and glass, the wood that gleamed as darkly brilliant as the surface of a pool of oil—all the glory of the marriage, the environment of the new estate. "You know I fight when it comes to fighting, Scratchy Wilson; but I ain't got a gun on me. You'll have to do all the shootin' yourself."

His enemy's face went livid. He stepped forward, and lashed his weapon to and from before Potter's chest. "Don't you tell me you ain't got no gun on you, you whelp. Don't tell me no lie like that. There ain't a man in Texas ever seen you without no gun. Don't take me for no kid." His eyes blazed with light, and his throat worked like a pump.— Stephen Crane, "The Bride Comes to Yellow Sky"

The writer in the passage below, however, owns and uses a

different language. It is a language that is both active (some fifteen verbs and a number of nouns or modifiers made from verbs—*spincasting, calling, shielded*) and easy, with familiar pronoun references and pleasantly varied sentences that range from six to fifty-seven words.

Trotlines from shore to shore get you more fish and bigger ones, but they're also more labor. After I'd finished with the line I worked along the beach, spincasting bootlessly for bass. Four Canada geese came diagonally over the river, low, calling, and in a moment I heard a clamor at the head of the island, shielded from me by the island's duned fringe and by willows. I climbed up through them to look. At least 200 more honkers took off screaming from the sand bar at the upper end of the bare plain. The passenger ran barking after them. Calling him back, I squatted beside a drift pile, and in the rose half-light of dusk watched through the field glass as they came wheeling in again, timid but liking the place as I liked it, and settled by tens and twenties at the bar and in the shallows above it where the two channels split.—John Graves, *Goodbye to a River*

An idiolect is not necessarily restrictive. A person who speaks or writes in a personal language can easily understand other languages that he hears and reads, and almost everyone can and regularly does shift from one idiolect into another and then another. It is possible, of course, for a personal language to shut a hearer or reader out, barring comprehension.

## Dialects

When a community of speakers and writers uses idiolects that have much in common in pronunciation, grammar, and vocabulary, the combined idiolects are often referred to as a *dialect*. It is common enough for us to think of a dialect only as a language common to a particular geographical region, but we can use the word to name any gathering of idiolects that have much in common. A dialect is almost like a code: speakers and writers of a dialect can converse with and write to speakers and writers of other languages usually, but they also know the special language of some group or region. Since a dialect is any gathering of languages that have much in common, then it is plain enough that there are many dialects. When Paul Simon wrote and sang that he was "Lookin' for fun and feelin' groovy," his language linked him to some people who used the language in a similar way. When Jerry Rubin wrote, "Young whites are dropping out of white society. We are getting our heads straight, creating new identities," he was using a dialect common to many young people—and sometimes slightly mystifying to their elders—in the 1960's. But dialects occur everywhere; people who grow food in the fields sometimes use distinguishable dialects, to be sure, and so do people who teach the third grade, and so do people whose language is often supposed to be remarkably proper. In the passage that follows, for example, a language is used that belongs to a dialect influenced by religious, psychological, and sociological studies:

How is the humanization of sex impeded? First it is thwarted by the parading of cultural-identity images for the sexually dispossessed, to make money. These images become the tyrant gods of secular society, undercutting its liberation from religion and transforming it into a kind of neotribal culture. Second, the authentic secularization of sex is checkmated by an anxious clinging to the sexual standards of the town, an era so recent and yet so different from ours that simply to transplant its sexual ethos into our situation is to invite hypocrisy of the worst degree.—Harvey Cox, *The Secular Society*

As we will see a little later, this passage, shown here as a kind of dialect, is close to still another kind of language that might be called *professional language*, or *craft language*, or *shoptalk*.

## Regional dialects

There are, of course, many *regional dialects;* some of them are readily recognizable. Migration habits, geographical, botanical, and zoological features, work habits, and other characteristics of a particular region sometimes help to create a language for the region that is easily distinguishable from other dialects. A regional dialect may be marked by special words; people in the Southwest, for example, have more occasion to talk about *canyons* and *mesas* than people in Virginia do, both because of southwestern topography and because of their exposure to Spanish languages. A regional dialect may be marked, too, by characteristic constructions (in the following passage, *she'd 'a' scanted herself*), by pronunciations *(creatur, Squer'ls),* and by words not commonly used elsewhere *(bangeing,* or lounging about):

"Sylvia takes after him," the grandmother continued affectionately, after a moment's pause. "There ain't a foot o' ground she don't know her way over, and the wild creatur's counts her one o' themselves. Squer'ls she'll tame to come an' feed right out o' her hands, and all sorts o' birds. Last winter she got the jay-birds to bangeing here, and I believe she'd 'a' scanted herself of her own meals to have plenty to throw out amongst 'em, if I hadn' kep' watch."—Sarah Orne Jewett, "A White Heron"

## Temporal dialects

Another kind of dialect might be called *temporal.* Language changes faster in some communities than in others; sometimes a person or a group preserves usages or words out of the past while another person or group hurries into acceptance of new words, new usages. Martin Luther King's speech in Washington, D.C., on August 28, 1963, as the passage below will testify, gained a part of its power to move and to exhilarate from its recollection of rhythms, words, and constructions from the King James Bible:

I have a dream that one day every valley shall be exalted, every hill and mountain shall be made low, the rough places will be made plane and crooked places will be made straight, and the glory of the Lord shall be revealed, and all flesh shall see it together.

This is our hope. This is the faith that I go back to the South with. With this faith we will be able to hew out of the mountain of despair a stone of hope. With this faith we will be able to transform the jangling discords of our nation into a beautiful symphony of brotherhood. With this faith we will be able to work together, to pray together, to struggle together, to go to jail together, to stand up for freedom together, knowing that we will be free one day.

## Occupational dialects

We have already mentioned professional languages, craft languages, and shoptalk, all of which might be called *occupational dialects.* A wide range of such dialects is before us a good part of the time. We frequently borrow words from occupations for use in conversation, less frequently for use in writing—for example, *feedback, input, bug, huddle, fade-in, fade-out, close-up,* or *program* (as used with computers). Occupational dialects, of course, would occur most frequently in speech or writing in the discussion of particular occupations and their work, but as the words listed above may suggest, parts of some occupational dialects have come into common use. When this happens, sometimes the parts of dialects that come into common use move into common daily language and after a while no longer call attention to themselves as forms of dialects. But occupational dialects occur in many ways. In professional journals and specialized books, for example, we may expect to find languages that are common to people within given occupations. The passage below, though it appeared in a popular magazine, *The Saturday Review,* depends heavily on a language taken from theological and psychological studies:

> The third dilemma I propose is that our highly vaunted sexual freedom has turned out to be a new form of puritanism. I define puritanism as a state of alienation from the body, separation of emotion from reason, and use of the body as a machine. These were the elements of moralistic puritanism in Victorian times; industrialism expressed these same characteristics of puritanism in economic guise. Our modern sexual attitudes have a new content, namely, full sexual expression, but in the same old puritan form—alienation from the body and feeling, and exploitation of the body as though it were a machine.—Rollo May, "Antidotes for the New Puritanism"

### Public dialects

We hear and read some special languages that we might call *public dialects.* Most of us hear, see, speak, read, and sometimes write words, phrases, and constructions that come from television, magazines, motion pictures, politics, and other forms of public communication. How many people said "At this point in time" instead of "now" during the Watergate hearings in the summer of 1973? How many people, following President Nixon, found themselves saying, "I want to make one thing perfectly clear"? How many people take over the language of Archie Bunker, or of Sanford and Son, or other popular television characters? The public language of television and magazine advertisements is a fantasy language, never quite specific, always full of promise—"This is an unretouched photograph of Bonnie wearing Cornsilk—the makeup that gives you the look of innocence," or "There's a skin cleanser that leaves your skin the way nature intended," or "You're going to be beautiful . . . both of you, in Palm Beach Formals."

### General English

Most of the language you hear or read in a week, however, probably doesn't belong to any one of these dialects, though the *public dialects* are extraordinarily pervasive. If we take into account all of the language you hear or read in a week, from television, classrooms, friends, overheard conversations, radio disc jockeys, newspapers, magazines, and elsewhere, a good part of it doesn't have the distinctive character of personal idiolect, regional dialect, occupational dialect, or even public dialect. Much of it is in that broad range of language so commonly used that it attracts no attention to itself, and of course there are varieties of language within that range. These varieties we might call *general dialects.* In writing, the vocabulary and sentence structure of the general dialects seem natural, and close to those of speech. Punctuation is usually relatively light, and sentences are likely to vary widely in length and complexity.

In the following passage the author talks about his people, the Kiowas, but the language he uses is community property:

Once there was a lot of sound in my grandmother's house, a lot of coming and going, feasting and talk. The summers there were full of excitement and reunion. The Kiowas are a summer people; they abide the cold and keep to themselves, but when the season turns and the land becomes warm and vital they cannot hold still; an old love of going returns upon them. The aged visitors who came to my grandmother's house when I was a child were made of lean and leather, and they bore themselves upright. They wore great black hats and bright ample shirts that shook in the wind. They rubbed fat upon their hair and wound their braids with strips of colored cloth. Some of them painted their faces and carried the scars of old and cherished enmities. They were an old council of warlords, come to remind and be reminded of who they were. Their wives and daughters served them well. The women might indulge themselves; gossip was at once the mark and compensation of their servitude. They made loud and elaborate talk among themselves, full of jest and gesture, fright and false alarm. They went abroad in fringed and flowered shawls, bright beadwork and German silver. They were at home in the kitchen, and they prepared meals that were banquets.—N. Scott Momaday, *The Way to Rainy Mountain*

The general dialects are not limited to transmitting matters of general interest; they will also carry specialized information:

Yet if our agriculture-based life depends on the soil, it is equally true that soil depends on life, its very origins and the maintenance of its true nature being intimately related to living plants and animals. For soil is in part a creation of life, born of a marvelous interaction of life and nonlife long eons ago. The parent materials were gathered together as volcanoes poured them out in fiery streams, as waters running over the bare rocks of the continents wore away even the hardest granite, and as the chisels of frost and ice split and shattered the rocks. Then living things began to work their creative magic and little by little these inert materials became soil. Lichens, the rocks' first covering, aided the process of disintegration by their acid secretions and made a lodging place for other life. Mosses took hold in the little pockets of simple soil—soil formed by crumbling bits of lichens, by the husks of minute insect life, by the debris of a fauna beginning its emergence from the sea. — Rachel Carson, *Silent Spring*

The most common defect in general English is flatness, though this often comes from flat or obvious subject matter as much as from the language. In this passage from a short story the language is a compressed form of what we all might say (except perhaps "the world leaps into proportion"), but it has the quality of feeling that we associate with literature:

The man who expected to be shot lay with his eyes open, staring at the upper left-hand corner of his cell. He was fairly well over his last beating, and they might come for him any time now. There was a yellow stain in the cell corner near the ceiling; he had liked it at first, then disliked it; now he was coming back to liking it again.

He could see it more clearly with his glasses on, but he only put on his glasses for special occasions now — the first thing in the morning, and when they brought the food in, and for interviews with the General. The lenses of the glasses had been cracked in a beating some months before, and it strained his eyes to wear them too long. Fortunately, in his present life he had very few occasions demanding clear vision. But, nevertheless, the accident to his glasses worried him, as it worries all near-sighted people. You put your glasses on the first thing in the morning and the world leaps into proportion; if it does not do so, something is wrong with the world. — Stephen Vincent Benét, "The Blood of the Martyrs," *Thirteen O'Clock*

## Dialect modifications

Most of the English that we hear, read, speak, and write falls within what we have called the *general dialects.* Some versions of language within this range are far more casual and informal than others. Many of us, even if our speech or writing shows no other distinguishing marks (such as our occupation, or the place where we live), use language that is breezy and often uncomplicated; sentences are often short, and words and phrases may be more characteristic of speaking than of writing (*cop, dead pan, iffy, chancy, phony, peeve, whodunit* — such words as these and others we use casually may be tagged as *colloquial* by some dictionaries, which means that they occur more often in speech than in writing).

When we are writing or speaking informally, we're likely to make some use of *slang,* newly made words *(peacenik, hippie, groupie, teenybopper),* or old words with new meanings *(cool, straight, trip, far-out),* or phrases conspicuously overused *(good deal, tell it like it is).* A continual flow of usually short-lived words and phrases comes into the language, for many reasons. Sometimes we want to be different; sometimes we believe that we have to have new words to name new experiences; sometimes we want to separate ourselves from some other group (parents, for example) by acquiring our own language. Some slang proves useful and becomes a part of the general vocabulary.

When we are being informal, we are likely to use a good many *localisms,* words or phrases characteristic of a particular region, taken perhaps from a *regional dialect.* We often use regional names for common things *(coal oil* or *kerosene; fried cake, cruller, fatcake,* or *doughnut; sack, poke,* or *bag),* special names for local occupations *(mule skinner, carhop),* or special names for features of the landscape peculiar to a region *(canyon, coulee, gulley, hogback, arroyo, bayou).* These words sometimes reflect the language of the early settlers of an area, as the Dutch in New York, the Germans in Pennsylvania, the Spanish in the Southwest.

## Edited American English

Many versions of the English language ring around us. No perfect system exists for classifying and naming all of them. The idiolects, dialects, and versions of language mentioned here are examples only. *All of them are versions of spoken English, and most of them can be written effectively.* No one of them is equivalent to what has been called *edited American English. Edited American English* is a version of the language that you may associate with textbooks and classrooms, especially English classrooms. It is an idiolect or dialect that has been modified to produce a uniformity in sound, a consistency with such grammatical standards as have traditionally been taught in English and American schools, and a vocabulary that can be shared by people in different places and different times. Edited American English is produced by a kind of filtering process. Motivations for promoting edited American English as *the* standard English are no doubt mixed, but some motivations are good. In the filtering process, what separates people from each other linguistically is supposed to be trapped and discarded, while what binds people together linguistically is left free for use. Few people speak edited American English; many write it. What we should remember, it seems clear, is that edited American English is another variety of language available to us.

And, for special reasons, the filtering process doesn't end there. There are versions of English still more formal and controlled than edited American English. The *formal variety* of usage, found chiefly in writing, is principally a development from the *general dialects* and still more fully edited, more complex than edited American English. It is more influenced by reading and follows more closely the conventions built up by writers and editors in the past. It usually occurs in discussions of specialized topics and in writing addressed to somewhat limited audiences.

The vocabulary of formal English includes most of the general words but few if any from informal English. Necessarily, formal English uses the specialized vocabulary of the subject matter being discussed; it also may use a good many abstract words. The grammatical constructions tend to be fuller than in general English, and ordinarily the sentences are somewhat longer and more complex. Formal writing tends to follow older practices in punctuation and to use *close* punctuation — more frequent marks than are typical in general English, and heavier ones, such as a semicolon where a comma might serve.

The formal English used in academic, scientific, technical, and scholarly writing is usually impersonal. Good formal writing, however, is not stilted or dull. This account of the mapping of Switzerland shows the single-minded attention to the subject, the compact and orderly statement of ideas, and the moderate use of technical terms that characterize good impersonal formal English:

The heroic task of making a topographic survey and map of Switzerland fell to the lot of General Guillaume Henri Dufour (1787–1875). Under his personal supervision the work was begun in 1830 and the first sheet was published in 1842. Thirty-four years later the entire survey, on a scale of 1:100,000, was finished and the last of the 25 sheets came from the press. Soon after, the map appeared in atlas form, published at Berne. Far from being a pioneering effort that would require immediate revision, the Dufour atlas proved to be a model of accuracy and artistic delineation, not only for future map makers of Switzerland, but for cartographers at large. The sheets of the atlas were used as a basis for later surveys on different scales, and on the sheets of Switzerland's new survey references were made to the corresponding sections and subsections of the original Dufour map. The art work and conventional signs on the new map were almost identical with those on the Dufour originals. The lettering and bench marks (figures denoting heights), prominent buildings, roads, boundaries and forests were printed in black. Small slopes and passes, ravines and narrow defiles that could not be shown by equally spaced contour lines were printed in brown hachures. Black hachures were used to indicate rocky prominences and precipices, the general effect being a pictorial representation by oblique lighting. Horizontal surveys were shown in bronze and water was indicated by shades of blue.—Lloyd A. Brown, *The Story of Maps*

A more personal type of formal English is shown in the following passage. Some of the words and phrases are formal—*inert knowledge, radical error,* and *delicate, receptive, responsive to stimulus.* The constructions are full: note the sentence beginning *Whoever was the originator* and the following sentence, beginning *But whatever its weight of authority.* But some constructions *(I appeal to you, as practical teachers. So far, so good.)* carry an unmistakable personal emphasis and keep us aware that the writer is expressing himself as an individual.

I appeal to you, as practical teachers. With good discipline, it is always possible to pump into the minds of a class a certain quantity of inert knowledge. You take a text-book and make them learn it. So far, so good. The child then knows how to solve a quadratic equation. But what is the point of teaching a child to solve a quadratic equation? There is a traditional answer to this question. It runs thus: The mind is an instrument, you first sharpen it, and then use it; the acquisition of the power of solving a quadratic equation is part of the process of sharpening the mind. Now there is just enough truth in this answer to have made it live through the ages. But for all its half-truth, it embodies a radical error which bids fair to stifle the genius of the modern world. I do not know who was first responsible for this analogy of the mind to a dead instrument. For aught I know, it may have been one of the seven wise men of Greece, or a committee of the whole lot of them. Whoever was the originator, there can be no doubt of the authority which it has acquired by the continuous approval bestowed upon it by eminent persons. But whatever its weight of authority, whatever the high approval it can quote, I have no hesitation in denouncing it as one of the most fatal, erroneous, and dangerous concepts ever introduced into the theory of education. The mind is never passive; it is a perpetual activity, delicate, receptive, responsive to stimulus. You cannot postpone its life until you have sharpened it. Whatever interest attaches to your subject-matter must be evoked here and now; whatever powers you are strengthening in the pupil, must be exercised here and now; whatever possibilities of mental life your teaching should impart, must be exhibited here and now. That is the golden rule of education, and a very difficult rule to follow. — Alfred North Whitehead, *The Aims of Education*

These are some versions of our language — countless idiolects, many dialects, regional, occupational, general, public, edited American English, formal language. Each can be used to move or to inform; each can be warm, generous, and powerful; each can be used with point and precision.

Each can also be used to mislead, to deceive, to betray, to oppress. Just here is a trouble we face with language. Each of the varieties of language we have mentioned can also be a *nonstandard English.* Nonstandard English is not defined by its vocabulary, its sound, or its grammatical construction. Perhaps, instead, we should learn to mark as nonstandard *any* language that violates itself, that fails in its purpose to communicate as effectively as possible. Some languages are *nonhuman* and thus self-violating. If a speaker says to us, "From the beginning of our session together, I want to get you programmed to give me instant feedback," then no matter what his intention is, he is thinking both of himself and of us as objects, electronic machines. When an educator says, "We must get the new students conditioned to the self-paced learning programs," he is, whether he intends to or not, visualizing students as Pavlov's dogs. Some languages are *mean-spirited.* They focus on the speaker, the speaker's interest and kindred, and they exclude others from any magic circle of human communication. Some languages are simply agencies for *falsehood* ("termination with extreme prejudice" substitutes for "execution"). And all of our idiolects, all of our languages, sometimes *fail their own possibilities,* fail to say all that they might say.

A final note on the varieties of English. In the Old Testament account of the building of the tower at Babel by the people who, as the story goes, had all one language, when the people in their vanity had gone too far in their effort to reach heaven, the Lord said, "Let us go down, and there confound their language, that they may not understand one another's speech." The words are among the most ominous ever uttered, yet full of promise. They foretell the scattering of people and the diversification of their languages and all the miseries that come to us because we cannot speak to each other.

## Some versions of American English—A summary

### Spoken language

**Idiolect:** an individual's personal language, influenced by environmental factors (geographical area, occupation) and internal factors (age, sex, personality).

**Dialect:** the combined idiolects of a *community of speakers*. Dialects can overlap, but can be classified by such terms as regional, temporal, occupational, public.

**Dialect modifications:** slang, localisms, fad words.

**General English:** includes the languages above. What might be called the dialect of the great majority of speakers of American English without the strong modifications of other dialectal factors.

### Written language

**Edited American English**
**Informal English:** characterized by short sentences, "breezy" style; includes personal and journalistic writing.

**General English:** characteristic of the constructions and vocabulary of general English, with more attention paid to grammatical conventions; includes most books, magazines, etc.

**Formal English:** characterized by full constructions and specialized vocabulary, it's generally impersonal and found mostly in academic, scientific, technical, scholarly, and other specialized forms of writing.

Sometimes our language is confounded even when we all claim to speak the same tongue. But the words are also rich with promise. A multitude of languages will let people say a multitude of things if they learn to use their languages well and listen generously when others speak their languages. Because there is a multitude of languages, anyone who writes faces a problem: Which language is a "good" language to use?

## Some qualities of good language

A "good" language is not just a gathering of specific practices in vocabulary, grammar, and usage that you must invariably follow. Many languages are available, all equally reputable and, in certain circumstances, all equally "good." The objective in writing is not first to conform to some previously established system of usages, but to use the resources of the language in order to speak fully, precisely, and honestly. Good writing is not born of a system of rules and usages; systems of rules and usages are born of good writing.

A language can enable us to remember our experiences and get them straight in our minds. A language can enable us to put our experiences in order and establish connections between them. A language can enable us to speculate on our experiences and draw conclusions from them. A language can enable us to praise or to blame. As the previous section suggests, many languages, many dialects, are available to serve these purposes, each suitable in particular circumstances. Each of these dialects may have its own distinct structure, and each can be written.

Just there writers encounter a major problem, already mentioned. When we speak to someone, we are there. We can "finish out" what we intend by our words. The tone of voice, the shift of shoulders, the gesture, the movement of eyes or hands—these complement the words. And when we speak to someone, often we can tell if he is comprehending or accepting what we say by his expression; if we sense that he is not, then we have the immediate opportunity to start over, speak in a new way, try a new direction.

But when we write, we are usually not there when someone

reads what we have written. Our meaning and intention rest in the words on the page, and they are sometimes bare and skimpy. Any language we use is incomplete: a language won't let us say two things at once under normal circumstances; when we say one thing, we're *not* saying another; if we acquire the capacity to use a formal language, we risk losing the rich words that name particular local features in a regional dialect. When we write, to complicate the problem, our written words have to be their own validation. We are not there to explain, to modify, to fill in, to shift emphasis. We should, then, expect to give our greatest care to writing, to insure if we can the precision and the fullness of our meaning. Writing is a kind of contract between writer and reader. The writer requires of readers the time they will spend in reading; to do so obliges the writer to give care to the writing. The reader requires of the writer some worth in what is written and owes the writer at least a little curiosity, a little patience, a little willingness to listen. Any language that takes care to insure the precision and fullness of meaning and to promote this bond between reader and writer is likely to be a "good" language.

## An appropriate language

This *Handbook,* however, will customarily recommend what we earlier called edited American English, for several reasons. In the first place, as we have already mentioned, no single handbook can fully describe all the versions of English; it's doubtful that a single handbook could describe *two* versions fully; it's doubtful, indeed, that a single handbook can describe a *single* version of the language fully. Since the book can't describe all, or even some, it sets out to describe and recommend the kind of language that appears most commonly in print, that is the primary medium of communication in most books, newspapers, and magazines. Edited American English is valuable because it is widely used, and it is widely used because it is flexible and will serve many purposes. It is a language suitable to sociological research and to cookbooks, to personal letters and to political commentary. We recommend it, finally, because it is a language we can hold in common, speak, hear, and read in common. Its widespread use in publications and in schools makes it more accessible to more people. The language does not belong to any single person, or to any single group or region. Even when a writer makes a language his or her own, controls it, mixes it with his or her own character, the language can still belong to all of us. Widely used and commonly accessible, edited American English is a language in which we can be together. We have not tried to list the hallmarks or characteristics of edited American English: the rest of this *Handbook* tries to show what edited usage is like. When we say, "Many writers prefer to . . ." or "It's usually best to say . . ." or "Try to avoid . . ." we are recommending a general American English edited for written use.

Any language you use can be a "good" language if it is used appropriately. Edited American English can also be governed by a standard of appropriateness. When you write a language, the choice of vocabulary, usage, and construction is, in a way, not yours alone. The subject you are talking about makes certain demands, and the audience you reach may be expected to have certain expectations and to deserve good treatment. When we make our choices from the range language offers, we must use words in trust and place ourselves in community with others. We cannot use language solely as if it were our private toy. Nor can we use language solely to please others. If we are to use a language well, we must use it so that it is appropriate to us as speakers or writers, appropriate to its audience, appropriate to the particular situation in which we find ourselves.

## Appropriateness to speaker or writer

As a writer, you dominate the writer-reader relationship. Your judgment and sense of fitness control the language you use. Whatever your purpose in writing, express your ideas in language that seems natural to you. Your writing should be an honest expression of your own character. Your language alone is what presents you to a reader; you cannot be everywhere your writing is, and only your language can bring a distant reader and you into any accord. The most fitting language for you is the language that gives you and your ideas fullest expression.

That doesn't mean that you should necessarily rest content

with the idiolect or dialect or language that you already speak. It means, rather, that you ought to make any language you use your own so that you understand it and feel easy using it. One place to start the process of choosing an appropriate language is in your own present language. How well do you understand the way you already speak and write? What is your present language like? Does it have special traits that you can't reasonably expect other people to understand? Are you sure of yourself in spelling, punctuation, sentence structure? When you write a paper for a college course, do you choose the best part of your natural language, or do you assume an entirely different sort of English? If you return to a paper that you wrote some time ago and read it aloud, does it sound at all like something you would or could say? If it doesn't, can you tell what happened to your language in the paper?

In your first papers in a composition course it is often best to write as naturally as you can, so that both you and your instructor can see the present state of your language and know what you need to do next. You don't have to write in the same way that all the other students do. You don't have to write as the instructor or a professional writer would. You don't have to go out of your way to write in a formal style (as students sometimes do, only to end up sounding pompous). Good English is not primarily a matter of rules, but of judgment. You are not struggling under a series of *don'ts* but trying to discover among the wide resources of modern English the language that best suits your purpose, your audience, and yourself. The suggestions and the pressures of teachers or critics may have some brief effect on the way you use language, but in the long run you set your own standard. The language you use is your responsibility.

## Appropriateness to listener or reader

If you are trying to reach particular types of readers, you may have to adjust your subject matter and your manner of expression more or less to their expectations. You have to be more than merely understandable; you may have to meet your readers largely on their own ground. Your readers are as real as you are. If the language you use as right for you is not a language your readers can use and respond to, then your meanings won't reach them. You can enjoy the small, cold comfort of knowing that you are right in what you say, but you probably shouldn't expect applause from readers who can't respond to your language. Meeting your readers on common ground, or on their ground, is not always difficult. You make some adjustments in your language almost automatically in letters, writing in somewhat different ways to different people. Trying to write without knowing who will read the words is difficult and discouraging. In writing a college paper, try to direct it to some particular audience such as the class of which you are a member. This will help you select material that will appeal to a considerable part of the group, and it will help you judge what words and what kinds of sentences are appropriate, and help lead to language that is clear, correct, and interesting.

## Clarity

Since your aim in writing is to communicate, use clear and exact words that your readers will understand. If the subject requires terms that may be unfamiliar, try to make them clear by the way you use them or add a tactful explanation. In a few instances you may have to provide a formal definition. Clarity also calls for sentences that are not too long and that have a natural, direct movement—though you must remember the demands of your subject and situation, as well. Experienced readers can grasp more elaborate sentences than those who read little or read hurriedly. But anyone will be pleased with direct, straightforward sentences.

Careful attention to punctuation is also necessary if you are to make your statements clear to your readers. The various marks—commas, semicolons, and periods—indicate the groups of words that are to be understood as units and often show the relationship between these units. Omissions or misused marks may force a reader to go over a passage two or three times to get its intended meaning; superfluous marks may keep him from grouping words that belong together or may slow the speed of reading to the point of exasperation.

## Correctness

Part of a writer's concern for readers is meeting their expectations in language. This means avoiding careless and elementary errors. Elementary errors may indicate to some readers that you just aren't bothering, that you aren't doing as well as you easily could and should. When you finish writing a paper, take time to check it carefully for errors in spelling, punctuation, and other matters of usage.

Interest

All readers will appreciate some liveliness in what they read, in the writer's expression as well as the choice of material. Too many students seem to feel that serious writing requires a flat and lifeless or a pompous sort of language. In striving for liveliness, you needn't try for novelty or use words that are out of the ordinary; draw on the vocabulary you might use in an intelligent, reasonably animated conversation. Avoid dragging and monotonous sentences; vary their length and pattern so that they suggest an active, alert mind. Attract your readers' interest by making reference, when appropriate, to things people have said and done, and use details to demonstrate your ideas.

One warning is needed: In gearing your writing to your readers' background and expectations, don't underestimate their intelligence, compromising yourself and insulting them. Visualize them at their best and write for them as they are then.

## Appropriateness to purpose and situation

If you are using this book (and it seems reasonable to assume that you are, if you just read that), you are probably in college, and more than likely in a college composition class. The teacher in your composition class may be interested in seeing essays and other forms of writing that you do using a wide variety of languages and methods. Your composition teacher may be glad enough for you to try out your own idiolect, any dialects that you can control, and even some formal language. But many of your other teachers, perhaps all of them, won't be so glad. On the papers that they assign, they will probably expect what we have called edited American English.

The standards of written usage in a composition course are about the same standards that would be expected in similar published material. This means that papers about personal experiences, college activities, your own private reflections, and so on might suitably be in some appropriate variety of general American English or its edited version. It also means that papers required in other college courses, where your writing will usually carry less of your own character and attitudes and will usually focus with greater concentration on an impersonal subject, may have to meet other expectations and be more nearly formal.

This expectation for college writing is not the result of an arbitrary decision that a given variety of language is nicer or more correct than others. When you are able to use a more formal variety of language, you have, by acquiring that ability, won a larger vocabulary for yourself, and probably a wider variety of sentence structures. The vocabulary and structure of formal language are often necessary if you wish to say anything about many academic subjects. Consider a single instance. Suppose that you are in a philosophy course; one of your assignments is to write a critique of a book on philosophy that will include an examination of the author's premises, the mode of his argument, and the style of his presentation. To complete the assignment means, among other things, that you must know what a *critique* is, and that you must command a language that will let you talk about *premises, modes of argument,* and *styles of presentation.*

The rather formal language that will enable you to discuss these things may not, however, be useful in a meditative reminiscence about the time you sat on a mesa at twilight among Comanche ghosts. If you pay attention to purpose and situation, you should be able to treat most subjects in the language they deserve. Inexperienced writers frequently use language that is too heavy to be appropriate to them or to their subjects. For example, a student who wanted to say that he had rebelled against his parents despite having come from a happy home wrote:

Although my domestic environment was permissive and munificent and my sibling relationships were good, I found it necessary to express my generation's mores in reaction to paternal supervision.

The student may seriously have believed that this kind of writing was better than a simple statement. He would almost certainly object to being told that his sentence was bad English, worse perhaps than if it contained some inaccurate or illogical expressions. But inaccuracies can be quite easily corrected, whereas inflated and pompous language must be completely rewritten to be effective. The artificial "formality" of such language is not found in good formal writing, and it should be avoided in student papers.

Once you find the tone that is right for your situation, you should stay with it unless there is some special reason for changing. Although the lines between the varieties of usage cannot be drawn precisely, conspicuous shifts from one to another should ordinarily be avoided, as in the second of these two sentences:

In the distant pines the rising wind whined as it played among the needles. And when the storm broke, the rain came down in buckets.

Superficial consistency is not so important as fundamental appropriateness, but ordinarily one variety of English should be used throughout a piece of writing.

Reading the work of practiced writers is one good way to increase your sensitivity to language and its various uses. Before attempting to write for an unfamiliar situation, read and study some good examples of writing done for a similar purpose. Don't try to write an article for a magazine that you have never read, and don't try to write a technical report or reference paper without ever having seen one. Try to learn what is typically done and follow the accepted practices unless you have a good reason for some other usage.

Some Writing: Voices

1. A mimic specializes in talking in other people's voices. Actually, we all command several different "voices," and experimenting with the language of other people can extend the range of language we can use in our writing.

   Here, for example, is the "voice" of a newspaper reporter:

   COMPANY FACES SEX BIAS CHARGE. (Pahrump, LPI)—The Pahrump department of Civil Rights has filed a sex bias charge against Rabbit Pellet Company of Pahrump.

   The department alleged that the company officials have maintained a "deeply rooted, systematic, and long-standing policy" of discriminating against women seeking executive-level posts with the company.

   The charge is a result of a complaint filed in 1971 by Sharon Allworthy, a secretary with the company for more than 13 years. "Men come to work for the company and work out on the pellet machines for a few years, and then move up the ladder to become foremen or even executives.

   "But a secretary is hired a secretary and stays a secretary, and all the secretaries are women. All of the executives are men," alleged Ms. Allworthy.

   The company's president, George L. Rabbit, denied the charges. "We have never discriminated against women," he told the Journal *today when contacted by phone. "We simply feel that it is unfair to burden a woman with the responsibilities of being an executive when she may have a home to manage as well as a job,"* Rabbit contended. *"Besides,"* he concluded, *"women are happiest when working for men."*

*If the sex bias charge is upheld, the company could be ordered to alter its promotion policies, job descriptions, and pay scales. A court hearing is set for next Tuesday morning.*

The voice of the reporter is neutral, factual. We have no indication of how the reporter *feels* about the situation.

**a.** Now imagine that you are an employee for the company. Write a brief letter (two paragraphs or so) to a friend, explaining what is happening where you work. Be sure to include how you feel about the sex bias charge. You can make up some details if you want.

**b.** Now imagine that you are a lawyer—either for Mr. Rabbit or for the Civil Rights department. Write a brief two-paragraph opening statement for the trial. Be sure to sound as "lawyerish" as possible: formal, educated, and persuasive. Remember that, as a lawyer, your job is to win the case.

**2.** You have probably heard and seen thousands of commercials, and you probably have a pretty good idea of the voice of a commercial. Listen to this commercial:

*MEAT-O-MATIC!!! This amazing little instrument does wonders for mom in the kitchen! It can slice, chip, chop, pound, dice, and cut—all with the turn of a dial! Watch it turn this thick steak into succulent hamburger in moments. See how it thin-slices this bologna for dad's sandwich—isn't it a miracle? Watch it tenderize an entire roast in only 46 seconds—can you believe your eyes? MEAT-O-MATIC has sold nationally for over 22 dollars, but you can have it for only $9.95 if YOU ACT NOW. Send $9.95 to this station by midnight tomorrow for your very own MEAT-O-MATIC. But remember, act now! This offer may never be repeated. That's $9.95 for the unbelievable MEAT-O-MATIC. . . .*

**a.** The voice of this commercial is shrill and urgent. We are used to hearing it in commercials, but it can sound odd in other circumstances. Imagine that your college is engaged in a big campaign to raise money and attract more students. Using the voice above, write a "commercial" for your college.

**b.** Now you are a very well-educated person from an extremely wealthy family. You have excellent taste and breeding, and have never worked a day in your life. Through no fault of your own, the family fortune has been lost, and you are forced to accept a job as a salesperson for Meat-O-Matic. You have too much class to use the shrill voice above, so write out your dignified, rational, and intelligent sales pitch. Make up any details that you want.

**3.** Pick a chapter from one of your textbooks for analysis. Since you will be dealing with a certain level of edited American English from now on, you might just as well consider how it works in some detail.

Consider the following in your rhetorical analysis: is the author young, middle-aged, or old? How can you tell? What is the "voice"? Are there certain words or phrases to which the author is partial? Could you pick the author's writing out of some unidentified writing samples written by different people? How? What is the author's attitude toward you, the reader? Does the author address you directly or keep a more formal distance? Does the author talk down to you, or straight across? Is the author enthusiastic about the subject or neutral or bored? Would you like to have dinner with the author? A friendly conversation?

You might organize your rhetorical analysis as follows: I. Author's attitude toward subject. II. Author's attitude toward audience. III. Author's voice.

# Part One

Resources for Composition

*. . . the right to utter a sentence is one of the very greatest liberties; and we are entitled to little wonder that freedom of utterance should be, in every society, one of the most contentious and ill-defined rights. The liberty to impose this formal unity is a liberty to handle the world, to remake it, if only a little, and to hand it to others in a shape which may influence their actions.* — Richard Weaver, The Ethics of Rhetoric

If a language serves to make communication possible between two people, it does so because both have agreed upon the language and can share it. If a language serves to make communication possible between one person and a group, or between two groups, it does so because both parties have some agreement about the language. If a person speaking or writing to a group uses forms of language that go beyond what the audience can agree upon, then the audience will not understand what the speaker has said. Some of the dialects and forms of general American English will not afford a writer a very large audience or an audience very different from himself or herself. While each of the forms of general American English can be spoken and written effectively, some of them can be agreed upon only by people who share some special commitment, identity, heritage, or geography. Remember that in this book we are recommending (with some variations) edited American English. While no claim can be made that it is inherently "the" right form of English, edited American English is extraordinarily serviceable. Because almost all of the public enterprises of government, education, and business are conducted in this medium, because it is the medium of public communication, this version of English affords the widest boundaries of agreement. More people can agree upon this language and within this language than upon and within any other version of English.

The *sentence* is the primary constructed unit in edited American English and in all other forms of English. Indeed, a sentence form of some kind exists in most, if not all, languages.

What appears to happen in the English sentence form is that two or more kinds of experience are put together so as to make a new kind of statement or experience. You can know what *pants* are and what *tearing* is, but when you read the sentence, "My pants are torn," you can understand it without stopping to think about the separate things, *pants* and *tearing.* The sentence is something new and different from the kinds of experience that it includes. In the common sentence form the two (sometimes more) kinds of experience are stated, usually one as a subject, the other as a verb. Sometimes, however, one or the other or both of the experiences are not stated, but supplied by the context.

He went to town yesterday. [In this sentence, the different kinds of experience or reality included are the person referred to as **He** and the act of **going.**]

Why weren't you there? [In this sentence, the two are the person referred to as **you** and the idea of **being in some place.**]

Please try to be on time. [In this sentence, one is omitted, but since we can understand that the speaker is talking directly to someone, we know that what is left out is **you.**]

Why not? [Here all of the experiences are omitted from the sentence, and we would have to depend on the circumstances in which the words appear to know what the experiences are. They might, for example, be a shortened form of "Why can't I go to town?"]

Good! [Here again we would have to depend on the circumstances in which the word appears to know what the statement is.]

All of these are sentences, though they may look remarkably different from each other. A written sentence is one or more words, punctuated as an independent unit, that say something. A sentence is made complete by its grammatical form and meaning or occasionally, in special circumstances, by the context in which it appears.

In the writing that you will do in college, you will be twisting and turning sentences this way and that to say what you know to say and want to say. It is useful to you in this work to understand different kinds of sentences and what each can do, the insides of sentences and the way the parts fit each other, and the possibilities for altering and controlling your sentences. This section reviews the basic grammatical terms you may need in analyzing and describing sentences and in discussing the relations between the words of which they are composed.

## Main sentence elements                    1.1

Most English sentences are made with a subject and a verb. You may see this pattern referred to as the "major" or "favorite" sentence type in English.

## The subject

The subject (s) of a sentence is a noun or noun equivalent (pronoun, noun clause, gerund, infinitive) that is the starting point of the sentence. The *simple subject* is a single word, like *students* in the first sentence below. The *complete subject* consists of the simple subject plus any words that modify it: *Hurried students*.

     s
Hurried **students** often make careless mistakes. [noun]
 s
**She** runs faster than her brother does. [pronoun]
     s
**What he doesn't know** is that he talks too much. [noun clause]
 s
**Talking** is his only exercise. [gerund]
 s
**To listen** is to suffer. [infinitive]

## The verb

A verb (v) is a word that has forms like *ask, asks, asked, asking* or *sing, sang, sung, singing* and in a sentence agrees with the subject. In the typical sentence the verb follows the subject and, like the subject, is often a nucleus for modifying words. The verb may consist of one or more words:

       s       v
Hurried students often **make** careless mistakes.
 v   s   v
**Does** he **listen** to what she says?
    s       v
Leslie Jones **has driven** for twenty years without getting a ticket.
      s       v
Perhaps the defendant **should be given** the benefit of the doubt.

Participles, gerunds, and infinitives *(taken, taking, to take)* cannot function as full verbs in making sentences. See §4, Verbals, and §8, Verbs.

   The *predicate* is the verb and whatever words are related to it, such as objects, complements, and modifiers. In the following sentences the complete predicate is in boldface type, the verb itself marked with a v:

      s       v
Hurried students **often make careless mistakes.**
    s   v
The doorbell **rang.** [The verb is the complete predicate.]

S       V

After finishing his second year, George **spent two long sessions talking with his advisor about his major.**

## The object

The *direct object* (O) of a verb is a noun or noun equivalent that completes the statement. It answers the question asked by adding "what" or "whom" after the verb. (Hurried students often make what? Careless mistakes.)

       S          V            O
Hurried students often make careless **mistakes.** [noun]
     S         V           O
The Sherwoods have decided **to buy a home.** [infinitive phrase]
 S   V
He wondered **what he should do.** [noun clause]

The *indirect object* (IO) is used with verbs of telling, asking, giving, receiving, and so on. It names the receiver of the message, gift, or whatever, answering the question "to whom or what" or "for whom or what." It comes *before* the direct object.

 S   V        IO               O
He gave the **church** a memorial window.

The same meaning can usually be expressed in a prepositional phrase placed *after* the direct object:

 S   V              O
He gave a memorial window **to the church.**

## The complement

A complement (C) is a noun or an adjective in the predicate which follows a linking verb (LV). In contrast to an object, a complement is related to the subject rather than to the verb, because a linking verb (sometimes called a *copula*) expresses a condition rather than direct action. A noun used as a complement is called a *predicate noun;* an adjective used as a complement is called a *predicate adjective:*

     S      LV           C
Mary Enderby is a skilled **architect.** [predicate noun]
    S      LV        C
The tenor sounded a little **flat.** [predicate adjective]

The most common linking verb is *be* in its various forms: *is, are, was, were, has been, might be.* Other linking verbs include *seem* and *appear* and, in some contexts, *feel, grow, act, look, smell, taste,* and *sound.*

See also §9.2, Predicate adjectives.

## Word order
In English we identify the main sentence elements chiefly by their position in the sentence—by their word order. Although the form of the words is the same, it makes a great deal of difference whether you say "the ball hit the boy" or "the boy hit the ball."

### Typical word order
The typical order of the main elements is subject–verb–object (or subject–linking verb–complement). This is the order in which we make most statements and the means by which we understand them.

In "The class congratulated Rachel" we know through experience that *class* is the subject of *congratulated* because it comes before the verb, and that *Rachel* is the object because it follows the verb. When the verb is in the *passive voice* (a past participle following some form of the verb *be*), the order of sentence elements remains subject–verb: Rachel was congratulated by the class.

So familiar is this order that we recognize it even though the statement itself may be gibberish, or "jabberwocky," as in these lines by Lewis Carroll:

> . . . the slithy toves
> Did gyre and gimble in the wabe. . . .

Whatever the meaning, most people would agree that because of the order of the words, the subject is *toves* and the verbs are *did gyre* and *gimble*.

### Inverted order
The typical order of sentence elements is reversed in questions, exclamations, and emphatic statements:

       V   S     O
**Question:** Have you a minute to spare?

                C           S    LV
**Exclamation:** How wasteful these meetings are!

                  O   S     V
**Emphatic object:** A better job I never had.

In sentences with *there* or *it* as an *anticipating subject* (**AS**), the real subject comes after the verb:

AS LV    C      S
It  is a difficult choice.

Main
sentence
elements
**37**

AS  LV  C    S
There are several reasons for the difficulty.

When the usual order of elements is reversed, you can find the subject of the sentence by locating the verb and then seeing what word answers the question formed by putting "who" or "what" before it. Thus in the expression "A lot he knows about it," *knows* is the verb, and since the answer to "*Who* knows?" is obviously *he, he* (rather than *lot*) is the subject.

## Secondary sentence elements                              **1.2**

In addition to the main sentence elements (subject – verb – object or subject – linking verb – complement), most sentences also contain secondary elements. Secondary elements are typically used as modifiers (M) – they describe, limit, or make more exact the meaning of main elements. The table on page 40 shows the various ways in which modifiers – single words, phrases, and clauses – might be used to qualify or expand a simple statement.

### Adjectives and adverbs as modifiers
Single words used as modifiers are ordinarily related to the element they modify by means of word order. *Adjectives* relate to nouns and usually stand before the words they modify, but sometimes they come immediately after; in both examples, *climb* is the word modified:

       M        M
It was a **slow, dangerous** climb.

                                  M              M
The steepness of the slope made the climb **slow** and **dangerous.**

*Adverbs* are more varied in position because often they relate to the sentence as a whole. However, when they modify a particular word (verb, adjective, or adverb) they usually stand close to it:

          M
They **particularly** wanted to go. [modifies **wanted**]
                                            M
He came home from the movies **quite** late. [modifies **late**]

See §9, Adjectives and adverbs.

## Other words and word groups as modifiers

In English a noun often modifies another noun: *glass* jar, *ski* pants, *dance* hall. Nouns used in this way can be called *modifiers* (not adjectives) or, more exactly, *nouns used attributively.* (See §6.4, Noun modifiers.)

Prepositional phrases function as modifiers in the majority of English sentences:

An apartment-dweller **in a large city** [modifies **apartment-dweller**] can
live **in the same place** [modifies **can live**] **for a year** [modifies **in the same place**] and never speak **to his next-door neighbor.** [modifies **speak**]

Verbal phrases and subordinate clauses also can function as modifiers:

**Finding no one at home,** he scribbled a note and left it under the front door. [participle phrase modifying **he**]

He needed a way **to make money.** [infinitive phrase modifying **way**]

People **who live in glass houses** shouldn't throw stones. [subordinate clause modifying **People**]

## Appositives

An appositive (A) is a noun or noun equivalent placed beside another noun to supplement or complement its meaning. It has the same grammatical function as the noun to which it relates. In speech, it is marked by a pause and a change in pitch:

Your lawyer, **Mr. Jenkins,** is on the telephone.

The story takes place in Thebes, **a city in ancient Greece.**

See §11.3, page 159, Appositives.

## Modifiers of modifiers

Words, phrases, and clauses that modify the main sentence elements may themselves be modified. These expressions are called modifiers of modifiers:

The **local** high-school orchestra played several difficult selections **very** well.

## Modifiers

### Modifiers of the subject

|  | | |
|---|---|---|
| **A word:** | The **local** orchestra played a selection.<br>M S | |
| **A phrase:** | The orchestra, **consisting largely of amateurs,** played a selection.<br>S · · · · M | |
| **A clause:** | The orchestra, **which had practiced hard for several weeks,** played a selection.<br>S · · · · M | |

### Modifiers of the verb

|  | | |
|---|---|---|
| **A word:** | The orchestra played the selection **badly.**<br>V · · · · M | |
| **A phrase:** | The orchestra played the selection **with more enthusiasm than technique.**<br>V · · · · M | |
| **A clause:** | The orchestra played the selection **as if they had never rehearsed together before.**<br>V · · · · M | |

### Modifiers of the object

|  | | |
|---|---|---|
| **A word:** | The orchestra played a **difficult** selection.<br>M O | |
| **A phrase:** | The orchestra played a selection **of old folk tunes.**<br>O · · · · M | |
| **A clause:** | The orchestra played a selection **which no one in the audience had ever heard before.**<br>O · · · · M | |

### Modifiers of the main clause

|  | | |
|---|---|---|
| **A word:** | **Nevertheless,** the orchestra played the selection.<br>M | |
| **A phrase:** | **Considering their lack of experience,** the orchestra played the selection fairly well.<br>M | |
| **A clause:** | **Since there were no other requests,** the orchestra played the selection.<br>M | |

English sentences are constructed of single words, phrases, and clauses. Main (or independent) clauses form the principal grammatical units of sentences; they express completed statements and can stand alone. Phrases and subordinate clauses, on the other hand, are dependent on other sentence elements and are used very much like single words.

## Phrases

Phrases are groups of related words connected to a sentence or to one of the elements in it by means of a preposition or a verbal. A phrase has no subject or predicate and cannot stand alone.

### Prepositional phrases

A prepositional phrase consists of a preposition (*at, from, by, in, of, under,* etc.) followed by a noun or noun equivalent, plus whatever modifiers it may have. It functions like an adjective or adverb, depending on what element it modifies:

He came **from a small town** [modifies the verb **came**] **in northeastern Minnesota** [modifies the noun **town**].

### Verbal phrases

A verbal phrase consists of a participle, gerund, or infinitive (none of which has full verb function) plus its object or complement and modifiers. A participle phrase functions as an adjective; a gerund phrase as a noun; and an infinitive phrase as either a noun, an adjective, or an adverb. (See §4, Verbals.)

Sentences **containing several unrelated ideas** [participle phrase modifying **Sentences**] are seldom effective.
**Containing the enemy** [gerund phrase used as subject] was their first objective.
The easiest way **to understand grammatical construction** [infinitive phrase modifying **way**] is **to analyze your own sentences** [infinitive phrase used as complement].

## Clauses

A *main* (or independent) clause contains a subject and predicate and is the grammatical core of a sentence. In the three sentences below, the main clauses are in bold-face. Each is a complete expression and could stand alone as a sentence:

S   V
**I laughed** because I couldn't help myself.
S   V   O   S   V   O
**She hated English,** but **she needed one more course to graduate.**

s  v          o
If I were you, **I would find a new job.**

A *subordinate* (or dependent) clause also has a subject and a predicate, but it functions as *part* of a sentence. It is related to the main clause by a connecting word that shows its subordinate relationship, either a relative pronoun *(who, which, that)* or a subordinating conjunction (*because, although, since, after, if, when*, etc.):

I laughed **because I couldn't help myself.**

Subordinate clauses are used like nouns (as subjects, objects, or complements), like adjectives (modifying nouns or pronouns), or like adverbs (expressing relationships of time, cause, result, degree, contrast, and so forth). The subordinate clauses are emphasized in the following examples:

He confessed **that he loved me.** [noun clause, object of **confessed**]

Many of the criminals **whose cases crowded the docket each year** were third- or fourth-time offenders. [adjective clause modifying **criminals**]

**After you plant the seeds,** you should water the garden right away. [adverb clause of time]

The peas in his garden were stunted **because he did not water soon enough.** [adverb clause of cause]

See §3, Subordinate clauses and connectives. Some exercises on working with phrases and clauses appear on page 49.

## Sentences classified by clause structure    **1.4**

Sentences may be classified according to the kind and number of clauses they contain as *simple, compound, complex,* or *compound–complex.*

### Simple sentences
A simple sentence contains one independent clause and no subordinate (dependent) clauses:

The man went across the street.

Although simple sentences contain only one clause, they need not be limited to a small, simple idea. They may contain any number of modifiers, and either the subject or the predicate (or both) may be compound:

Someday, with a telescopic lens an acre in extent, we are going to see something not to our liking, some looming shape outside there across the great pond of space. . . . For the first time in four billion years a living creature had contemplated himself and heard with a sudden, unaccountable loneliness, the whisper of the wind in the night reeds. — Loren Eiseley, *The Immense Journey*

Journalism professors, books, editors and reporters often explain news in terms of characteristics or values. — Ivan and Carol Doig, *News: A Consumer's Guide*

Colleges and universities do not exist to impose duties but to reveal choices. — Archibald MacLeish, "Why Do We Teach Poetry," *The Atlantic Monthly*

### Compound sentences

Compound sentences contain two or more main clauses and no subordinate clauses:

The nations of Asia and Africa are moving with jet-like speed toward gaining political independence [first main clause], but we still creep at horse-and-buggy pace toward gaining a cup of coffee at a lunch counter. — Martin Luther King, Jr., "Letter from Birmingham Jail"

Each clause in a compound sentence is independent and is *coordinate* (of equal rank) with the other clauses. The clauses may be joined (or separated) in one of three ways:

### With coordinating conjunctions

Independent clauses are most frequently linked by the coordinating conjunctions *and, but, or, nor, for, yet* or the correlatives *either . . . or, neither . . . nor, both . . . and, not only . . . but (also):*

It rained all morning, **but** it cleared up for the picnic.
**Either** you play to win **or** you don't play at all.

### Without connectives

Independent clauses not joined by coordinating conjunctions are conventionally separated by semicolons:

They are generous-minded; they hate shams and enjoy being indignant about them; they are valuable social reformers; they have no notion of confining books to a library shelf. — E. M. Forster, *Aspects of the Novel*

### With conjunctive adverbs

The clauses in a compound sentence are sometimes linked by a conjunctive adverb such as *accordingly, also, consequently, however, nevertheless, therefore, then*. However, the connective function of these adverbs is weak, and a semicolon should be used before them:

The urban renewal program has many outspoken opponents; **nevertheless,** some land has already been cleared.

See §12.1, Semicolons.

## Complex sentences

A complex sentence consists of one main clause and one or more subordinate clauses:

As far as I could determine [subordinate clause], Paris hadn't changed at all [main clause] since I last visited it ten years before [second subordinate clause].

In published writing today, complex sentences are used far more frequently than the other three types are. Often, as many as half of the sentences in a particular piece of writing are complex. Complex sentences offer more variety than simple sentences do; it is often possible, for example, to shift subordinate clauses around in the sentence in order to get different emphases or different rhythms. Look at the example above again. It could be changed in various ways, keeping essentially the same words but changing the emphasis: *Since I last visited Paris ten years ago* [subordinate clause], *it hadn't changed at all* [main clause], *as far as I could determine* [second subordinate clause]. Or, *Paris hadn't changed at all* [main clause], *as far as I could determine* [subordinate clause], *since I last visited it ten years ago* [second subordinate clause]. The tone changes slightly in these examples: in the first example the idea emphasized is that Paris hadn't changed at all; the second sentence emphasizes the visit ten years before; and the third places more doubt on the idea of Paris not changing because *as far as I could determine* gets heavier emphasis. And complex sentences are often more precise than compound sentences are: a compound sentence treats two ideas equally, while a complex sentence establishes a more exact relationship.

## Compound-complex sentences

A compound–complex sentence contains two or more main clauses and one or more subordinate clauses:

When two men fight a duel [first subordinate clause], the matter is trivial [first main clause], but when 200 million people fight 200 million people [second subordinate clause], the matter is serious [second main clause]. Bertrand Russell, *The Impact of Science on Society*

Compound–complex sentences occur very seldom in English because they are likely to sound awkward.

Some Study and Writing: Clauses into Sentences appears on page 50.

## Sentences classified by purpose          1.5

Sentences are conventionally classified by meaning or purpose as follows:

*Statements* (often called *declarative sentences*):

Jim laughed.
Most of the sentences we speak and write are declarative.

*Questions:*

At what temperature does water boil?
Why do you ask?

*Commands* (including requests and instructions):

Write soon.
When the liquid boils, remove it from the heat.

*Exclamations* (feelings, facts, or opinions expressed in an emphatic way):

How lucky you are!
He should be thrown out!

## Minor sentence types          1.6

While the great majority of written sentences contain both subjects and verbs, some do not. In speech, we may express ourselves by a single word ("Yes." "Oh?"), a phrase ("In a minute."), or a clause ("If you say so."). Similarly, we occasionally find single words, phrases, and subordinate clauses as sentences in published material:

And so on to Bangkok. Spit and hiss of water, the gramaphone quiet. The lights out along the deck, nobody about.—Graham Greene, *The Shipwrecked*

We do not have to supply any "missing" words to get the author's meaning (such as "And so *the ship sailed* on to Bangkok."). Such statements are meaningful and complete as they stand. But they are minor types, exceptions to the typical English sentence with subject and predicate. When they appear in print, they are used deliberately and for a special purpose (for dialog, for emphasis, or to avoid colorless or repetitious verbs).

## Subjectless sentences

Commands and requests generally do not have subjects:

Don't let me hear you say that again.
Please try.

The subject is sometimes omitted in informal writing (seldom in serious writing) when it is easily carried over from the preceding sentence by the context:

They took no interest in civilized ways. Hadn't heard of them, probably. — Clarence Day, *Life with Father*

## Verbless sentences

Several types of sentences without a main verb are used in all levels of speaking and writing. The verbs are not left out; they are not thought, spoken, or written. The statements are complete and independent without them.

### Exclamations

*Ouch!, Oh!,* and similar words make complete exclamations, as do such phrases as *What luck!* and *How terrible!*

### Answers to questions

Short answers without a main verb *(Yes. No. Not if I can help it.)* are considered complete sentences. Occasionally a writer may use a verbless construction to answer a question he has raised himself:

What is a hero? **The exceptional individual.** How is he recognized, whether in life or in books? **By the degree of interest he arouses in the spectator or the reader.** — W. H. Auden, *The Enchaféd Flood*

### Descriptive details

In fiction especially, descriptive details are sometimes set off for emphasis or to avoid colorless verbs like *is, are, has:*

I was watching a bunch of men hold their fingers to their lips and shush each other to keep quiet. **Every one of them haw-hawing and tittering under their breath and pointing to a kid asleep on the floor.** He was about twenty. **Little white cap from the ten-cent store, a pair of old blue washed-out pants, shirt to match, a set of dirty heels caked over with the dust of many railroads, and a run-over pair of low-cut shoes.** He was hugging his bed roll and moving his lips against the wool blanket. I saw him dig his toes in the dust and kiss the bundle. — Woody Guthrie, *Bound for Glory*

## Thought movement

To convey the speed and pattern of mental activity, verbs are often omitted in passages portraying a character's thought:

Getaway, no chances tonight. Down the fire escape to the next floor. No light. Another window open. Taking candy from a baby. — John Dos Passos, *Manhattan Transfer*

## Appositional sentences

A phrase that stresses the meaning of the preceding statement or looks forward to the next one is sometimes written as a complete sentence:

So much for the contemplative aspect of a man's place in a scientific cosmos. I come now to the practical aspect. — Bertrand Russell, *The Impact of Science on Society*

**Some Writing and Practice with the Grammar of the Sentence (for §1.1–1.2)**

Let's begin by admitting that you already know English grammar. You could not understand the words you are now reading if you did not, nor could you talk nor understand English speech if you did not (at least subconsciously) possess the rules which dictate word order in English. The popular name for these rules is "grammar." Another, more formal, term is "syntax."

The terror that many students feel when they come to study grammar is really unnecessary, as mostly you are simply learning names for the processes that you employ every day when you read, write, speak, or listen. This section of the book that you have just read is designed to give you some grammatical terms which will be helpful to you as you discuss your writing with your instructor and/or you read more about effective writing.

As this part of this book explains, spoken language is often quite different from formal written representations of it. It is helpful if you master some of the formal terms which will be used if your writing strays beyond the bounds of acceptable grammar in edited American English.

One way to accomplish this is by tapping the knowledge you already have about English grammar.

1. Subjects
   Pick five different words, each of which will fit in the blank, and make a sentence:

          s     v

   a. The old _____ walks slowly up the hill.
   Each of the five words you picked is a *noun,* and each is also the *subject* of the sentence. If you didn't know English grammar, you could not supply those missing words like *woman, duck, man,* etc.

2. Verbs and Predicates
   Finish the following sentences in *one* word (you must make a sentence):

   s
   **a.** The fish _____.

   s
   **b.** The woman _____.

   s
   **c.** The ice _____.

   The one-word sentence-stoppers are all *verbs;* here, they are also predicates.

   Supply words which will finish each of the following sentences:

   s                    O
   **d.** The boy _____ the cake.

   s                    O
   **e.** The man _____ the dog.

   s                    O
   **f.** The author _____ the book.

   These verbs can't stop sentences; instead, they *transfer* something from the *subject* to the *object* (also a noun or nouns). Verbs which transfer are called "transitive," and verbs which can stop sentences without an object are called "intransitive."

3. Sentence-Stretching: Adjectives
   Sentences are something like rubber bands. They can be very short (*Birds fly.*), but they can also be stretched wide to encompass large amounts of meaning.

   One way sentences are stretched is by use of adjectives. This is one kind of *modification.* To see how this works, find *one* word which will fit *both* of the blanks below and still make some sense:

   M                    M
   **a.** The _____ baker is very _____.

   You will find that words such as *happy* and *tired* fill these adjective blanks, while a word like *two* is unacceptable (*The two baker is very two* doesn't make sense). Now try two more:

   **b.** The _____ dog is rather _____.

   **c.** The _____ man is very _____.

   This test will often help you tell whether a word is an adjective. Notice that this adjective slot is *reduplicative;* that is, you can keep piling the adjectives up:

                                    M
                    M             grubby
   The *grubby old* man is very old.

                                        M
           M     M     M              tired
   The *tired, dirty, drunken* man is very dirty.
                                      drunken

   You can go on, almost forever, stretching the sentence with adjectives. Fill in the blanks below to create a sentence:

<pre>     M     M     M              S      V       O</pre>
**d.** The ___ ___ ___ circus performer gobbles the fire from the blazing torch.

**4.** More Sentence-Stretching

Of course piling up adjectives is only one way in which sentences are expanded. No one would want to read or listen to those kinds of sentences for very long. Consider the sentence-expanding below:

<pre>     S   V</pre>
The girl sang.

<pre>                        S</pre>
The delicately beautiful girl, made even more attractive by her ner-
<pre>     V</pre>
vousness, sang so sweetly that every person in the audience hoped she would win the contest.

Here a simple three-word sentence is transformed into a twenty-six word sentence by using a variety of grammatical rules. You can do the same thing. Expand the following sentences to at least twelve words each.

**a.** Birds chirp.
**b.** The cake tastes good.
**c.** The car runs.

**5.** Analysis: Naming the Parts

You should be ready now to firm up your control over the basic sentence grammar terms presented in this section of the book. Find five sentences of ten to thirty words each in a book or magazine and analyze them in terms of subjects, verbs, objects, complements, modifiers, etc. Keep this book handy so that you can look up the tricky items. If something is beyond the scope of the presentations thus far, put a question mark over it.

**Some Work with Phrases and Clauses (§1.3)**

**1.** Remember that a phrase does *not* contain the basic sentence elements of subject and predicate. Phrases and clauses serve as powerful sentence-expanders which can make a sentence more descriptive and explicit. These sentence elements are precisely ordered by the rules of English grammar. Adverbial phrases and clauses, for example, may be ordered like this:

Sentence (subject + verb) + adverbial phrase or clause of location + adv. of manner + adv. of time + adv. of reason.

Thus, we could have

Sentence — She walked
adv., location — up the hill (phrase)
adv., manner — very slowly (phrase)
adv., time — at five o'clock (phrase)
adv., reason — because she was so tired (clause).

Now write a sentence based on these models:
a. Sentence (subject + verb) + adv. location + adv. manner + adv. time + adv. reason. Now notice that you can "hop over" some rules.
b. Sentence + location + manner.
c. Sentence + manner + reason.
d. Sentence + location + time.
   Elements can also be moved around to create different effects and vary the patterns still further:

    (REASON)      (SENTENCE)  (MANNER)
Because she was so tired, she walked very slowly.

Try writing sentences based on these models:
e. Reason + sentence + manner.
f. Time + sentence + location.

## Study and Writing: Clauses into Sentences (§1.4)

Your instructor may at times note that you should, in your writing, vary your sentence structure. This usually means that you have fallen into a pattern of writing the same sentence type over and over—a sure way to put your reader to sleep.

1. To improve your control over longer sentences, try combining these short sentences into single sentences by reducing some to phrases or subordinate clauses. Switch the parts around in any way necessary to create sentences.
a. People do learn and think. Sometimes a man cannot think for himself. He cannot go beyond the ideas of others. He is enslaved by their ideas.
b. We learn from painful experience. Freedom is never voluntarily given by the oppressor. It must be demanded. The oppressed have to demand it.
c. The wind died. It was sunset. The night was clear. Its wisp of moon was not out yet. There were stars. It was still. I found myself resenting the fire's snapping sound.

2. To be sure that you understand the various sentence types introduced in this section, write one sentence on each model below. An example of each model is given for you to refer to, but be sure to write your own sentences or the exercise will be meaningless.
a. Compound: Main clause, + conjunction (yet, and, or, nor, but, for) + main clause.
   He was happy, and he was successful.
b. Complex: Subordinate clause, + main clause.
   Because he was successful, he was happy.
c. Compound-Complex: Subordinate clause, + main clause, + conjunction + main clause. Because he had a positive outlook, he was happy, and he was successful.

Except for misspelled words, which sooner or later will attract someone's attention, probably the three most conspicuous errors in sentence construction are fragmentary sentences, comma faults, and fused sentences.

A *fragmentary sentence* is an incomplete statement — a phrase or a subordinate clause — punctuated as a complete sentence, as in this example:

**Fragment:** The two girls built a tree house in the old oak. **Because they felt they needed a secret place where they could get away from their families for a while.**

**Possible revision:** The two girls built a tree house in the old oak because they felt they needed a secret place where they could get away from their families for a while.

**Possible revision:** Because they felt they needed a secret place where they could get away from their families for a while, the two girls built a tree house in the old oak.

A *comma fault* occurs when two sentences that are distinctly separate have been put together in a sentence with only a comma separating them. A comma isn't a strong enough signal for the reader to know that a complete statement is on either side. A comma is a signal for slowing, hesitating; between two complete statements the reader needs a signal to break or come to a full stop.

**Comma fault:** The war provided the setting for many novels, three of them were especially outstanding.

**Possible revision:** The war provided the setting for many novels. Three of them were especially outstanding.

**Possible revision:** The war provided the setting for many novels, three of which were especially outstanding.

**Possible revision:** The war provided the setting for many novels, including three that were especially outstanding.

A *fused sentence* occurs when two sentences have been run together with no separating punctuation at all:

**Fused sentence:** The war provided the setting for many novels three of them were especially outstanding. [This could be revised as the comma fault was revised.]

These three faults are common, but if they occur often in your writing they are considered serious because they suggest either that you are not recognizing and distinguishing between separate complete statements, or that you are not checking your writing carefully.

## Fragmentary sentences

> **Frag** Correction: Revise the fragment marked by joining it to another sentence, by making it into a complete sentence, or by rewriting the passage.

Fragmentary sentences occur frequently in our speech, and they often make good enough sense there, as responses to what someone else has said, for example, or as additions to what we have already said. A coach might say to his players in practice, "Let's take a ten-minute break to get these last two plays straight. And to give you a chance to catch your breath." His players would probably have no difficulty in understanding him even though the latter statement is a fragment. But they are listening to him and watching him and can tell that while he was talking about the two plays he saw their tongues hanging out. As a consequence, he adds the fragment. When you write something down, however, you can't give it extra gestures and tone; a reader has only the written words as a guide to your meaning. A fragmentary sentence is likely to be a fragmentary idea that needs to be finished or added to another idea.

A sentence fragment can be corrected in various ways—by joining it to another sentence, by supplying a subject and a predicate, or by rewriting the passage in which it occurs, as shown below. (See § 1.6, Minor sentence types, for a discussion about the occasional effective use of fragmentary sentences.)

### Joining a fragment to another sentence
A fragmentary sentence usually should be part of the preceding sentence. If you read the passage aloud, you will notice that you pause only slightly before the sentence fragment and do not drop your voice as noticeably as you do at the end of complete sentences. This means that the fragment should be joined to the preceding sentence, usually with a comma. Sometimes it should also be rephrased.

| Sentence fragment | Revised |
|---|---|
| The next afternoon we made our way through the harbor of Okinawa. **That island, which had made history during World War II.** | The next afternoon we made our way through the harbor of Okinawa, the island which had made history during World War II. |

*Phrases* are subordinate sentence elements and should not be punctuated as complete sentences:

| Sentence fragment | Revised |
|---|---|
| I cite these examples to show you how interesting accounting can be. **And to give you an idea of the kind of problems an accountant has to solve.** [infinitive phrase] | I cite these examples to show you how interesting accounting can be and to give you an idea of the kind of problems an accountant has to solve. |
| For the past five years I have been contributing a small amount annually to the March of Dimes. **Without ever suspecting that one day a member of my own family might benefit from this foundation.** [prepositional phrase] | For the past five years I have been contributing a small amount annually to the March of Dimes, without ever suspecting that one day a member of my own family might benefit from this foundation. |
| Professor Brown suddenly glanced up from his notes. **His eyes twinkling with suppressed laughter.** [**Twinkling** is a participle, not a full verb.] | Professor Brown suddenly glanced up from his notes, his eyes twinkling with suppressed laughter. |

*Explanatory phrases* beginning with *such as, for example, that is, namely,* and similar expressions often belong in the same sentence as the statement they explain:

| Sentence fragment | Revised |
|---|---|
| Their mother had a hard time cooking for them because they disliked so many foods. **For example, squash, sweet potatoes, beets, okra, cabbage, apricots, and peaches.** | Their mother had a hard time cooking for them because they disliked so many foods, for example, squash, sweet potatoes, beets, okra, cabbage, apricots, and peaches. |

*Subordinate clauses* are only parts of sentences and should not stand alone without definite reason. A relative pronoun *(who, which, that)* or a subordinating conjunction (such as *although, because, if, when, while*) indicates that what follows is a subordinate clause and that it should be combined with a main clause.

| **Sentence fragment** | **Revised** |
|---|---|
| At the time, my old rowboat with its three-horsepower motor seemed a high-speed job to me. **Although it only attained a speed of about twelve miles an hour.** [adverb clause, beginning with **Although**] | At the time, my old rowboat with its three-horsepower motor seemed a high-speed job to me, although it only attained a speed of about twelve miles an hour. |
| The whole area is honeycombed by caves. **Many of which are still unexplored.** [adjective clause, introduced by **which**] | The whole area is honeycombed by caves, many of which are still unexplored. |

## Making a fragment into a sentence

If the fragment deserves special emphasis, it can be made into a sentence by inserting a subject and a predicate:

| **Sentence fragment** | **Revised** |
|---|---|
| He talked for fifty minutes without taking his eyes off his notes. **Apparently not noticing that half the class was asleep.** [**Noticing** is a participle, not a verb.] | He talked for fifty minutes without taking his eyes off his notes. Apparently he did not notice that half the class was asleep. [The subject is **he**; the predicate is the verb **did notice** plus the words related to it.] |
| National elections and student elections may be compared as closely as an object and its photograph. **The only difference being in size.** [**Being** is a participle, not a verb.] | National elections and student elections may be compared as closely as an object and its photograph. The only difference is in size. [**Is** is the verb, and **difference** is the subject.] |

## Rewriting a fragment

Sometimes involved or hopelessly snarled sentence fragments have to be completely revised. The following long "sentence" has three phrases that seem to be subjects, but there is no verb:

| **Sentence fragment** | **Revised** |
|---|---|
| **The people** who only said, "Oh, too bad," on seeing the lifeless puppy, **the small boy** who removed the dead puppy from the gutter, and the **middle-aged man** who kept saying that people were making a greater fuss about this incident than had been made over his own accident at this same corner a year ago, when he was almost run over by a taxi. | When the small boy removed the dead puppy from the gutter, some people only said, "Oh, too bad." But the middle-aged man kept saying that people were making a greater fuss about this incident than they had made over his own accident at this same corner a year ago, when he was almost run over by a taxi. |

**CF** Correction: Change the comma marked to a period or semicolon or revise the passage to make an acceptable sentence or sentences.

A comma fault (sometimes called a *comma splice* is two or more independent clauses not joined by a coordinating conjunction and written with only a comma between them. The result is that one clause is simply backed up against the other:

The card catalog is the key to the books in the library, many large libraries have separate catalogs for certain collections of books.

Each of the two clauses joined here is a main clause that could stand alone as a simple sentence. The clauses should be separated by a period or joined into a compound sentence by a semicolon or an appropriate connective.

If you understand clause structure and are aware of when you use clauses, your writing probably won't have many comma faults. If you make this error often, review §1.4, Sentences classified by clause structure. You may also find it helpful to read your papers aloud. If your voice drops or if you pause noticeably at a comma, check the sentence to see if it is actually two independent statements. For example, read this sentence aloud to see how much more marked the pause is at the comma following *past* (a comma fault) than at the comma following *five-thirty:*

The long shopping days of Front and Market streets are a thing of the past, the stores now open for business at ten in the morning and close at five-thirty, including Saturdays.

The marked pause indicates that there are two separate statements here; a new sentence should begin after *past*.

## Making two sentences

A comma fault may be removed by using a period instead of the comma, making two full sentences:

| **Comma fault** | **Repunctuated** |
|---|---|
| He took a couple of steps, stopped, reached out, and turned a valve, as he did so he told us the valves had to be checked daily. | He took a couple of steps, stopped, reached out, and turned a valve. As he did so, he told us the valves had to be checked daily. |

This is usually the best solution when the ideas are clearly distinct or when there are many commas in either or both statements. However, correcting a comma fault by putting a period between two very short, closely connected statements may result only in two weak sentences:

I opened the door noisily, he didn't move. [Here joining the clauses by **but** is preferable to making each a separate sentence.]

## Using a semicolon

Comma faults may sometimes be corrected by substituting a semicolon for the comma. This is appropriate when the ideas expressed in the two clauses are closely related:

| Comma fault | Repunctuated |
|---|---|
| Charley then crossed the room and threw a switch which started the motor, returning, he wiped the sweat from his forehead with the back of his hand. | Charley then crossed the room and threw a switch which started the motor; returning, he wiped the sweat from his forehead with the back of his hand. |

A great many comma faults in student papers occur with "conjunctive" adverbs (such as *accordingly, consequently, however, therefore*). When such adverbs appear at the junction of two independent clauses, the conventional punctuation is a semicolon. Although such words show the connection between ideas in the clauses, their connective function is weak.

| Comma fault | Repunctuated |
|---|---|
| The person with a college education has training far beyond that which can be obtained solely from books, **therefore** his or her chances for success may be greater than are those of a person without this education. | The person with a college education has training far beyond that which can be obtained solely from books; therefore his or her chances for success may be greater than are those of a person without this education. |

Other uses of adverbs like *however* and *therefore* are discussed on page 170.

## Revising the passage

Usually the best way to remove a comma fault is to revise the sentence, using a connective that will show the relation between the statements. The connective may be a coordinating conjunction (such as *and* or *but*), a subordinating conjunction *(although, because, if, since, when . . .),* or a relative pronoun *(who, which, that . . .)* referring to a noun in the first statement. Sometimes one statement can be revised as a phrase, as in the third example:

**Comma fault**

It is a personal matter, everyone has to cope with it sooner or later.

I enjoy being in the midst of a party, particularly if I feel some responsibility for its success, conversation is a stimulant more powerful than drugs.

Many companies are looking for experts in pollution control, this is a rapidly expanding field.

**Revised**

It is a personal matter **that** everyone has to cope with sooner or later.

I enjoy being in the midst of a party, particularly if I feel some responsibility for its success, **because** conversation is a stimulant more powerful than drugs.

Many companies are looking for experts in pollution control, a rapidly expanding field.

There are many ways of correcting comma faults. The method of revision you choose probably ought to depend as much as possible upon what you are trying to do in the passage where the fault occurs. Look at the comma fault we mentioned earlier:

The war provided the setting for many novels, three of them were especially outstanding.

Suppose this occurs in the opening paragraph of a paper in which you intend to review a number of war novels very briefly and then focus at some length on three that you think are outstanding. You might revise the sentence as shown below to show that the review of several novels is less significant in the paper than the close study of three:

While the war provided the setting for many novels, three of them were especially outstanding.

If you intend in your paper to give equal time and attention to the review of several novels and to the close study of three, you might revise the fault in this way:

The war provided the setting for many novels. Three of them were especially outstanding.

If the review of a number of novels is what is most important in your paper, and the three novels are simply being used as examples, then you might revise in this way:

The war provided the setting for many novels, including three that were especially outstanding.

**FS** Correction: Use a period or semicolon between the two statements, or revise the passage to make an acceptable sentence or sentences.

A fused sentence is the same kind of error as a comma fault, except that no punctuation at all appears between the main clauses. It should be corrected in the same way as a comma fault: making two sentences of the fused sentence; using a semicolon to separate the two parts; or rewriting the passage.

**Fused sentence**
Two volumes of this work are now completed the first will be published next year.

**Possible revisions**
Two volumes of this work are now completed. The first will be published next year.

Two volumes of this work are now completed, the first **of which** will be published next year.

## Mixed constructions **2.4**

**Mix** Correction: Revise the mixed construction to make an acceptable sentence or sentences.

When several sentence faults are combined or when a construction is not one of the standard sentence types, the result is sometimes called a mixed construction. Repunctuating cannot correct errors of this kind; the whole passage must be rewritten into acceptable sentence units.

**Mixed construction**
I had always admired his novels, and when I had a chance to meet him, a real delight. [independent and subordinate clauses improperly joined by **and**]

**Possible revision**
I had always admired his novels and was delighted when I had a chance to meet him.

Charles was a hard worker, but I wondered how was he going to get everything finished on time? [shift from statement to question]

Although Charles was a hard worker, I wondered how he could finish everything on time.

| | |
|---|---|
| Of course the Haitian diet is quite different from ours, this is obvious consisting largely of beans and rice. [a comma fault and a misplaced modifying phrase] | Of course the Haitian diet, consisting largely of beans and rice, is quite different from ours. |

Since mixed constructions usually involve a combination of errors, their variety is almost infinite. The only sure way to avoid them is to be sure you understand the principles of sentence construction.

**Applications: Fragments, Comma Faults, and Fused Sentences**

1. Advertisements often use sentence fragments for directness and brevity. As you have just learned, these constructions are usually not appropriate in more formal writing. Turn the following series of sentence fragments into normal sentences.

   a. Hartley Wine. Not for kids. Feel tall. Feel cool. Paris, Rome — from your bar stool or couch. Mellow. Meant for lovers. And adventurers. Hartley Wine.
   Here is another ad, written out in sentences. Turn this into fragmentary advertising copy. This should help you be more aware of the differences between sentences and fragments.

   b. Turtle eggs are both delicious and good for you. When boiled, they are delicious in salads; when they are fried, their lovely lemony yolks contrast with bacon and toast. Turtle eggs are always plentiful and a good buy at the price. You should have turtle eggs for breakfast, lunch, or dinner every day. A day without a turtle egg is like a zoo without an aardvark.

2. As you have just read, fragments and comma faults often turn out to be merely punctuation problems. Follow these models and repair the sentences below:

   *frag.:* The angry boy kicked the professional boxer on the shin. Which was a mistake. [change the period to a comma and make the *W* lower case]
   *comma fault:* The Braves traded Hank Aaron, it was a big mistake. [change the comma to a period or semicolon or rewrite the sentence]

   a. I'd like to own a bigger car. Although I don't think I could afford the gas.
   b. I'd like to own a bigger car, I don't think I could afford the gas.
   c. She likes quiet hobbies. Like collecting string.
   d. Abraham Lincoln said, "Never argue with the newspapers, they always have the last word."
   e. Bricklayers were hired on a contingency basis, that is, they weren't paid until the building was finished.

3. The fused sentence is the opposite of a comma fault, but it is still often just a punctuation problem. Follow the model below and repair the fused sentences.

*fused:* She passed the math test easily there were three more tests left.

*revised:* She passed the math test easily. There were three more tests left.

*or:* She passed the math test easily; now there were three more tests left.

**a.** The birds began to sing it was late in the afternoon.

**b.** The steak was very expensive lots of prices have been going up lately.

**c.** "What is the purpose in this?" he asked he did not believe in fraternity initiations.

4. You can sharpen your "sentence sense" by looking through magazine ads for fragments and rewriting them. You can also reduce comma faults and fused sentences by careful proofreading after you have finished a paper. Check some of your previous writing for these common mistakes; rewrite the sentences correctly for practice.

# Subordinate clauses and connectives 3

A subordinate clause has a subject and a predicate, but it is shown to be an incomplete statement—a subordinate part of the sentence—by a special kind of connective that relates it to the main clause. In the following sentence, *when* and *that* are the connectives; *few people thought* is the main clause:

**When Truman ran for re-election in 1948,** few people thought **that he could win.**

Subordinate (dependent) clauses are used in sentences as modifiers, subjects, objects, or complements. Depending on the grammatical function they serve, they are classified as adjective clauses (§3.1), adverb clauses (§3.2), or noun clauses (§3.3).

About half the sentences in most kinds of writing contain one or more subordinate clauses, for subordination shows the relationship between ideas much more exactly than a series of simple or compound sentences. Effective use of subordinate clauses is discussed at the end of this section. For a further discussion of subordination, see §25.2, Subordination to control and clarify meaning.

## Adjective clauses 3.1

A clause that modifies a noun or pronoun is an adjective clause. The relative pronouns *who, which,* and *that* (p. 102) are the words most frequently used to introduce adjective clauses; these pronouns also serve as subjects or objects within the clause:

Some people **who buy modern paintings** are interested in them more as investments than as art. [**Who** is the subject of the clause, which modifies **people.**]

The goals **for which he had fought all his life** no longer seemed important to him. [**Which** is the object of the preposition **for;** the clause modifies **goals.**]

Many books **that are commercially successful** often do not qualify as serious literature. [**That** is the subject of the clause, which modifies books.]

He received a letter from an uncle **whom he had not seen for twenty years.** [**Whom** is the object of the verb **had seen;** the clause modifies **uncle.**]

Adjective clauses may also be introduced by the relative adverbs *when, where,* and *why:*

It was a day **when everything went wrong.** [The clause modifies **day.**]

She returned to the town **where she had lived as a girl.** [The clause modifies **town.**]

The reason **why these early settlements disappeared** has never been explained satisfactorily. [The clause modifies **reason.**]

See §11.3 for a discussion of adjective clauses as restrictive and nonrestrictive modifiers.

### Clauses without relative words

Sometimes an adjective clause is a restrictive modifier, a modifier that is essential to the sentence because it limits the meaning. In this case, the relative word is often omitted, especially when the following word is a pronoun or proper name:

The only books [that] Alice read in high school were those [that] her teacher assigned.

He is a person [whom] everyone admires.

These clauses without relatives (they are still subordinate clauses) have long been used in English and are acceptable in all varieties of writing.

### *and which*

*And* is sometimes needlessly used between an adjective clause and the rest of a sentence. The relative pronoun *who, which,* or *that* is the only connective needed; the use of *and* or *but* is superfluous and defeats the subordination:

| Careless | Revised |
|---|---|
| The sea anemone is a fascinating creature **and which** looks more like a plant than an animal. | The sea anemone is a fascinating creature which looks more like a plant than an animal. |

## Adverb clauses   **3.2**

A subordinate clause that modifies a verb, adjective, adverb, or a main clause is an adverb clause. It usually expresses a relationship of time, place, direction, cause, effect, condition, manner, or concession:

He lived abroad for three years but returned to the United States **when war broke out.** [The clause modifies the verb **returned.**]

During her husband's absence she managed the business better **than he had.** [The clause modifies the adverb **better.**]

He becomes very stubborn **when he meets opposition.** [The clause modifies the predicate adjective **stubborn.**]

**Because she was a woman of principle,** even her opponents respected her. [The clause modifies the main statement, **even her opponents respected her.**]

English has many connectives for expressing these adverb relationships. The following are among the most common:

| | | | |
|---|---|---|---|
| after | because | since | unless |
| although | before | so | until |
| as | if | so that | when |
| as if | in order that | though | where |
| as long as | provided that | till | while |

See also §3.4, page 66, Using exact connectives.

## Noun clauses     **3.3**

Because they function as nouns, subordinate clauses used as subjects, objects, complements, and appositives are called noun clauses. Most noun clauses are introduced by *that,* but *whatever, whoever, who, what, why, when, where,* and *whether* are also used.

### As objects
Noun clauses are most frequently used as direct objects:

The President said **that his meeting with the Arab heads of state had been fruitful.**

No one knows **why these early settlements disappeared.**

They wondered **what would happen next.**

Noun clauses also serve as objects of prepositions:

From **what you have told me,** I think he is making more money than he deserves.

There is a prize for **whoever gets there first.**

In the last sentence, *whoever* is the correct form rather than *whomever* because the pronoun is the subject of the clause.

## As appositives

Noun clauses are quite often used as appositives:

Most people still accept the myth **that progress is inevitable.**
The fact **that he might lose** never occurred to him.

## As subjects

Sentences beginning with a subject clause introduced by *that* or *whether* sometimes seem rather stilted, especially if the clause is relatively long. In most kinds of writing, constructions of this kind can more easily appear *after* the verb:

**Stilted**
**That he could raise his grade by studying harder** had never occurred to him.

**Whether or not we should revise our foreign policy** was the principal topic of discussion.

**Revised**
It had never occurred to him **that he could raise his grade by studying harder.**

The principal topic of discussion was **whether or not we should revise our foreign policy.**

Subject clauses introduced by other words are common in all levels of writing:

**Whatever is worth doing at all** is worth doing well.
**Where he disappeared** is a matter of conjecture.

## As complements

Noun clauses sometimes occur as complements, particularly in definitions and explanations. Such constructions are often awkward, however, and it is often better to substitute a different wording:

**Awkward**
A common belief is **that toads cause warts.**

**Better**
It is commonly believed that toads cause warts. *Or:* It is a common belief that toads cause warts.

Usually the winner is **whoever has the most endurance.**

The person with the most endurance usually wins. *Or:* Whoever has the most endurance usually wins.

Our materialism is **why some Europeans criticize us.**

Some Europeans criticize us for our materialism. *Or:* Our materialism is criticized by some Europeans.

A thermostat is **what controls temperature.**

A thermostat is a device for controlling temperature. *Or:* Temperature is controlled by a thermostat.

After "The reason *is* (or *was*) . . . " the preferred connective in formal and general writing is *that* rather than *because* (*because* means "the reason that"):

The reason he lost the election was **that** [preferable to **because**] he lacked organized support.

## Subordination for exact statement    **3.4**

> **Sub** Correction: Show the intended relationship between ideas by using appropriate subordination, or correct the faulty subordination.

Ideas that deserve equal emphasis should be grammatically coordinate (as in *My son is in high school and my daughter is in college*). But an important part of writing is discriminating among ideas that do *not* deserve equal emphasis. Statements that describe or explain another statement or tell how, when, where, or why something happened should be expressed in subordinate constructions whenever the relationship is not immediately clear from context. For example, there is no reason why three separate sentences should be made of these obviously related ideas:

Mozart made his first trip to Italy in 1769. He was thirteen years old. His father went with him.

If the first statement is the one the writer wants to emphasize, the others could be subordinated in this way:

In 1769, **when he was thirteen years old** [subordinate clause], Mozart made his first trip to Italy [main clause], **accompanied by his father** [verbal phrase].

### Showing the relative importance of ideas

A subordinate clause usually indicates that the matter subordinated is less important to the subject being discussed than the main statement. To judge the rightness of subordination it is necessary to know what the emphasis of the passage is. For instance, in joining the two statements "The lightning struck the barn" and "Mother was setting the table for supper," the first would be the main statement in a general account of the event:

The lightning struck the barn [main clause] just as Mother was setting the table for supper [subordinate clause].

But if the point to be emphasized is what Mother was doing when the lightning struck, the sentence would probably be written:

When the lightning struck the barn [subordinate clause], Mother was setting the table for supper.

The paragraph would then probably go on to tell what Mother did in the crisis.

In revising sentences, then, it is important to see that the parts are related according to their relative importance.

## Using exact connectives

Subordinate clauses are exact because their connectives show a precise and specific relationship to the main clause. Coordinating conjunctions, especially *and,* are much less definite in meaning than adverb connectives like *because, since, when, while* or the adjective connectives *who, which, that:*

| **Coordinate statement** | **One statement subordinated** |
|---|---|
| Sandra was waiting for the bus and she saw a purse on the sidewalk. | **While she was waiting for the bus,** Sandra saw a purse on the sidewalk. |
| "I, Too, Sing America" is one of Langston Hughes' best-known poems, and it has been reprinted in many textbooks. | "I, Too, Sing America," **which is one of Langston Hughes' best-known poems,** has been reprinted in many textbooks. |

In speaking we tend to rely on only a few of the conjunctions available for expressing adverb relationships (see §3.2), but in writing greater exactness is required. Particular care should be taken so that the common conjunctions *as* and *so* are not overused.

*as*

The conjunction *as* may introduce various kinds of adverb clauses:

Degree or manner: I went as fast **as I could go.**
Time: Our guests arrived **as the clock struck nine.**
Cause: **As it was getting dark,** we made for home.
Comparison: Lettuce is not as fattening **as avocados are.**
Attendant circumstance: **As the fire spread,** the sky grew darker.

The variety of its meanings makes *as* a word to be watched in writing. In some instances it is the proper and only connective to use—to express comparisons, for example (We went as far *as the others did*), or in clauses of manner (*As Maine goes,* so goes the nation). But in many other constructions, *while, when, since,* or *because* would be more exact and emphatic:

**While** [not **as**] we were walking, he told us stories.
The war was almost over **when** [not **as**] he was drafted.

*As* is especially weak in the sense of *because.* To introduce clauses of reason, purpose, or result, *since* or *because* is better in most writing:

He refused to join in the square dancing **because** [not **as**] he was afraid of making a fool of himself.

*so*

Like *as,* the word *so* (or *and so*) is an overworked and often inexact connective. In most writing it should be replaced by a more definite word:

| Inexact | Revised |
|---|---|
| She couldn't find a job, **so** she decided to go to summer school. | **Since** she couldn't find a job, she decided to go to summer school. |
| He was new to the neighborhood, **so** he had few friends. | **Because** he was new to the neighborhood, he had few friends. |

In clauses of purpose, *so that* is usually preferable to *so:*

He went to New York **so that** [not **so**] he could find a job in publishing.

## Faulty subordination     3.5

Faulty subordination is no more effective than excessive coordination. It usually results from a careless stringing together of ideas as they happen to come into the writer's mind. Consider, for example, the haphazard use of dependent constructions in the following sentence:

Because her mother died when Barbara was five years old, and since her father lived a solitary life, Barbara had a very unhappy childhood, having no family to confide in.

The elements in this cluttered statement might be rearranged to establish a better sense of order and proportion:

Barbara had a very unhappy childhood. She was five years old when her mother died, and since her father led a solitary life, she had no family to confide in.

When you go over the first draft of your papers, revise any

subordinate elements that weaken your sentences or obscure their meaning.

## Tandem subordination

It is usually best to avoid statements in which a series of dependent clauses are strung together, one after another. Too many clauses beginning with similar connectives *(who, which, that; when, since, because)*, each built upon the preceding one, are called tandem subordination, or "house-that-Jack-built" constructions:

| **Tandem subordination** | **Revised** |
|---|---|
| He had carefully selected teachers **who** taught classes **that** had a slant **that** was specifically directed toward students **who** intended to go into business. | He had carefully selected teachers who specifically slanted their courses toward students intending to go into business. |
| The recordings **which** I bought last week were scarce items **that** are essential to people **who** are making collections of folk music **which** comes from Spain. | Last week I bought some scarce recordings that are essential to collectors of Spanish folk music. |

Sentences that begin and end with the same kind of subordinate clauses are awkward because of their seesaw effect:

**When** he came home from work, Dad would always complain **when** the children weren't there to meet him.

Such constructions can be improved by changing one of the connectives. Usually it is possible to choose a connective that is more exact:

When he came home from work, Dad would always complain **if** the children weren't there to meet him.

## Inverted subordination

Putting the main idea of a sentence in a subordinate clause or phrase ("inverting" the proper relationship between statements) may result in an awkward or incongruous statement:

| **Inverted** | **More accurate** |
|---|---|
| She was eighteen when her hands were severely burned, which meant that she had to give up her dream of becoming a concert pianist. | When she was eighteen, [main clause:] **her hands were severely burned.** As a result, [main clause:] **she had to give up her dream of becoming a concert pianist.** |

Inverted or "upside-down" subordination frequently occurs in sentences that trail off into weak participle phrases:

The road was blocked, **causing us to make a twenty-mile detour.**

Such sentences can be improved by putting the less important statement in an adverb clause:

We had to make a twenty-mile detour **because the road was blocked.**

### Applications: Practice with Subordination

**1.** The pairs of sentences below can be turned into single sentences using the key word provided in parentheses:

*ex.: (who)* Some people attend church every Sunday to be seen. They are more interested in appearances than in religion.
*revised:* Some people *who* attend church every Sunday to be seen are more interested in appearances than in religion.

**a.** *(which)* The hamster is a handsome animal. It looks like a bundle of fur.
**b.** *(because)* He was a strong man. He was feared and admired.
**c.** *(because)* The rain has fallen for two days. It has washed the bridge away.
**d.** *(who)* Those delegates are not here yet. They attended a big party last night.
**e.** *(when)* He was fourteen years old. He began to shave.

**2.** The following paragraph consists of simple sentences. Rewrite it, using a subordinate clause or two in each sentence.

The man approached quietly. The millionaire sat in front of the fire. He was reading a book. He did not hear anything. The man's fingers grasped the millionaire's throat. The millionaire struggled. The lights came on suddenly. A voice said, "Stop him!" It was Inspector Hanson. The police stopped the attempted murder. The millionaire said he was all right. The man went to jail. He had tried to murder the millionaire. He served ten years in jail. The end.

**3.** The following paragraph suffers from faulty and excessive subordination. Decide what statements deserve the most emphasis and rewrite the passage so that the relationship between main and secondary ideas is clear.

Everyone who has studied the Bible has found some book that appeals to the sense which he has of life and that appeals to the sense which he has of great literary style. For the man who feels that he is confounded by the bewildering multiplicity of life which he finds everywhere, the book of Genesis is likely to have great appeal as it conveys a massive but simple unity which characterizes creation. Its aura of awesome mystery is what causes the book of Job to appeal to the man who is oppressed by the scientific rationalism which characterizes the modern world. The book of Matthew is able to release in the cold man great reserves of emotion and the reason is because it sets forth with such moving humility the trials and character of Christ.

# Verbals 4

Because *verbals* are forms of *verbs,* you can sometimes confuse the two. *Verbs* (see §8) are often described as finite. *Verbals,* which are discussed in this section, are described as nonfinite. It may help to get the distinction clear if we note differences between finite and nonfinite forms.

If we say, "Joe went to the movie this afternoon," or "Joe went to the movie yesterday," the verb *went* (a form of *go*) is finite. That means that we can tell from the form of the verb that the action took place at a particular time in the past. The verb is *finite;* it is limited, for this form can only be used to record past action. If we say, "Joe will go to the movie tomorrow," the verb *will go* is finite; the form can only be used to tell of future action. Other forms of *verbs* are finite in similar ways.

*Verbals* are not limited in this way; for that reason we can say that they are nonfinite. We can say, "Joe has always liked to go to the movies" (in past time), or "Joe likes to go to the movies" (present time), or "Joe will always like to go to the movies" (future time). In each instance the infinitive *to go* keeps the same form because it is nonfinite. The gerund *going* is nonfinite also; it can be used in any time reference:

**Going** to the movies was his favorite entertainment when he was young. [Past time]

He likes **going** to the movies more than any other entertainment. [Present time]

He will enjoy **going** to the movies when he is too old for anything else. [Future time]

The participle *going* can also be used in any time reference:

Joe has always been a **movie-going** nut [past time]; he may be the city's number-one **movie-going** fan [present time].

*Verbals* are nonfinite verb forms that are used in sentences as nouns (subjects, objects, complements) or modifiers. They have many qualities of verbs; they can show tense and take objects, for example, but they cannot serve as full, finite verbs to make sentences or clauses. In many sentences, however, verbal phrases function very much like subordinate clauses in showing the relationship between main and subordinate ideas:

**When she graduated from college,** she went to New York in search of a job. [subordinate clause]

**Having graduated from college,** she went to New York in search of a job. [verbal phrase, modifying **she**]

Verbals are classified by form and function as (1) infinitives *(to ask, to buy),* which can serve either as nouns or as modifiers; (2) participles *(asking, asked, buying, bought),* which modify nouns and pronouns; and (3) gerunds *(asking, buying),* which are verbal nouns. Although the present participle and the gerund are identical in form, they can be distinguished by the way they are used in sentences, the participle as a modifier (a *dancing* figure) and the gerund as a noun (*dancing* takes skill). The forms and principal uses of verbals are illustrated in the table on page 74. See also §8, Verbs.

## Verbal phrases      **4.1**

Like full verbs, verbals can take objects, complements, and adverbial modifiers. In some constructions they also take a subject, if the meaning of that term is stretched a little.

**Slowly weaving her way from twig to twig,** the spider built her nest. [**way** is the direct object of the participle **weaving,** which is modified by the adverb **slowly; way** is modified by the prepositional phrase **from twig to twig;** the entire participial phrase modifies **spider,** the subject of the sentence]

He avoided the accident by **running his car onto the shoulder of the road.** [**car** is the direct object of the gerund **running,** which is modified by the phrase **onto the shoulder of the road;** the verbal phrase is the object of the preposition **by**]

She wanted **to be an architect or industrial designer.** [**architect** and **designer** are complements of the infinitive **to be;** the verbal phrase serves as object of the verb **wanted**]

### Subjects with infinitives

An infinitive phrase often has an expressed subject:

He wanted **the whole department** [subject of the infinitive] **to be reorganized.**

If the subject of an infinitive is a pronoun, it is in the object form:

They asked **him** [subject of the infinitive] **to be chairman.**
Their mother told **them** [subject of the infinitive] **to behave.**

## Subjects with gerunds

When a noun or pronoun precedes a gerund, serving as its "subject," some questions of usage arise: sometimes the genitive (possessive) form is used, sometimes the common form. The writer must depend partly on the sound in choosing the form that seems more natural, but the following principles should serve as guides:

1) When the subject of a gerund is a personal pronoun or a proper noun, the genitive form is generally used:

The less said about **his** singing, the better.
They insisted on **Bob's** playing the piano.

2) When the subject is a plural noun, the common form is usually preferred:

The manager disapproves of **people** smoking in meetings.
The staff will not tolerate **visitors** coming and going at will.

3) If the subject is abstract, the common form is used:

It was a case of **panic** getting the upper hand.
There is a danger of the **temperature** dropping suddenly.

4) When the subject is modified by other words, the common form is used:

There was something suspicious about the **daughter** of the sponsor winning the $10,000 prize.
At the outbreak of the Civil War no one in Washington foresaw the possibility of **Grant,** who had failed in so many undertakings, leading the Union forces.

5) When the subject is stressed, the common form is usually preferred with nouns and the object form with pronouns:

Did you hear about the **mayor** being arrested for speeding?
I can't imagine **him** winning an award.

6) With other noun forms, usage is divided. If you are writing something that needs to be formal, it is usually best to use the possessive form, but the common form of the noun is widely used in general English:

**Formal:** The neighbors complained about the **dog's** barking at night.
**General:** The neighbors complained about the **dog** barking at night.
**Formal:** Jones worried about his **secretary's** taking another job.
**General:** Jones worried about his **secretary** taking another job.

Sometimes we say things in a particular way, not because it is grammatically proper, but simply because it is a way of speaking or writing that has for a long time been customary. When we say that we *put up with* something, the expression doesn't make much sense grammatically, but we know that it means *tolerate* because it is an *idiom,* a customary way of speaking, that we are familiar with.

 Some expressions are regularly completed by infinitives (privileged *to attend*), others by gerunds (the privilege *of attending*). When one form is substituted for the other, the result is an unidiomatic construction: for example, "eager *to join*" is a standard idiom, but "eager *of joining*" is not. Here are typical expressions, some that call for a gerund, others for an infinitive. You will find others in your dictionary under the key (main) word of the construction.

| Gerund | Infinitive |
|---|---|
| cannot help going | compelled to do |
| capable of working | able to work |
| skilled in writing | the desire to write |
| the habit of giving | the tendency to give |
| successful in getting | manage to get |
| ignore saying | neglect to say |
| my object in paying | my obligation to pay |
| satisfaction of doing | satisfying to do |

With many words, especially common ones, either a gerund or an infinitive is idiomatic: a way *of doing* it, a way *to do* it.

## *the* and *of* in gerund phrases
Gerunds are more direct when they are not preceded by *the* and when they are completed by a direct object rather than an *of* phrase:

**Awkward:** In **the** revising **of** the first draft, the writer should check his spelling.

**Direct:** In revising the first draft, the writer should check his spelling.

## *to* with infinitives
Most infinitive constructions are introduced by *to,* "the sign of the infinitive":

She needed time **to think.** They hoped **to get** home before dark. His efforts **to be promoted** failed.

# Forms and uses of verbals

## Infinitives

An infinitive is (1) the base form of a verb (with or without *to*) or (2) any verb phrase that can be used with *to* to function in a sentence as a noun, an adjective, or an adverb.

| Forms: | Active | Passive |
|---|---|---|
| **Present** | (to) ask, (to) be asking | (to) be asked |
| **Past** | (to) have asked, (to) have been asking | (to) have been asked |

**Principal uses:**

**Subject:** *To be called* to the principal's office makes little boys nervous.

**Object:** He does not like *to express his opinion.*

**Modifier (adjective):** I have plenty of work *to do.* (Modifies *work*)

**Modifier (adverbial):** The students came *to learn Russian.* (Modifies *came*)

**Absolute phrase modifying the main clause:** *To tell the truth,* she is a bore.

## Participles

A participle is a verb form, typically ending in *-ing* or *-ed*, used as a modifier.

| Forms: | Active | Passive |
|---|---|---|
| **Present** | asking | being asked |
| **Past** | having asked | asked, having been asked |

**Principal uses:**

**Modifier of a noun:** a *smiling* candidate; a *clogged* drain

**Participial phrase modifying a noun:** The candidate *getting a majority of the votes* will be nominated.

**Absolute phrase modifying the main clause:** *Everything considered,* a portable typewriter seems the most practical gift.

## Gerunds

A gerund is a verb form, typically ending in *-ing* or *-ed*, used as a noun.

| Forms: | Active | Passive |
|---|---|---|
| **Present** | asking | being asked |
| **Past** | having asked | having been asked |

**Principal uses:**

**Gerund as subject:** *Having been asked* made him happy.

**Gerund phrase as subject:** *Taking anthropology* opened a whole new field.

**Gerund as object:** She taught *dancing.*

**Gerund as complement:** Seeing is *believing.* (*Seeing* is also a gerund.)

**Gerund as a modifier of a noun:** the *dining* room, a *fishing* boat

**Gerund as appositive:** He had only one hobby, *collecting stamps.*

*To* is not used, however, after auxiliary verbs *(can, may, must, shall, will)*:

I can **see**. You must **try** it. We may **go** to Europe next fall.

With a few verbs *(do, dare, help, need,* etc.) usage varies:

I did **see** him. It did me good **to see** him.
I helped him [**to**] **learn** to drive.

## Split infinitives

If an adverb comes between *to* and an infinitive (I don't want *to ever see* him again) the phrase is called a *split infinitive*. A writer should avoid split infinitives that are obviously awkward or that call undue attention to themselves:

| **Awkward** | **Better** |
|---|---|
| I will not describe the circumstances of our meeting, or even attempt **to** physically **describe** her. | I will not describe the circumstances of our meeting, or even attempt **to describe** her physically. |
| After a while I was able **to,** although not very accurately, **distinguish** the good customers from the sulky ones. | After a while I was able **to distinguish** — although not very accurately — the good customers from the sulky ones. |

But constructions of this sort are not always awkward. When the normal position of the adverb is after the word *to,* a split infinitive is standard usage (The receptionist asked them *to please sit* down). Putting the adverb modifier immediately before or after the infinitive would be unnatural or misleading in some statements:

**Unnatural:** Autumn is the time **really to see** Europe.
**Better:** Autumn is the time **to really see** Europe.

## Misrelated Modifiers                    **4.3**

> **MM** Correction: Revise the sentence so that the expression marked is clearly related to the word or statement that it modifies.

Verbals, either as single words or in phrases, are most often used as modifiers of individual words:

I first noticed him **sitting alone in a corner.** [present participle, modifying **him**]

The town hall, **completely renovated four years ago,** always impresses visitors. [past participle, modifying **town hall**]

He still had three years **to serve in prison** before he would be eligible for parole. [infinitive, modifying **years**]

Like other modifiers, verbal modifiers should be clearly related to the words that they modify. When a verbal construction seems from its position to refer to a word that it cannot sensibly modify, it is said to be *misrelated*. Participial phrases usually give writers the most trouble:

| **Misrelated** | **Revised** |
|---|---|
| On the other side of the valley, **grazing peacefully like cattle,** we saw a herd of buffalo. [the participial phrase seems to refer to **we**] | On the other side of the valley we saw a herd of buffalo, **grazing peacefully like cattle.** [the phrase clearly refers to **buffalo**] |

Misrelated modifiers may be momentarily confusing to the reader (or unintentionally humorous) and should therefore be avoided. Sometimes the correction can be made by putting the modifier immediately before or after the word it is meant to modify, as in the example above, but often it is better to rewrite the sentence completely:

| **Misrelated** | **Revised** |
|---|---|
| One early-day western senator is said to have passed out campaign cards to the voters **pinned together with five-dollar bills.** [the participle phrase seems to refer to **voters**] | One early-day western senator is said to have pinned five-dollar bills to the campaign cards he passed out to voters. |

Occasionally modifiers are placed so that they seem to refer to either of two elements in the sentence. These constructions (sometimes called *squinting modifiers*) can be avoided by changing the position of the modifier or by otherwise revising the sentence:

| **Ambiguous** | **Revised** |
|---|---|
| The woman who was standing in the doorway **to attract attention** dropped her purse. | The woman who was standing in the doorway dropped her purse **to attract attention.** *Or:* The woman, standing in the doorway **to attract attention,** dropped her purse. |

Other types of misrelated modifiers are discussed in §9.5, Position of adverbs.

> **DM** Correction: Revise the sentence to include the word to which the dangling modifier refers.

Dangling modifiers refer to a word that is implied rather than actually stated in the sentence. Like misrelated modifiers, they can make a sentence confusing or ludicrous:

**Having moved at fifteen,** his home town no longer seemed familiar.

This error often occurs when passive rather than active verbs are used:

| Dangling | Revised |
|---|---|
| **In painting four of these pictures,** his wife was used as his model. | **In painting four of these pictures,** he used his wife as a model. |
| **To find the needed information,** the whole book had to be read. | **To find the needed information,** I had to read the whole book. |

Usually the easiest way to correct a dangling modifier is to name the agent or the "doer" of the action immediately after the phrase, as in the revisions shown above. It is often better, however, to revise the sentence entirely, making the relationships more accurate by using other constructions. Changing the verbal phrase to a subordinate clause often improves the sentence:

| Dangling | Revised |
|---|---|
| **Having been delayed by a train accident,** the leading role was played by a local actress. | **Because the leading lady was delayed by a train accident,** her role was played by a local actress. |
| **Coming down the road,** an old-fashioned green house caught his eye. | **As he was coming down the road,** an old-fashioned green house caught his eye. |

## Absolute modifiers 4.5

A writer should distinguish clearly between verbal modifiers that obviously dangle, such as those cited above, and *absolute modifiers*—participle or infinitive phrases that modify the statement as a whole and thus do not need a specific reference word in the main clause. A number of absolute constructions are commonly used expressions:

**Everything considered,** this plan seems best.
**To make a long story short,** we bought the house.
**Considering the cost of labor,** the price is reasonable.

An absolute phrase with a subject is sometimes called a *nominative absolute*. This construction is often used effectively in descriptive and narrative prose for adding details or parenthetical material:

He stalked like the specter of a soldier, **his eyes** [subject] **burning** [participle] with the power of a stare into the unknown. — Stephen Crane, *The Red Badge of Courage*

The Portuguese listened with his head cocked to one side, **his dark eyes** [subject] **ringed** [participle] with ash-gray circles, and now and then he wiped his damp veined dead-white hands on his stained apron. — Carson McCullers, *Member of the Wedding*

**For Study and Writing**
1. *Finite and Nonfinite.* Identify the italicized verb forms below with an *F* for "finite" or an *NF* for "nonfinite."
a. Joe *went* to the movies.
b. It has always been a pleasure *to be* invited.
c. *Going* to church is important.
d. He *ate* dinner yesterday.
e. I like *to go*.

2. Some of these sentences contain misrelated or dangling modifiers. Rewrite these sentences to clear up the relationships. Those with *absolute modifiers* need no revision.

   *ex.:* Having grown tired of them, their actions no longer concerned me.
   *revised:* As I had grown tired of them, their actions no longer concerned me.
   *or:* Having grown tired of them, I felt that their actions no longer concerned me.

a. Being thoroughly persuaded of them myself, the beliefs I hold seem to me to be obviously true.
b. My spirits often sink in despair, however, trying to find ways to convince others of these truths.
c. After having convinced a friend against his will, both he and I find that our friendship is in doubt.
d. It does not really persuade anyone to accept my beliefs by citing authorities to prove my point.
e. To be honest about it, my friends have grown weary of my arguments and often try to avoid me.
f. After having satisfied my own mind in every detail of an argument, the decision I reach seems incontrovertible.
g. My position tends to harden very rapidly, my decision having been reached, and I am not likely to change my mind.

**h.** To be perfectly frank, it is unwise for you to pretend that you are convinced by what I say to be polite.

**i.** Above and beyond the call of mere friendship, being more important, truth is what matters.

**j.** To do justice to any friendship based on truth, it takes absolute candor on both sides.

# Agreement of subject and verb 5

**Subj.-Verb Agr.** Correction: Make the verb marked agree in form with its subject.

In English, parts of speech that change form to show number, gender, or person should agree or correspond when they are related to each other. Pronouns agree with their antecedents (see §7.2) and verbs with their subject. When we say that words should agree or correspond, we mean, for example, that if a subject is plural, then its verb ought to be plural as well.

Agreement between subject and verb is not a common problem in general English because our verbs don't change form much. The verb *be,* of course, changes nearly every time you notice, but other verbs have only two forms in the present tense and only one form in the past tense. We say *I swim* and *you swim,* and then change the form for the third person singular, *he swims, she swims, it swims.* In the past tense, we would use the same form for all. There are some variations from this practice in some English dialects. Some, for example, consistently use only one form in the present tense: *I do, you do, he do, she do, it do.* See §8, Verbs, for a discussion of English verb forms.

Since English verbs don't change their form very much, questions about agreement of subject and verb are not likely to arise frequently except when verbs have compound subjects or collective nouns as subjects, or when the number of the subject (whether it is singular or plural) is blurred by other words between the subject and verb. These problems are discussed in the following sections.

## Verbs with compound subjects 5.1

A compound subject is made up of two or more words, phrases, or clauses joined by *and, or, nor.* The number of the verb depends on which conjunction is used and on the meaning of the subject.

## Subjects joined by *and*

The conjunction *and* is used to join coordinate items, to add them together. Thus subjects joined by *and* usually take a plural verb:

**Bob, Ted,** and **Sandra swim** with the varsity team.

The first **draft** of your paper and the **version** finally turned in might **differ** in several ways.

*Exception:* When the words of a compound subject refer to the same person or are considered together as a unit, the verb is usually singular:

His warmest **admirer** and severest **critic was** his wife.

**Law and order means** different things to people with different political opinions.

## Subjects joined by *or, nor*

Compound subjects joined by *or, nor, either . . . or, neither . . . nor* sometimes take singular verbs and sometimes plural. Here are some ways to tell the difference:

1) When both subjects are singular, the verb ordinarily is singular:

**One** or the **other is** certainly to blame.

Neither **Senator Jackson** nor **Senator Kennedy has been invited** to debate the health-care bill.

*Exceptions:* In questions, where the verb precedes the subject, general usage tends to use a plural verb:

**Are** [formal: **Is**] either **Stevenson** or **Percy** supporting the bill?

In general usage a plural verb may also follow two singular subjects if they are not considered as separate:

Neither **radio** nor **television provide** [formal: **provides**] adequate news coverage.

2) When both subjects are plural, the verb is plural:

No artificial **colorings** or **preservatives are used.**

3) When one subject is singular and the other plural, usage varies. In formal writing the verb usually agrees with the nearer subject:

One major **accident** or several minor **ones seem** to occur at this corner every weekend.

Neither the **revolutionists** nor their **leader was** to blame.

In general usage a plural verb is often used even if the nearer subject is singular:

Neither the **revolutionists** nor their **leader were** to blame.

4) When the subjects are pronouns in different persons, formal usage requires that the verb agree in person and number with the nearer subject. In general usage (and even in formal usage if the alternative is awkward) the verb is usually plural:

**Formal:** Either **you** or **she is** likely to be elected.
**General:** Either **you** or **she are** likely to be elected.

**Formal and general:** Neither **you** nor **I are** trained for that job. [**Am** would sound unnatural.]

Such problems of agreement can usually be avoided by substituting a different, more natural construction:

**One** of you **is** likely to be elected.
**Neither** of us **is** trained for that job.

### Subjects followed by *as well as*

In formal usage a singular subject followed by a phrase introduced by *as well as, together with, along with, in addition to* ordinarily takes a singular verb:

The **treasurer as well as the president was held** responsible for the mismanagement of the company.

But a plural verb is often used in these situations when the added phrase is clearly intended as a compound subject:

Both the **production** of small cars, **together with the supply** in the dealers' showrooms, **have been outstripped** by the demand.

A simple solution—and one that may make the statement more direct—is to use *and* wherever appropriate:

Both the **production** of small cars and the **supply** in the dealers' showrooms **have been outstripped** by the demand.

### Verbs with collective nouns as subjects    **5.2**

Words that refer to a group of people or objects but are singular in form are called collective nouns or group nouns: *army, audience, choir, committee, crowd, faculty, gang, group, government, jury, mob, orchestra, public, team.* Verbs and pronouns used with collective nouns are either singular or plural, depending upon the meaning of the group word.

## Nouns referring to the group as a unit

Singular verbs and singular pronouns are used with collective nouns that refer to the group as a unit:

**Class is** dismissed.
The **committee has** already held **its** first meeting of the year.
The **audience is** requested to remain seated during intermission.

## Nouns referring to individuals in a group

When a collective noun refers to the members of the group, especially if it represents them as acting individually, a plural verb and plural reference words are used:

The graduating **class have** all agreed to have **their** pictures taken.
The **committee are** arguing among **themselves.**
The **audience have** taken **their** seats.

Sentences like these often sound rather unnatural, and in most cases it is better to substitute a clearly plural subject (the committee *members,* the *members* of the audience).

## Verbs with measurements and figures

Expressions signifying quantity or extent *(miles, liters, years, pounds)* take singular verbs when the amount is considered as a unit:

**Five dollars is** too much to pay for a book in that condition.
**Four quarts** of oil **is** all the crankcase holds.
**Three months passes** in no time at all on a dude ranch.

When the amount is considered as a number of individual units, a plural verb is used:

**Two more dollars are** missing from the till this morning.
There **are three quarts** of milk in the refrigerator.
The last **three months have been** the driest in California's history.

In expressions of addition and multiplication, usage is evenly divided:

Five and seven **is** [or **are**] twelve.
Five times seven **is** [or **are**] thirty-five.

A singular verb is used in expressions of subtraction:

Twenty-five from thirty-one **leaves** six.

## Verbs with *data, number, public*

*Data* is a plural form and is generally so considered in formal, particularly scientific, writing; but since the singular *datum* is rarely used, *data* is often used for both singular and plural in general writing; agreement often depends on context:

**Singular idea:** The **data** the president needs **has been analyzed** by his assistant. [**data** refers to a body of facts]

**Plural idea:** After the **data** [individual facts] **have been gathered** and **analyzed,** you can decide which elements are most essential to your study.

*Number* as a collective noun may be either singular or plural: preceded by *the*, it refers to the total sum and takes a singular verb; preceded by *a*, it refers to the individual units and takes a plural verb:

**A number** of pages **are** badly torn.

**The number** of pages assigned for daily reading **was** gradually increased to twelve.

Physicians were disturbed to find that **an** alarming **number** of bacteria **were** developing a tolerance to penicillin.

*Public* takes a singular verb if the writer wishes to signify the whole group (The *public is* invited to attend); it takes a plural verb if the writer is considering the individual members (The *public are* invited to express their opinions).

## Words ending in *-ics*

*Physics, mathematics, economics, civics, linguistics,* and similar *-ics* words that refer to a science, art, or a body of knowledge are usually considered singular; other words ending in *-ics* that refer to physical activities or qualities *(athletics, acrobatics, tactics)* are generally treated as plurals.

| Singular forms | Plural forms |
|---|---|
| **Physics was** my most difficult subject in high school. | **Athletics have** been virtually abolished from some smaller schools. |
| **Ballistics is** the study of the motion of projectiles. | His motives may be good, but his **tactics are** deplorable. |

Some words ending in *-ics (ethics, politics, acoustics)* may be used either in a singular or plural sense:

| Singular idea | Plural idea |
|---|---|
| In almost every group, **politics is** a controversial subject. | Radical **politics were** offensive to the Federalists. |
| **Acoustics is** a branch of science that is growing fast. | The **acoustics** in this room **are** not all they might be. |

When you are in doubt about the number of a word ending in *-ics,* consult a dictionary.

Sometimes writers make a verb agree with a nearby expression rather than with its actual subject. Since this often occurs when a writer accepts the nearest convenient word or phrase that looks like a subject, it is frequently referred to as "blind agreement." The error usually occurs in the following situations:

### Plural nouns between subject and verb

A singular subject followed by a phrase or clause containing plural nouns is still singular:

Here and there a **man** [subject] such as Columbus, Galileo, and others **has** [not **have**] ventured into the unknown physical and intellectual worlds.

The **lumberman** [subject] who previously sold only to carpenters and builders now **finds** [not **find**] hundreds of amateurs eager to build their own homes.

I decided to see exactly how **one** of those new cars **is** [not **are**] put together.

### one of those who

In formal English, the verb in clauses that begin *one of those who* (or *that*) is plural:

He is one of those men who never **care** how they look. [The verb is plural because its subject **who** refers to **men,** not to **one.**]

"The Lottery" is one of those stories that **leave** you more puzzled when you finish than when you began. [**Stories** is the antecedent of **that.**]

Although a singular verb is common in spoken English ("one of those girls who *plays* in the band") and in a good deal of published material, the plural verb is customarily used in formal English.

*Exception:* When *the only* precedes *one of those who* the verb is singular, since the pronoun *who* then refers to a single person or thing:

She is the only one of those women who **plays** bridge well.

### there is, there are

When a sentence begins with the introductory (or "dummy") word *there* (sometimes referred to as an "anticipating subject"), the number of the verb is determined by the subject which follows:

There **are** conflicting **opinions** [subject] about smoking in the class-rooms.

There **is** great narrative and dramatic **power** [subject] in the first part of this novel.

At our camp there **were** at least a dozen **men** [subject] who were familiar with the mountain trail.

In this construction a singular verb is frequently used before a compound subject, especially if a plural verb would be un-idiomatic, as in the second example below:

There **is food** and **drink** enough for everyone.
There **was nothing** he could do and **little** he could say.

## Verb and complement

A verb agrees with its subject and not with its complement or its object:

Our chief **trouble** [subject] **was** [not **were**] the black flies that swarmed about us on the trip.

The **black flies** [subject] that swarmed about us on our trip **were** [not **was**] our chief trouble.

The **material** [subject] that was most interesting to me when I worked on my reference paper **was** [not **were**] the books that stated the facts forcefully.

When subject and complement differ in number, the sentence usually sounds less awkward if the subject and verb are plural, as in the second example above.

## Inverted word order

When the word order is inverted, care must be taken to make the verb agree with its subject and not with some other word:

Throughout the story **appear** thinly disguised **references** [subject] to the author's own boyhood.

**Is** any **one** [subject] of these pictures for sale?

Accompanying the senator **were** her **secretary** and two **members** of her legal staff. [The verb has a compound subject.]

## *series, portion, part*

Subjects like *series, portion, part, type* take singular verbs even when modified by a phrase with a plural noun:

A **series** of panel discussions **is** scheduled for the convention.

A substantial **portion** of the reports **is** missing.

The most interesting **part** of the investigations **was** the discovery and identification of the forged letters.

## Applications: Agreement of Subject and Verb

1. Find the subject of the italicized verbs in the following paragraph. If the subject is a pronoun, indicate what word or idea it refers to.

(a) *Suppose* it *were* perfectly certain that the life and fortune of every one of us *would,* one day or other, *depend* upon his winning or losing a game of chess. (b) *Don't* you *think* that we *should* all *consider* it to be a primary duty to learn at least the names and moves of the pieces; to have a notion of a gambit, and a keen eye for all the means of giving and getting out of check? . . . (c) Yet it *is* a very plain and elementary truth, that the life, the fortune, and the happiness of every one of us . . . *do depend* upon our knowing something of the rules of a game infinitely more difficult and complicated than chess. . . . (d) The chessboard *is* the world, the pieces are the phenomena of the universe, the rules of the game *are* what we *call* the laws of Nature. (e) The player on the other side *is hidden* from us. (f) We *know* that his play *is* always fair, just, and patient. (g) But we also *know,* to our cost, that he never *overlooks* a mistake, or *makes* the slightest allowance for ignorance. — Thomas H. Huxley, *Science and Education*

2. Determine the subject of each of the following sentences and select the verb form that agrees with it. If there is any problem of agreement, explain your choice of verb in terms of the points made in this section.
a. The wages of sin (is, are) death.
b. All (is, are) well.
c. Comparison of things that are unlike and that, by their uniqueness (produces, produce) a sense of wonder in us, (show, shows) that the writer is just displaying his or her own cleverness.
d. Too many metaphors (is, are) a sign of a young writer.
e. "Patience and fortitude," though describing virtues, (is, are) a motto often used to counsel sloth.
f. These United States of ours (has, have) become a great nation.
g. He is one of those people who (is, are) always making trouble.
h. To have loved and lost (is, are) an experience most of humanity (has, have) suffered.
i. The bulk of our tax dollars (go, goes) to defense spending.
j. Neither metaphor nor simile (is, are) useful if the image is confused.

3. Examine the following student theme for errors in agreement between subject and verb or between pronoun and antecedent. Rewrite the theme, making the necessary corrections. What do you think about this writer's use of analogy? Is it as effective as Huxley's in exercise 1?

The faculty of a college are like a pick-up team in a sandlot game; the members will have varying degrees of competence. The inequality of their skills do not matter much, provided that each of the key players do the assigned job well.

Some faculty teams are more important than others. Thus the English department is central, for if they do not do their job well, the student body as a whole are bound to suffer. The whole curriculum depends on the abilities that the student show in reading and listening. If the students at a lecture were to fail to catch the "pitch" made by the teacher, it would be like catchers on a team which were fielding only eight men, no one of whom were behind the plate.

Committees are the staff which run such faculty teams; these are made up of both administrative officials and faculty members. Their collective jobs is to do one thing: to map the strategy for winning the student body's minds and spirits. They may seek advice from individual players on the faculty, which, after all, are in the best positions to know how the players on the student team is going to act in given situations; but overall, everyone, when the chips are down, defer in judgment to the committees.

The public are the alumni and the parents. Its job is to follow the whole complex of what is going on, to cheer when things at the school is going well, and to boo, by sending letters and criticism, when they are dissatisfied with the particulars that the management have decided on.

**4.** The most common agreement problems in student writing involve -s and -ed endings. One reason may be that some of these endings are not pronounced in speech, and the writer may simply not realize that they must be present in written English.

**a.** The -s (and -es) endings indicate the third person singular, present tense, as this section of the book explains:

1st person singular: I walk
2nd person singular: you walk
3rd person singular: she walks, he walks, it walks

To practice getting the -s endings in the correct places, write a story about a page long, using the third person singular, present tense. The story begins like this: *The deputy enters the carnival. He has a job: he looks for fraud—for cheaters. First, he approaches the shooting-gallery where. . . .*

**b.** The -ed endings are even more tricky. These endings have to do with tense or time:

Present: Today, I *ask* for justice.
Past: Yesterday, I *asked* for food.

Write a page in the past tense, using correctly as many -ed endings as you can. The story begins like this: *The fire burned the warehouse. Men screamed. Sirens from the fire trucks wailed in the distance. Suddenly, a masked figure appeared. . . .*

# Nouns 6

Nouns are words used in sentences chiefly as subjects of verbs, objects of verbs or prepositions, as complements following a linking verb, as appositives, or as modifiers of other words. They change their form to show number (by adding -s, -es, etc.) and possession ('s, s'). A noun may designate a person *(George Washington, child)*, place *(Spain, home)*, thing *(pencil, steak)*, quality *(beauty, rage)*, action *(hunting, logrolling)*, or idea *(justice, reality)*.

The table on page 90 shows the forms, functions, and customary ways of classifying nouns. The following sections focus on the common problems that writers may have with nouns: how to use plural and possessive forms conventionally, when to use *a* or *an* before nouns, and how to spot unidiomatic or clumsy noun modifiers.

## Plurals of nouns 6.1

> **Pl**  Correction: Change the noun marked to a standard plural form.

Most English nouns form the plural simply by adding -s to the singular form *(cats, girls, books, things)*. If the plural makes an extra syllable, -es is added to the singular form *(bushes, churches, kisses, Joneses)*.

A few nouns preserve older methods of forming the plural, adding -en *(children, oxen)* or changing the vowel *(feet, teeth, geese, mice)*. Some nouns have the same form for both singular and plural: (1) all words ending in -ics, such as *athletics, civics, mathematics;* (2) the names of some animals, such as *deer, fish, mink, sheep;* (3) a number of words rarely or never used in the singular, such as *barracks, headquarters, measles, pants, scissors.*

The following sections consider some groups of nouns whose plurals are likely to cause trouble. There are few hard-and-fast rules, however, and the writer should learn to consult the dictionary whenever he or she is unsure of a plural form. If the plural of a noun is irregular, it will be shown under the entry for the singular form; if no plural is given, the plural is formed in the usual way, by adding -s or -es.

# Nouns: Forms, Functions, and Classes

## Forms

**Singular and plural forms**
Singular: boy, mother, box, child, goose, hero, baby, phenomenon
Plural: boys, mothers, boxes, children, geese, heroes, babies, phenomena

**Compound nouns or group words,** two or more nouns (written as one word, as two words, or hyphened) that function as a single unit: bookcase, football; pine tree, high school; father-in-law, hangers-on

**Genitive or "possessive" form:** boy's, Harriet's, girls', cats'

**Gender.** A few nouns in English have one form for the masculine, one for the feminine: actor, actress

## Functions

**Subject of a verb:** The *tires* squealed as the *car* skidded around the corner.

**Object of a verb:** The new company manufactured *toys*.

**Complement:** A whale is a *mammal*. He became *president*.

**Object of a preposition:** The acrobats were performing inside the *tent*.

**Indirect object:** He gave the *church* a memorial window.

**Appositive:** Mr. McDermott, the insurance *agent*, is here.

**Modifier of a noun:** He thought *cigarette* holders looked silly. *Mr. Tyler's* car was stolen.

**Modifier of a statement:** *Each year* we make new resolutions.

## Classes

**Proper nouns,** names of particular people, places, and things, written with capitals: Anne, George W. Loomis, London, Monday, Monroe Doctrine

**Common nouns.** In contrast with these proper nouns, all the other groups are common nouns and are written with lower-case letters

**Concrete nouns,** names of objects that can be seen and touched: leaf, leaves, road, panda, manufacturer

**Abstract nouns,** names of qualities, actions, ideas that are perceived mentally: kindness, hate, idealism, fantasy, concept

**Collective nouns,** names of groupings of individuals: fleet, army, company, committee, bevy

**Mass nouns,** names of material aggregates or masses not defined as individual units: food, money, intelligence, justice

**Count nouns,** names of things perceived as individual units: car, shelf, pencil, cow, vase

## Nouns ending in *-y*, *-o*, or *-f*

Nouns ending in *-y* following a vowel form the plural regularly by adding *-s (toys, bays, joys, monkeys)*. But nouns ending in *-y* preceded by a consonant change *y* to *i* and add *-es*:

| | | |
|---|---|---|
| apolog**y**, apolog**ies** | curiosit**y**, curiosit**ies** | librar**y**, librar**ies** |
| compan**y**, compan**ies** | ferr**y**, ferr**ies** | stud**y**, stud**ies** |

*Exception:* In forming the plural of proper names, the *-y* is retained and *-s* added: all the *Kellys,* both *Marys.*

Nouns ending in *-o* preceded by a vowel form the plural by adding *-s (folios, studios, tattoos)*. If the final *-o* is preceded by a consonant, the plural is usually formed by adding *-es*, but a few nouns add *-s* only:

| | | | | |
|---|---|---|---|---|
| ech**oes** | potat**oes** | | pian**os** | sopran**os** |
| her**oes** | tomat**oes** | But: | sol**os** | tobacc**os** |
| Negr**oes** | vet**oes** | | banj**os** | Eskim**os** |

A few nouns ending in *-o* add either *-s* or *-es* to form the plural: *cargos, cargoes; hobos, hoboes; zeros, zeroes.* Because no rule can be given for adding *-s* or *-es*, a writer must either memorize the plurals or consult a dictionary.

Nouns ending in *-f* or *-fe* often form the plural regularly *(beliefs, chiefs, fifes, roofs)*. But some common words ending in *-f* form their plurals by changing *-f* to *-ves*:

| | | |
|---|---|---|
| cal**f**, cal**ves** | kni**fe**, kni**ves** | sel**f**, sel**ves** |
| hal**f**, hal**ves** | lea**f**, lea**ves** | thie**f**, thie**ves** |

The plural of a few nouns ending in *-f* may be either *-s* or *-ves: elfs, elves; hoofs, hooves; scarfs, scarves; wharfs, wharves.*

## Words with foreign plurals

Some nouns have two forms for the plural: a foreign plural and the anglicized form ending in *-s* or *-es*. The foreign plural is characteristic of formal usage, particularly in scientific and academic writing:

| Singular | Formal plural | General plural |
|---|---|---|
| antenna | antennae (zoology) | antennas (radio, TV) |
| appendix | appendices | appendixes |
| cactus | cacti | cactuses |
| curriculum | curricula | curriculums |
| formula | formulae | formulas |
| index | indices | indexes |
| maximum | maxima | maximums |
| medium | media | mediums |
| radius | radii | radiuses |

| Singular | Formal plural | General plural |
|----------|---------------|----------------|
| sanatorium | sanatoria | sanatoriums |
| stratum | strata | stratums |
| syllabus | syllabi | syllabuses |
| vertebra | vertebrae | vertebras |

Although some dictionaries list alternate plural forms for *phenomenon* and *criterion, phenomena* and *criteria* are preferred in both formal and general writing.

Certain nouns derived from Greek or Latin and ending in *-is* form their plurals by changing *-is* to *-es:*

| Singular | Plural | Singular | Plural |
|----------|--------|----------|--------|
| analysis | analyses | neurosis | neuroses |
| axis | axes | parenthesis | parentheses |
| basis | bases | psychosis | psychoses |
| crisis | crises | synopsis | synopses |
| diagnosis | diagnoses | thesis | theses |

The word for a person who has been graduated from a college has four forms:

alumnus (ə lum′nəs): one male graduate

alumni (ə lum′nī): two or more male graduates or a combination of male and female graduates

alumna (ə lum′nə): one female graduate

alumnae (ə lum′nē): two or more female graduates

The simplest way out of this confusion of forms is to use the term *graduate* or *graduates.*

## Group words and compound nouns

Most compound words and group words form their plurals by adding *-s* to the last word of the group, whether the expression is written as one word or two:

| Singular | Plural |
|----------|--------|
| baby sitter | baby sitters |
| cross-examination | cross-examinations |
| major general | major generals |

But when the significant word is the first term (as it often is in hyphened compounds), that word is the one made plural:

| | |
|---|---|
| daughter**s**-in-law | passer**s**-by |
| **men**-of-war | president**s**-elect |

The plural of nouns ending in *-ful* is made by adding *-s* to the last part of the word: two *cupfuls*, three *tablespoonfuls.*

**6.2** | **Noun**

**6.2**

Case refers to the form a noun or pronoun takes that shows its relationship to other words in the sentence. In English, nouns have only two case forms, the common form *(dog, book, John)* and the genitive, which is the common form plus an *s* or *z* sound *(dog's, book's, John's)* or a plural form with no additional sound *(dogs', books')*. An *of* phrase *(of the dog, of the book, of John)* can function as a genitive and is usually regarded as an alternate form.

## Uses of the genitive

The genitive case of nouns is commonly called the "possessive" because its most frequent function is to show possession (a *student's* book, a mannerism *of the professor*). But the genitive case also shows other relationships:

1) Description: a *day's* work, a suit *of wool, yesterday's* paper.

2) Doer of an act ("subjective genitive"): the *wind's* force, the *dean's* permission, the permission *of the dean.*

3) Recipient of an act ("objective genitive"): the *bill's* defeat, the execution *of a spy.*

4) Subject of a gerund (see page 72): the *doctor's* warning, the *play's* closing.

## Forms of the genitive

In speech, genitive and plural forms are identical, and we can distinguish between them only by the way they are used: the genitive is followed by another noun (The *boy's work* was finished), whereas the plural is not (The *boys worked* hard). It is impossible to distinguish between the singular and plural genitive except in the larger context of what is being said.

In writing, the apostrophe signals the genitive case, and the position of the apostrophe *(boy's, boys')* ordinarily tells us whether a genitive is singular or plural.

V̌ Correction: Insert an apostrophe where it belongs in the word marked or take out the unnecessary apostrophe.

Position of the apostrophe

Most singular nouns form the genitive by adding *'s*, as do the few plural nouns that do not end in *-s* (such as *men, women, children*):

the **teacher's** remarks (the remarks **of the teacher**)
a **day's** work (the work **of a day**)
the **children's** playground (the playground **of the children**)

Plural nouns ending in *-s* form the genitive by adding an apostrophe alone:

the **teachers'** meeting (the meeting **of teachers**)
the **musicians'** union (the union **of musicians**)
the **Joneses'** relatives (the relatives **of the Joneses**)

Singular nouns ending in *-s* usually form the genitive by adding an apostrophe alone, just as plural nouns do, or by adding *'s* if an extra syllable would be pronounced. Either is correct, but you should be consistent in whichever form you use.

Mr. **Jones'** [or **Jones's**] business    the **hostess'** [or **hostess's**] gown
**Delores'** [or **Delores's**] father    the **actress'** [or **actress's**] role

Group words

With group words or compound nouns the *'s* is added to the last term:

The **Queen of England's** duties    the **attorney general's** job
her **mother-in-law's** address    **someone else's** responsibility

Nouns in series

When two coordinate nouns (joined by *and, but,* or *nor*) are in the genitive, the apostrophe usually is added only to the last one if there is joint possession: *Barbara and Tom's* mother. But if there is individual possession, the apostrophe is used with both nouns: *Barbara's and Tom's* bicycles, *neither Barbara's nor Tom's* teacher.

Plural nouns as modifiers

The apostrophe is not used in some expressions in which the plural noun is considered a modifier: *teachers* college, *Veterans* Administration, *United States* Post Office. Substitution of plural noun modifiers for the genitive is increasing today, so you should carefully note letterheads, signs, official publications, and the like to determine customary usage.

*of* phrases and *'s* forms

The *'s* form of the genitive is customarily used with living things (my *uncle's* house, a *cat's* paw, a *robin's* nest) and an *of* phrase with inanimate objects (the door *of the room,* an angle *of inclination,* the beginning *of the end*). But in many instances either form may be used, the choice depending largely upon the sound and intended emphasis of the expression (the *book's* cover, the cover *of the book*). Some idiomatic expressions are usually stated in one form only (a *week's* wages, a *moment's* hesitation, an embarrassment *of riches,* the wages *of sin*).

Awkward use of *'s* forms

An *of* phrase is sometimes preferable to an *'s* form to avoid a clumsy or unidiomatic expression or a statement that may be ambiguous. When the modifying noun is separated from the word it refers to by a phrase or a clause, an *of* phrase should be used:

The apartment **of the woman** who won the contest was ransacked last night. [not **The woman who won the contest's apartment** nor **The woman's apartment who won the contest**]

The *of* phrase is useful in distinguishing between the recipient and doer of an act (between the subjective and objective genitive), particularly if the meaning is unclear in context. *John's photographs* might mean either photographs *of* him or photographs *by* him, but *the photographs of John* would ordinarily mean that John was the subject of the pictures.

The double genitive

In a few statements both the *of* and *'s* forms of the genitive are used, an idiom of long standing in English: that boy *of Henry's,* some friends *of my father's,* a remark *of the author's.*

## Use of *a* and *an* with nouns  6.3

The choice between *a* and *an* depends on the initial sound of the word that follows rather than the initial letter. *A* is used before words beginning with a consonant sound (long *u* has the sound of the consonant *y*):

a car   a European country   a *D*   a used car

*An* is used before words beginning with a vowel sound:

an ape   an *F*   an hour   an honor   an oar

When an adjective is the customary form in an expression, it should be used in place of a clumsy or unidiomatic noun modifier:

After graduating from St. Olaf, Karen took her **medical** [not **doctor**] training at Northwestern.

After sparking his team to victory in the city championship, Les went on to play with a **Canadian** [not **Canada**] team.

But for words that do not have exact adjective equivalents, the noun forms are freely used as modifiers: a *murder* mystery, *kitchen* utensils, *radio* reception, *prison* walls. In some expressions either the noun or adjective form may be used: *atom* bomb, *atomic* bomb.

Noun forms used as modifiers — particularly units of measurement — are ordinarily singular: a ten-*ton* truck, a six-*foot* jump. (Used as nouns, the forms would be plural: ten *tons* of coal, a jump of six *feet*.)

**Applications: Nouns**

1. Nouns have formal properties, as you have just learned. They are, for example, either *count* or *mass:*

   *count:* one rock, two rocks, etc.
   *but not:* one gravel, two gravels, etc.

   Nouns are *concrete* (fence, for example) or *abstract* (justice). Some nouns have *gender* (masculine, feminine, neuter), and nouns may be *animate* or *inanimate* (living or not living). Finally, nouns may be *human* or *nonhuman*. (See the chart on p. 90 for further information.)
   Here are sample analyses of two nouns:

   *animal:* count + concrete + neuter + animate + nonhuman
   *hostility:* mass + abstract + neuter + inanimate + nonhuman

   Now analyze in the same way each of the following nouns: (a) *aunt,* (b) *trumpet,* (c) *radio,* (d) *king,* (e) *taste*

2. Read each sentence below and then select the noun form you consider appropriate. If the choice is optional, explain the context in which each form would be used. Consult your dictionary if necessary to find the standard plural form.
   a. Delicately the proud (man-of-wars, men-of-war) dipped their masts and fired (eight-gun, eight-guns) salutes.
   b. Their (enemies, enemys) stood towering on the crests of the hills and then stormed thunderously into the unprotected (valleys, vallies).

**c.** The (atom, atomic) blast flowered evilly behind the desert dotted with pale (cactuses, cacti).

**d.** (A, An) awful explosion set the (axis, axes) of the earth quivering like a slackening top.

**e.** The chessboard is the world; the pieces are the (phenomena, phenomenas) of the universe; the rules of the game are what we call the (laws, lawes) of nature.

**3.** Distinguishing between plural and genitive forms of nouns is important to the reader's understanding of your meaning. Indicate which of the italicized nouns in these sentences are correctly written with *s* endings and which should have *'s* or *s'*.

**a.** The *energies* of our system will decay, the *suns* glory will dim, and the earth will no longer tolerate the race which has disturbed *its* peace.

**b.** One of Sir James *Barries* humorous characters said, "Facts were never pleasing to him. . . . He was never on *terms* with them until he stood them on their *heads*."

**c.** As flies to wanton *boys,* are we to the *gods;* they kill us for their sport.

**d.** When the *childrens* laughter began to peal in the garden, the *Joneses* neighbors closeted themselves in the air-conditioned family room.

**e.** The king was "the *peoples* prayer . . . the young *mens* vision and the old *mens* dream."

**4.** The sentences below contain various errors in noun forms. Read the sentences carefully, as if you were proofreading a theme or composition, making the necessary corrections. You will probably need your dictionary.

**a.** The father's-in-laws brow assumed a supercilious arch when the bride's-maid appeared in lavender organdy.

**b.** The kingdom of vertebrae embraces ourselfs and all beasts, birds, reptiles, efts, frogs, and fishes.

**c.** The family down the street's neurosis are as brightly iridescent and exotically ocellated as preening peacocks tails.

**d.** Years like great black oxes tread the world and God, the herdsmen, drives them on.

**e.** The doctor's last bill's effect upon the declining editor's-in-chief health was mortal.

# Pronouns 7

The word *pronoun* means *for a noun.* A pronoun is a word similar to a noun in function, but it does not specifically name a person, place, thing, or idea. Usually it is used as a substitute for a previously stated noun, called its antecedent. A pronoun refers to its antecedent for its specific meaning, which is generally evident from its context:

My uncle phoned last night. **He** is coming by plane.
Men over forty are invited to join. **They** may apply by mail.
Joe heard that credit cards cause many financial problems. **This** interested **him.**
My friend and I are invited to a party with her cousins. **We** are going to **it** with **them.**

Pronouns free you from the necessity of repeating nouns every time you wish to designate a person, place, thing, or idea. They also help bind statements together. When a pronoun in a sentence refers to a noun in the preceding sentence, there is a natural connection between the two sentences. Notice how the emphasized pronouns in the following passage help give it continuity:

If the history of the earth's tides should one day be written by some observer of the universe, it would no doubt be said that **they** reached **their** greatest grandeur and power in the younger days of Earth, and that **they** slowly grew feebler and less imposing until one day **they** ceased to be. For the tides were not always as **they** are today, and as with all that is earthly, **their** days are numbered. — Rachel Carson, *The Sea Around Us*

Pronouns should be used more carefully in writing than they sometimes are in speaking. Remember that a pronoun does not name anything specifically by itself and that a reader cannot see you point or hear the change in your tone. Readers need to see pronouns in the form that indicates their function, and they need to be able to follow a pronoun's reference to its antecedent without confusion. The following sections discuss the most common problems in using pronouns. The table on page 101 lists the various kinds of pronouns and their forms.

> **Ref**   Correction: Change the pronoun marked so that its reference will be exact and obvious; if necessary, substitute a noun for the pronoun or revise the sentence.

## Pronouns referring to a definite antecedent

The antecedent of a pronoun should be clearly stated, not merely implied, and the pronoun should refer specifically to this antecedent:

| Inaccurate | Accurate |
|---|---|
| He had been vaccinated against typhoid, but **it** did not protect him. [No antecedent for **it.**] | He had a typhoid **vaccination,** but **it** did not protect him. [**Vaccination** is the antecedent of **it.**] |

Instead of changing the antecedent, it is often better to substitute a noun for the inexact pronoun:

| Inaccurate | Accurate |
|---|---|
| She couldn't understand how to make the cake until I wrote **it** out. | She couldn't understand how to make the cake until I wrote out **the recipe.** |

A simple test for accurate reference is to see whether the antecedent could be substituted for the pronoun. If not, the sentence needs revision.

| Inaccurate | Accurate |
|---|---|
| She talked a lot about the technique of horsemanship, although as a matter of fact she had never ridden **one** [horsemanship?] in her life. | She talked a lot about the technique of horsemanship, although as a matter of fact she had never ridden **a horse** in her life. |

The antecedent of a pronoun should not be a noun used as a modifier or a noun in the possessive form:

| Inaccurate | Accurate |
|---|---|
| To make an attractive tulip border, plant **them** close together. [**Tulip** is used as a modifier.] | To make an attractive border of **tulips,** plant **them** close together. |
| Bill provided more excitement one afternoon when he was skipping rocks across the pond and cut open a young **girl's** head **who** was swimming under water. [A noun in the possessive functions as a modifier.] | Bill provided more excitement one afternoon when he was skipping rocks across the pond and cut open the head of a young **girl who** was swimming under water. |

## Ambiguous reference

Sometimes the meaning of a pronoun is unclear because the pronoun could refer to two different antecedents. To eliminate such ambiguity, either substitute a noun for the pronoun or clarify the antecedent:

**Confusing**
When Stanton visited the President in February, **he** did not know that **he** would be dead within two months.

**Clear**
When Stanton visited the President in February, **he** did not know that **Lincoln** would be dead within two months.

Sometimes ambiguous reference may be avoided by making one of the antecedents singular and the other plural:

**Ambiguous**
In the nineteenth century many businessmen [plural] exploited the workers [plural] at every point, not caring whether **they** were making a decent living wage, but only whether **they** were getting a lot of money.

**Clear**
In the nineteenth century many businessmen [plural] exploited the worker [singular] at every point, not caring whether **he** or **she** was making a decent living wage, but only whether **they** were getting a lot of money.

Using the same pronoun for different implied antecedents is particularly annoying to a reader and should be avoided:

**Confusing**
We pulled out our spare, which was under the seat, and put **it** on. **It** dampened our spirits for a while, but we decided to go on with **it**. [The first **it** refers to the tire, the second to the mishap, the third to the trip.]

**Revised**
We pulled out our spare, which was under the seat, and put the tire on. The flat dampened our spirits for a while, but we decided to go on with the trip.

Identifying the antecedent by repeating it after the pronoun is a makeshift practice that should be avoided:

**Clumsy**
Boswell first met Johnson when **he** (Johnson) was fifty-four.

**Revised**
Johnson was fifty-four when Boswell first met **him.**

Ambiguity sometimes results from a careless use of possessive pronouns:

**Ambiguous**
Mrs. Hurst was a very popular woman and **her accusation** scandalized everyone in town. [Was Mrs. Hurst the accuser or the accused?]

**Revised**
Mrs. Hurst was a very popular woman and **the accusation she made** [or **the accusation made about her**] scandalized everyone in town.

# Kinds of pronouns

## Personal pronouns

|  | Subject | Object | Possessive |
|---|---|---|---|
| First person |  |  |  |
| Singular | I | me | my, mine |
| Plural | we | us | our, ours |
| Second person |  |  |  |
| Singular and plural | you | you | your, yours |
| Third person |  |  |  |
| Singular |  |  |  |
| masculine | he | him | his |
| feminine | she | her | her, hers |
| neuter | it | it | its (of it) |
| Plural | they | them | their, theirs |

## Relative pronouns

|  |  |  |
|---|---|---|
| who | whom | whose |
| that | that |  |
| which | which | whose, of which |

## Interrogative pronouns

|  |  |  |
|---|---|---|
| who | whom | whose |
| which | which | whose, of which |
| what | what |  |

## Reflexive and intensive pronouns
myself, yourself, himself, herself, itself, oneself
ourselves, yourselves, themselves

## Demonstrative pronouns: this, these, that, those

## Indefinite pronouns

| all | both | everything | nobody | several |
|---|---|---|---|---|
| another | each | few | none | some |
| any | each one | many | no one | somebody |
| anybody | either | most | nothing | someone |
| anyone | everybody | much | one | something |
| anything | everyone | neither | other | such |

## Reciprocal pronouns: each other, one another

## Numeral pronouns: one, two, three . . . first, second, third . . .

## Pronouns referring to ideas and statements

*This, that, which,* and *it* are often used to refer to ideas or situations expressed in preceding statements:

Always do right. **This** will gratify some people and astonish the rest. — Mark Twain

Nor is the way in which a speech community rounds off its numbers haphazard; rather **it** is explainable as an interplay between language and culture. — Peter Farb, *Word Play*

Perhaps the enjoyment of music is always suffused with past experience; for me, at least, **this** is true. — Ralph Ellison, "Living with Music"

In such constructions, the idea to which the pronoun refers should be obvious.

## Use of *who, which, that*

*Who* refers to persons, *which* generally refers to things, and *that* refers to either persons or things.

Students **who** [or **that**] plan to enter the university in the fall quarter should forward transcripts of their records to the registrar.

In five minutes he solved a problem **that** [or **which**] I had struggled with for nearly five hours.

This is a matter about **which** more information is needed.

*That* usually introduces restrictive clauses. *Who* and *which* are used both restrictively and nonrestrictively. See §11.3.

The use of *which* to refer to persons is not desirable. Although *who* has no specific meaning, almost everyone who uses the pronoun uses it almost every time to refer to a person. *Which* doesn't have the same customary connection with persons, and is more often associated with nonliving or nonhuman things. *Which* is often used, however, to refer to impersonal organizations of people like groups, clubs, companies, and so on:

The state legislature, **which** [not **who**] passed the act despite the governor's protest, had its eye on politics.

The Maryland Company, **which** manufactured farm implements, has gone into bankruptcy.

## Use of *he* or *she*

The masculine pronoun *(he, him, his)* has customarily been used when referring to a noun or pronoun that includes persons of both sexes *(student, teacher, clerk, everyone, anyone, somebody):*

Each entering freshman is required to report promptly for **his** scheduled physical examination.

Everyone who is eligible to vote should make certain that **he** has registered before the deadline.

There is no particular reason why the masculine pronoun should be used in such situations. It has for a long time been a customary practice. It is more convenient and less cumbersome to use a single pronoun than it is to use two pronouns to signify both sexes:

Everyone who is eligible to vote should make certain that **he or she** has registered before the deadline.

It seems likely (if predictions aren't out of place in a handbook) that the use of both masculine and feminine pronouns will become more common, or plural constructions used more frequently:

**Every student** who wishes to can get **his or her** textbooks at the University Store immediately after registration.

**All students** who wish to can get **their** textbooks at the University Store immediately after registration.

## Agreement of pronoun and antecedent                    7.2

**Pron Agr**    Correction: Make the pronoun marked agree in form with the word to which it is related.

To be clear in meaning, a pronoun must agree in number with its antecedent—the particular noun to which it refers. When a pronoun serves as subject, the number of the verb is similarly determined by the pronoun's antecedent. (See also §5, Agreement of subject and verb.)

### Personal pronouns

Personal pronouns, like nouns, have both singular and plural forms, as listed in the table on page 101. A personal pronoun referring to a singular antecedent should be singular; one referring to a plural antecedent should be plural. Errors in agreement are most likely to occur when a pronoun is separated from its antecedent by some intervening element:

| Inaccurate | Accurate |
|---|---|
| Although the average **American** believes theoretically in justice for all, **they** sometimes fail to practice it. [**American** is singular; **they** is plural.] | Although the average **American** believes theoretically in justice for all, **he or she** sometimes fails to practice it. [**American** and **he or she** are both singular, as are their verbs.] |
| After reading his **arguments** in favor of abolishing property, I found that I was not convinced by **it**. [**Arguments** is plural; **it** is singular.] | After reading his **arguments** in favor of abolishing property, I found that I was not convinced by **them**. [Both **arguments** and **them** are plural.] |

When a pronoun's antecedent is a collective noun, the pronoun may be either singular or plural, depending on the meaning of the noun (see §5.2):

The **class** planned **its** next field trip.
The **class** had **their** pictures taken.

A pronoun referring to coordinate nouns joined by *and* is ordinarily plural:

When **Cynthia and Barbara** returned, **they** found the house empty.

Usually a singular pronoun is used to refer to nouns joined by *or* or *nor:*

**Dick or Stan** will lend you **his** car.

In general, the principles governing agreement between a pronoun and coordinate nouns are the same as those governing agreement between a compound subject and verb; see §5.1.

### Relative pronouns

When a relative pronoun is used as subject, the antecedent of the pronoun determines the number of the verb and of all reference words:

George is one of those people who **have** trouble making up **their minds**. [The antecedent of **who** is **people**.]
George is a person who **has** trouble making up **his mind**. [The antecedent of **who** is **person**.]

### Indefinite pronouns

A number of words of greater or less indefiniteness often function as pronouns: *some, all, none, everybody, somebody, anybody, anyone.* Some of these words are considered singular; others may be singular or plural, depending on the meaning of the statement. In revising your papers be sure that verbs and reference words agree in number with indefinite pronouns.

*everyone, anybody, somebody*
*Everyone, everybody, anyone, anybody, someone, somebody, no one, nobody* are singular forms and are used with singular verbs (Everyone *has* left; Somebody *was* here; Nobody ever *calls*).

Spoken usage and written usage, however, often differ in the form of the pronouns used with these words. In writing, a singular reference word is standard (Everyone brought *his* book); in speaking, a plural reference word is often used.

| **Written** | **Spoken** |
|---|---|
| Not everyone is as prompt in paying **his** bills as you are. | Not everyone is as prompt in paying **their** bills as you are. |

But in some statements a singular reference word would be puzzling or nonsensical with the indefinite pronoun:

When I finally managed to get to my feet, everybody was laughing at me, and I couldn't blame **them** [**him** would be impossible] because I was a funny sight.

*all, some, none*
*All, any, some, most, more* are either singular or plural, depending upon the meaning of the statement:

All of the turkey **has** been eaten.
All of these questions **were** answered.
Some of the dialog **is** witty.
Some of the farmers **have** opposed price supports.

*None* may be either singular or plural, depending upon the context. In current usage it is commonly used with a plural verb, but formal usage still prefers a singular verb unless the meaning is clearly plural.

None of our national parks **is** more scenic than Glacier.
None of the charges **has** been proved.
None of the new homes **are** as well constructed as the homes built twenty-five years ago. [The sentence clearly refers to all new homes.]

The emphatic *no one* is always singular:

I looked at a dozen books on the subject, but no one **was** of any use to me.

*each*

*Each* is a singular pronoun and usually takes a singular verb and singular reference words:

**Each** of the players on the football team **has his** own idea about physical training.

Every year thousands of women adopt some current fashion in dress, yet **each thinks her** attire is unique.

Although the use of the plural form to refer to *each* is considered informal (*Each* of the boys ran as fast as *their* legs could carry *them*), this construction is sometimes found in writing when the plural idea is uppermost:

Each of these peoples undoubtedly modified Latin in accordance with **their** own speech habits. — Albert C. Baugh, *History of the English Language*

However, unless you are prepared to justify your use of plural forms with *each,* you should use singular verbs and pronouns. See also §9.3, Demonstrative adjectives, for agreement of *this* and *that (this kind, that sort).*

## Case of pronouns                                    **7.3**

**Case**   Correction: Change the form of the pronoun marked to show how it functions in the sentence.

### Subject and object pronouns
Most personal pronouns and the relative or interrogative pronoun *who* have one form when they are used as subjects *(I, she, he, we, they, who)* and another when they are used as objects *(me, her, him, us, them, whom).* The distinction between these forms (or *cases*) is sometimes disregarded in speech (There were no secrets between Mother and *I*), but writers are expected to follow conventional use (There were no secrets between Mother and *me*). Subject and object forms are listed in the table of pronoun forms on page 101.

### After prepositions
The object form of a personal pronoun is used after a preposition (a letter for *him;* among *us* three). When a pronoun

immediately follows a preposition, there is seldom any question about the proper form, but when there are two pronouns, or when a noun is used with the pronoun, writers are sometimes tempted to use a subject form.

| Incorrect | Revised |
|---|---|
| After all, those men are human beings, like you and **I**. | After all, those men are human beings, like you and **me**. |
| The same is no doubt true of what European and Asiatic nations have heard about **we** Americans. | The same is no doubt true of what European and Asiatic nations have heard about **us** Americans. |
| The work was divided between **she** and **I**. | The work was divided between **her** and **me**. |

After *than* in comparisons

In written English, *than* is considered a conjunction, not a preposition, and is followed by the form of the pronoun that would be used in a complete clause, whether or not the verb appears in the construction:

I am older than **she** [is].
John dances better than **I** [do].
I like him better than **she** [does].
I like him better than [I like] **her**.

In speech the object form is common with *than* when the pronoun stands alone (I am older than *her;* My roommate was taking more courses than *me*). It is occasionally found in general writing, especially fiction, but in most college writing the subject form is preferable in these constructions.

*it is I, it's me*

Formal English prefers the subject form after the linking verb *be* (It is *I;* that is *he*). But educated as well as uneducated people usually say and write "It's me" or "That's him." *Me* is more natural in this expression because the pronoun stands in the object position, immediately after a verb. All authoritative grammars and dictionaries consider *it's me* acceptable general usage. Fortunately, this construction seldom occurs in writing, except in dialog, where "It is *I*" would sound stilted.

The notion that *I* is somehow more "correct" or polite than *me* sometimes leads people to use the subject form even when the pronoun is the object of a verb: Father took Jerry and *I* to the game. The object form should be used in such constructions: Father took Jerry and *me* to the game.

*who, whom*

The distinction between *who* and *whom* has practically dropped from speech (the *Oxford English Dictionary* says *whom* is "no longer current in natural colloquial speech"), and it may eventually disappear in writing. For example, in this construction — *Who* are you taking to the concert? — most would agree that *who* seems natural, since it's in the subject position, although formal usage would require *whom,* as the direct object (You are taking *whom* to the concert?).

In most college papers it is probably best to make the distinction between *who* and *whom: whom* is the standard form when it is the object of a preposition and comes immediately after the preposition (To *whom* were you speaking? He was a man in *whom* we placed great trust). In other objective constructions *whom* is also used; use *who* when it is the subject of a verb, even in subordinate clauses which may themselves be in the objective case:

Taxes will go up no matter **whom** we elect [**whom** is the direct object of the verb **elect**].

Taxes will go up no matter **who** is elected [**who** is the subject of the verb **is elected**].

The easiest way to check your usage is to arrange the elements in the clause in a subject – verb – object order (we elect *whom; who* is elected); *whom* serves as object, *who* as subject. Sometimes intervening words cause problems, but the principle still holds: He made a list of all the writers *who* [subject of *were*] he thought were important in that century.

Possessive pronouns

In writing, the chief problem in the use of possessive forms of pronouns is the apostrophe. Remember that an apostrophe is not used with the possessives of personal pronouns (a relative of *ours;* the tree and *its* leaves), nor with the possessive of the relative pronoun *who* (a boy *whose* name was Tom).

Possessive of personal pronouns

Personal pronouns have two forms for the possessive (see p. 101): one is used (as a modifier) before a noun (*my* roommate, *her* favorite hat) and the other is used (by itself or in a phrase) after a noun (That pencil is *mine;* a friend of *hers*). While either form may be used in many statements (*our* government, this government of *ours*), there are some constructions in which one form is obviously better than the other:

| Clumsy | Revised |
|---|---|
| We decided to pool **their** and **our** resources. | We decided to pool their resources with **ours.** |

*its, it's*

*Its* without the apostrophe is the possessive form of *it; it's* with the apostrophe is the contraction for *it is* or *it has:*

Everything should be in **its** proper place.
**It's** [it is] an ill wind that blows no good.
**It's** [it has] been a long time.

One of the mistakes most frequently marked on student papers is using *it's* for *its.* If you tend to confuse these two forms you should check each instance of *its (it's)* when revising your papers: for example, if you've used *it's,* read the word as *it is* or *it has;* your meaning will reveal any errors.

Possessive of indefinite pronouns

Several of the indefinite pronouns *(all, any, each, few, most, none, some)* are used only in *of* phrases for the possessive:

They were both happy when things were going well, but adversity brought out the best side **of each.**

The apostrophe and *s* are used with the possessive forms of other indefinite pronouns, just as they are with nouns:

**Anyone's** guess is as good as mine.
One man's meat is **another's** poison.
**Somebody's** books were left in the classroom.

When indefinite pronouns are used with *else,* the apostrophe and *s* are added to *else* and not to the preceding word:

These notes are somebody **else's.**
Anyone **else's** offer would have been accepted.

Possessive of *who* and *which*

*Whose* is the possessive form of the relative pronoun *who. Who's,* the informal contraction for *who is* or *who has,* is not used in most writing.

Best known of American primitives is Grandma Moses, **whose** paintings are familiar to thousands.
It is the white-collar worker **who is** [informal: **who's**] least likely to be affected by seasonal unemployment.

Although *whose* usually refers to persons and *of which* to things, *whose* is regularly used to refer to inanimate things when *of which* would be awkward.

. . . we would cross a room in which no one ever sat, **whose** fire was never lighted, **whose** walls were picked out with gilded mouldings. . . . — Marcel Proust, *Remembrance of Things Past*

## Reflexive and intensive pronouns 7.4

The reflexive form of a personal pronoun is used to refer back to the subject in an expression where the doer and recipient of an act are the same:

I had only **myself** to blame.
He hurt **himself** skiing.

The same pronoun form is sometimes used as an intensive to make another word more emphatic:

The award was presented by the governor **himself.**
Life **itself** is at stake.

In certain constructions *myself* is mistakenly considered by some people as more polite than *I* or *me* (My wife and *myself* accept with pleasure), but in standard English the reflexive form is not used as the subject or as a substitute for *me:*

Another fellow and **I** [not: **myself**] saw the whole thing.
Sam invited John and **me** [not: **myself**] to dinner.

*Hisself* and *theirselves* are not standard English forms.

## Choice of personal pronoun form 7.5

Personal pronouns indicate the person or persons speaking (first person: *I, we*), the person spoken to (second person: *you*), or the person or thing spoken of (third person: *he, she, it, one, they*). In writing, the choice of form may be a problem since the writer can refer to himself or herself as *I, one,* or *we*. Some questions that frequently arise in using these pronouns are considered here.

### *I, we*

There is no reason to avoid the pronoun *I* in any situation where it is needed. Some writers, perhaps through excessive modesty, try to get around the natural use of *I* by devices that only call attention to themselves.

| Awkward | Revised |
|---|---|
| After exploring the subject, **the writer** finds that mass hysteria is a rather common occurrence. | After exploring the subject, I find that mass hysteria is a rather common occurrence. |

*We* is useful for general reference (*We* are living in an atomic age), but as a substitute for *I,* the "editorial" *we* is out of place in most writing.

| Awkward | Revised |
|---|---|
| The conclusions in **our** paper are based upon information **we** obtained from the local police. | The conclusions in **my** paper are based upon information I obtained from the local police. |

*you*

Overuse of the generalizing *you* (meaning people in general) should be avoided. Its implied reference to the reader may sometimes be irritating:

| Awkward | Revised |
|---|---|
| When **you** begin reading *The Waste Land,* **you** are totally confused. | When I began reading *The Waste Land,* I was totally confused. |

Use of the generalized *you* should be confined to situations which genuinely apply to everyone:

When **you** suddenly enter a dark room, it takes a while for **your** eyes to adjust.

*You* can be used successfully, as in a familiar essay, when the writer seeks to establish a close relationship with the reader.

*one*

*One* is used, particularly in formal writing, to refer either to people in general or to the writer:

Watching the scene on television, **one** senses the drama of the situation.

But this use of *one* is impersonal, rather stiff, and often ungainly, especially when *one* is repeated several times. General English characteristically uses personal pronouns in such expressions:

Watching the scene on television, I [or **you**] can sense the drama of the situation.

In current American usage, it is standard practice to refer to *one* (meaning the writer or anyone) by the third-person *he* and *his* or *she* and *her:*

One should be cautious if **he** wants to avoid offending **his** friends.

## Avoiding shifts in pronoun form

**Shift**   Correction: Make the words or constructions marked consistent in form. Pronouns should be consistent in person and number; verbs should be consistent in tense.

In using pronouns for general reference, be consistent and do not make unnecessary shifts from singular to plural forms or from *we* to *you* or *one.*

**Inconsistent**

After **one** has selected the boat **he** is going to learn in, it would be a good idea if **you** first learned the theory of sailing. Most of **us** have at least seen a sailing boat, but seeing one and sailing one are two different things. **One** might think that a boat can sail only with the breeze and not against it. Or **they** might think that a stiff breeze is necessary to sail a boat.

**Consistent**

After **you** have selected the boat **you** are going to learn in, it would be a good idea if **you** first learned the theory of sailing. **You** have probably seen a sailing boat, but seeing one and sailing one are two different things. **You** may think that a boat can sail only with the breeze and not against it. Or **you** may think that a stiff breeze is necessary to sail a boat.

The pronoun *one* is more likely to lead to shifted constructions than are the other forms. Unless you intend to be impersonal and feel confident in your use of *one*, use *you, we, he,* or a noun substitute in these situations.

**Applications: Pronouns**

1.  Use pronouns to replace the repetitious nouns and make a single, smoother sentence.

    *example:* John saw the sports car. John knew at once that he must own the sports car.
    *rewritten:* John saw the sports car and he knew at once that he must own it.

    **a.** The Duchess lit the Duchess' cigar. The cigar glowed brightly.
    **b.** ''Heavens, yes,'' said the Duchess, ''the Duchess will tell you about the Duke. The Duke is now dead.''
    **c.** ''The Duke was unwilling to take orders from the Duchess,'' said the Duchess. ''The Duke thought that the Duke would run the castle and the kingdom.''

**d.** "But the Duchess had other ideas. Now the Duke sleeps permanently in the garden, and the Duchess runs the kingdom and the castle."

**e.** "The castle and the kingdom are well run now. The castle and the kingdom are efficient. The Duchess is happy and, come to think of it, the Duke is probably better off, too," concluded the Duchess.

**2.** Rewrite the following sentences, changing the words indicated. Make all other changes that would naturally occur, including those in pronoun, noun, and verb forms.

*example:* Change *an athlete* to *athletes.* When an athlete gets out of shape, he is probably insuring the end of his career and the end of his team's winning record.
*rewritten:* When *athletes* get out of shape, *they* are probably insuring the end of *their* careers and the end of *their* team's (or *teams'*) winning record (or *records,* if *teams'*).

**a.** Change *a person* to *people.* When a person weaves in and out of traffic lanes, he is endangering the lives of other motorists as well as his own.

**b.** Change *Another* to *Other.* Another grocery store also reports that its meat sales have fallen off.

**c.** Change *anyone* to *everyone.* My sister wanted to be able to help anyone who looked insecure or troubled, and to make him feel at ease, no matter who it happened to be.

**d.** Change *one* to *some.* One actor may interpret the role of Hamlet one way, another another way; if one decides that the role is pathetic, another may decide that his view—the tragic one—is correct.

**e.** Change *each* to *all.* Until the law determining the age of legal majority was changed, each student was expected to provide her home address so that her grades could be sent to her parents.

**3.** Revise each of the following sentences in which the reference of pronouns seems to you inexact, misleading, or otherwise faulty.

*example:* A general interest bookstore would probably do better in this town than an obscure one.
*revised:* A general interest bookstore would probably do better in this town than a bookstore that specializes in obscure books.

**a.** After he had studied *kung fu* for three months, he began to boast that he was an expert one.

**b.** An exercise room is available in the basement of the new physical education building which can be used by both students and faculty.

**c.** Tolliver's wild flower text is useful, but its descriptions of the high-plains ones are vague.

**d.** Football is a more complex game now than in the past, with its play books and game movies, but many are still brutally rough.

e. When the women were about to leave the exhibit of quarter horses, they ran into their mates.

4. Revise the following sentences to correct the needless shifts in person or number.

   *example:* The modern car is very complex, and they are always breaking down.
   *revised:* The modern car is very complex, and *it is* always breaking down.
   *Or:* Modern *cars are* very complex, and they are always breaking down.

   a. Some writers think teachers use grammar as a means to block your creative abilities.
   b. When a person has worked for a year in Washington, one is reluctant to return home to an ordinary job.
   c. When a student has spent a lot of time on his compositions, they are apt to be disgruntled if all they get is grammatical criticisms. Anybody would feel the same way if you had a teacher like mine.
   d. Although a pocket dictionary can give some help, they cannot replace a standard desk dictionary.
   e. Nobody in the class seemed very sure of their ability to analyze style.

5. Read the following sentences and correct any pronouns not in good edited form.

   *example:* She answered the phone, trying to sound very dignified, and said, ''Would you like to leave a message with I?''
   *revised: I* should be *me.*

   a. She divided what was left of the cake equally between Margaret and I.
   b. A book in which a man and a woman collaborate should deal accurately with human nature, for between him and her they represent the two sexes.
   c. Most of the other actors have had more experience than me and make fun of my stage fright.
   d. Whom do you think is going to be chosen as editor?
   e. A letter came for Paul and I inviting us to a committee meeting.

# Verbs 8

**Vb**  Correction: Change the verb form marked so that it conforms to standard usage.

The emphasized words in these sentences are verbs:

The hunter **shot** a deer.
Our next speaker **will be introduced** by the chairperson.
**Are** you ready?

Except in questions, verbs usually follow the subject. In meaning, they indicate action *(run, manufacture, write)*, condition *(am, feel, sleep)*, or process *(become, grow)*. In form, they may be one word *(do)* or a phrase *(should have done)*, and may add letters (prove*s*, prove*d*) or change internally (s*i*ng, s*a*ng, s*u*ng) to indicate person, number, tense, and voice. The table on page 117 lists the terms used to describe the principal characteristics of verbs.

  The following sections discuss some of the most common problems in the use of verb forms. See also §4, Verbals, and §5, Agreement of subject and verb.

# Tense 8.1

**T**  Correction: Make the tense of the verb marked conventional in form or consistent with others in the passage.

By means of the different tenses, a writer sets the time of the situation he is describing (as happening in the past, going on at present, or occurring in the future) and also shows the continuity of the action or explanation. Consistent and conventional use of tense keeps the sequence of your writing in order and enables a reader to follow the sequence.

## Tense forms
The appropriate form of a verb should be used to indicate each of its tenses. Problems seldom arise with regular verbs, because they have only two forms: the infinitive or base form

used for the present tense *(walk, imagine, sleep)* and a form ending in *-ed, -d,* or *-t* for the past tense and past participle *(walked, imagined, slept).* See §8.2 for the forms of irregular verbs.

Except for the simple present and past tenses, English verbs show distinctions of time by various phrase combinations *(have walked, had walked, will walk,* etc.), often supported by adverbs (for example, "he is *about* to go" as a future). The table on page 118 lists the most frequently used active tenses and the verb phrases most commonly associated with time distinctions.

### Sequence of past tenses

The various past tenses in English serve to distinguish degrees of past time. In simplified terms, they may be described as follows: the *past* expresses indefinite past time (he *finished*); the *perfect* expresses past time extending to the present (he *has finished*); the *past perfect* expresses past time before some other past time (he *had finished*); the *past progressive* (he *was finishing*) expresses a more extended period of past time. These tenses should be used accurately to express differences in past time.

He **has finished** supper [perfect] and **is looking** [present progressive] at television.

He **had finished** supper [past perfect] and **was looking** [past progressive] at television.

He **had finished** supper [past perfect] when I **arrived** [past].
He **finished** supper [past] when I **arrived** [past].

When the verb of a main clause is in the past or past perfect tense, the verb in a subordinate clause is also past or past perfect:

They slowly **began** to appreciate what their teacher **had** [not **has**] **done** for them.

Up to that time I **had** never **seen** Slim when he **hadn't** [or **didn't have**; not **hasn't**] a wad of tobacco in his mouth.

*Exception:* A present infinitive is usual after a past verb:

I **would have liked** very much **to attend** [not **to have attended**] her wedding, but I was out of town.

# Terms used in describing verbs

**Verb forms** (§8.1). English verbs have three principal parts:

| Infinitive (the base form) | Past tense | Past participle |
|---|---|---|
| ask (to ask), go (to go) | asked, went | asked, gone |

**Regular and irregular verbs** (§8.1 and §8.2). Regular verbs add -*ed* to form the past tense and past participle (ask, asked, asked). Irregular verbs change form in other ways (sing, sang, sung; go, went, gone).

**Tense** (§8.1). The "time" of a verb's action as expressed in the form of the verb:
**Past:** I went      **Present:** I go      **Future:** I will go
(For other tenses, see the table on p. 118.)

**Transitive and intransitive.**
A verb is **transitive** when it has an object: The teacher *demanded*(v) *order*(o).
A verb is **intransitive** when it does not have an object: He *slept*(v) well.

**Active and passive voice** (§8.3).
A **passive** verb is a form of *be* and a past participle: *is believed, was believed, had been believed, will be believed.*
All other verbs are **active.**

**Mood** (§8.4). The manner in which a statement is expressed (an almost obsolete distinction now):
The **indicative mood** expresses a fact or a statement: I *am* thrifty.
The **subjunctive mood** is used in some conditions and in clauses like the following: It is necessary that he *be* twenty-one.

**Auxiliary verb** (§8.2). A verb used in a verb phrase to show tense, voice, etc.: *am* going; *had* gone; *will* go; *should have been* done.

**Linking verb or copula** (§1.1). A verb that "links" its subject to a predicate noun or an adjective: She *is* a teacher. The days *became* warmer.

**Finite and nonfinite verbs.**
**A finite verb** (from the Latin *finis*, meaning "end" or "limit") can be limited (§5 and §8):
In **person** by a pronoun or subject (I *sing*, she *sings*)
In **time** by a tense form (she *sings*, she *sang*)
In **number,** singular or plural (he *sings*, they *sing*)
Finite verbs are full verbs in sentences and clauses: I *had gone* before he *came*.

**The nonfinite verb forms** (participles, infinitives, gerunds) are not limited in person or number and are ordinarily used in phrases (§4): Before *leaving* I thanked our host. She needed a hat *to wear* to the party.

## Most frequently used active verb tenses

| | I | he, she, it | we, you, they |
|---|---|---|---|
| **Present tenses** | | | |
| **Present** (immediate present) | ask | asks | ask |
| **Present progressive** (continuing present) | **am** asking | **is** asking | **are** asking |
| **Past tenses** | | | |
| **Past** | asked | asked | asked |
| **Past progressive** (continuing period in past) | **was** asking | **was** asking | **were** asking |
| **Perfect** (past time extending to the present; past participle plus *have* or *has*) | **have** asked | **has** asked | **have** asked |
| **Past perfect** (a time in the past before another past time; past participle plus *had*) | had asked | had asked | had asked |
| **Future tenses** | | | |
| **Future** (future time extending from the present) | will ask / **am** going to ask | will ask / **is** going to ask | will ask / **are** going to ask |
| **Future perfect** (past time in some future time; future tense of *have* plus past participle) | will have asked | will have asked | will have asked |

## Consistent use of tenses

**Shift**  Correction: Make the words or constructions marked consistent in form. Verbs should be consistent in tense; pronouns should be consistent in person and number.

Unnecessary shifts in tense (as from the present to the past, or the past to the future) confuse the sequence of your writing:

**Unnecessary shifts**
I **sit** down at my desk early with intentions of spending the next four hours studying. Before many minutes **passed,** I **heard** a great deal of noise down on the floor below me; a water fight **is** in progress. I **forgot** about studying for half an hour, for it **is** quite impossible to concentrate on Spanish in the midst of all this commotion. After things **quieted** down I **began** studying again, but **had** hardly **started** when a magazine salesman **comes** into my room. [mixture of present and past]

**Consistent**
I **sat** down at my desk early with intentions of spending the next four hours studying. Before many minutes **had passed,** I **heard** a great deal of noise down on the floor below me; a water fight **was** in progress. I **forgot** about studying for half an hour, for it **was** quite impossible to concentrate on Spanish in the midst of all that commotion. After things **had quieted** down I **began** studying again, but **had** hardly started when a magazine salesman **came** into my room. [past tense throughout]

In single sentences inconsistencies in verb tenses often occur when a writer shifts the form of two or more verbs that should be parallel:

**Shifted**
For years I **have been attending** summer camp and **enjoyed** every minute of it.

**Consistent**
For years I **have been attending** summer camp and **enjoying** every minute of it.

## Irregular verbs and auxiliaries                                    **8.2**

Some of the most commonly used verbs in English create problems in writing because of their irregular forms or optional uses.

## Irregular verb forms

Writers sometimes depart from the standards of edited American English when they form some tenses of the irregular ("strong") verbs. This is most likely to happen when a writer uses some dialect form or other unedited form (He *seen* the show last week) or when a writer confuses forms with similar spellings *(choose, chose).* The following list shows the principal parts of irregular verbs that sometimes cause problems. The *past tense,* second column, is used in the simple past (She *wrote* a letter). The *past participle,* third column, is used with auxiliaries to form verb phrases (The bird *had flown* away; Soon this *will be forgotten:* The chimes *are being rung*). The past participle cannot be used alone as a full verb in the past tense.

When two forms are given, both are acceptable (He *lighted* a cigarette; He *lit* a cigarette). Verbs marked with an asterisk (*) are discussed in the sections following. For verbs not given here, consult a recent dictionary. Caution: If your dictionary labels a form in question *nonstandard, obsolete, archaic, dialect,* or *rare* it is not suitable for most general writing.

| Infinitive | Past tense | Past participle |
| --- | --- | --- |
| arise | arose | arisen |
| bear (carry)* | bore | borne |
| bear (give birth to)* | bore | borne, born |
| begin | began | begun |
| bite | bit | bitten, bit |
| blow | blew | blown |
| break | broke | broken |
| bring | brought | brought |
| burst | burst | burst |
| catch | caught | caught |
| choose | chose | chosen |
| come | came | come |
| dig | dug | dug |
| dive | dived, dove | dived, dove |
| do* | did | done |
| drag | dragged | dragged |
| draw | drew | drawn |
| dream | dreamed, dreamt | dreamed, dreamt |
| drink | drank | drunk |
| drive | drove | driven |
| eat | ate | eaten |
| fall | fell | fallen |
| fly | flew | flown |
| forget | forgot | forgotten |

| Infinitive | Past tense | Past participle |
|---|---|---|
| freeze | froze | frozen |
| get* | got | got, gotten |
| give | gave | given |
| go | went | gone |
| grow | grew | grown |
| hang (a person) | hanged, hung | hanged, hung |
| hang (an object) | hung | hung |
| know | knew | known |
| lay (place)* | laid | laid |
| lead | led | led |
| lend | lent | lent |
| lie (recline)* | lay | lain |
| light | lighted, lit | lighted, lit |
| lose | lost | lost |
| pay | paid | paid |
| prove | proved | proved, proven |
| ride | rode | ridden |
| ring | rang, rung | rung |
| rise | rose | risen |
| run | ran | run |
| see | saw | seen |
| set* | set | set |
| shake | shook | shaken |
| shine | shone, shined | shone, shined |
| show | showed | showed, shown |
| shrink | shrank, shrunk | shrunk |
| sing | sang, sung | sung |
| sink | sank, sunk | sunk, sunken |
| sit* | sat | sat |
| slide | slid | slid, slidden |
| speak | spoke | spoken |
| spring | sprang, sprung | sprung |
| stand | stood | stood |
| steal | stole | stolen |
| swim | swam, swum | swum |
| take | took | taken |
| tear | tore | torn |
| throw | threw | thrown |
| wake | waked, woke | waked, woke |
| wear | wore | worn |
| wring˙ | wrung | wrung |
| write | wrote | written |

## Forms of the verb be

The verb be has eight forms, three more than any other verb in English. In addition to the infinitive, there are three forms in the present tense, two in the past tense, the present participle, and the past participle:

| | I | he, she, it | we, you, they |
|---|---|---|---|
| **Present tense** | am | is | are |
| **Past tense** | was | was | were |
| **Present participle** | being | | |
| **Past participle** | been | | |

The forms of *be* are not troublesome in ordinary situations, at least not if you are reasonably well acquainted with edited American English. Some dialects do use *be* differently, for example, *she be singing.* These forms are usually not found in general written English, however.

*ain't*

*Ain't* is an idiolect and dialect contraction; *aren't* and *isn't* are the standard forms. In questions with *I, am I not* is formal; *Aren't I* is the form most often used. Since the forms are rarely needed in writing except in dialog, the form most natural to the speaker would be used.

### Choice of *can* or *may*

In all levels of usage *can* is used for ability (This car *can* do better than 80 miles an hour; He *can* walk now with crutches), and *may* for possibility (That *may* be true; We *may* get there before dark).

To express permission, formal English generally uses *may* (*May* I go now? You *may* have any one you like); general English increasingly uses *can* in such expressions (*Can* I go now? You *can* have any one you like), but many people object to this usage. In writing it is best to use *may.*

### *do, did, done*

Some idiolects and dialects use *done* alone (He *done* his best to please her) when edited American English calls for standard forms. Particular care should be given to the past tense and the past participle:

Present tense: I, we, you, they **do**; he, she, it **does**

Past tense: I, you, he, she, it, we, they **did**

Past participle: I, you, we, they have (had) **done**; he, she, it has (had) **done**

### *don't, doesn't*

*Don't* is the contraction for *do not* (I do not, I don't), *doesn't* is the contraction for *does not* (he does not, he doesn't). The substitution of one form for the other (*Don't* she look pretty?) is not consistent with edited forms of the language.

## Idioms with *do*

*Do* is used in many standard idioms (set expressions): *do without*, *do away with*, *make do*. In college writing it's best to avoid informal expressions with *do*, like these:

When the Dean of Women arrived, she seemed **done in** [**exhausted**]. They **did** [**cheated**] the government out of $50,000.

Consult a dictionary whenever you are unsure about the appropriateness of a particular expression with *do* or *done.*

## *born — borne*

The past participle of *bear* in the sense of "carry" is spelled *borne:* a leaf *borne* by the wind, he had *borne* many hardships. In the sense of "give birth to," the spelling is *born* in the passive voice, *borne* in the active: *born* in Miami, a *born* loser, a child *born* to her (but, she had *borne* a child).

## *get, got, gotten*

The principal parts of the verb *get* are *get, got,* and *gotten* or *got.* Both forms of the past participle are used in the United States:

He could have **gotten** [or **got**] more for his money.
Her efforts had **gotten** [or **got**] no results.

Used with *have* to show possession (see below), the form is always *got.* In other constructions, *gotten* is more common.

### *have got, have got to*

*Have got* in the sense of possession (I *haven't got* a black tie) or obligation (We *have got* to finish this experiment today) is widely used in speech and is acceptable in most kinds of writing. Some writers of formal English avoid the expression, regarding *got* as redundant and preferring *have* alone (I *haven't* a black tie; We *have* to finish this experiment today). Although *have* alone carries the meaning, it is so frequently used as a mere auxiliary of tense that we do not often consider it as a verb of full meaning, and either *have* or *have got* is usually considered acceptable.

### Idioms with *get*

In many common idioms *get* is standard usage for all levels of speaking and writing:

get up                                    get along with (someone)
get away from                             get over (an illness)
get ahead                                 get tired

Other expressions with *get* are considered informal and would best be avoided in college writing:

Long-winded discussions **get** on my nerves.
This modern music **gets** me.
Some people seem to **get** away with murder.
A stray bullet **got** him in the shoulder.

When you are in doubt about the standing of an idiom with *get,* consult a recent dictionary.

### *lie — lay*
*Lie,* meaning to recline, does not take an object. Its principal parts are *lie, lay, lain:* You *lie* down for a rest, or *lie* down on the job; Yesterday he *lay* in bed all morning; The log had *lain* across the road for a week. The present participle of *lie* is *lying:* The log was *lying* in the road; I found him *lying* in bed.

Lay, meaning to put or place, takes an object. Its principal parts are *lay, laid, laid:* He should *lay* down his cards; She *laid* her purse on the table; The cornerstone was *laid.* The present participle of *lay* is *laying:* He was *laying* the foundation. The same forms are used when *lay* means to produce an egg.

### *sit — set*
The verb *sit* (as in a chair) does not take an object. Its principal parts are *sit, sat, sat:* I like to *sit* in a hotel lobby; He *sat* there an hour; I have *sat* in the same chair for three semesters.

The verb *set,* meaning to put something down, takes an object. Its principal parts are *set, set, set: Set* the soup on this pad; They *set* the trunk in the hall yesterday; She has *set* candles in the windows.

For correct uses of *set* in its many other meanings, consult the dictionary.

### *shall — will*
In current American usage, *will* is generally used with all persons of the verb for the future tense (I *will* leave tomorrow. He *will* arrive at six. We *will* return later). To express determination or for emphasis, usage is divided about *will* and *shall* (I *will* not permit it. They *shall* pass). Some formal writers make the following distinctions between *shall* and *will:*

**Simple future**

| First person: | I shall ask | we shall ask |
| --- | --- | --- |
| Second person: | you will ask | you will ask |
| Third person: | he, she, it will ask | they will ask |

**Emphatic future**

| First person: | I will ask | we will ask |
| --- | --- | --- |
| Second person: | you shall ask | you shall ask |
| Third person: | he, she, it shall ask | they shall ask |

These distinctions are seldom made today except by the most conservative formal writers.

*shall* and *will* in questions

In questions, *will* is used in all persons, but *shall* is often used, especially in formal English, if there is a notion of propriety or obligation:

**Will** I go? Where **will** we go next? What **will** you do now?
Obligation: **Shall** I go? What **shall** she wear?

In the negative, *won't* is the regular form:

What **won't** they think of next?
Why **won't** you go?

Overuse of *shall*

*Shall* should not be used in statements where *will* is the standard form:

Whether or not Congress **will** [not **shall**] pass the bill is not for me to guess.

Some people apparently think that *shall* is a more correct (or elegant) form than *will.* It isn't.

*should—would*

*Should* and *would* are used in statements that carry a sense of doubt or uncertainty:

It **should** be cooler by evening. [Contrast with the meaning of: It **will** be cooler by evening.]
I wasn't ready as soon as I thought I **would** be.

*Should,* like *shall,* is often used to express the idea of propriety or obligation:

You **should** wash your hands before meals.·
I **should** answer her letter this week.

In polite or unemphatic requests, both *would* and *should* are used for the first person and *would* for the second person:

I **would** be much obliged if you could help me.
I **should** be much obliged if you could help me.

**Would** you please give this your earliest attention?
I wish you **would** write more often.

In indirect discourse *would* and *should* serve as the past tenses of *will* and *shall:*

| Direct discourse | Indirect discourse |
|---|---|
| Mary said, "I will go." | Mary said that she would go. |
| "Shall we adjourn?" the chair-man asked. | The chairman asked if they should adjourn. |

## Active and passive voice     **8.3**

We frequently have a choice of making a noun either the subject or object in a sentence, with a resulting difference in verb form:

Active verb: Jim's father **gave** him a car.
Passive verb: Jim **was given** a car by his father.

The passive consists of a form of *be* plus the past participle *(is given, are chosen, was taken, have been corrected).*

### Appropriate passives

The great majority of English sentences use active verbs, but sometimes the passive is appropriate. Passive constructions are natural if the actor is unknown or unimportant to the statement:

The game **was postponed** because of rain.

The expressway **will be completed** by spring.

The entire fuel-handling operation **is conducted** by remote control, of course, and fresh fuel assemblies **can be delivered** to the storage rack or spent ones **removed** from it while the reactor is in operation.—T. R. Bump, "A Third Generation of Breeder Reactors." *Scientific American*

A passive verb may also be appropriate if the writer wants to emphasize the object or the act rather than the doer:

The fire **was discovered** by the night watchman.
The bill **is supported** by congressmen of both parties.

### Inappropriate passives

| **Pass** | Correction: Change the passive verb or verbs to active. |
|---|---|

Often passive constructions are weak or awkward and should be changed to the more direct active form:

| **Weak passive** | **Active** |
|---|---|
| A distinction **is made** by sociologists between achieved and ascribed status. | Sociologists **make** a distinction between achieved and ascribed status. |
| All of the major Russian novelists **were studied** in my comparative literature course. | I **studied** all of the major Russian novelists in my comparative literature course. |

It is sometimes awkward to combine an active and a passive verb in the same sentence:

| **Awkward** | **Revised** |
|---|---|
| The city **needs** more money to build new schools, and it **will** probably **be raised** through a bond issue. | The city **needs** more money to build new schools and **will** probably **raise** it through a bond issue. |

## Use of the subjunctive mood        8.4

Certain instances of untypical verb forms are known as the subjunctive mood: He *ask* instead of *asks;* I, he, she *were* instead of *was;* I, he, she *be asked* instead of *is* or *was asked.* The use of these forms in current English is quite limited and inconsistent, even in formal English. There is almost always an alternative construction, and writers seldom need to use the subjunctive.

### In conditions
The subjunctive is sometimes used, especially in formal English, to express contrary-to-fact, impossible, or improbable conditions:

If I **were** in your position [I'm not], I wouldn't accept his offer.
He said if he **were** President [he isn't], he would remove them.

The subjunctive is sometimes found in simple conditions:

If the subject of a verb **be** impersonal, the verb itself may be called impersonal.

This use does not contribute to meaning and seems unimportant.

### In *that* clauses
The subjunctive is used in many set expressions (usually in a

formal, often legal, context) for recommendations, demands, and so on:

| Formal | General edited form |
|---|---|
| It is required that the applicant **be** under twenty-one. | The applicant must be under twenty-one. |
| It is necessary that every member **inform** himself of these rules. | Every member should inform himself of these rules. *Or:* It is necessary for every member to inform himself of these rules. |
| I ask that the interested citizen **watch** closely the movements of these troops. | I ask the interested citizen to watch closely the movements of these troops. |

### In formulas

The subjunctive is found in numerous formulas and set phrases, locutions surviving from a time when the subjunctive was used freely:

| | | |
|---|---|---|
| If I were you | Be that as it may | Heaven forbid |
| Come what may | God bless you | As it were |

## Idioms with verbs                                    **8.5**

| **Id** | Correction: Change the word or expression marked so that it will be idiomatic. |
|---|---|

Verbs and verb phrases should be both idiomatically correct and appropriate to the general level of a writer's usage. Some of the verb forms in the following list should be avoided because they are clumsy or not good edited form. Others are acceptable in informal or general usage but are sometimes frowned upon in formal English.

**able to:** A clumsy and unidiomatic expression when used with a passive infinitive: "This shirt **can be** [not **is able to be**] washed without shrinkage."

**aggravate, irritate:** In formal usage **aggravate** means to intensify or make worse; **irritate** means to vex or annoy: "The seriousness of his crime was **aggravated** by the prisoner's implication of innocent people." "Stop **irritating** me with those silly questions." Informally **aggravate** is used in the same sense as **irritate:** "I was never so **aggravated** in my life." The distinction between the two words should be observed in college writing.

**being that:** To introduce a dependent clause of reason or cause, **being that** is an unacceptable substitute for **because, since,** or **for:** "Randy decided to major in pharmacy **because** [not: **being that**] his uncle was a successful pharmacist."

**contact:** Many people dislike this verb as a substitute for "get in touch with someone," although it is widely used in business: "Will you **contact** our Mr. Hubble?" In general and formal writing "call" or "see" is ordinarily used.

**enthuse:** Dictionaries label this verb colloquial and prefer **be enthusiastic about** or **show enthusiasm.** While **enthuse** is in fairly common use, it is generally better to use another form in college writing.

**fix:** In general usage **fix** commonly means repair or prepare (**fix** a broken clock, **fix** lunch for three). It also means to make fast or establish (**fix** the tent to its pegs, **fix** tariff prices). **Fix** is informal in the sense of to **get even with** (I'll **fix** you for that).

**leave, let:** **Leave** means to depart or to abandon; **let** means to permit: "**Let** us **leave** this place." Using **leave** for **let** is inconsistent with edited forms of the language.

**predominate, predominant:** **Predominate** is a verb: "The captain's will **predominated** throughout the voyage." **Predominant** is an adjective: "His **predominant** characteristic is laziness."

**suspect, suspicion:** **Suspect** is the verb meaning to distrust or imagine: "The police **suspected** foul play." **Suspicion** is a noun, and when used for **suspect** is a localism, inappropriate to college writing except in dialog.

**try and, try to:** Both are accepted idioms: **Try and** is the more common in general English (**Try and** get your work in on time); **try to** is the preferred form in formal English (**Try to** get your work in on time).

**want, want to, want that:** In the sense of **ought** or **should, want** is informal: "You **should** [rather than: **want to**] review your notes before the test." In statements of desire or intention, **want to** is the standard idiom: "I **want you to get** [not **for you to get** or **that you get**] all you can from this year's work." In such constructions **want that** and **want for** are not standard.

### Some Study and Writing: Verbs

1. A common complaint about student writing is that it lacks directness. Often this is because the student has fallen into the habit of using the passive voice, or is postponing the subject in some way. Revise the sentences below so that they still mean the same thing, but in the more emphatic and direct active voice.

   *example:* It has always been felt by me that the study of biology is boring.
   *revised:* I have always felt that studying biology is boring.

   a. Biology is thought by students to be very time-consuming.
   b. It is also felt that cutting up dead frogs is disgusting to some students.

**c.** Sometimes tests are given by biology professors which are thought to require too much memorizing.

**d.** Also, it is costly to some to pay the lab fees.

**e.** For these reasons, it is an opinion of mine that the abolishment of required biology should be considered by school authorities.

**2.** Supply the proper form of the verbs in parentheses in each of these sentences. Some of the constructions call for an infinitive, participle, or gerund (see §4).

*example:* Last night, the wind (whip) the leaves so that they (spin) like the arms on a windmill. (whipped, spun)

**a.** In the saloon the yellow-bearded cowboy pushed aside his beer and slowly (draw) his gun.

**b.** Tim's fear-(bite) face (whiten) sickeningly.

**c.** Outside a buzzard (hang) ominously just below the louring clouds.

**d.** At the hitching post Old Paint nervously (shake) his mane and (paw) the dusty ground.

**e.** Suddenly a sharp crack (rend) the air.

**f.** Tim's hat (spin) crazily for a moment over the bar and then (sink) languidly into a pool of (spill) beer.

**g.** A low moan was (wring) from Tim's quavering lips.

**h.** Old Paint (begin) a piteous (whinny).

**i.** The yellow-bearded cowboy brandished his weapon menacingly and (blow) on the smoking barrel.

**j.** Thereupon the care-(ride) sheriff (ride) up.

**k.** He had (rid) the town of many varmints heretofore.

**l.** He suspected that the cowboy was a drunk drover who needed to be (drive) out of town.

**m.** Passing the door of the saloon, the sheriff (lay) a cautious ear to the (work)-iron window grill, wondering what (lie) within.

**3.** For practice with the various tenses of verbs, rewrite this paragraph, filling in the proper forms of the verbs indicated in parentheses, including any necessary auxiliary verbs. You may want to consult the chart of active verb tenses on p. 118 and the list of irregular verbs on p. 120.

As the action begins, it is clear that the old man (perfect of *rise*) and (perfect of *bid*) the young soldier enter. The audience is aware that the young soldier (perfect of *know*) for a long time that it was the old man who (past perfect of *slay*) his father. When the soldier (past perfect of *return*) from the war, his mother (past perfect of *forsake*) her deathbed to tell him how the old man (past perfect of *steal*) into the house, (past perfect of *find*) the loaded gun on the night table, and, even as the mother (past of *shrink*) into the corner of the room, (past perfect of *shoot*) her husband. (Past participle of *lade*) with this heavy sorrow, her heart (past perfect of *burst*). Within the next few moments of action the young soldier (future perfect of *bind*) the arms of the old man and (future perfect of *begin*) to lead him from the room.

4. Correct any faulty verb forms that you find in the following sentences. Some of the constructions call for verbals (see §4).

   *example:* He often had came to the same bar.
   *revised:* He often *had come* to the same bar.

a. The students were not use to seeing the Chancellor in Duffy's Tavern, ordinarily a student hangout.
b. It was raining hard, and he had almost drownded before he come upon a place to find shelter.
c. He was wet through and through, and he said that his feet were nearly froze.
d. Having rode across the prairie all day, Lonesome Jim was thoroughly wore out and could not get his legs unbended.
e. Early in the day the TV stations broadcasted the news that the President was going to make a speech that night.
f. Having born a pack, a shovel, a canteen, a map case, and a notebook for thirty miles, Jim laid down and went to sleep immediately.
g. There don't seem to be any way to keep him from sleeping when he is tired.
h. His grandfather believed that the family had originally came from northern Georgia.
i. He sat the overdue books on the counter and waited to pay the fine.
j. They got up before dawn, drunk coffee and ate rolls, checked the map, and taken back roads west for the next stage of their journey.

5. The story below is told by someone speaking an informal variety of English and sometimes getting mixed up in his use of tenses. Rewrite the sentences, especially the parts that are italicized, so that it sounds like a well-educated person speaking very formally.

a. As I *lay* here on the cold floor, I do not doubt *but what* my host is insane.
b. Why else did he contact my wife and *led* me into this trap?
c. Of course, I should *of suspicioned* that something was amiss when he walked me straight from the front hall to this clammy cell.
d. But I have *got* to stop dwelling on the past and think of a way out.
e. Above, an aggravating fly keeps *hurling* himself futilely against the wall.
f. My situation is desperate, *being that* the ceiling, which is slowly descending, *will do me in.*
g. If only my fears will *leave me be* momentarily, I will *try and* concentrate on escape.
h. To face a situation like this, a man wants *that he should* be as clear-headed as if he was fresh from a long rest.
i. But I *have got unnerved* listening *at* the malicious cackling of my host beyond the door!
j. Should I get out of here alive, I *aim to fix* that inhuman monster.

**6.** Here is a brain-teasing exercise in improving a piece of writing. Read this passage carefully, looking for errors or shifts in tense (time). Make a list of changes that you think would improve the passage. Find at least five changes and then compare them with someone else's list, if possible. If you are ambitious and eager to improve your writing even more, try rewriting the passage to make it clear and consistent.

Our last solid food was gone a week earlier. I lagged now and almost feel freezing from time to time. John Tolliver, my companion, and I tie a line from our remaining dog to each of our waists. Nothing seems to stop this dog, a black female named Friday. Each time she tugged at me I am reminded that, like her, I must not give up. Three weeks before, we had started from Repulse Bay, 150 miles to the southeast, with nine dogs. One by one they had give out after the food was gone, and we had left them, hoping that some might survive. Now we, too, were close to the edge of disaster. We can not afford another of the bitter storms that had pinned us down for days on end. We had shed all our equipment except sleeping bags and a knife. We rest only two or three minutes at a time; longer stops threatened frostbite. The effort of walking warms us and made us thirsty. We eat snow.

> **Adj./Adv.** Correction: Use the appropriate form of the adjective or adverb marked.

Nouns and verbs can be used without adjectives and adverbs. Adjectives and adverbs are not usually used without nouns and verbs. That seems to indicate the value and the function of adjectives and adverbs. They are secondary to nouns and verbs. What they contribute to sentences, however, is genuine and useful. Note the difference in meaning the adjectives make in the following sentence:

The can on the shelf contains gas.

The **red** can on the **lowest** shelf contains a **poisonous** gas.

By *expanding* the sentence, the adjectives *restrict* its meaning: the sentence is a statement about a particular can on a particular shelf containing a particular substance.

Adjectives and adverbs are essential to writing because the basic parts of a sentence—the simple subject, the verb, the object—do not always convey the exact meaning one wishes to give. They enable a writer to specify, to distinguish (not *shelf,* but *lowest shelf*). These modifiers may enable a reader to locate the experience you are talking about. Modifiers may add descriptive details (a scene of *pleasant* memories; he laughed *loudly*), limit or make more definite the meaning of a key word (the *first* book; he left *immediately*), or qualify statements (*Perhaps* you've had enough).

As parts of speech, adjectives and adverbs typically are words that are compared by adding -er or -est *(fast, faster, fastest)* or by being preceded by *more* or *most (luckily, more luckily, most luckily).* In sentences we identify an adjective or an adverb by finding the word or word group to which it is related: it is an adjective if it modifies (relates to) a noun or pronoun, an adverb if it modifies (relates to) a verb, adjective, another adverb, or the whole sentence.

**Adjective**
the **lucky** dog (modifies the noun **dog**)

The car is **fast** (modifies the noun **car**).

**Adverb**
He **luckily** won the third round (modifies the verb **won**).

She drove **fast** (modifies the verb **drove**).

Other examples of use are discussed in the sections that follow.

## Position of adjectives                                  **9.1**

Adjectives offer few problems in English because of their simple forms and relatively fixed positions. The typical position of adjectives (and of participles and nouns used as adjectives) is immediately before the words they modify, though other positions are sometimes possible:

The **red** sunset, with **narrow, black cloud** strips like threats across it, lay on the **curved** horizon of the prairie. The air was **still** and **cold,** and in it settled the **mute** darkness and **greater** cold of night. High in the air there was wind, for through the veil of the dusk the clouds could be seen gliding rapidly south and changing shapes. A **queer** sensation of torment, of **two-sided, unpredictable** nature, arose from the stillness of the **earth** air beneath the violence of the **upper** air. Out of the sunset, through the **dead, matted** grass and **isolated weed** stalks of the prairie, crept the **narrow** and deeply **rutted** remains of a road. In the road, in places, there were crusts of **shallow, brittle** ice. There were **little** islands of an **old oiled** pavement in the road too, but most of it was mud, now **frozen** rigid. The **frozen** mud still bore the **toothed** impress of great tanks, and a wanderer on the **neighboring** undulations might have stumbled, in this light, into **large,** partially **filled-in** and **weed-grown** cavities, their banks **channelled** and beginning to spread into badlands. These pits were such as might have been made by **falling** meteors, but they were not. They were the scars of **gigantic** bombs, their rawness already made a **little** natural by rain, seed, and time. Along the road, there were **rakish** remnants of fence. There was also, just visible, one portion of **tangled** and **multiple** barbed wire still **erect,** behind which was a **shelving** ditch with **small** caves, now very **quiet** and **empty,** at intervals in its **back** wall. Otherwise there was no structure or remnant of a structure visible over the dome of the **darkling** earth, but only, in **sheltered** hollows, the **darker** shadows of **young** trees trying again. — Walter van Tilburg Clark, "The Portable Phonograph"

Two or more adjectives are often placed after the word they modify to gain emphasis or to avoid a clumsy expression:

Except for a boy, **tall** and rather **gangly,** the room was deserted.

. . . the sailors thronged the streets in flapping blues and spotless whites — **brown, tough,** and **clean.** — Thomas Wolfe, *Look Homeward, Angel*

If an adjective is modified by other words, it often comes after the noun:

The old man, exceedingly **weary** from his trip, lay down to rest.

In some set phrases or conventional expressions, the adjective always occurs after the noun (accounts *receivable,* attorney *general,* president-*elect,* battle *royal*).

## Predicate adjectives    **9.2**

Predicate adjectives—adjectives that follow linking verbs— refer back to the subject (§1.1). The common linking verbs are *be (am, is, are, was, were, has been), seem, appear, become, grow, prove,* and verbs describing sensations like *taste, feel, smell, look, sound.*

Sometimes these verbs are followed and modified by adverbs. (The weeds grew *rapidly*). To determine whether a predicate adjective or an adverb should be used, see whether the word modifies the subject or the verb. When it modifies or refers to the subject, use an adjective; when it modifies the verb, use an adverb:

The children looked **unhappy.** [predicate adjective describing **children**]

As the rain continued to fall, the children looked **unhappily** out the window. [adverb modifying **looked**]

He turned **abruptly** when he heard his name called. [adverb, describing the way in which he **turned**]

Overnight the weather turned **cold.** [predicate adjective modifying **weather**]

### *good, well*

*Good* is an adjective (a *good* time; This cake tastes *good*). *Well* is either an adjective (He was a *well* boy; Are you feeling *well?* All is *well*), or an adverb (He writes *well*). Either *good* or *well* may be used as a predicate adjective with the verb *feel,* but with different connotations:

Don't you feel **well?** [referring to a state of health, "not ill"]

It made him feel **good** to pack his own bag and get into the front seat and drive his own car. [referring to a general attitude or bodily sensation—comfort, happiness, well-being]—John Dos Passos, *The Big Money*

Since *good* is an adjective, it shouldn't be used in place of the adverb *well:*

The team played **well** [not **good**] for five innings.

*bad, badly*

As an adjective, *bad* is the usual form after linking verbs:

She feels **bad.** The milk tastes **bad.** The situation looks **bad** to me.

But *badly* is also used when the emphasis is on the verb: I feel *badly* [or *bad*] about your troubles. Many people object to such uses of *badly*, however, and it is just as well to avoid them in writing.

## Demonstrative adjectives    **9.3**

*This* and *that* (called demonstrative adjectives) are the only adjectives with plural forms: *this* idea, *these* ideas; *that* project, *those* projects. They are often used with *kind* and *sort,* which are singular nouns and should be preceded by singular modifiers (*this* kind of clouds, *that* sort of people). In spoken English *these* or *those* is sometimes used with *kind* or *sort* when a plural noun occurs in a following phrase (I like *these* kind of *records* best; *Those* sort of *jokes* annoy me). But in formal and general usage both words should be treated as singular:

I like **this** kind of records best.
Jokes of **that sort** annoy me.

## Forms of adverbs    **9.4**

A number of common adverbs *(now, quite, there, too)* have no distinctive forms, but the majority of adverbs are made by adding *-ly* to an adjective: *accidental-ly, particular-ly, real-ly, sincere-ly.* A few adjectives ending in *-ly (early, likely)* are also used as adverbs.

Although adverbs can be made by adding *-wise* to a noun *(lengthwise, sidewise),* this practice has been greatly overused *(budget-wise, economy-wise).* It is better to avoid such words.

### Long and short forms of adverbs

Some adverbs have two forms: one with an *-ly* ending (long

form), the other without (short form): *slow—slowly, loud—loudly, tight—tightly.* Adverbs used with or without the *-ly* ending include:

| | | | |
|---|---|---|---|
| bright | even | rough | straight |
| cheap | fair | second | tight |
| close | loose | sharp | wrong |
| deep | loud | slow | |
| direct | quick | smooth | |

The long and short forms are often interchangeable:

Go **slow.** Go **slowly.**
Don't talk so **loud.** Don't talk so **loudly.**
The rope was drawn **tight.** The rope was drawn **tightly.**

But in some situations the long and short forms are not interchangeable. The long forms are used between *to* and the base form of a verb *(to wrongly accuse,* not *to wrong accuse)* and generally between the subject and verb (They *closely* watched). The short forms are used more with short words: *new* found friends, but *newly* acquired rank. Formal writers tend to use the long forms, general writers more of the short forms. But since comprehensive rules cannot be given, each writer has to choose between the forms largely on the basis of the tone and sound of the sentence.

## Bobtailed adverbs

When an adverb has only the *-ly* form, care should be taken not to drop the ending. Some temptations are *considerably, seriously,* and *differently:*

Twenty-five dollars is **considerably** more than I want to pay. [not **considerable**]
People often told him that he should take things more **seriously.** [not **serious**]
She worked **differently** from the others. [not **different**]

Dropping the *-ly* in such words is a characteristic of some dialects and of informal conversation. A dictionary will tell what the standard adverb form is.

The bobtailed adverbs most likely to be found in writing are *bad, real, sure.* In general or edited English these forms are adjectives only; the adverbs have *-ly:*

He danced **badly.**
It was a **really** outstanding performance.
They were **surely** enjoying themselves.

## most, almost

In formal and general English *most* is not used for the adverb *almost,* meaning "very nearly":

I **almost** lost my mind. [adverb, modifying the verb **lost**]
The train was **almost** always on time. [adverb, modifying the adverb **always**]
**Most** fishermen are optimists. [adjective, modifying **fishermen**]
**Almost** all fishermen are optimists. [adverb, modifying the adjective **all**]

## Position of adverbs　　　　　　　　　　　　　　**9.5**

### Adverbs modifying a single word

Unlike adjectives, adverbs can have various positions in the sentence. But they should be placed in a position that clearly indicates the writer's intended meaning and desired emphasis.

When an adverb modifies a single word, its typical position is immediately before that word:

a **quite** late party [modifies **late**]
They **never** finished the job. [modifies **finished**]

This often puts the modifier of a verb between an auxiliary and participle:

He had **quietly** withdrawn.

A modifier of a verb often follows the verb or comes after the verb and its object:

He withdrew **quietly.**
　　　　v　　　　　　　o
They finished the job **hurriedly.**

See also §4.2, p. 75, Split infinitives.

### Sentence adverbs

A good many adverbial modifiers—single word adverbs, phrases, or clauses—cannot sensibly be related to another single word in a sentence. It is conventional to say that these adverbs "modify the whole sentence" and to call them *sentence adverbs.* Their position is variable:

**Unfortunately** they had already left.
They had already left, **unfortunately.**
They had **unfortunately** already left.

This flexibility makes it possible to shift the position of many sentence adverbs for variety as well as for emphasis.

## Misplaced adverbial modifiers

> **MM**  Correction: Revise the sentence so that the expression marked is clearly related to the word or statement it modifies.

A writer should be careful not to misplace a modifier so that the meaning of a statement becomes ambiguous or even ludicrous:

**Ambiguous:** Using several pen names, the two editors have almost written every article in the magazine. [**almost** seems to modify **written**]

**Clear:** Using several pen names, the two editors have written **almost** every article in the magazine.

Modifiers are sometimes placed so that they could refer to either one of two elements; these are sometimes called "squinting modifiers":

Although it was often said that the old boat would sink **somehow** it seemed blessed with unsinkability. [**Somehow** might modify the preceding verb **sink** or the following clause. Adding a comma after **sink** would clear up the ambiguity.]

In some constructions, misplacing the modifier may alter the intended meaning:

The way I can stand in front of a store window and persuade myself that I need useless articles **even** surprises me. [intended meaning: **surprises even me**]

See also §4.3, Misrelated modifiers, and §4.4, Dangling modifiers, for a discussion of the placement of verbal modifiers.

## Position of *only* and similar adverbs
In formal usage, limiting adverbs like *only, merely, hardly, just* are placed immediately before the element they modify:

I need **only** six more to make a full hundred.
The audience seemed **hardly** to breathe when the girl began speaking.

In spoken usage limiting adverbs usually stand immediately before the verb:

I **only** need six more to make a full hundred.
The audience **hardly** seemed to breathe when the girl began speaking.

This pattern, typical of spoken English, is usual in general writing, when no misunderstanding of the author's meaning will occur:

When the brilliant lightweight boxer, Kid Lewis, stood for Parliament in his native borough, he **only** scored a hundred and twenty-five votes. — George Orwell, *The English People*

He **only** remembers one verse of the song and he has been repeating it. — Eugene O'Neill, *A Moon for the Misbegotten*

It is possible to misplace *only* so that it seems to belong to a word that it cannot sensibly modify:

**Nonsensical:** He had **only** a face a mother could love.
**Accurate:** He had a face **only** a mother could love.

## Double negatives                                      **9.6**

A statement in which a second negative needlessly repeats the meaning of the first negative is called a *double negative:* "The trip will *not* cost you *nothing*." Such constructions, once acceptable in English, are not used in edited American English and should be rephrased: "The trip will cost you *nothing*" or "The trip will *not* cost you anything."

Writers usually make few mistakes with obvious double negatives like *not* and *nothing,* but they need to watch the concealed ones, when *not* is combined with *but* or with adverbs of negative meaning such as *hardly, barely, scarcely.*

*can't hardly, couldn't scarcely*
Such common expressions as "I can't hardly hear you" and "There wasn't scarcely enough money left to pay the taxes" are double negatives, because *hardly* and *scarcely* in this sense mean *almost not.* The standard idioms that should be used in writing are "I *can* hardly hear you" and "There *was* scarcely enough money left to pay the taxes."

## can't help but

The construction *can't help but* (or *cannot help but*) is an established idiom. Many writers, however, avoid it, using instead one of the expressions in the following sentences:

I **cannot but** feel sorry for him. [formal]
I **can't help feeling** sorry for him. [general]

## irregardless

*Regardless* is the standard usage. The suffix *-less* is a negative ending; the addition of the negative prefix *ir-* in *irregardless* creates a double negative.

## Comparison of adjectives and adverbs 9.7

| **Comp** | Correction: Make the comparison of adjectives or adverbs more accurate or more appropriate. |
|---|---|

Most adjectives and adverbs have three different forms to indicate degrees of the characteristic they name. The positive degree (or simple form of the modifier) expresses no comparison *(red, slow, seriously);* the comparative degree represents an increase or decrease of the positive form, or makes a specific comparison between two things *(redder, slower, more seriously,* or *less seriously);* the superlative indicates the greatest (or least) degree among three or more things (the *reddest* apple of all, the *slowest* runner on the team, the *most* — or *least* — seriously presented argument).

### Forms of comparison

Most adjectives and adverbs are compared in one of two ways: by adding *-er, -est* to the positive form, or by prefixing *more, most* (or *less, least*).

| | **Positive** | **Comparative** | **Superlative** |
|---|---|---|---|
| **Adjectives** | hot | hotter | hottest |
| | brilliant | more brilliant | most brilliant |
| | expensive | less expensive | least expensive |
| **Adverbs** | near | nearer | nearest |
| | sincerely | more sincerely | most sincerely |
| | often | oftener, more often, less often | oftenest, most often, least often |

In general, the *-er, -est* forms are used with words of one syllable *(longer, driest),* and *more, most* with words of more than two syllables *(more interesting, most rapidly).* With two-syllable words a writer often has a choice of either form *(abler, more able; easiest, most easy).* The sound of the expression may determine which form is used:

His step was **steadier** and **more elastic.** Even his bloodshot eyes looked **fresher,** and his hair and beard were **softer.** — Eyvind Johnson, *Return to Ithaca*

A few common modifiers form the comparative and superlative degrees irregularly:

| | | |
|---|---|---|
| bad | worse | worst |
| good, well | better | best |
| far | farther, further | farthest, furthest |
| little | less, lesser, littler | least, littlest |
| many, some, much | more | most |

*worse, worst*

*Worst* is the appropriate form for the superlative: That was the *worst* [not *worse*] show I have ever seen.

*farther, further*

In formal English a distinction is sometimes made between *farther,* referring to physical distance (It was six miles *farther* to town), and *further,* referring to abstract degree (We will study these suggestions *further*). In general English, *further* is commonly used for both distance and degree.

## Use of the comparative form

The comparative form of an adjective or adverb is ordinarily used when two things are compared:

You're a **better** man than I am, Gunga Din!
Blood is **thicker** than water.
She works **more diligently** than her roommate.

But in some expressions the comparative form is used when no actual comparison is mentioned (higher education, the lower depths, Better Business Bureau). In others, the reader is left to supply the comparison (Look younger, live longer . . . than what?). Writers of advertising copy are particularly fond of this absolute use of the comparative because of the favorable inferences the reader may draw: Smoke a *milder* cigarette; More protection for *fewer* dollars; Sudso gets clothes *cleaner*. This construction is meaningless and should generally be avoided.

## Use of the superlative form

The superlative form ordinarily indicates the greatest degree among three or more persons or things:

He was voted the member of his class **most likely** to succeed.

Many critics consider *King Lear* the **greatest** of Shakespeare's tragedies.

In spoken English the superlative is sometimes used for comparing two things (Put your *best* foot forward). The same construction is occasionally seen in writing, but in college writing, it is usually better to keep the superlative for comparisons among three or more.

Superlative forms also occur in expressions in which no direct comparison is implied (*best* wishes, *deepest* sympathy, *highest* praise, *most* sincerely yours). The form with *most* is frequently used as an intensive to signify a high degree:

For example, Herbert Spencer (1820–1903), a **most** influential English philosopher. . . . —Melvin Rader, *Ethics and Society*

The informal use of a heavily stressed superlative to indicate nothing more than general approval should be avoided in serious writing:

Hasn't she the **sweetest** voice? (Better: Hasn't she a **sweet** voice?)

## Comparison of *unique* and similar words

Some people regard words such as *unique, perfect, dead, empty* as logically incapable of comparison or qualification because their positive forms express absolute states. Ordinarily, we wouldn't expect to say that something is *more unique,* or *emptier,* but in actual usage these terms are often qualified or modified by comparative forms, as in the following examples:

We, the people of the United States, in order to form a *more perfect* union. . . . —Preamble to the Constitution of the United States

. . . The *more unique* his nature, the more peculiarly his own will be the coloring of his language. —Otto Jespersen, *Mankind, Nation, and Individual from a Linguistic Point of View*

Whether words like *unique* should or should not be qualified is a matter that can be determined only by appropriateness. In college writing, they should ordinarily be used without qualification; invested with their full meaning, they are valuable words that say something precisely.

# Making comparisons idiomatic

**Id** Correction: Change the expression marked so that it will be idiomatic.

In writing, expressions of comparison should be more carefully and more fully stated than they often are in speaking. Expressions that might pass unnoticed in conversation (such as *all the higher the ladder will reach* or *the slowest of any runner on the team*) are too slipshod to be used in careful writing (where the same ideas would be expressed: *as high as the ladder will reach* and *the slowest runner on the team*).

## Comparing comparable things

When using comparisons in your writing, make certain that the things compared are of the same kind and actually comparable:

| **Terms not comparable** | **Comparable terms** |
|---|---|
| The rhinoceros has a hide almost as tough as an alligator [**hide** and **alligator** are not comparable]. | The rhinoceros has a hide almost as tough as that of an alligator [or **as an alligator's**]. |
| One reviewer compared these short stories to O. Henry. | One reviewer compared these short stories to those written by O. Henry [or **to O. Henry's**]. |

## Completing comparisons

Statements involving comparisons should be written out in full, particularly if any misunderstanding might arise through shortening one of the terms:

| **Ambiguous** | **Clearer** |
|---|---|
| I owe him less than you. | I owe him less than I owe you. *Or:* I owe him less than you do. |
| He admires Eliot less than other modern poets. | He admires Eliot less than other modern poets do. *Or:* He admires Eliot less than he does other modern poets. |

Double comparisons with *as . . . as, if . . . than* should be filled out in writing.

He is **as** tall **as, if** not taller **than,** his brother. [*not:* He is as tall if not taller than his brother.]

The styles vary **as** much **as, if** not more **than,** the colors.

Since the *if . . . than* construction tends to interrupt sentence movement, it is usually preferable to complete the first comparison and then add the second, dropping *than:*

He is as tall as his brother, if not taller.
The styles vary as much as the colors, if not more.

## Use of *other* in comparisons

*Other* is used when the comparison involves things of the same class, but not when the things being compared belong to two different classes:

She is a better dancer than the **other** girls.
She dances better than any [not **any other**] boy in school.
*Blithe Spirit* was more successful than the **other** plays we produced.
I think movies are more entertaining than any [not **any other**] book.

*Other* is not used with superlative comparisons:

Pavlova was the best of all the [not **all the other**] Russian ballerinas.
The Egyptians had attained the highest skill in medicine that had up to that time been achieved by any [not **any other**] nation.

## Use of *like* or *as* in comparisons

To introduce a prepositional phrase of comparison, *like* is standard usage:

They are **like** two peas in a pod.
He looks **like** his father.
Bicycle riding, **like** golf, can be enjoyed at almost any age.

In college writing, *as* should not be substituted for *like* or *such as* in prepositional phrases like this:

Some writers **like** [not **as**] Faulkner and Caldwell take their material from a particular region.

To introduce a clause of comparison with a definite subject and verb, formal and general English both prefer *as, as if, as though* to *like:*

He acted **as if** he didn't feel well.
He wanted to be a doctor **as** his father had been.
She took to skiing **as** a duck takes to water.

The use of *like* as a conjunction has increased in recent years and is gaining respectable status:

"Suddenly everybody wanted to look like he came from Harvard, or like he thought everyone looked at Harvard," says Grossman.—*Time,* Feb. 28, 1964

However, many people are prejudiced against the use of *like* to introduce clauses, and the preferred forms *as, as if, as though* should ordinarily be used in college writing.

## Some Practice and Writing: Adjectives and Adverbs

1. Native speakers seldom make serious errors in adjectives and adverbs. Sometimes an *-ly* ending gets left off in informal writing, or a *good* replaces a *well.* Learning to tell the difference marks "edited" writing from less formal varieties. The following type of "test" may help you choose the proper form:

The *slow* car is very *slow.* [adjective]
You should drive *slowly.* [adverb of manner]

Now try your hand at this exercise. Choose the adjective or adverb form that seems appropriate. If both forms are possible, indicate when each would be used.

A Hollywood studio presents a scene that defies description. Side by side, you can see, (clear, clearly) as day, sets from Morocco and Antarctica. Much of the construction is made so (cheap, cheaply) that it will not last (long, for long) but it looks (real, really) (good, well) at first glance. As you swing down the main street of a western town, you can imagine yourself in a two-man gunfight, drawing your six-shooter out (smooth, smoothly) as silk; you have no fears about the outcome, for you know that the (best, better) man always wins because he shoots (straighter, straightest). Around the corner you stop and stare at one of the (goldarndest, most goldarn) sights you ever saw—a great ape driving a limousine (worse, more badly) than a Keystone cop would. Past that, you come upon a grim, gaunt building set in a swamp, and you hold your arms (close, closely) to your sides in fear. It looks so real you shiver, (slow, slowly) at first, and then with (increasing, increasingly) rapid shudders. Broadway chorus girls dancing (high and mighty, highly and mightily) on a great raised stage next catch your eye and hold it (fixed, fixedly). With so much to see, it is difficult to know what to look at (most, mostly).

2. Study the following sentences carefully and state where you would place the indicated modifier within each sentence. If more than one position is possible, explain what change of emphasis would result from shifting the modifier.

*example:* Add *almost:* The fire had burned down to nothing.
*with modifier:* The fire had *almost* burned down to nothing.
*or:* The fire had burned down to *almost* nothing.

a. Add *certainly:* The fields were carpeted with snow that had fallen in the night, for there had been none yesterday.
b. Add *scarcely:* Some had landed, oddly enough, on the back patio, where the wind was now blowing.
c. Add *almost:* Farther out in the yard, the doghouse was covered to the roof so that it looked like a small mound of cotton.
d. Add *even:* The garden walks were so obliterated by drifts that my father, who had laid out the garden, did not know where they were.

**e.** Add *more or less:* You could tell where one path went by following the clothesline, which had a ridge of snow that made it visible from the house.

**f.** Add *only:* Yesterday I had seen the yard with a few flowers growing.

**g.** Add *definitely:* "It's beautiful to look at," my father said, "but you'll have to shovel the walks because your mother will want to hang out the wash she did last night."

**h.** Add *better:* Picking up the old battered shovel, I went out into the bitter wind, knowing I would be able to get the job done before the snow hardened.

**i.** Add *hardly:* Although I walked on the white snow-blanket softly, I had taken a few steps when I fell in a position from which I could extricate myself.

**j.** Add *merely:* Because it was a moderate snowfall, I laughed and went on with my work.

**3.** Some of the adjective and adverb forms and expressions of comparisons in these sentences would be inappropriate in most college writing. Revise each sentence and explain briefly the reasons for each change.

**a.** The ship lay in the harbor like it was a natural fixture.

**b.** It had been there so long that the weather had turned it more wharf-colored.

**c.** Many things would be needed to refurbish it, as calking, paint, new masts, and glass for portholes.

**d.** All in all, it was the most 19th-century sight in the town.

**e.** The ship looked as much if not more pathetic than an old hound lying forgottenlike nearby a deserted farmhouse.

**f.** Still, the scene was real fine artwise, and camera enthusiasts were taking pictures most every clear day of the year.

**g.** Picturesque as the sight was, everyone agreed it was the saddest.

**h.** I thought wistfully of how trim and noble the ship must have been in her heyday, what with her tall masts and most every sail stretching out to catch the wind.

**i.** The reason for its being there was most unique; the owner had died of a sudden before he could make it into a museum.

**j.** A sailing ship is the most romantic, because it pits man against the elements more than any other motorized boat does.

**k.** To sit on the wharf and watch the old ship rot, that's what made me feel badly.

**l.** Much the most dreariest of sights is watching anything lose its former beauty.

**m.** I only wished I could have seen her in her prime, when she was shipshape.

**n.** Her prow was cut sharp back, so that she could cleave the waves like a knife through hot butter.

**o.** She was clearly the best of all the other ships I have ever seen, bar none.

4. Fill in the modifiers called for in the paragraph below, choosing modifiers that will help create a melancholy tone for the paragraph. Then, going through the paragraph again, try converting it into an adventurous statement by changing the modifiers.

Sometimes, late in the evening, when I have worked (adverb) and (adverb) at my desk, I stop and lean back in my (adjective) chair and hear night sounds (adjective) and (adjective) in the distance. Sometimes I hear a (adjective) car passing, or someone calling far away, or (adjective) music from some car radio, or a bird song, (adjective) and (adjective). Then I remember that there is a world outside my window (adjective) (adverb), and I go to the door and stand a moment, looking out (adverb).

# PUNCTUATION
## AND
## OTHER
## CONVENTIONS

# End punctuation 10

Every complete sentence requires a mark of punctuation at the end, either a period, a question mark, or an exclamation mark. The great majority of sentences are statements, requiring a period (.). Direct questions are followed by a question mark (?), and emphatic or exclamatory statements are ended with an exclamation point, or mark (!).

Periods and question marks also have several conventional uses in addition to their function as end stops.

## Periods 10.1

10.1

> ⊙ Correction: Insert a period at the place marked.

Periods are the most common end stops; they mark the end of all sentences that are not direct questions or exclamations.

### After statements

Madagascar is an island off southeast Africa.
"Where is he now?" she asked. "Tell me."
"Oh."

### After indirect questions and courtesy questions

An indirect question is really a statement *about* a question, and is never followed by a question mark.

He asked us where we got the money. (A direct question would be **Where did you get the money?**)

They wanted to know what I had been doing since I graduated.

Will you please return this copy as soon as possible. (This is a courtesy question, a polite request phrased as a direct question, but followed by a period.)

May we hear from you at your earliest convenience.

### After abbreviations

A period is conventionally used after most abbreviations:

| | | |
|---|---|---|
| Mr. H. L. Matthews | Oct. | Ph.D. |
| St. Paul, Minn. | D.D.S. | etc. |

An abbreviation within a sentence may be followed by additional punctuation (After she gets her M.A., she might go on to get her Ph.D.), but at the end of a sentence no additional mark is needed unless the sentence is a question or exclamation (Does he have a Ph.D.**?**)

Periods are sometimes omitted from abbreviations, especially if they are made from initial letters: UNESCO, GOP. Consult an up-to-date dictionary for the preferred form of particular abbreviations. If usage is divided (A.W.O.L., AWOL, or a.w.o.l.), follow a consistent style throughout your paper. (See §17.1, Abbreviations.)

### With figures
A period (decimal point) is used before fractions expressed as decimals and between whole numbers and decimals, and to separate dollars and cents:

| .05 | 4.6 | 3.14159 | 95.6% |
|-----|-----|---------|-------|
| $4.98 | $.98 | **but** 98 cents | 98¢ |

See §14.3 for periods used as ellipses to mark the omission of words.

## Question marks                                    **10.2**

> **?**  Correction: Punctuate this sentence or sentence element with a question mark.

### After direct questions
A question mark is used after a sentence expressing a direct question:

What can we do**?**
Did Napoleon dislike Elba**?**
Really**?**

When a sentence begins with a statement but ends with a question, the ending determines the punctuation:

Perhaps this explanation is poor, but is there a better one**?**

### After questions within a sentence
A question mark stands immediately after a question that is included within a sentence:

Someone once remarked (wasn't it Mark Twain**?**) that old second-hand diamonds are better than no diamonds at all.
"Are you engaged**?**" he blurted.

When a question mark and quotation mark occur together, the question mark falls inside if only the quotation is a question, outside if the whole sentence is a question:

He asked himself, "Is this the best of all possible worlds**?**"
Do you agree that this is "the best of all possible worlds"**?**

## To indicate a doubtful statement
A question mark is used, with or without parentheses, to show that a statement is approximate or questionable:

Geoffrey Chaucer, 1340**(?)** – 1400
Geoffrey Chaucer, 1340**?** – 1400

Sometimes writers place a question mark in parentheses to indicate humor or mild sarcasm:

She gave him an innocent **(?)** wink over her menu.

The question mark is better omitted. If humor or sarcasm requires a signal for the reader to recognize it, it would probably be better to revise the entire passage.

**!**

**10.3**

## Exclamation marks                                    **10.3**

> **!** Correction: Insert or remove exclamation mark at the place indicated.

An exclamation mark is used after an emphatic interjection (Oh! Ouch! Fire! Help! No, no, no!) and after statements that are genuinely exclamatory:

The building had disappeared overnight!
What torments they have endured!

There is seldom a need for exclamation marks unless you are writing dialog. Don't use an exclamation mark unless the statement is genuinely emphatic; it will not lend weight to a simple statement of fact, nor will the use of double and triple marks add anything.

# Commas                                                11

∧
,

**11.1**

Commas mark a slight separation between grammatical units, similar to brief pauses in speech. They are highly important to the meaning of all kinds of writing, and they are important in determining the pace and tempo of writing. About two-thirds of all punctuation marks used are commas.

To use commas well, you must know not only when to use them but also when to omit them. When units that should run consecutively are broken up by commas so that the movement of a passage is unnecessarily interrupted, the effect can be annoying. Long sentences may be perfectly clear without any commas at all, as in this example of over forty words:

> I had hoped that the white moderate would understand that law and order exist for the purpose of establishing justice and that when they fail in this purpose they become the dangerously structured dams that block the flow of social progress.—Martin Luther King, Jr., "Letter from Birmingham Jail"

The principal uses of the comma are described in the following sections and summarized in the table on page 155. The table also lists some constructions in which commas should *not* be used, as discussed in §11.8, Misused commas.

## Between coordinate clauses                           **11.1**

A comma is customarily used before the conjunction linking the coordinate clauses in a compound sentence, especially when the clauses are long or when it is desirable to emphasize their distinctness. Notice that the comma always comes *before* the coordinating conjunction, not after it:

> But generalities require illustration, and for this purpose, I choose the business school of a university.—Alfred North Whitehead, "Universities and Their Function"

> This town does not actually exist, but it might easily have a thousand counterparts in America or elsewhere in the world.—Rachel Carson, *Silent Spring*

> The village was to the scale of the town of Lilliput, and I could have straddled over Toad Hall.—Aubrey Menen, "Dazzled in Disneyland"

# Commas

Commas are used:

1. Between coordinate clauses (§11.1)
   a. When they are joined by *and, or, nor* if the clauses are long or not closely related
   b. When they are joined by *but* or *yet*
   c. When they are joined by *for*
2. After long introductory elements (§11.2)
   a. When an adverb clause precedes the main clause (usually optional if the introductory clause is short and closely related)
   b. When a long modifying phrase precedes the main clause (usually optional if the phrase is short and closely related)
3. With nonrestrictive modifiers (§11.3)
   a. To set off subordinate clauses and phrases that do not limit or restrict the meaning of the term they modify
   b. To set off appositives
4. To set off interrupting and parenthetical elements (§11.4)
5. To separate coordinate items in a series (§11.5)
   a. In a series of words, phrases, or clauses not joined by conjunctions (optional before *and* joining the last item in a series)
   b. In a series of coordinate adjectives, all modifying the same noun
6. To separate constructions for clarity (§11.6)
7. In certain conventional places (§11.7)
   a. In numbers
   b. In dates
   c. In addresses
   d. With titles and degrees
   e. In correspondence
   f. With phrases identifying direct quotations

Commas should not be used (§11.8):

1. Between main sentence elements
2. Between two words or phrases joined by *and*
3. Between main clauses without a connective
4. With restrictive modifiers
5. After the last item in a series

### Short clauses joined by *and, or, nor*

The comma may be omitted before the conjunctions *and, or, nor* in compound sentences if the coordinate clauses are short and closely related in thought:

Life is short [ ] and time is fleeting.
He had to get home [ ] or his father would be furious.
Nancy didn't like her [ ] nor did I.

General writing often omits the comma where formal writing would use one, as between the two independent clauses in this example:

I remembered being taken for a haircut and scraping my knee on the footrest and I remembered my father's face as he soothed my crying and applied the stinging iodine.—James Baldwin, "Notes of a Native Son"

### Clauses joined by *but, yet*

In both formal and general writing a comma is used between independent clauses joined by *but* or *yet* in order to emphasize the contrast:

This was not the man they had known, but they had scarcely expected to be confronted with him. . . .—Ibid.
It is an imperfect system, yet it is better than none.

### Clauses joined by *for*

A comma is necessary between clauses joined by *for* used as a conjunction, so that it won't be confused with the preposition *for:*

He was an easy target, for anyone could pull the wool over his eyes. [**for** as a conjunction]
He was an easy target for anyone who wanted to take advantage of him. [**for** as a preposition]

## After long introductory elements     **11.2**

Adverb clauses and long modifying phrases are usually set off by a comma when they precede the main clause. When these elements come at the end of a sentence, a comma may or may not be necessary.

### Adverb clauses

Adverb clauses (see §3.2) are often placed at the beginning of a sentence for variety or emphasis. In this position they are usually separated from the main clause by a comma:

**When he said that we would be expected to write a theme every day,** I nearly collapsed.

**Before penicillin and other antibiotics were developed,** pneumonia was often fatal.

The comma is frequently omitted when the introductory clause is short and closely related to the main clause, especially if both clauses have the same subject:

**When I lived in New York** [ ] I went to the theater every month.
**After he seized control** [ ] the situation changed drastically.

When an adverb clause *follows* the main clause, no comma is used if the subordinate clause is closely related to the meaning of the sentence:

I nearly collapsed [ ] **when he said that we would be expected to write a theme every day.**

Pneumonia was often fatal [ ] **before penicillin and other antibiotics were developed.**

If a following subordinate clause is only loosely related to the main clause and would be preceded by a distinct pause in speech, it is separated from the main clause by a comma:

The new wing will be finished by spring, **unless, of course, unexpected delays occur.**

I have known readers who find Huxley unreadable, **although they have found it impossible to explain why.** — Colin Wilson, "Existential Criticism"

## Long modifying phrases

Long modifying phrases are generally punctuated in the same way as adverb clauses. When they come before the main clause, they are followed by a comma:

**To fully understand the impact of Einstein's ideas,** one must be familiar with those of Newton. [infinitive phrase]

**Leaning far out over the balcony,** he stared at the waves below. [participle phrase]

**In such a situation,** speakers of the creole often deny their mother tongue. [prepositional phrase] — Peter Farb, *Word Play*

When the phrases are relatively short and closely related to the clauses they modify, general writing often omits the comma:

**In this context** [ ] the meaning is entirely different.
**To evade the draft** [ ] he moved to Costa Rica.

When the modifying phrase *follows* the clause, commas are unnecessary if the thought seems to flow smoothly from one to the other. But if the phrase is only loosely related to the clause or if it modifies some distant expression, a comma should be used to prevent confusion:

One must be familiar with Newton's ideas [] **to fully understand the impact of Einstein's.**

Special treatment may be necessary [] **in cases of severe malnutrition.**

The local residents often saw Elgin [] **wandering among the ruins.**

Wilson nervously watched the man**, alarmed by his silence.** [The phrase modifies **Wilson,** not **man.**]

## With nonrestrictive modifiers          **11.3**

> **Rest**   Correction: If the modifier marked is nonrestrictive, set it off with a comma or commas; if it is restrictive, do not separate it from the term it modifies.

### Subordinate clauses and phrases

A *nonrestrictive* modifier is a subordinate clause or a phrase that does not limit or define the term it modifies. In other words, it does not *restrict* the term's meaning; if it was omitted, the meaning of the sentence would not change much. The most persistent problems occur with clauses introduced by *who, which,* or *that,* but nonrestrictive phrases may also cause difficulty. Nonrestrictive modifiers are set off by commas to indicate their subordinate function in the sentence:

Last night's audience**, which contained a large number of college students,** applauded each number enthusiastically.

The people of India**, who have lived in poverty for centuries,** desperately need financial and technical assistance.

Vasari's history**, hovering between fact and fiction,** is not a reliable source of data.

Notice that the modifiers in the three preceding sentences are not essential to the terms they modify. Although some information would be lost if they were removed, the central meaning of each sentence would not change.

A *restrictive* modifier limits or defines the meaning of a term; without it, the sentence would take on a different meaning or become difficult to understand. Since it is essential to the sentence, it is *not* set off by commas:

He is a man **who thinks for himself.**
Ortiz discovered many temples **which were pre-Toltec in origin.**
The questions **that he did not answer** were the most interesting ones.

Almost all clauses beginning with *that* are restrictive. All clauses in which the relative pronoun can be omitted are restrictive (the questions *he failed to answer,* the book *I read*).

In distinguishing between restrictive and nonrestrictive modifiers, the writer must carefully consider the nature of the term modified and the context in which it occurs. If the term is fully defined in itself and cannot be confused with another, the modifier that follows is nonrestrictive. But if the term is vague or ambiguous without the modifier, the modifier is restrictive. Compare the function of the modifier in each of these passages:

Children **who can't swim very well** should stay off the diving board.
Children**, who can't swim very well,** should stay off the diving board.
Last month I read a novel and a biography. The novel**, which especially appealed to me,** was written by Hawthorne.
Last month I read several novels and a biography. The novel **which especially appealed to me** was written by Hawthorne.
While in Rome, I took photographs in the vicinity of St. Peter's. The square**, designed by Michelangelo,** is perfectly symmetrical.
While in Rome, I took photographs of squares designed by Michelangelo, Bernini, and Borromini. The square **designed by Michelangelo** is perfectly symmetrical.

A good test to apply in distinguishing between restrictive and nonrestrictive modifiers is to read the passage aloud. If your voice drops slightly in pitch and hesitates briefly before and after the modifier, the modifier is probably nonrestrictive and requires commas. If you read the passage smoothly without a pause, the modifier is probably restrictive and needs no commas.

## Appositives

Appositives—nouns or noun equivalents that extend the meaning of a preceding expression—are usually nonrestrictive modifiers and are set off by commas:

Thomas Malthus**, author of the first serious study of population growth,** foresaw one of our greatest modern problems.
Lincoln delivered a famous address at Gettysburg**, site of a crucial Civil War battle.**

Notice that such appositives, like other nonrestrictive modifiers, must be set off by *two* commas when they occur in the middle of the sentence.

Restrictive appositives and those used as part of a person's name require no commas:

I thought the question referred to Lewis **the novelist** rather than to Lewis **the union leader.**

William **the Conqueror** invaded England from Normandy.

---

## 11.4 To set off interrupting and parenthetical elements  **11.4**

A word, phrase, or clause that interrupts the movement of a sentence is usually set off by commas or other appropriate marks. Whether or not the degree of interruption is sufficient to require commas depends on tone and emphasis. Formal English uses commas more frequently than general English for this purpose:

There are**, however,** few college subjects in the humanities and the social sciences in which forty-five hours of the teacher lecturing and the students listening can be useful.—Nathan Glazer, "The Wasted Classroom"

The city**, after all,** is not just a collection of buildings and services.—Barbara Ward, "The City May Be as Lethal as the Bomb"

**As I have said before,** I believe that now as in the days of the founding fathers, even the faintest possibility of achieving such an order depends upon the steadfast faith of this country.—Adlai Stevenson, Speech on United Nations Charter Day

To decide whether or not to set off short phrases with commas, read the passage aloud with the kind of emphasis you want to give it. If your voice drops and you pause slightly before and after the phrase, commas should be used. If the phrase seems to run naturally into the rest of the sentence, probably no commas are necessary:

Cybernetics, **on the other hand,** has attracted many students.
Machines are useful, **of course,** in doing complex calculations.
Machines are **of course** incapable of what we call creative thought.

### Adverbs that compare or contrast

Adverbs that compare or contrast some preceding idea *(however, therefore, consequently, too, also)* are generally set off by commas when they occur within a sentence:

It was in Paris, **too,** that we felt the spirit of the American expatriots of the 'twenties.

The largest single group of terms in the dictionary, **however,** is that in the general vocabulary, which belongs to all speakers of American English. — Patrick E. Kilburn, "Ruckus in the Reference Room"

When such words appear at the beginning of a sentence, they may or may not be followed by a comma, depending on the emphasis desired:

**Thus** the way was cleared for further explorations.
**Nevertheless,** work did not always proceed according to plan.

When a clause beginning with such an adverb is joined to a preceding clause, the *semicolon* must be used, since these words are weak connectives. They relate ideas to one another but do not join them grammatically (see §12.1, page 170, Clauses linked with a conjunctive adverb):

Business recessions take place periodically; **however,** they are generally short-lived.

The natives are incredibly poor; **moreover,** they have little hope of bettering their lot.

When adverbs that closely modify the verb or the entire sentence *(perhaps, so)* begin the sentence, they should not be followed by a comma. Similarly, conjunctions are part of the clauses they introduce and should not be set off from them:

**Perhaps** a solution can still be found.
**But** the average American cannot afford such luxuries.

## Weak exclamations

Weak exclamations *(well, oh, say)* and *yes* and *no* sometimes occur as modifiers, particularly at the beginning of a sentence. They are conventionally separated from the sentence they modify by commas:

**Well,** not much can be done about it now.
**Yes,** times have changed.

It is doubtful whether the ordinary city-dweller is more grasping than the French peasant, **say,** or even the sturdy New Englander. — Herbert Muller, *The Uses of the Past*

## Names in direct address

Names which occur as interrupters in direct address are also set off by commas:

I firmly believe, **fellow citizens,** that justice will prevail.
It seems to me, **George,** that your attitude is poor.
**Workers of the world,** unite!

## Words, phrases, or clauses in a series

A comma is the mark ordinarily used to separate coordinate words, phrases, or clauses in a list or series:

> Body, senses, mind, and soul are only partial aspects of man, but they cannot be separated; they all operate together in health and in sickness. — C. A. Doxiadis, "The Coming Era of Ecumenopolis"

> He remembered these feelings as precisely as he remembered the clothes, the cars, the furniture, the songs, the slang. — Arthur Mizener, *The Far Side of Paradise*

> We were taught how to sit gracefully, how to walk, how to converse politely.

Although usage is divided, most writers prefer to use a comma before a connective joining the last item in a series:

> We had hot dogs, potato salad, soft drinks, and watermelon at the class picnic.

> It was left to the House of Representatives to decide whether the Presidency should go to Jackson, Adams, or Crawford.

In some informal writing, especially in newspapers, the final comma is omitted if no misinterpretation is possible:

> Further tornado damage was reported in Libertyville, Barrington, Palatine and Arlington Heights.

However, because there is quite often the possibility of misreading, it's generally better to use a final comma:

> At the rock concert we heard Blackberry Wine, Golden Gate Bridge, Red Eye and the Bull Dogs. [Is Red Eye and the Bull Dogs one group or two?]

If each of the items in a series is joined by a conjunction, commas are ordinarily omitted. The following sentence illustrates series with and without connectives:

> Scenes down on the farm **or** among raftsmen poling their flatboats **or** among the prairie schooners and Indians of the West were present in the canvasses of painters like George Caleb Bingham, William Sidney Mount, and Alfred Jacob Miller. — Holman Hamilton, "The American Renaissance"

See also §12.1, page 171. Semicolons to separate elements containing other marks.

## Coordinate adjectives

Commas are used to separate adjectives in a series when they modify the same noun. Since each performs the same function, such adjectives are called *coordinate*. In a coordinate series each member could sensibly be joined by *and* instead of a comma, or the order of modifiers could be reversed:

He spoke of the **violent, exciting, challenging** era that followed the Civil War.

Commas are not used when the adjectives are arranged so that each one modifies the entire following expression. Such items cannot be joined by *and* or reversed in order:

She made a **tasty** [ ] **Hungarian** goulash.
He spoke longingly of the **good** [ ] **old** [ ] **prewar** days.

Notice that a comma is never used between the last adjective in a series and the noun it modifies.

## To separate for clarity                     **11.6**

Commas tend to keep distinct the constructions they separate and should be used wherever necessary to prevent misreading. They are useful in the following situations:
1) When the subject of a clause may be mistaken for the object of a verb or preposition that precedes it:

As far as I can **see, the results** have not been promising.
When the rains are **over, the fields** are plowed in preparation for planting.

2) When a word has two possible functions, a comma can guide the reader in interpreting it properly. Words like *for, but,* and *however,* for example, may be used in several ways:

The surgeon's face showed no emotion, **but** anxiety and a little nervousness must have been hiding behind that impassive mask. [. . . showed no emotion but anxiety . . .]
Sharon was thoroughly embarrassed, **for** her parents treated her like a child. [. . . was thoroughly embarrassed for her parents . . .]
**However,** I interpreted his remarks liberally and continued my work.
**However** [ ] I interpreted his remarks, they made no sense.

3) A comma is sometimes necessary for clarity when one expression might be mistaken for another:

After he broke his **hand, writing** was very difficult for him.

4) When the same word occurs consecutively, a comma may be used, although usage is divided on this:

Whatever **is, is** right.

5) When the writer wishes to call attention to the second half of a compound predicate or to differentiate between them:

Though Dolly Sinatra has eighty-seven godchildren in Hoboken, and still goes to that city during political campaigns, she now lives with her husband in a beautiful sixteen-room house in Fort Lee, New Jersey. — Gay Talese, "Frank Sinatra Has a Cold"

This practice should be used only to avoid confusion in long sentences or to show contrast between the two parts of the predicate.

## In conventional places 11.7

Current practices should be followed in the use of commas in conventional places. Such commas help the reader quickly recognize distinct units of information.

1) Commas are conventionally used to group numbers into units of threes in separating thousands, millions, etc.:

2,853                84,962                3,542,869

Commas are not generally used in round numbers of four figures, serial numbers, or street addresses:

There were about 2000 words in the article.
The serial number of my typewriter is 11-6445793.
He lives at 11085 Champagne Point Road.

2) Commas are used to separate the day of the month and the year:

February 8, 1928                November 21, 1975

When only the month and year are given, a comma is not necessary, although it is frequently used:

October 1929                October, 1929

The form favored in military usage — 16 March 1962 — is more common in British than in American writing.

3) Commas are used in addresses to separate towns, counties, states, and districts:

Toledo, Ohio
Hamilton, Madison County, New York
He was born in Washington, D.C., in 1937.

4) Commas are used to separate proper names from titles and degrees:

Marshall Field, Jr.
Jerome Blum, M.A., Ph.D.
Gen. H. L. Matthews, U.S.M.C., Ret.
David Franklin Moore, Esq.

Notice that the final element in dates, addresses, and titles is followed by a comma if it falls within a sentence:

He was born on December 7, 1929, twelve years before we entered World War II.
She was born in Miami, Ohio, and lived there for seven years.
Sammy Davis, Jr., followed his father into show business.

5) Commas are conventional after the salutation of informal letters (Dear Shirley, Dear Uncle Joe,) and after the complimentary close of most letters (Yours truly, Sincerely yours,). A colon is used after the salutation of a formal or business letter (Dear Mr. Miller:).

6) A comma is customarily used after expressions that introduce direct quotations:

Sherman said, "Only a fool would carry on like that."

If the phrase interrupts a sentence in the quotation, it is set off by two commas:

"Only a fool," Sherman said, "would carry on like that."

No comma is needed with very short quotations, exclamations, or phrases closely built into the structure of the sentence:

Father always said "Time is money."
She began to scream "Fire!" as soon as she saw the smoke.
One famous writer called slavery a "peculiar institution."

Misused commas                                   **11.8**

> **No** $\wedge$   Correction: Remove the superfluous comma at the place marked.

Students frequently use too many commas because of a mistaken notion that the more punctuation, the better. Remember that too many commas are as bad as too few, and be prepared to justify every comma you use. The most common errors in using commas are described below.

## Between main sentence elements

Since a comma is a mark of separation, it should not ordinarily be used between those elements of a sentence that naturally go together: subject and verb, verb and object (or complement), preposition and object. There should be no marks where the brackets stand in the following sentences:

**Subject and verb:** Sometimes students who have attended expensive preparatory schools[ ] have trouble adjusting to large public universities.

**Verb and object:** I have often noticed[ ] that a person's physical characteristics may influence his personality.

**Verb and complement:** Whenever the dogs in the kennel appeared[ ] restless or hostile the trainer took steps to pacify them.

**Preposition and object:** Nothing troubled her except[ ] that her friendship with Swift was causing gossip.

## Between two words or phrases joined by *and*

Be careful to distinguish between coordinating conjunctions joining independent *clauses* and those joining other sentence elements, such as compound subjects or verbs. Except for coordinate clauses (§11.1), two items joined by *and* or by one of the other coordinating conjunctions are not ordinarily separated by a comma. Commas would be out of place in the following compound constructions:

Primitive agricultural tools[ ] and bits of clay pottery were found. [compound subject]

He either talked too much[ ] or else said nothing at all. [compound predicate]

In his senior year he was captain of the football team[ ] and secretary of his class. [compound complement]

She wanted more time for study [ ] and contemplation. [compound object of preposition]

Occasionally a comma is used for clarity between the two parts of a compound predicate; see §11.6.

## Between main clauses without a connective

A comma alone is an inadequate mark of separation between two main clauses. If the clauses are not joined by a coordinating conjunction, they must be separated by a semicolon or punctuated as individual sentences. See §2.2, Comma faults.

## With restrictive modifiers

A restrictive modifier is one that is essential to the meaning of the sentence (see §11.3); it should not be separated from the element it modifies by a comma. The boldface elements in the following example are restrictive and should stand as they are here, without commas:

The conenose, or kissing bug, is an insect **whose painful bite can draw blood.**

The book **that I left at home** is the one I really need for class.

## After the last item in a series

A comma is never used between the last adjective in a series and the noun it modifies:

He imagined himself as a **rich, handsome, successful**[ ] man of the world.

A comma is also not used after the last item in other kinds of lists or series:

The work of such modern masters as Picasso, Matisse, van Gogh, and Gauguin [ ] shocked conservative critics when it was introduced at the famous New York Armory show in 1913.

**Applications: Commas**
1. Read the following sentences carefully. In which of the places marked with brackets would you insert a comma? In which do you consider a comma optional? Not appropriate? Give specific reasons for your choice of punctuation.
a. If a man can write a better book [1] preach a better sermon [2] or make a better mousetrap [3] than his neighbors [4] though he builds his house in the woods [5] the world will make a beaten path to his door. — Ralph Waldo Emerson
b. There is a tavern in the town [1]
And there my true love sits him down [2] sits him down [3]
And drinks his wine mid laughter free [4]
And never [5] never thinks of me.
c. When a man assumes a public trust [1] he should consider himself as public property. — Thomas Jefferson
d. Put your trust in God [1] my boys [2] and keep your powder dry. — Oliver Cromwell (attributed)
e. Let us all be happy and live within our means [1] even if we have to borrow money to do it. — Artemus Ward
f. When I was a child [1] I spake as a child [2] I understood as a child [3] I thought as a child; but when I became a man [4] I put away childish things. — I Corinthians
g. Whenever punctuation problems arise [1] it is a good idea to consult the text [2] and determine the appropriate usage.
h. In 1958 [1] they moved to Santa Fe [2] New Mexico [3] and their third child [4] a daughter [5] was born there on October 27 [6] 1959.
i. Professor Tillman [1] author of several books [2] gave a series of lectures [3] on the depression.
j. Walk right in [1] and sit right down.

2. The following sentences contain both restrictive and nonrestrictive modifiers. Punctuate each sentence appropriately. If the sentence makes sense either way, explain the difference in meaning between the restrictive and the nonrestrictive modifier.

*example:* The alligator which was often hunted for its hide is in danger of becoming extinct.
*correction:* insert commas after *alligator* and *hide*

Exer

a. The wall which was built by Hadrian served its purpose for many years.
b. Abraham Lincoln sometimes called "The Great Emancipator" has become a symbol to many groups which crave independence.
c. Diamonds which are synthetically produced are more perfectly formed than natural diamonds which have serious flaws.
d. American movies that are exported abroad are popular in countries that have no native movie industry.
e. The French chef whose accomplishments are well known is eagerly sought by expensive restaurants and hotels.
f. Cockfighting outlawed by the Mexican authorities still takes place in areas where the police seldom turn up.
g. The oboe which is a woodwind instrument is played by means of a reed inserted in the mouthpiece.
h. The early settlers who were exposed to severe winters and who expected Indian attacks usually constructed forts many of which can still be found.
i. Drunk drivers who are responsible for many traffic fatalities obviously do not consider the value of human life.
j. The common belief that science can solve everything is another example of the naive optimism that most people are prey to.

3. Commas have been omitted from the following passages. Copy the paragraphs, punctuating with commas wherever you think appropriate; be prepared to account for the commas you insert. The first passage is from a version of "Rapunzel," the second from *Huckleberry Finn*.

a. There was once a man and his wife who had long wished in vain for a child and at last they had reason to hope that heaven would grant their wish. There was a little window at the back of their house which overlooked a beautiful garden full of lovely flowers and shrubs. It was however surrounded by a wall and nobody dared to enter because it belonged to a witch who was feared by everybody.
b. Mornings before daylight I slipped into cornfields and borrowed a watermelon or a mushmelon or a punkin or some new corn or things of that kind. Pap always said it warn't no harm to borrow things if you was meaning to pay them back sometime; but the widow said it warn't anything but a soft name for stealing and no decent body would do it.

## Semicolons 12.1

> ∧
> , Correction: Use a semicolon at the place marked to
> separate coordinate sentence elements.

∧
,

**12.1**

The semicolon is a mark of separation much stronger than a
comma and almost as full as a period:

Our haunted house was not strictly in the best haunted-house tradition. It was not a ramshackle pile standing at a lonely crossroad; it
was on a street inside the town and was surrounded by houses that
were cheerfully inhabited. It was not tumble-down; it was a large,
well-built mansion of brick, and it still stands, good as new.—Frank
Sullivan, *The Night the Old Nostalgia Burned Down*

Although the constructions requiring a semicolon are clearly
defined and relatively few, many student writers have trouble
with this mark of punctuation. Probably the most general fault
is that of using a semicolon where a comma or other mark
would be better. The semicolon is a heavy mark of separation
that makes a sentence move rather slowly. It occurs more frequently in formal writing, which is likely to use long, aggre-
gating sentences, than it does in general writing, which usually moves quite rapidly. In deciding between a semicolon or
another mark, consider the requirements of your own style
and of the material you are presenting.

The few constructions in which a semicolon is required are
listed below. Notice that in all its uses the semicolon marks a
separation between *coordinate* elements—expressions of
equal rank.

### Between main clauses without an expressed connective

A semicolon must be used to separate main clauses that are
not joined by one of the coordinating conjunctions *(and, but,
for, or, nor, yet):*

The penalty for not turning work in on time is a lowered grade; the
penalty for not turning it in at all is failure.

These clauses are clearly separate in thought and structure
and could be punctuated as separate sentences. A semicolon

is used to combine such clauses when the writer considers them parts of one idea. Sometimes the second clause continues the thought of the first:

Alfred Hitchcock was probably the first director to place *himself* at a slightly ironic distance from the action of his films; his own subtle mockery helped him confect high-gloss thrillers that serious people might enjoy without losing their sense of identity. — Jacob Brackman, "Onward and Upward with the Arts"

Sometimes the second clause presents a contrasting idea:

But however immature they are, these lovers are not dull characters; on the contrary, they are hauntingly and embarrassingly real. — Arthur Mizener, *The Far Side of Paradise*

The use of a comma rather than a semicolon or period between main clauses without an expressed connective is considered a serious error in writing. (See §2.2, Comma faults.)

## Between main clauses linked with a conjunctive adverb

A semicolon is used before heavy conjunctive adverbs like *however, therefore, consequently,* and *nevertheless* when they occur between clauses. Although such adverbs show a connection between the ideas, their connective function is weak and a semicolon must be used to separate the clauses:

The investigative jurisdiction of the FBI is limited to those cases in which the stolen automobile has been transported from one state to another; **however,** through cost-free services provided by the FBI Laboratory and Identification Division, the FBI has been able to assist state and municipal law enforcement agencies in identifying and convicting numerous auto thieves whose operations have not yet extended across state lines. — J. Edgar Hoover, "Auto Theft Is Big Business"

And, in fact, absense of intellectual content is the mark of the sentimental genre; **conversely,** it is because of her intellect that Jane Austen is never sentimental. — Brigid Brophy, "A Masterpiece, and Dreadful"

The use of heavy conjunctive adverbs between long clauses is characteristic of a sober, very formal style, as the examples above may indicate. They do appear in other places, of course, as in the following lines from Keats' "Ode on a Grecian Urn":

Heard melodies are sweet, but those unheard
　Are sweeter; **therefore,** ye soft pipes, play on;
Not to the sensual ear, but, more endeared,
　Pipe to the spirit ditties of no tone.

12.1

You may do well to follow the practice of many current writers, who use these adverbs as transitions between sentences rather than as transitions between clauses:

My mother had included drawing lessons in the advantages she had wrested for me out of the various strange environments in which we lived, and I had enough talent to be encouraged to become a painter. **However,** when I was told by my artist cousins that in order to become a painter I should go to art school and skip college, I gave up the idea. — Margaret Mead, *Blackberry Winter*

It is no secret that organized crime in America takes in over forty billion dollars a year. This is quite a profitable sum, especially when one considers that the Mafia spends very little for office supplies. Reliable sources indicate that the Cosa Nostra laid out no more than six thousand dollars last year for personalized stationery, and even less for staples. **Furthermore,** they have one secretary who does all the typing, and only three small rooms for headquarters, which they share with the Fred Persky Dance Studio. — Woody Allen, *Getting Even*

## With coordinating conjunctions

A semicolon is sometimes used between main clauses connected by coordinating conjunctions if: (1) the clauses are unusually long, (2) the clauses are not closely related, (3) one or more of the clauses contain commas, or (4) the writer wishes to show an emphatic contrast between statements:

I have known many black men and women and black boys and girls who really believed that it was better to be white than black, whose lives were ruined or ended by this belief**; and** I myself carried the seeds of this destruction within me for a long time. — James Baldwin, ''Unnameable Objects, Unspeakable Crimes''

In most cases these individualists are corporate executives, bankers, Wall Street lawyers**; but** they do not, as the economic determinists seem to believe, simply push the button of their economic power to affect fields remote from economics. — Robert Lubar, ''The Prime Movers''

## To separate elements containing other marks

Semicolons are often used in lists and series to separate elements that contain commas or other marks. In the following sentence, for example, the semicolons are necessary for clarity:

Here are a few: Theodore Dreiser, of German extraction; Eugene O'Neill, of Irish ancestry; Fannie Hurst, of Jewish blood; Carl Sandburg, a Swede; John Dos Passos — his name is Portuguese; James T. Farrell, an Irishman; O. E. Rolvaag, another Scandinavian; Archibald MacLeish, and that looks Scotch; Paul de Kruif — I suppose that to be Dutch; Carl Van Doren — another Dutch name; Saroyan, an

Armenian—and so on indefinitely.—Howard Mumford Jones, *Ideas in America*

Notice that here, just as with main clauses, the semicolon separates *coordinate* elements. It is never used between elements of unequal rank, such as phrases and clauses or main and subordinate clauses.

## Colons    12.2

> ∧ **Correction:** Insert a colon at the place marked, or
> ∵ change the misused colon.
> ∨

A colon is a mark of anticipation, directing attention to what follows:

Molecular biologists have now provided a fairly complete picture of how genes carry out their primary function: the specification of protein structure.—William B. Wood and R. S. Edgar, "Building a Bacterial Virus"

Students sometimes confuse colons and semicolons, but their functions are entirely different. The distinction is simple: a colon introduces or indicates what is to follow; a semicolon separates coordinate elements. The following passage illustrates the correct use of both marks (as does the sentence of the text immediately above):

Smaller birds were less elusive: a pair of blue-winged warblers scolded us for coming so close to their nest, as the juncos had along the higher trail; a winter wren, reminiscent of the Long Trail in Vermont, lit up the woods with song; a kingfisher shot downstream with his loud rattle.—Paul Brooks, "The Great Smokies"

### Anticipatory use

A colon may be used after a main clause to indicate that a list, an illustration, or a summation is to follow:

There are three kinds of open code: the jargon code, the null cipher, and geometrical systems like the Cardano grille.—David Kahn, *The Codebreakers*

What made Poe particularly acceptable to the French, however, was what had distinguished him from most of the other Romantics of the English-speaking countries: his interest in aesthetic theory.—Edmund Wilson, *Axel's Castle*

The colon is used as an anticipatory mark only after grammatically complete expressions. Do not use a colon between verbs and their objects or complements, or between prepositions and their objects.

| Colon | No colon |
|---|---|
| He visited the following cities: Boston, Dallas, Chicago, Miami, and Seattle. | He visited Boston, Dallas, Chicago, Miami, and Seattle. [objects of verb] |
| The string section consists of four instruments: violin, viola, cello, and bass. | The four instruments in the string section are violin, viola, cello, and bass. [complements of verb] |

## Between main clauses

A colon may be used between two main clauses when the second clause is an illustration, a restatement, or an amplification of the first:

The Great Books have about them much more, I feel sure, than mere snob appeal: they have a kind of dim religious light, a sense of the Serious Call, of the medieval scholar-saint. — Louis Kronenberger, *Company Manners*

I was impractical: I wanted to marry a poet. — Lillian Hellman, *Pentimento*

## Before quotations

A colon is generally used between an introductory statement and a grammatically complete quotation, especially if the quotation is more than one sentence. If the quotation runs to several sentences, it may be paragraphed separately:

In "A Cooking Egg," the poet demands, after a call upon a very mild, dull spinster: "Where are the eagles and the trumpets?" and himself returns the saddened answer: "Buried beneath some snow-deep Alps." — Edmund Wilson, *Axel's Castle*

. . . Take one of the passages I have already quoted from Yeats: "We make out of the quarrel with others, rhetoric, but out of the quarrel with ourselves, poetry. Unlike the rhetoricians, who get a confident voice from remembering the crowd they have won or may win, we sing amid our uncertainty, and, smitten even in the presence of the most high beauty by the knowledge of our solitude, our rhythm shudders." — Ibid.

When a short quotation is built closely into a sentence, it may be preceded either by a comma or by a colon, depending on how it is introduced:

As Alexander Pope said, "A little learning is a dangerous thing."

She reminded him of the words of Pope: "A little learning is a dangerous thing."

## Colons in conventional places

A colon is customary in the following places:

1) After an expression introducing examples or a large body of material (as after *places* in the preceding sentence).

2) Between hours and minutes expressed in figures: 11:30 a.m.

3) In formal footnotes and bibliographies:

Between volume and page — *The Nation*, 98:295
Between chapter and verse of the Bible — Matthew 4:6
Between the title and subtitle of a book — *China: A Modern Enigma*

4) After the formal salutation in a letter:

Dear Sir:                          Dear Professor Jones:

See page 206 for use of capital letter after colons.

∧
:
∨

**12.2**

## Dashes 13.1

/--/ Correction: Use a dash (or dashes) to set off the expression marked.

Dashes are used to set off parenthetical expressions and abrupt interruptions in thought. The dash is a useful mark of separation, but since it is a more emphatic way of setting off elements than either commas or parentheses, it should not be used to excess or in places where another mark (or none) would be more appropriate. Dashes are customarily used in the situations shown below.

1) To set off parenthetical expressions and abrupt interruptions:

All it means—**but it does mean that**—is that these millions of peasants are slowly putting aside their heritage of vague, mystical thoughts about the world around them (in which, for instance, an iron plow made the earth "sick") and entering the world of rational technological thinking.—Hans Konigsberger, "A Reporter at Large: China Notes"

Note: on the typewriter a dash is made with two unspaced hyphens; there should likewise be no space on either side of the dash, between it and the words it separates.

2) To mark sharp turns in thought:

He praised Ann's intelligence, her efficiency, her good taste—**and then proposed to her sister.**

He is a humble man—**with a lot to be humble about.**

3) To enclose parenthetical elements (usually to give greater emphasis to elements that could also be set off with commas):

Still we do condemn—**we must condemn**—the cruelties of slavery, fanaticism, and witch-burning.—Herbert Muller, *The Uses of the Past*

With our love of record keeping—**doubtless a mark of our business society**—the origin of almost everything is known or easily discoverable.—Jacques Barzun and Henry Graff, *The Modern Researcher*

For clarity, dashes are sometimes used instead of commas to set off parenthetical elements that have internal punctuation.

Note that *two* dashes are necessary to enclose a parenthetical element that falls in the middle of a sentence:

While Joe, Barney, and I were enjoying college and considerable leisure, three of our high-school friends—George Matthews, Herb Friedson, and Walt Moran—had been drafted and were awaiting transportation overseas.

4) To set off an expression that summarizes or illustrates the preceding statement:

He founded a university, and devoted one side of his complex genius to placing that university amid every circumstance which could stimulate the imagination—**beauty of buildings, of situation, and every other stimulation of equipment and organisation.**—Alfred North Whitehead, "The Idea of a University"

5) To serve some special uses:

a. To precede a credit line, as at the end of the quoted passages in this book.

b. After introductory words that are to be repeated before each of the lines following:

We pledge—
    To uphold the Constitution.
    To obey the laws of this state.

c. To separate questions and answers in testimony:

Q.—Did you see him?
A.—No.

d. To indicate interrupted dialog (usually *two* dashes separated by a space are used):

"Well, I had always assumed that— —"
"I don't care what you assumed," John snapped.

## Parentheses **13.2**

**Correction: Use parentheses to enclose the expression marked.**

Parentheses are curved marks used chiefly to enclose incidental or explanatory remarks as shown below.

1) To enclose incidental remarks:

He was adored **(I have spent some time looking for the right verb, and that's it)** by the members of the *Journal* staff, who greeted him each afternoon, in a sudden silence of typewriters, as if they hadn't seen him for a long time. —James Thurber, "Franklin Avenue, U.S.A."

2) To enclose details and examples:

For seven long years **(1945–1952)** austerity was the key word in British economic life.

The changes can be seen by comparing the profits made before 1929 **(upper diagram)** with those made after 1929 **(lower diagram).**

3) To enclose figures or letters used to enumerate points:

The main questions asked about our way of life concern **(1)** the strength of our democracy, **(2)** our radical practices, **(3)** our concept of modern economy, and **(4)** the degree of materialism in our culture. —Vera Dean and J. B. Brebner, *How to Make Friends for the U.S.*

**(/)**

**13.2**

No punctuation marks are used before a parenthetical statement that occurs within a sentence. If a comma or period is needed after the parenthetical material, it is placed *outside* of the *closing* marks:

There is talk with music (tapes and records**),** talk with film and tape (movies and television**),** talk with live public performance (demonstrations and "confrontation"**).** —William Jovanovich, "A Tumult of Talk"

When the parenthetical statement comes between sentences, the appropriate end punctuation is placed *inside* the closing mark:

Fearing federal intervention, Vincent Columbraro, the Buttered Toast King, called for a truce. (Columbraro has such tight control over all buttered toast moving in and out of New Jersey that one word from him could ruin breakfast for two-thirds of the state.) —Woody Allen, *Getting Even*

**Some Study and Practice: Reviewing Punctuation**

1. In each numbered space in the following sentences, which mark of punctuation would you consider most appropriate: a comma, a semicolon, a colon, a dash, or a parenthesis? Is punctuation necessary in all cases? If more than one choice is possible, list the marks in order of your preference.

a. Let us begin by looking [1] at the two countries where population pressures are most severe [2] India and Pakistan.

b. The finalists in diving were [1] Wilkins [2] U.S.A. [3] and Oyama [4] Japan [5] no one else had qualified.

c. To Ahab the white whale became an obsession [1] even Starbuck [2] the first mate [3] could do nothing to shake him out of it.

d. Reisman divides behavior into two major classes [1] inner-directed [2] directed toward pleasing the self [3] and other-directed [4] concerned with pleasing others [5].

e. The Edsel was [1] the most carefully planned and lavishly promoted new car in automobile history [2] but it was a total failure.

f. Someone [1] was it Carlyle [2] ironically used a truss factory [3] as a symbol [4] of modern [5] industrial progress.

g. Some industries have established good relations with their unions by increasing benefits [1] vacations, insurance, pension plans [2] but many manufacturers feel that there is only one permanent solution to their chronic labor problems [3] increased automation.

h. The key word in the essay [1] *faction* [2] is carefully defined by Madison at the beginning [3] then he goes on to explain [4] what forms it may take.

i. An audience is basically one of three things [1] although various mixtures are also possible [2] friendly, hostile, or indifferent.

j. He played [1] the guitar, the banjo, and the piano [2] so badly [3] that everyone in the musical felt it was doomed [4] unless they could think of some tactful way to get him out of the show.

# Quotation marks, brackets, ellipses, and italics

In general the more common punctuation marks—periods, question marks, commas, semicolons, colons, dashes, and parentheses—indicate intonation and degrees of interruption that would occur if the material was read aloud. They show how the writer wants the words grouped together for meaning and emphasis.

The four marks discussed in this section—quotation marks, brackets, ellipses, and italics—are somewhat different in purpose. They are visual guides that tell the reader at a glance such things as whether the words are a writer's own and whether they are being used in a special way. Compare the following pairs of sentences:

He said I was a fool. [He accused the **writer** of being a fool.]
He said, "I was a fool." [He called **himself** a fool.]

He spoke of Watson's moral decline. [the moral decline of Watson]
He spoke of Watson's *Moral Decline*. [a book by Watson]

Although quotation marks, brackets, ellipses, and italics are used less often than other punctuation, it is important to know how to use them correctly. They are often necessary in college papers, which are likely to contain references to the writing of others.

## Quotation marks

> ˅˅ Correction: Make the quotation marks and accompanying punctuation conform to conventional usage.

Quotation marks are necessary to set off direct speech and material quoted from other sources. They are also used around some titles and around words used in special ways.

Usage varies, but double quotations (" ") are the usual marks in American publications. Students should follow this convention, using single marks (' ')—made on the typewriter with apostrophes—only for a quotation within a quotation (see p. 181). Whether double or single, quotation marks are always used in *pairs,* before and after the quoted material.

## Quotation marks to enclose direct discourse

Statements representing actual speech or conversation are enclosed by quotation marks. The following passage illustrates typical punctuation for direct discourse. Notice not only the quotation marks but the punctuation used with them:

> When we got home, Cathy asked, "Did you win the game?"
> David said, "You'd better believe it. I got four hits, and we won 8 to 5."
> I hobbled to my chair.
> "And Daddy hit a triple," Mindy said. "You should have seen him run."

In dialog the words of each speaker are customarily indented like paragraphs, as in the example above. But when short speeches or statements are quoted to illustrate a point in exposition, they are usually included in the paragraph where they are relevant rather than being set off:

> When he is not playing adman, businessman, referee and editor, Cerf devotes a good part of his time to keeping his authors happy. Fortunately, he enjoys it, even when his high-strung writers curl into knots. He likes to tell about the time that Sinclair Lewis spent a night at the Cerf apartment. "He had dinner," Cerf recalls, "and we were all sitting at the table. Then Bill Faulkner called up and said he was in town. I told Lewis and asked him, could Bill come over? Lewis said, 'Certainly not. This is my night!' Then at 9:30, Lewis went to bed. At 10:30, he shouted downstairs, 'Bennett!' I answered him, and he said, 'I just wanted to see if you sneaked out to see Faulkner.' " — *Time,* December 16, 1966

Only *direct discourse,* which represents the actual words of the speaker, is enclosed by quotation marks. *Indirect discourse,* which gives the substance of what the speaker said but not his exact words, is *not* enclosed in quotes:

| Direct discourse | Indirect discourse |
|---|---|
| The coach said, "Get in there and fight." | The coach told us to get in there and fight. |
| "At the present time," the senator replied, "I haven't made up my mind about the bill." | The senator replied that he had not yet made up his mind about the bill. |

## Quotation marks around quoted material

Words taken directly from another writer or speaker must be clearly set apart, either by quotation marks or by some other conventional typographic device such as setting them in reduced type. Whether a writer is quoting a phrase or several paragraphs, he should make certain that he follows the exact

Quotation
marks,
brackets,
ellipses,
italics
180

wording and punctuation of his source.

## Short quotations

Quotation marks are used around quoted phrases and statements that are included within the body of a paragraph. The quoted material may be worked into the structure of a sentence or may stand by itself:

Another immortal pun is Eugene Field's comment on the actor Creston Clarke that "he played the king as though he were in constant fear that somebody else was going to play the ace." — Max Eastman, *The Enjoyment of Laughter*

While Iago, for example, is gulling Roderigo, he scoffs at him with superb disdain: "I have rubb'd this young quat almost to the sense / And he grows angry" (Othello, 5.1.11 – 12). — Maurice Charney, *How to Read Shakespeare*

## Long quotations

When quoted material is relatively long — more than one full sentence from the original source or more than four lines in your paper — it is usually indented and single spaced but not enclosed in quotation marks. In published material, long quotations are often set in smaller type.

## A quotation within a quotation

Use single quotation marks around quoted material that appears within a quotation which is itself enclosed in double marks:

If they depended solely on economic theory to guide them, they would be in the position of the man John Williams mentions: "About the practical usefulness of the theory, I have often felt like the man who stammered and finally learned to say, 'Peter Piper picked a peck of pickled peppers,' but found it hard to work into conversation." — C. Hartley Grattan, "New Books"

In the rare instances when a third quotation occurs within a second, double and single marks are alternated, like this:

In the next passage he gives an example of Mill's uncontrolled temper: "Mill attacked Beaton with a poker after reading his comment that 'A work of genius is not, as Mr. Mill says, "a spontaneous outflowing of the soul"; it is the product of intellectual discipline, a quality Mr. Mill notably lacks.'"

Such a proliferation of quotation marks is confusing and can usually be avoided, either by indenting and single spacing the main quotation or by paraphrasing some of the material:

In the next passage he gives an example of Mill's uncontrolled temper, telling how Mill attacked Beaton with a poker after reading his comment that "A work of genius is not, as Mr. Mill says, 'a spontaneous overflowing of the soul'; it is the product of intellectual discipline, a quality Mr. Mill notably lacks."

### Quoted verse
A phrase or portion of a line of verse may be built into a sentence and enclosed by quotation marks, as is this phrase from *Romeo and Juliet:*

> "A plague on both your houses" was the general attitude toward the parties in any conflict, no matter what the outcome. — Percy Finch, *Shanghai and Beyond*

**14.1**

If the quoted passage extends over several lines of the poem, it is best to line it off exactly as it appears in the original, single-spaced and indented. Quotation marks are unnecessary:

Milton opens *Paradise Lost* by announcing that he will write

> Of Man's first disobedience, and the fruit
> Of that forbidden tree whose mortal taste
> Brought death into the World. . . .

If two or three lines of verse are incorporated into a paragraph, the passage is enclosed in quotation marks and the line breaks are indicated by diagonal lines (/):

Milton opens *Paradise Lost* by announcing that he will write "Of Man's first disobedience, and the fruit / Of that forbidden tree whose mortal taste / Brought death into the World."

### Quotation marks around titles
Quotation marks are used to set off the titles of short written works such as single poems, essays, short stories, and magazine articles. The titles of books and the names of newspapers and magazines are italicized:

**The Oxford Book of English Verse** includes only two poems by Oliver Goldsmith: **"Women"** and **"Memory."**

Judith Blake and Kingsley Davis have contributed an article titled **"Norms, Values, and Sanctions"** to **The Handbook of Modern Sociology,** edited by Robert E. L. Faris.

See §14.4, Italics, and §28, The reference paper.

A few titles are neither set off by quotation marks nor underlined for italics: the Bible, Old Testament, the Constitution of the United States, Lincoln's Gettysburg Address, Montgomery Ward Catalog, the Denver Telephone Directory (or any other catalog or directory).

Quotation
marks,
brackets,
ellipses,
italics
**182**

## Quotation marks to set off words

Words used in some special way within a sentence are often set apart by quotation marks or by italics (underlining).

### A word used as a word

A word used as a word or as an example rather than for its meaning in a passage is either italicized or enclosed by quotation marks. Use one or the other consistently:

People often confuse the meanings of words that sound alike, such as **"allusion"** and **"illusion."**

I have trouble typing *artificial* and *expectation.*

### Apologetic quotes for slang and colloquial expressions

In serious writing, an expression associated with unedited or colloquial forms of English is sometimes put in quotation marks to show that the writer knows it is not considered appropriate in formal usage:

The disheartening outcome of recent international conferences has convinced some of our statesmen that certain nations consider us as little more than "fall guys."

The trouble with apologetic quotes is that they focus the reader's attention on the expression and make him wonder why the writer chose to use it. If you think a word or phrase is right for what you are saying, it's best to use it without apology.

When a real or imaginary person is frequently referred to by his or her nickname, it is not set off by quotation marks:

Abe Lincoln    Huck Finn    Babe Ruth    Ivan the Terrible

In general writing there is seldom any need to use apologetic quotes about a word or expression. If the word is appropriate, use it without quotation marks. If it is not, use another.

### Words used derisively

Sometimes a writer may use quotation marks around a term to show that it is being used derisively or sarcastically.

This remarkable piece of "art" consists of a large canvas covered with mud and old bus transfers.

She was so "genteel" that she avoided any reference to the human body.

It's generally better to try to make the whole tone of the passage derisive rather than to rely too much on quotation marks as signposts.

## Quotation marks with other punctuation

The following conventions govern the use of other punctuation with quotation marks:

1) Commas and periods are always placed *inside* the closing quotation mark:

"Yes," Roger agreed, "it's too late to worry about that now."

Her watch case was described as "waterproof," but "moisture-resistant" would have been more accurate.

2) Semicolons and colons are placed *outside* the closing quotation mark:

This critic's attitude seems to be "I don't like any movie"; on a few occasions, though, he has said kind words for a travelog or a documentary film.

Fully a third of the railroad passengers were what trainmen call "deadheads": people who ride on passes and never tip.

3) Question marks, exclamation points, and dashes are placed inside *or* outside the final quotation mark, depending upon the situation. They come *inside* when they apply to the quotation only:

Mother looked at me and asked, "Why do you say that?"

He gave me a skeptical look which seemed to mean "Look who's talking!"

Terrence interrupted, "No, listen to this—" and proceeded to recite a poem none of us had ever heard before.

They are placed *outside* the final quotation mark when they apply to the entire statement:

Who was it who said that "good guys finish last"? [The whole sentence is a question.]

And to top it all off, she refers to her automatic dishwasher as "essential equipment for gracious living"!

End punctuation marks are never doubled. If a quotation ends your sentence, the end punctuation within quotation marks also indicates the end of the sentence:

Ever since I moved to Boston to conduct symphony concerts exclusively, one of the principal questions put to me in interviews is "How much do you miss opera?"—Erich Leinsdorf, "What Makes Opera Run"

Notice that no period is added after the final quotation mark, even though the sentence is a statement, not a question. Occasionally it is necessary to use double marks *within* a

Quotation
marks,
brackets,
ellipses,
italics
184

sentence to avoid a possible misreading, as in the sentence following the one quoted above, but such instances are rare:

Mind you, not "Do you miss opera?", because the questioner takes it for granted that it is impossible for one who has conducted so much opera to live without it, but "How much?" — *Ibid.*

## Brackets     14.2

> **[/]**    Correction: Use brackets to set off any insertion in quoted material.

Brackets are used to insert brief editorial comments and explanations in material quoted from other writers:

Lest it be thought that I am exaggerating, listen to Mencken: "The impact of this flood [of common-speech, non-fashionable Americanisms] is naturally most apparent in Canada, whose geographical proximity and common interests completely obliterate the effects of English political and social dominance." — Eric Partridge, *Slang Today and Yesterday*

Comments or directions may be bracketed in conversation or in other quoted material to show that the speaker didn't actually say the enclosed words:

For the first few minutes the practiced speaker, therefore, fills in time with his "Thank you" to the chairman introducing him. . . . Then come his formal salutations, "Mr. President, honored guests [if there are any], ladies and gentlemen." — *Amy Vanderbilt's Complete Book of Etiquette*

The Latin word *sic* (meaning *thus* or *so*) is sometimes inserted in brackets within quoted material to mark an error in spelling, usage, or fact that appeared in the original:

The author's next letter was headed "Danbury, *Conneticut* [*sic*] Oct. 6, 1854."

Most current writers feel that the insertion of *sic* to mark the errors of others is more snobbish than scholarly, and the practice has declined.

In this book brackets are used with examples of writing to enclose words that might better be left out of a sentence, to suggest an improved expression, and to comment on a construction. These special uses are illustrated below:

At the end of an hour and a half we arrived at [the spot where] the red flag [was situated].

He looks **similar to** [**like**] his father.
**Most** fishermen are optimists. [adjective, modifying **fishermen**]

Occasionally brackets are used for parenthetical material that falls within parentheses—thus ([ ])—but such constructions are awkward and can usually be avoided. Do not confuse the normal uses of parentheses and brackets; see §13.2, Parentheses.

/. . ./     Correction: Use an ellipsis to indicate any omission in quoted material.

A punctuation mark of three spaced periods, called an ellipsis (plural: *ellipses*), indicates that one or more words have been omitted from the quoted material. If an ellipsis comes at the end of a sentence, the sentence period (or other end punctuation) is retained, and the three periods of the ellipsis follow it. There is no space between the last word and the end punctuation:

Fourscore and seven years ago our fathers brought forth upon this continent a new nation . . . dedicated to the proposition that all men are created equal. Now we are engaged in a great civil war. . . . We are met on a great battlefield of that war. . . .—Abraham Lincoln, Gettysburg Address

Does this sound harsh today? . . . Yes, but I cannot sell my liberty and my power, to save their sensibility.—Ralph Waldo Emerson, "Self-Reliance"

To indicate that an entire paragraph or more or an entire line or more of poetry has been omitted, a full line of ellipses is used:

That's my last Duchess painted on the wall,
Looking as if she were alive. . . . [two words are omitted here]
. . . . . . . . . . . . . . . . . [two lines omitted]
Will 't please you sit and look at her?
                        —Robert Browning, "My Last Duchess"

Ellipses are sometimes used, especially in narrative, to indicate interruptions in thought, incomplete statements, or hesitation in speech, as in this description of the dying words of John Wilkes Booth, the assassin of Lincoln:

Quotation
marks,
brackets,
ellipses,
italics
**186**

/. . ./

**14.3**

Water was poured into his mouth. He blew it out feebly, opened his eyes and moved his lips to shape the words: "Tell . . . mother. . . ." Then he fainted again. When he came to, he finished his sentence: "Tell . . . mother . . . I . . . died . . . for . . . my country." — Eleanor Ruggles, *Prince of Players*

## Italics 14.4

> **Ital** Correction: Underline the word or expression marked to correspond to the conventions for using italic type.

Words are set off or emphasized in most published works by printing them in slanting type called *italics*. In handwritten or typed papers, such words are underlined:

The article first appeared in Harper's Magazine and was reprinted in The Reader's Digest.

### Italics for titles

The names of newspapers and magazines and the titles of books, plays, films, and other complete works published separately are conventionally italicized (or underlined):

*Newsweek*
*The Great Gatsby*
the novel *Huckleberry Finn*
*Webster's Eighth New Collegiate Dictionary*

*The Chicago Tribune* (or: the Chicago *Tribune*)
*Hamlet,* Act III
the movie *Ben Hur*
Dante's *Divine Comedy*

Titles of articles, short stories, poems, and other short pieces of writing that are part of a larger work are usually enclosed in quotation marks:

"The Easy Chair" was a regular feature in *Harper's Magazine.*

See §14.1, page 182, Quotation marks around titles, and §28, The reference paper.

### Italics for words and phrases used as examples

Words used as words or as examples rather than as parts of a sentence should be italicized or set off by quotation marks. (See also §14.1, Quotation marks to set off words.)

Even on a sophisticated level there is some variation in word usage. For instance, what in other parts of the country is called a **sidewalk** was and may still be called in my native section of Maryland a **pavement,** and what is elsewhere called a **pavement** was in our usage the **street** if in town and the **road** if in the country. — Thomas Pyles, *Words and Ways of American English*

## Italics for foreign words

Ital

Words from foreign languages that have not been absorbed into English should be italicized, not set off by quotation marks:

**14.4**

In Antiquity every tree, every spring, every stream, every hill had its own **genius loci,** its guardian spirit. — Lynn White, Jr., "The Historical Roots of Our Ecological Crisis"

Sometime soon after he arrives in Hawaii, a sweet lassitude creeps over the **malihini** (newcomer). — *Time,* December 16, 1966

Foreign expressions that would ordinarily be underlined for italics include terms like *coup d'état, Weltschmerz, deus ex machina, mañana.* In most books and formal writing, the accents and other marks are used.

Scientific names for plants, insects, and so forth are also italicized:

The mistletoe **(Phoradendron flavescens)** is the state flower of Oklahoma.

Words from other languages that are now widely used in general English are not considered foreign terms and so are not underlined or otherwise set off:

| | | | |
|---|---|---|---|
| bourgeois | debut | laissez faire | sputnik |
| chalet | debutante | prima donna | status quo |
| chic | fiancee | slalom | vice versa |

Although dictionaries usually designate words that are now anglicized (have become part of the English language) and those that are not, their usage tends to be conservative. If you are certain that an expression marked "foreign" is familiar to your readers, you need not underline it.

Abbreviations of the less common Latin words and phrases used mainly in reference works are sometimes italicized, but Latin abbreviations in general use are not:

e.g.    et al.    etc.    ibid.    i.e.    vs.    viz.

## Italics for emphasis

Italics are used in printed material to indicate an emphatic word or stressed statement:

Quotation
marks,
brackets,
ellipses,
italics
188

Since we cannot have our fill of existence by going on and on, we want to have *as much life as possible* in our short span.—Susanne K. Langer, "Man and Animal: The City and the Hive"

Italics should be used sparingly for emphasis. When used excessively or with words that do not deserve stress, this device may strike a reader as affected.

**Some Study and Practice: Quotation Marks, Brackets, Ellipses, Italics**

1. All the quotation marks and indentions have been removed from the following passage from a short story. Rewrite the passage, using quotation marks and indentions to show dialog and changes in speaker.

Ital

14.4

They do say, Mr. Adams said to Old Man Warner, who stood next to him, that over in the north village they're talking of giving up the lottery. Old Man Warner snorted. Pack of crazy fools, he said. Listening to the young folks, nothing's good enough for *them*. Next thing you know, they'll be wanting to go back to living in caves, nobody work any more, live *that* way for a while. Used to be a saying about Lottery in June, corn be heavy soon. First thing you know, we'd all be eating stewed chickweed and acorns. There's *always* been a lottery, he added petulantly. Bad enough to see young Joe Summers up there joking with everybody. Some places already quit lotteries, Mrs. Adams said. Nothing but trouble in *that,* Old Man Warner said stoutly. Pack of young fools.

adapted from Shirley Jackson, "The Lottery"

2. The passage that follows is part of a student paper on H. L. Mencken, the famous American journalist. The four marks discussed in this chapter—quotation marks, brackets, ellipses, and italics—have been omitted, as have typographical devices such as indention and single-spacing for quotations. The sources which the student refers to in this passage are reprinted on pages 190–191. Notice carefully all uses of direct quotation from the sources, omissions, and remarks or explanations inserted by the student. Then copy the student's passage, adding appropriate punctuation and typographical devices. For purposes of simplicity, you need not add the footnotes that would be necessary.

To Mencken, nothing was sacred. He attacked hypocrisy and stupidity wherever he found it. In his essay on Being an American, for example, he had this to say about social life in the White House: And the current Chief Magistrate of the nation Harding—its defiant substitute for czar and kaiser—is a small-town printer who, when he wishes to enjoy himself in the Executive Mansion, invites in a homeopathic doctor, a Seventh Day Adventist evangelist, and a couple of moving-picture actresses.

In another essay from Prejudices: Third Series, Star-spangled Men, he ridiculed the pretensions of popular fraternal organizations: The Nobles of the Mystic Shrine, chiefly paunchy wholesalers of the Rotary Club species, are not content with swords, baldrics, stars, garters and jewels; they also wear red fezes. The Elks run to rubies. There is an undertaker in Hagerstown, Md., who has been initiated eighteen times. When he robes himself to plant a fellow joiner he weighs three hundred pounds and sparkles and flashes like the mouth of hell itself. Put beside this lowly washer of the dead, General Pershing newly polished would seem almost like a Trappist.

Mencken's talent for invective was enormous, and nothing pleased him more than to fill pages scourging America's buffooneries, ribaldries, imbecilities, and grotesqueries. Such forceful language was bound to arouse animosity. Frederick Lewis Allen, in Only Yesterday, reports that when Mencken denounced the residents of Dayton during the Scopes trial, the Reverend A. C. Stribling replied that Mencken was a cheap blatherskite of a pen-pusher; and to such retorts there was a large section of outraged public opinion ready to cry Amen. A few years later Mencken published a Schimpflexicon, an anthology of abusive remarks made by his critics.

Although he was an unflagging critic of America, Mencken delighted in the satirical material it provided him. He maintained that in America only the man who was born with a petrified diaphragm can fail to laugh himself to sleep every night. Many Americans apparently agreed, for the circulation of the Mercury was over 77,000 in 1927, perhaps because, as Allen says, the magazine crystallized the misgivings of thousands. At any rate, in 1927 Walter Lippmann called Mencken the most powerful personal influence on this whole generation of educated people.

**Sources**

And here, more than anywhere else that I know of or have heard of, the daily panorama of human existence, of private and communal folly—the unending procession of governmental extortions and chicaneries, of commercial brigandages and throat-slittings, of theological buffooneries, of aesthetic ribaldries, or legal swindles and harlotries, of miscellaneous rogueries, villainies, imbecilities, grotesqueries, and extravagances—is so inordinately gross and preposterous, so perfectly brought up to the highest conceivable amperage, so steadily enriched with an almost fabulous daring and originality, that only the man who was born with a petrified diaphragm can fail to laugh himself to sleep every night, and to awake every morning with all the eager, unflagging expectation of a Sunday-school superintendent touring the Paris peepshows. — H. L. Mencken, "On Being an American" from *Prejudices: Third Series,* pp. 13 – 14

And the current Chief Magistrate of the nation — its defiant substitute for czar and kaiser — is a small-town printer who, when he wishes to enjoy himself in the Executive Mansion, invites in a homeopathic doctor, a Seventh Day Adventist evangelist, and a couple of moving-picture actresses. — Ibid., pp. 21 – 22.

The Nobles of the Mystic Shrine, chiefly paunchy wholesalers of the Rotary Club species, are not content with swords, baldrics, stars, garters and jewels; they also wear red fezes. The Elks run to rubies. The Red Men array themselves like Sitting Bull. The patriotic ice-wagon drivers and Methodist deacons of the Ku Klux Klan carry crosses set with incandescent lights. An American who is forced by his profession to belong to many such orders — say a life insurance solicitor, a bootlegger, or a dealer in Oklahoma oil stock — accumulates a trunk full of decorations, many of them weighing a pound. There is an undertaker in Hagerstown, Md., who has been initiated eighteen times. When he robes himself to plant a fellow joiner he weighs three hundred pounds and sparkles and flashes like the mouth of hell itself. He is entitled to bear seven swords, all jeweled, and to hang his watch chain with the golden busts of nine wild animals, all with precious stones for eyes. Put beside this lowly washer of the dead, Pershing newly polished would seem almost like a Trappist. — H. L. Mencken, "Star-Spangled Men," *Prejudices: Third Series,* p. 138

The *Mercury* made an immediate hit. It was new, startling, and delightfully destructive. It crystallized the misgivings of thousands. Soon its green cover was clasped under the arms of the young iconoclasts of a score of college campuses. Staid small-town executives, happening upon it, were shocked and bewildered; this man Mencken, they decided, must be a debauched and shameless monster if not a latter-day emissary of the devil. When Mencken visited Dayton to report the Scopes trial and called the Daytonians yokels, hillbillies, and peasants, the Reverend A. C. Stribling replied that Mencken was a "cheap blatherskite of a pen-pusher"; and to such retorts there was a large section of outraged public opinion ready to cry Amen. After a few years so much abuse had been heaped upon the editor of the *Mercury* that it was possible to publish for the delectation of his admirers a *Schimpflexicon* — a book made up entirely of highly uncomplimentary references to him. Meanwhile the circulation of his magazine climbed to more than 77,000 by 1927; and in that same year Walter Lippmann called him, without exaggeration, "the most powerful personal influence on this whole generation of educated people." — Frederick Lewis Allen, *Only Yesterday,* pp. 231 – 232

**Sp**

*This recommendation of steadiness and uniformity* [in spelling] *does not proceed from an opinion that particular combinations of letters have much influence on human happiness; or that truth may not be successfully taught by modes of spelling fanciful and erroneous. . . . Language is only the instrument of science, and words are but the signs of ideas; I wish, however, that the instrument might be less apt to decay, and that signs might be permanent.* — Samuel Johnson

**15.1**

> **Sp**    Correction: Correct the spelling of the word marked.

For- college writing, and for much of the other writing that you may do, we have been recommending what we call *edited American English.* One purpose of editing is to make language consistent with itself, so that, for example, if a writer uses the word *theatre* seven times in an essay, it will always be spelled in the same way. Another purpose of editing is, if it does not interfere with some purpose of the writer, to eliminate errors and unconventional usages. One feature of language that often requires careful editing is spelling.

Sometimes people talk about spelling as if it were some monstrous and unnatural act. It isn't that, but it isn't always easy. Some people spell well; others don't. Accurate spelling doesn't appear to have any direct connection with good writing. But good edited writing is characterized by accurate spelling. Out of regard for yourself and for your reader, you should make certain that whatever you write is as free from error as possible. You want your reader to see the same word that you intended to write, and your reader is entitled to expect that you will follow the conventions of spelling. Misspelled words seldom interfere with meaning, but they may distract your reader from what you are trying to say, or, worse, lead your reader to assume that if you don't care about your spelling you don't care about what you are saying.

## Overcoming spelling problems                **15.1**

English spelling would be easier if each sound used in speaking were represented by a single letter or even by a combination of letters. But the way a word is pronounced and the way it is spelled do not always match. The same letter or combination of letters may represent a variety of sounds, as does the *a* in *fare, hat, many, lay, far, war, human,* or the *ou* in *though, bough, enough, through.* And one sound may be represented in a variety of ways: b*ee*, bel*ie*ve, prec*e*de, s*ea*, mach*i*ne. As a further complication, a number of English words are written with silent letters: lam*b*, *p*sychology, *k*nife, r*h*ythm, *w*rote. Others, called *homonyms,* sound alike but are spelled differently: *meat, meet, mete; sight, site, cite; write, right, rite; its, it's; peace, piece.*

Obviously, absolute correctness in spelling is not easy to achieve in English. Most mistakes can be avoided, however, if you are willing to take the time and effort necessary to learn the spelling of difficult words, to use the dictionary when you are in doubt, and to proofread what you have written.

## Eliminating careless mistakes

Carelessness undoubtedly accounts for the majority of misspelled words in student papers. It may result from too rapid writing (as in papers written in class) or from failure to proofread the finished copy carefully. Typical examples of careless misspelling are *their* for *there, to* for *too, who's* for *whose, it's* for *its, fourty* for *forty*—basic words that you learned before entering high school. Most people make careless mistakes when writing rapidly, but conscientious writers eliminate them by proofreading.

Accurate proofreading requires careful word-by-word reading. If you have difficulty checking your own writing, try following each line with a pencil point, so that you have to look at every word separately. Some people find it helpful to read their papers aloud, pronouncing each word distinctly. Any method is useful if it makes it easier for you to see the way that the words have actually been put down on paper.

## Using a dictionary

If you are uncertain about the spelling of a word, consult your dictionary. The trial-and-error method of writing a word several ways until it "looks right" *(curiousity? couriousity? curiosity?)* is unreliable.

For papers written outside class, it's probably best to check spelling in *revision.* If you stop to look up the spelling of every doubtful word while you are writing a first draft, you may lose the flow of thought or interrupt the sentence movement. Put a check in the margin or over the word as you are writing; then when you are ready to revise, look up each word you have marked.

### Learning to visualize words

People who do a good deal of reading tend to be better spellers than those who read little, for seeing a word on the printed page tends to fix it in the mind. Sometimes, however, we learn to recognize a word in reading without really noticing how it is spelled. Very few Americans, for example, ever learned to spell the last name of Nikita Khrushchev, the former Soviet premier, though they saw it in their newspapers every day for years. Many people have a similar problem with such common English words as *occasion, occurrence,* and *precede.* When you meet a new word — or when you have to look up a familiar word — look at it carefully, noticing each syllable, and try to fix it in your mind for future use.

### Writing practice

If you are willing to take the time, you can often get the spelling of troublesome words straight in your mind by writing them until you spell them right without hesitation. It sounds like a tedious process, but it's probably worth the time if it enables you to become comfortable with words so that you can use them. If you are uncertain about the spelling of *embarrass,* for example, write or type the word ten, twenty, or more times, in its various forms, until the spelling becomes automatic: *embarrass, embarrassed, embarrassment, embarrassing.*

Separate into syllables words that you find difficult to spell (consult your dictionary for the proper divisions). Stress those letters or combinations of letters that trouble you:

| | |
|---|---|
| em baR Rass | par aL Lel |
| oC Ca sion al ly | preJ U dice |
| o MiT Ted | rep E ti tion |
| op tl mist | sep A rate |

It helps to say the word as you write it, either aloud or to yourself. The combination of (1) seeing a word letter by letter, (2) writing it carefully, and (3) pronouncing it will overcome most spelling problems.

### Learning new words

Learn to spell new words correctly as you meet them in your college courses. A new or unfamiliar expression is useless in writing until you can spell it with confidence. Make a note of the words you will probably have to write in reports or in examinations. Underline key words in textbooks and observe their spelling on the blackboard. Then write them out in syllables, pronouncing them as you do so:

Sp

15.2

ba cil lus  
bi par tite  
car bon if er ous  
de men tia prae cox  

Gen ghis Khan  
me tath e sis  
pro pri e tar y  
u ni cel lu lar  

When instructors in various courses complain that their students can't spell, they are usually referring either to very common words or to words that make up the essential vocabulary of their subject.

### Keeping a spelling list

You can help yourself in proofreading if you will keep a list of words you have misspelled or that you have trouble spelling. The words should be spelled correctly and should be easy to find so that you can refer to them when proofreading your papers. The purpose of such a list is to prevent the same mistakes from occurring in one paper after another. When the same word occurs more than once in your list, list it in some way that will call it to your attention.

## Common spelling errors                     15.2

The following list contains one hundred words frequently misspelled in student papers. Each word is divided into syllables so that you can see more clearly how it is put together.

ac com mo date  
ac quaint ed  
a cross  
a gree ment  
all right  
al read y  
a nal y sis  
ap pear ance  
ar ti cle  
ath let ics  

at tend ance  
be lieve  
ben e fit ed  
Brit ain  
bus i ness  
change a ble  
choose  
com par a tive  
con ceive  
con science  

con tin u ous  
de ci sion  
def i nite  
de pend ent  
de scrip tion  
de vel op  
din ing room  
dis ap pear ance  
dis ap point  
dor mi to ry

em bar rass
en vi ron ment
e quip ment
ex ag ger ate
ex ist ence
ex treme ly
fa mil iar
fas ci nate
for eign
for mer ly
for ty
gram mar
height
hin drance
im ag i nar y
im me di ate ly
in ci den tal ly
in de pend ent
in tel li gent
ir re sist i ble
judg ment [or judge ment]
knowl edge
lei sure
li brar y

lik a ble [or like able]
main te nance
man u fac tur er
mis spelled
mo not o nous
mys te ri ous
nec es sar y
no tice a ble
oc ca sion al ly
oc cur rence
o mit ted
op por tu ni ty
par tic u lar ly
pas time
per form
pre ced ing
prej u dice
priv i lege
prob a bly
pro ce dure
pro nun ci a tion
pro por tion
psy chol o gy

quan ti ty
re ceive
re fer ring
rep e ti tion
re sem blance
sched ule
sec re tar y
seize
sep a rate
sim i lar
soph o more
suc ceed
sym pa thize
tem per a ment
tend en cy
there fore
trag e dy
tru ly
un doubt ed ly
un til
u su al ly
val u a ble
writ ing

You may find this list useful in testing your spelling ability and in checking and correcting errors in your papers. A spelling list of your own, however, will be more profitable to study than lists made by others, because it will help you to concentrate on your individual problems.

## Errors caused by faulty pronunciation

Although faulty pronunciation is not a major cause of misspelling, it is responsible for some very common mistakes:

| Correct spelling | Misspelling |
|---|---|
| ath **let** ics | ath**a**letics |
| priv **i** lege | priv**l**ege |
| en vi **ron** ment | envi**rom**ent |
| mis chie **vous** | mischiev**io**us |
| **pre** scribe | **per**scribe |
| dis **g**ust | dis**c**ust |

Pronounce each syllable to yourself when writing longer words (ac-com-pa-ny-ing, par-tic-u-lar-ly, stud-y-ing). Also notice that many longer words contain letters that are blurred or lost in speech: tem-per-a-men-tal, ac-ci-den-tal-ly, lab-o-ra-to-ry.

## Omission of final -ed

One of the most common spelling errors is the omission of -ed at the ends of words. This sometimes occurs because of analogy to speech, where the -ed sound often is lost in rapid conversation or is assimilated by the following sound. To catch such errors in writing, you will have to rely on your eye rather than your ear. There are three principal trouble areas:

### In verb forms

Regular verbs form their past tenses and past participles by adding -ed. Be careful not to drop these letters, especially before words beginning with *t*, like *to. Used to* and *supposed to* are commonly misspelled:

I **used to** (not **use to**) misspell words.
He is **supposed to** be (not **suppose to** be) an authority.

### In verbal modifiers

The past participle is often used as a modifier *(stewed prunes, raised platform)*. Here too the tendency in pronunciation is to drop the -ed, and many such shortened forms have become established: *grade school, oilcloth, cream cheese, roast chicken.* Others are sometimes found in print but are debatable: *bottle beer, whip cream, advance headquarters.* In college papers it is better to use only shortened forms that are generally accepted. In less formal writing, more latitude is allowed, but dictionaries, current written practice, and appropriateness to the paper should serve as guides.

### In modifiers from nouns

Adjectives are often formed by adding -ed to nouns: *long-haired, heart-shaped, two-faced.* When the -ed is dropped in such forms — a growing tendency in current English — the result is a noun modifier (see §6.4): *king-size bed, hard-surface road, high-heel shoes.* Established forms like these are appropriate in all writing. It's usually better, however, to keep the -ed (as in *advanced courses, middle-aged, old-fashioned*) unless you have seen the form in print without the -ed.

## Confusion of words that sound alike

Be careful not to confuse words of identical or similar sound. It is easy when writing rapidly to put down *their* for *there, its* for *it's, maybe* for *may be,* but a conscientious writer will check his or her finished work closely for errors of this sort. Substituting one form for another may suggest an idea that the writer did not intend:

Psychiatric treatment changed Bobby from a withdrawn, unhappy child to a normal, happy boy **excepted** by his group.

The following pairs of words are often confused in writing. See if you can distinguish between them.

| | |
|---|---|
| accept—except | lead—led |
| advice—advise | loose—lose |
| affect—effect | passed—past |
| aisle—isle | peace—piece |
| allusion—illusion | personal—personnel |
| birth—berth | principal—principle |
| capital—capitol | quiet—quite |
| choose—chose | stationary—stationery |
| cite—site | than—then |
| conscience—conscious | their—there |
| coarse—course | to—too |
| credible—creditable | weather—whether |
| desert—dessert | who's—whose |
| its—it's | |

If you have trouble keeping any of these forms clear in mind, try making up sentences that will illustrate plainly the differences in meaning:

Everyone **except** Sam **accepted** the invitation.
**It's** difficult for the leopard to change **its** spots.
The ceremonies wll be held **whether** or not the **weather** is fair.

## Separate words and combined forms

Observe the distinctions between expressions that are written as one word and those written as two. These forms frequently need to be checked in revision:

**all ready** [adjective phrase]: The girls were at last **all ready** to leave.

**already** [adverb of time]: It was **already** dark when they arrived.

**all right** [adjective phrase, conventionally written as two words]: The seats seemed **all right** to me. (The forms **alright** and **alrite** are not accepted in edited usage.)

**all together** [adjective phrase]: We were **all together** at the depot.

**altogether** [adverb, meaning wholly]: That's **altogether** another matter.

**a while** [noun]: They talked for **a while.**

**awhile** [adverb]: Can't you stay **awhile** longer?

**may be** [verb phrase]: He **may be** the next mayor.

**maybe** [adverb, short for **it may be**]: **Maybe** you'll have better luck next time.

Certain phrases may be mistakenly written as one word

through analogy with other forms or because they are often run together in speech:

The assignment was **a lot** more difficult than I expected. [not: **alot**]
The judge **threw out** his testimony. [not: **throughout**]
The puppy was always there at his owner's **beck and call.** [not: **beck-on call**]

## Some principles of spelling 15.3

Chaotic as spelling is in English, some principles are helpful for spelling common words. Listed below are guides to spelling that you have probably heard before. If you *know* that you know them, you might better spend your time on some other aspect of writing. But if you aren't quite certain about these general principles, review them and perhaps also consult the spelling section in the front pages of your dictionary for more detailed information.

### Final -e

Words ending in silent -e generally retain the -e before additions (called *suffixes*) beginning with a consonant *(-ment, -ly, -some, -ness)*, but drop the -e before additions beginning with a vowel *(-ing, -able, -ous, -ary)*.

*-e retained before a consonant*

| | |
|---|---|
| arrange — arrange**m**ent | nine — nine**t**y |
| awe — awe**s**ome | require — require**m**ent |
| definite — definite**l**y | shape — shape**l**ess |
| hope — hope**l**ess | spite — spite**f**ul |

**Exceptions:**

| | | | | |
|---|---|---|---|---|
| arg**um**ent | **awf**ul | d**ul**y | **ni**n**th** | tr**ul**y |

*-e dropped before another vowel*

| | |
|---|---|
| argue — arg**u**ing | imagine — imagina**r**y |
| arrive — arri**v**al | shape — sha**p**ing |
| conceive — concei**v**able | value — valu**a**ble |
| grieve — grie**vous** | write — wri**t**ing |

**Exceptions:** In a few words silent -e is retained before a vowel to avoid confusion with other forms:

| | | |
|---|---|---|
| dye | dyeing | (compare **dying**) |
| singe | singeing | (compare **singing**) |

Words ending in -ce or -ge retain the final -e before additions beginning with *a, o,* or *ou* (so that the final *-c* or *-g* will not suggest the "hard" sound):

| | | |
|---|---|---|
| chang**ea**ble | notic**ea**ble | unmanag**ea**ble |
| courag**eou**s | outrag**eou**s | veng**ea**nce |

*-ie-* and *-ei-*

The familiar jingle learned by most school children is helpful in spelling *-ie-* and *-ei-* words: "Write *i* before *e* except after *c*, or when sounded as *a* as in *neighbor* and *weigh*."

Words with *-ie-*

Words with *-ie-* are more common than words with *-ei-*. The typical sound of *-ie-* is ē:

| | | | |
|---|---|---|---|
| achieve | chief | grievous | niece |
| believe | field | hygiene | siege |

Other *-ie-* words are *mischief, sieve,* and *view*.

Words with *-ei-*

After *c*, and also to spell the sound ā, *-ei-* is generally used:

| | | | |
|---|---|---|---|
| ceiling | perceive | eight | reign |
| conceive | receipt | freight | vein |
| deceive | receive | neighbor | weigh |

The long ē sound is spelled *-ei-* (rather than *-ie-*) in a few words: *either, leisure, neither, seize, weird*. Other sounds spelled *-ei-*: *counterfeit, foreign, height, heir*.

## Doubling the final consonant

Double the final consonant before a suffix beginning with a vowel (*-able, -ed, -er, -ing*) with (1) words of one syllable ending in a single consonant after a single vowel (*brag, hit, sit*) and (2) with words of more than one syllable, ending the same way and accented on the last syllable (*commit, forget, prefer*).

| One-syllable words | | | Words of more than one syllable | | |
|---|---|---|---|---|---|
| bat | batter | batting | commit | committed | committing |
| grip | gripping | gripped | control | controllable | controlled |
| pin | pinned | pinning | occur | occurrence | occurred |
| spot | spotty | spotted | omit | omitted | omitting |
| wet | wetter | wettest | prefer | preferred | preferring |

The consonant is *not* doubled (1) in words with two vowels before the final consonant *(daub, daubing; keep, keeper; spoil, spoiled)*, or (2) in words ending with two consonants *(help, helped; peck, pecking; lurk, lurked)*, or (3) when the accent of the lengthened word shifts to an earlier syllable *(infer', in'ference; prefer', pref'erence; refer', ref'erence)*.

Usage is divided about doubling the final consonant of some words not accented on the last syllable, but American spelling generally favors the single consonant.

| | |
|---|---|
| bias — biased | quarrel — quarreling |
| counsel — counseled, counselor | travel — traveler, traveled |
| diagram — diagramed | worship — worshiped, worshiping |
| kidnap — kidnaping, kidnaper | |

## Final -y

A final -y preceded by a consonant regularly changes to *i* before all suffixes except those beginning with *i:*

| | |
|---|---|
| body — bodies | happy — happiness |
| busy — business | lonely — loneliness |
| carry — carried, carrying | marry — marriage, marrying |
| duty — dutiful | mercy — merciful |
| easy — easily | study — studious, studying |
| envy — envious | Tory — Tories |

Final -y preceded by a vowel remains unchanged when a suffix is added:

| | |
|---|---|
| boy — boys, boyish | enjoy — enjoyable, enjoyment, enjoying |
| delay — delayed, delayer | play — playful, playing, played |

## -cede, -ceed, -sede

Only one word ends in -*sede: supersede.* Only three end in -*ceed: exceed, proceed, succeed.* All other words of this sort end in -*cede: precede, recede, intercede, secede,* etc.

## -able, -ible, -ance, -ence

Words with these endings should be carefully checked for correct spelling. Words ending in -*able* (like *advisable, desirable, improbable, suitable*) are much more common than those ending in -*ible* (such as *audible, divisible, horrible, visible*). But since no rules govern the formation of these endings, the individual words should be looked up whenever the writer is in doubt.

A few words are spelled with either -*able* or -*ible* endings. Dictionaries indicate the more common or preferred spelling by putting it first *(collapsible, collapsable; preventable, preventible).*

The spelling of words ending in -*ance, -ant; -ence, -ent* must also be watched, since pronunciation does not distinguish them (attend*ance,* confid*ence;* defend*ant,* exist*ent*).

See also §6.1, Plurals of nouns, especially page 91, Nouns ending in -y, -o, or -f.

## Variant spellings    15.4

When a word is currently spelled in two ways *(extol, extoll)*, it is usually a good idea to use the more common form.

Many words have secondary spellings, usually British or simplified forms generally labeled in dictionaries as *Brit., Variant, Archaic,* and so on, so that you can choose the form appropriate to your subject and style. Most people writing today, and certainly anyone who has difficulty with spelling, will ordinarily prefer:

1) The more modern of two equally reputable spellings: *draft, mold, plow* instead of *draught, mould, plough.*

2) The simpler form of a specialized word if it has attained currency among the people who use it most: *anesthetic, catalog, medieval, program, sulfur* rather than *anaesthetic, catalogue, mediaeval, programme, sulphur.*

Although it is possible to simplify the spelling of many common words (as *thoro* for *thorough, enuf* for *enough*), conventional spelling is expected in most kinds of writing.

3) American rather than British spellings: *center, labor, pajama* rather than *centre, labour, pyjama.*

For the spelling of proper names (the British *Labour* Party) and for direct quotation (the Prime Minister described it as "a *humourless* situation"), British spelling should be followed, but in other situations the American forms should be used.

**Study and Practice: Spelling**

1. Read the following passage carefully, noting and correcting the misspellings that have been inserted. Look especially for faulty -*ed* forms:

Nor should we be surprise that the historical record gives us this verdict. In its roots and aspirations, Western civilization is turn toward the future, not the pass; toward experiment, not the status quo; toward creation; toward "a new heaven and a new earth," not a safe and static world. It is precisely this quality of inventiveness, of vision, of the courage to dream that has made Western society, for good and evil, the catalyst and prime mover in a world of magnificent but somnolent civilisations. If that quality were lost today, if no vision of the future informed its policies, no lift of hope encourage its efforts, no faith to go further and do better inspire its aims, then the hulk of its greatness might survive. But the spirit would be dead. The trial of soul we face today is to outdream the communist visionaries, outwork the communist fanatics, and outdare the voices of defeatism and discouragment within our own society. And this is precisely the challenge which Western man, again and again in his millenial record, has met and measure and triumphantly overcome. — Barbara Ward, "In Time of Trial"

2. This exercise should help to fix some of the general principles of spelling in your mind. Copy the words in each of the following groups, making the additions or changes indicated:

   a. Supply -ei- or -ie- as required for correct spelling:

   | | | |
   |---|---|---|
   | all--d | fr--ght | s--ve |
   | bel--ve | h--ght | s--ze |
   | conc--ve | l--sure | th--r |
   | counterf--t | n--ther | v--l |
   | for--gn | p--ce | w--rd |

   b. Add -ed to the following verbs to show whether the final consonant is doubled or not. If there is a choice of forms, indicate both of them:

   | | | |
   |---|---|---|
   | bargain | droop | quarrel |
   | bias | drop | question |
   | chide | kidnap | refer |
   | clot | list | travel |
   | dine | play | whelp |

   c. Add -ing to each of these words, making any necessary changes in the root form of the word:

   | | | |
   |---|---|---|
   | become | endure | prove |
   | control | hope | use |
   | dine | hurry | write |

   d. Change each of these words to an adjective ending -ous:

   | | | |
   |---|---|---|
   | continue | dispute | mischief |
   | courage | glory | outrage |
   | courtesy | grieve | sanctimony |

3. Add -able or -ible to the following words, changing letters wherever necessary to conform with accepted spellings:

   | | | |
   |---|---|---|
   | accept | digest | repair |
   | advice | force | sense |
   | contempt | justify | train |

   Add -ance, -ant or -ence, -ent to these words, making any other necessary changes:

   | | | |
   |---|---|---|
   | ascend | dally | provide |
   | compete | defend | revere |
   | confide | maintain | vigil |

4. To help you learn to recognize misspelled words in your own writing, read through the following paragraph, correcting the misspelled words. Feel free to consult a dictionary; you may want to see how many mistakes you can find and correct without a dictionary first, however.

Exer

The principal that every great man is a national calamity is easily defensable. It is difficult to concieve that strong men will not irresistably impose upon their countrymen their own eccentricities and prejadices. Napoleon, for example, beleived that he had a definate destiny to succede, a mysterous "star" guiding him and France to great heighths. He did not dream of any hinderance from the other nations of Europe. His plans were to seperate them one by one and to sieze all power and priveledge. Only Britian refused to acommodate itself to his grandiose schemes. His temperment was characteristic of his enviroment; massively fasinated by Romantic psycology, he had an exagerated consciousness of the independant existance of his charisma. Napoleon was tradgically disappointed in his hopes, as were his spiritual forebears, Alexander the Great, Caesar, Louis XIV, and his inheritors, Hitler and Mussolini.

5. Make up sentences that will show clearly the differences between these pairs of words of similar sound (for example: "The *morale* of the troops overseas was high"; "There seems to be no *moral* to this tale"). Pay particular attention to those words that have given you trouble in writing:

| | |
|---|---|
| accept — except | may be — maybe |
| affect — effect | plain — plane |
| angle — angel | principal — principle |
| boarder — border | quite — quit |
| desert — dessert | stationary — stationery |
| discrete — discreet | than — then |
| its — it's | they're — their |
| loose — lose | to — too |

# Capital letters, hyphens, and apostrophes 16

## Capital letters 16.1

**Cap** Correction: Capitalize the word marked; be consistent in use of capital letters.

**lc** Correction: Write the word marked with a lowercase (small) letter.

Most uses of capital letters are standard conventions that every writer is expected to follow. Writing in which capitals are improperly used may seem sloppy and eccentric to the reader because it focuses attention on the wrong words and interrupts the natural flow of thought.

The following sections describe the most frequent uses of capital letters. A complete listing of all forms is obviously impossible. In general, formal English tends to use more capitals than general English, and newspaper usage tends to cut them to a minimum. Consult a recent dictionary or style manual if you are in doubt whether to capitalize a particular word. If usage is decided, choose the form that seems most appropriate to your paper and follow it consistently.

You may use proofreading marks to correct capitalization in your papers. Three lines under a small letter means: make this a capital. A slanting line drawn through a capital letter means: make this a lowercase (small) letter.

`march 15    He came from West of Buffalo.`

### To mark units of expression
Capital letters are used to draw the reader's attention to the beginning of a statement or to individual words in titles.

### First word of a sentence
Capitalize the first word of every sentence or expression punctuated with an end stop (period, question mark, or exclamation mark):

**H**as the change helped? **N**ot much. **T**he reason is obvious.

### First word of a line of poetry

In traditional verse style, the first word of each line is capitalized:

Full many a gem of purest ray serene,
  The dark unfathomed waves of ocean bear;
Full many a flower is born to blush unseen,
  And waste its sweetness on the desert air.

### First word of a quotation

The first word of a direct quotation that is in itself a complete sentence is capitalized:

He said, "The future of mankind cannot be left to chance."
"The crisis is here," she said. "We must act now."

But no capital is used when the quotation is fragmentary or built into the structure of the sentence, or when the second part of a quoted sentence is interrupted by an expression such as *he said:*

According to the advertisement, it was the "most spectacular picture of the year."
Rousseau maintained that "the love of happiness is the sole principle of all human actions."
"The argument is based," he said, "upon a false premise."

### In parentheses

A complete sentence enclosed in parentheses is always capitalized when it stands alone, but when enclosed *within* another sentence, it usually is not:

The broadcast, sponsored by a local bank, was frequently interrupted by lengthy commercials. (Apparently the sponsor doesn't believe that silence is golden.)
Fitzhugh was the member of a prominent family (his mother was the granddaughter of Sir Thomas Wyatt) and was received in the highest circles.

### After a colon

A complete sentence standing after a colon is not usually capitalized when the connection with the preceding clause is close:

Indeed, if Galileo had not been so expert an amateur theologian he would have got into far less trouble: the professionals resented his intrusion. — Lynn White, Jr., "The Historical Roots of Our Ecological Crisis"

The sentence after the colon is often capitalized when it is distinctly separate or when the writer wants to give it emphasis:

Quite a few teachers in the departments of science would tell the student: **We** scientists deliver the laws of nature to the philosopher, who has to interpret them. —Philipp Frank, *Relativity: A Richer Truth*

In titles of written material

The first word, the last word, all important words (nouns, pronouns, verbs, adjectives, and adverbs), and all prepositions of more than five letters are capitalized in the titles of books, magazine articles, themes, and so forth:

"The **B**attle **H**ymn of the **R**epublic"    *Of **M**ice and **M**en*
*Pottery Through the Ages*    *Tender Is the Night*

*I* and *O*

The pronoun *I* and the exclamation *O* are always capitalized to prevent reading them as parts of other words:

Give a man a girl he can love,
    As **I, O** my love, love thee. . . .   —James Thomson, "Gifts"

The exclamation *oh* is not capitalized unless it stands first in a sentence.

For proper nouns and their derivatives

The names of specific people, places, and things, and the words derived from them are conventionally capitalized (Karl Marx — Marxism; Africa — African sculpture; Lent — Lenten menu). Examples of the most frequent types of proper nouns are given in the following sections.

In a few cases, words originally derived from proper nouns have dropped the capital in the course of frequent use (pasteurized milk, a jersey blouse, french fries). Usage differs about the capitalization of others (diesel, levis). Up-to-date dictionaries provide a guide in such matters, as do the practices of current publications.

Names and titles of people

A person's name or nickname is capitalized:

**F**ranklin **D**elano **R**oosevelt    **E**udora **W**elty    **H**ank **A**aron
**S**hirley **C**hisholm    **M**indy    **D**izzy **G**illespie

A title should be capitalized when it is used as part of a person's name, but not when it is used as a descriptive term. A few titles of high rank are capitalized whether or not the officeholder is named: the President (of the United States), the Pope, the Queen of England, the Chief Justice of the Supreme Court. Titles referring to a position or an office rather than to the specific person holding it are not capitalized:

| Capitals | No capitals |
|---|---|
| **P**rofessor **T**ownsend | Francis Townsend is a professor. |
| **S**ergeant **D**avid **M**oore | A sergeant maintains discipline. |
| **J**udge **R. A. S**now | She was elected judge. |
| The **P**resident [of the U.S.] vetoed the bill. | The president of the company resigned. |
| The **Q**ueen addressed the opening session of Parliament. | England has had several queens. |

Names of family relationships are usually capitalized when used with a person's name or when used as proper nouns standing for the name. They are not capitalized when used as common nouns or when preceded by a possessive:

| Capitals | No capitals |
|---|---|
| **G**randma Moses | She is a grandmother. |
| **A**unt Sarah | My aunt's name is Sarah. |
| I showed **M**other the card. | I showed my mother the card. |
| Whatever **F**ather said, we did. | His father was demanding. |

### Names of groups

Names referring to racial, national, linguistic, political, or religious groups are capitalized:

| | | | |
|---|---|---|---|
| **N**egro | **S**wede | **D**emocrat | **C**atholic |
| **E**nglish | **I**talian | **R**epublican | **J**ew |
| **F**rench | **F**inn | **C**ommunist | **M**oslem |
| **L**atino | **I**ndian | **S**ocialist | **B**aptist |

Names of social and economic groups are not capitalized (except occasionally for stylistic emphasis):

the middle class    the intelligentsia    the bourgeoisie

### Names of organizations

Names and abbreviations of business associations, clubs, fraternities, and other voluntary organizations are capitalized:

| | |
|---|---|
| **N**ational **A**ssociation of Manufacturers **(NAM)** | **B**oy **S**couts |
| **R**otary **I**nternational | League of **W**omen **V**oters |
| **N**ational **O**rganization for **W**omen **(NOW)** | **U**nited **A**uto **W**orkers **(UAW)** |
| | Phi **B**eta **K**appa |

The words *freshman, sophomore, junior, senior* are capitalized only when they refer to organized groups and their functions (the Freshman Class, the Junior Prom), not when they refer to an academic status (She is a sophomore; The seniors must write a thesis).

## Names of places

Words that designate specific geographical divisions or particular places and areas are capitalized:

| | | |
|---|---|---|
| Asia | Ghana | Hyde Park |
| European | Texan | the Bowery |
| Latin America | Boston | Third Avenue |

When the names of directions are used to identify geographic areas, they are generally capitalized. When they merely indicate direction, they are not:

| Capitals | No capitals |
|---|---|
| the old West | west of Suez |
| a Southerner | a southern exposure |
| the Far East | eastern Tennessee |

## Names of institutions and their divisions

The names of specific public and private institutions and their divisions and departments are capitalized. Names that apply to a whole class of institutions are not:

| Capitals | No capitals |
|---|---|
| Chicago Public Library | a public library |
| U.S. Public Health Service | public health problems |
| Rock Falls High School | our high school |

Specific high-school or college academic courses are capitalized; general subjects are not, except for language courses:

| Capitals | No capitals |
|---|---|
| Modern French Literature | literature |
| Advanced Narrative Writing | composition |
| Chemistry 101 | chemistry |
| Abnormal Psychology 410 | psychology |

## Names of specific objects

Names of specific objects, such as ships, planes, structures, famous documents and artifacts, and brand-name products are capitalized:

| | | |
|---|---|---|
| the *S.S. Independence* | the Golden Gate Bridge | the Sphinx |
| the Super Chief | the Lincoln Memorial | Cleopatra's Needle |
| a Gremlin | Magna Charta | a Royal typewriter |

## Names of units in time

Capitalize words designating specific periods, events, months, days, and holidays:

| | | |
|---|---|---|
| the Stone Age | the Norman Conquest | Thursday |
| the Renaissance | the Battle of Waterloo | Labor Day |
| the Civil War | January | |

Names of seasons are not generally capitalized:

winter    summer    spring    fall    autumn

### Sacred names

References to deities and to sacred texts are capitalized. Pronouns referring to the Christian Trinity are also usually capitalized:

**Cap**

**16.1**

| | | |
|---|---|---|
| God | Holy Ghost | Talmud |
| the Savior | Bible | Koran |
| Virgin Mary | New Testament | the Buddha |

### Abstractions

Abstractions like ideas, qualities, or conditions may be capitalized, especially in formal and sentimental writing, to show that they are being discussed in some ideal or absolute state. Sometimes abstractions are personified, particularly in poetry:

Throughout recorded history, Man has responded to the challenge of Nature.

The pursuit of the Good Life is a persistent human preoccupation.

Eternal Spirit of the chainless Mind!
Brightest in dungeons, Liberty! thou art. . . .
— Lord Byron, "Sonnet on Chillon"

In general writing, capitalized abstractions are seldom appropriate. College students should confine them to formal papers of critical analysis or philosophical theory and follow the practices found in readings assigned in the course for which the papers are written.

### Distinguishing proper and common forms

Some words can be spelled either with or without capitals. It is important to distinguish between these forms because they often have different meanings:

| **Capitals** | **No capitals** |
|---|---|
| a Democrat (member of the Democratic Party) | a democrat (one who believes in democracy) |
| a Republican principle (of the Republican Party) | a republican principle (of a republic) |
| Orthodox beliefs (of the Greek Orthodox Church) | orthodox beliefs (conventional) |
| Catholic sympathies (of or with the Catholic Church) | catholic sympathies (broad; universal) |
| Romantic poetry (of the Romantic Period) | romantic poetry (concerning romance or love) |

> **Hyph**   Correction: Insert or remove hyphen between the words marked to conform to current usage.

Hyphens are used to connect two or more words used as a single expression *(heavy-hearted, will-o'-the-wisp)* and to keep parts of other words distinct *(anti-inflation, re-examine)*.

Hyphens are needed in some instances to prevent misreading *(un-ionized)* or to differentiate between the same words used in different ways (a *drive in* the evening, a *drive-in* theater). But generally they are used as a matter of convention *(brother-in-law, hocus-pocus)*.

In printed matter the use of hyphens varies considerably: newspapers and general English use relatively few hyphens; formal English uses more. The important thing to look for in proofreading is consistency. If an expression is hyphenated the first time it occurs, it should be hyphenated throughout.

This section lists the most common uses of hyphens. See also §21.2, page 304, Spelling and word division.

### In compound words

A hyphen is used between two or more words considered as a single unit in certain expressions, as discussed below.

Names for family relationships

Some compound names for family relationships are hyphenated; others are not:

**Hyphenated:** father-in-law, great-grandfather, sister-in-law
**One word:** stepson, stepmother, grandfather
**Two words:** half brother, second cousin

### Compound numbers

A hyphen is used in numbers from twenty-one to ninety-nine. Fractions are hyphenated except when the fraction already contains a hyphenated number:

| | |
|---|---|
| thirty-three | four-fifths of a box |
| one hundred twenty-eight | one-half inch |
| twenty-first birthday | one thirty-second of an inch |

### In compounds with *self*

Most group words beginning with *self* are written with hyphens *(self-contained, self-pity, self-support, self-govern-ment);* some may be written with a hyphen or without *(self support, self government).* A very few words beginning with *self* are written as one word: *selfsame, selfless, selfhood.* Consult a recent dictionary to find out which form is preferred.

### Standard compound nouns

A number of compound nouns are regularly written with a hyphen: *bull's-eye, good-for-nothing, jack-o'-lantern, secretary-treasurer.* Other similar compounds are written as one word *(beeswax, newsprint, policyholder)* or as two words *(intelligence test, labor union, shipping point, water cooler).*

Since practice is likely to vary with many of these forms, you often have the option of using or not using a hyphen. Where no confusion of terms is apt to arise, most writers would omit the hyphen. If you are in doubt whether a hyphen is necessary, consult a good recent dictionary.

### In group modifiers

When two or more words act as a closely linked modifier immediately before another word, they are often hyphenated to suggest the close relationship:

**gray-green** eyes     a **nineteenth-century** poet
a **well-kept** lawn     an **all-out** effort

A hyphen should always be used to prevent a possible misreading:

a **slow-motion** picture     a **pitch-dark** room
a **navy-blue** uniform     some **reclaimed-rubber** plants

When the first word of a group modifier is an adverb ending in *-ly,* no hyphen is used after it:

richly deserved praise     openly antagonistic attitude

Compound modifiers formed with present or past participles are usually hyphenated when they precede a noun:

a **good-looking** man     a **well-planned** attack

Such phrases are not usually hyphenated in other positions:

Her father was good looking.     The attack was well planned.

Long phrases or clauses used as modifiers are hyphenated:

. . . and he offers dramatic recitals about guerrillas (whom he didn't meet) and possible ambushes (which he didn't find), all of it pretty much in the **gosh-we-could-even-hear-the-guns-in-the-distance** school of war reporting. — G. Barrett, "Korean Scenario"

This type of construction is most likely to be found in informal writing. It is not effective if overused.

## With prefixes

Hyphens are used between certain prefixes and the root word either as a matter of convention or to prevent ambiguity. Dictionaries list most of these forms.

1) Between prefix and a proper name:

| | |
|---|---|
| pre-Renaissance | post-Civil War |
| anti-Communist | un-American |
| ex-President Truman | pro-German |

2) Between some prefixes that end with a vowel and a root word beginning with a vowel, especially if the root word begins with the same vowel:

re-elected    semi-independent    re-ink

When the parts have become merged in general use, no hyphen is necessary, though it is often still found:

cooperation    coordinate    preexistent

3) To prevent possible confusion with a similar term or when the prefix is stressed:

to **re-cover** a sofa (to **recover** from an illness)
a **run-in** with the police (a **run in** her stocking)
to **re-sort** buttons (a seaside **resort**)

Stressed prefixes occur in terms like *ex-wife, all-American, do-gooder.*

## Suspension hyphens

The suspension hyphen is often used to carry the modifying expression from one word over to the next:

Two-word forms first acquire the hyphen, later are printed as one word, and not infrequently the transition is from the **two-** to the **one-word** form, bypassing the hyphen stage. — *GPO Style Manual*

## Unnecessary hyphens

Don't hyphenate a term that is currently written as a single word or as two words. Even if your dictionary lists as alternatives such old-fashioned forms as *to-night* and *post-man,* use the first or preferred form. Here is a brief list of words that students are sometimes tempted to hyphenate:

| One word | Separate words |
|---|---|
| Anybody (pronoun) | all right |
| basketball, baseball, football | class president |
| bookkeeping | grade curve |
| footnotes | high school |
| himself, myself, ourselves | "How do you do?" |
| nevertheless | motion picture |
| outdoor | no one |
| outwit | press agent |
| overlooked | report card |
| percent (or per cent) | school days |
| roundabout | second in command |
| semicolon | six o'clock |
| taxpayer | tax rate |
| today, tomorrow | water pressure |
| throughout | |
| uphold | |
| whatever | |

## Apostrophes    16.3

>  Correction: Insert an apostrophe where it belongs in the word marked, or take out the unnecessary apostrophe.

An apostrophe (') is used in contractions, to mark the plural form of some expressions, and to indicate the genitive (possessive) case of nouns. Although it is a minor mark that seldom affects the reader's interpretation of a statement, its omission or misuse is noticeable.

### In contractions

Contractions are an attempt to represent the rhythms of speech. They are appropriate in dialog, informal writing, and much general writing. They are used frequently in this book; we believe that they are appropriate in almost any kind of writing. You should remember, however, that many teachers, editors, and readers think that contractions are out of place in formal writing and academic papers.

When a contraction is appropriate in writing, an apostrophe is used to indicate the omission of one or more letters:

| | | | |
|---|---|---|---|
| can't | I'll | it's (it is) | we're |
| don't | I'm | o'clock | won't |
| haven't | isn't | shouldn't | |

Notice that *till* (as in "from morning till midnight") is *not* a shortened form of *until* and no apostrophe is used with it.

An apostrophe is used with dates from which the first figures are omitted (the class of '59, the spirit of '76). In formal writing, dates should usually be written in full.

## With genitive (possessive) case forms

An apostrophe is used with the singular and plural forms of nouns and indefinite pronouns to mark the genitive case:

| | |
|---|---|
| John's car | children's games |
| New York's parks | your parents' permission |
| a stone's throw | anybody's guess |

An apostrophe is *not* used with the possessive forms of the personal pronouns *his, hers, its, ours, yours, theirs:*

the city and **its** suburbs      these seats are **ours**

See §6.2, p. 93, Forms of the genitive, and §7.3, pp. 108–109, Possessive pronouns.

## For plurals of letters and figures

An apostrophe is generally used before an *s* to form the plurals of figures, letters of the alphabet, and words considered as words:

the early 1900**'s** [*or* 1900s]
several size 16**'s** [*or* 16s]
a .44 pistol and two .22**'s** [*or* .22s]
There are four *s***'s,** four *i***'s,** and two *p***'s** in *Mississippi*

## For letters dropped in representing speech

An apostrophe is commonly used to indicate the omission of sounds in representing speech:

"But J. C. he wouldn't let me be until I brought him over. Just kept on sayin', Mamie I'm not a-goin' to move until I see where I'm goin'." — Ann Petry, *The Narrows*

It is not necessary in representing conversation to indicate all such omissions, and frequent apostrophes make for difficult reading.

**Applications: Conventions of Writing**
1. The writer of the following paragraph capitalized some words that shouldn't be capitalized and did not capitalize some that should be capitalized. He or she also used (and didn't use) apostrophes carelessly. Pretend you're the writer's eagle-eyed editor and correct every error you can find.

Whether one reads the germanic prose of Carlyle or Emersons epigrammatic aphorisms, one finds a similar theory of the "great man." It is he who embodies the principle of order (Order is the supreme principle of civilization) and who imposes his shaping spirit on the shapelessness of time. "Lives of great men all remind us," as Longfellow oracularizes, that

We can make our lives sublime,
and, departing, leave behind us
footprints in the sands of time.

Did not the marching feet of Napoleon and his liberating armies beat the path to Greatness over the Continent of Europe! From the piedmontese in the South to the Northern swedish realm of count Bernadotte, the symmetries of the napoleonic code exerted a salutary influence on the dissolving chaos of the holy Roman empire. Without the chastening clarity of Napoleons conservatism, the jacobinical excesses of the French revolution would have succeeded in accomplishing what they had already begun: exporting a Universal reign of Terror. Burke in his *Reflections on the French Revolution* failed to foresee that out of the destroying flame's of the directoire would emerge Frances' immortal Phoenix.

2. Indicate which of the following expressions should be written as separate words, which should be one word, and which should be hyphenated. The words in parentheses indicate the sense in which the expression is intended.

a lot (of work to do)
base ball
dark horse
every one (is present)
flame thrower
gilt edged
give and take
hydro therapy
in so far as
jet black
left overs (food)
man hunt
man of war (a ship)
may be (perhaps)
never the less

non communist
not with standing (a conjunction)
over look (to slight or neglect)
out and out (outright)
Ping Pong
re written
school board
self satisfied
semi colon
some body (is missing)
space craft
ten word (telegram)
three quarters (of an inch)
un American
where abouts (at what place)

> **Ab** Correction: Write in full the abbreviation marked or, if an abbreviation is appropriate, change it to the correct form.

Abbreviations are useful and appropriate in business and legal documents, reference works, scholarly footnotes, and other places where it is important to save space. But in college papers and most other general writing, all but a few kinds of words should be written out in full.

Dictionaries list most current abbreviations, either as regular entries or in a separate section, but they don't indicate when these forms should be used. The following sections discuss the kinds of abbreviations that are appropriate in formal and general writing as well as some forms that should not be used. If you are in doubt whether a particular abbreviation is appropriate, you will usually do better to avoid it.

### Titles, degrees, and given names

The courtesy titles *Dr., Mr., Mrs.,* and *Mssrs.* are always abbreviated when used with proper names, as are *Jr.* and *Sr.: Mrs.* Lester H. Holt, *Mr.* Claude C. Sampson, *Jr.* The new and convenient *Ms.,* used as a courtesy title equivalent to *Mr.* in addressing a woman without regard for her marital status, must remain an abbreviation, since it was devised as an abbreviation and does not stand for any word. Academic degrees are also generally abbreviated: *M.A., Ph.D., LL.D., M.D., D.D.S.* If a degree or honorary title is added after a name, it is the only title used:

William Carey, **M.D.,** *or* **Dr.** William Carey [*not* Dr. William Carey, M.D.]
James T. Holloway, **Esq.,** *or* **Mr.** James T. Holloway [*not* Mr. James T. Holloway, Esq.]

In formal writing, titles like *Reverend, Professor, President, Senator, Admiral* are usually written out in full. In most other styles they may be abbreviated *if* the first name or initials of the person are used:

| Standard forms | Forms to avoid |
|---|---|
| The Reverend James T. Shaw | The Rev. Shaw |
| The Reverend Mr. Shaw | Rev. Shaw |
| Rev. J. T. Shaw | The Reverend delivered a sermon. |
| | |
| Professor John Moore | Prof. Moore |
| Professor Moore | John Moore is an English Prof. |
| Prof. John R. Moore | |
| General Westmoreland | Gen. Westmoreland |
| Gen. William Westmoreland | The Gen. was given a new command. |

Spell out given names (sometimes called Christian names) or use initials. Avoid such abbreviations as *Geo., Thos., Chas., Wm.:*

George Harriman *or* G. F. Harriman [*rather than* Geo. F. Harriman]

*Saint* is almost always abbreviated when it is used with a name:

**St.** Francis, **Ste.** Catherine, **SS.** Peter and Paul, Sault **Ste.** Marie

## Government agencies and other organizations

If a government agency or other organization is known primarily by its initials (or by some other shortened name), the writer should generally use the familiar abbreviation rather than the full name:

| FBI | TVA | AFL-CIO | NBC Network |
|---|---|---|---|
| CIA | GOP | SPCA | MGM Studios |
| FHA | ROTC | 4-H Club | GPO Style Manual |

Abbreviations that are pronounced as words (called *acronyms*) have become very common: UNESCO, CARE, VISTA, NATO, SETO, Amvets.

See page 221 for discussions of the use of capitals and periods in abbreviations.

## Place names and dates

The names of countries, states, months, and days are usually written out except in journalistic writing and reference works:

| United States | Ghent, Belgium | Wednesday, November 3 |
|---|---|---|
| South America | Portland, Oregon | Christmas [**not** Xmas] |

Words like *Street, Avenue,* and *Boulevard* should be written out in general writing, not abbreviated as they might be in addressing a letter.

A few unusually long place names are customarily abbreviated even in rather formal writing: the *USSR;* Barbados, *B.W.I.* (for British West Indies); Washington, *D.C.*

## Units of measurement

In consecutive writing, most expressions for time, weight, and size are customarily written out:

| in a minute | **rather than** | in a min. |
|---|---|---|
| hour | | hr. |
| several pounds | | several lbs. |
| four grams | | 4 gr. |
| weight | | wt. |
| a half inch | | ½ in. or ½″ |
| sixty centimeters | | 60 cm. |

These units are abbreviated in directions, recipes, references, and technical writing when they are used with figures: ¼ lb. butter, 16 ft. 3 in.

## Scientific words, technical terms, trade names

Some scientific words, trade names, and other expressions are referred to by their abbreviations when they are familiar to readers and would be needlessly long if written out:

DDT (in place of **d**ichloro-**d**iphenyl-**t**richloro-ethane)
ACTH (in place of **a**drenocorticotropic **h**ormone)
Rh factor (**Rh**esus factor)
DNA (**d**eoxyribo**n**ucleic **a**cid)
FM radio (**f**requency **m**odulation radio)

If an abbreviation is to be used repeatedly and may not be familiar to every reader, explain it the first time it is introduced:

The International Phonetic Alphabet, commonly known as the IPA, provides a more precise method of recording speech than does our conventional alphabet.

Measurements expressed in technical terms are abbreviated when they are used with figures:

Tests show the car's highest speeds to be 34 **mph** [miles per hour] in low gear, 58.7 **mph** in second, and 93.5 **mph** in third.

The turntable can be adjusted to play records at either 78, 45, or 33⅓ **rpm** [revolutions per minute].

Expressions of this kind are written with either three periods or none (m.p.h. or mph). They are not abbreviated when used without figures:

The speed of a ship is usually given in knots rather than in **miles per hour.**

## Other standard abbreviations

There are a few standard abbreviations that are used in all levels of writing:

*a.m., p.m.*

The expressions *a.m. (ante meridiem,* "before noon") and *p.m. (post meridiem,* "after noon") are always abbreviated: 6:00 a.m., 12:24 p.m. Current usage prefers small letters for these abbreviations, but they may be capitalized.

The abbreviations *a.m.* and *p.m.* are used only in referring to a specific time:

**Standard:** He had an appointment at 3:00 p.m.
**Not:** He had an appointment in the p.m.

*B.C., A.D.*

These expressions are used to distinguish dates in history in reference to the birth of Christ; they are always abbreviated. B.C. means "before Christ," and follows the date; A.D. stands for *anno Domini,* "in the year of our Lord," and *precedes* the date.

836 B.C.        A.D. 76        A.D. 1984

## Commonly used Latin expressions

English has absorbed a number of Latin expressions that are conventionally abbreviated. The following are in common use and should not be italicized:

cf.     *confer* — compare (with another source)
e.g.    *exempli gratia* — for example
etc.    *et cetera* — and so forth (never *and etc.*)
i.e.    *id est* — that is

Many writers prefer the English equivalents for these and similar expressions. In college writing, the overworked catchall *etc.* should generally be avoided. Substitute *and so forth (and so on, and the like)* or rephrase the list, introducing it with *such as* or a similar qualifier. See also §28.8, page 483, Abbreviations in footnotes.

## The ampersand

In college writing the ampersand (&) should not be used as a substitute for *and* unless it appears in an expression or title that you are copying: *U.S. News & World Report,* Doubleday & Company, Inc.

## Capitals with abbreviations
Abbreviations are capitalized when the words they stand for are capitalized or when the abbreviation represents a title:

DAR (**D**aughters of the **A**merican **R**evolution)
USAF (**U**nited **S**tates **A**ir **F**orce)
Lt. Col. Brown
St. Matthew, St. Thomas Aquinas
100 degrees F. (**F**ahrenheit)

When an abbreviation stands for words that would not be capitalized if they were written out, no capitals are needed unless the abbreviation begins a sentence.

## Periods with abbreviations
A period should be put after the abbreviation of a single word and usually between the letters of abbreviations for longer terms:

| | | | |
|---|---|---|---|
| p. | doz. | N.Y. | c.o.d. |
| ch. | Lt. | B.A. | A.T. and T. |
| Nov. | hp. | e.g. | P.S. |

Usage is divided about the punctuation of abbreviated names made of two or more letters written as a unit. Some publications prefer periods *(P.T.A., B.B.C.)*, but a growing number are using the solid form *(PTA, BBC)*, especially when the abbreviation is generally used instead of the full name. Some dictionaries list optional forms. It doesn't make much difference which form you use as long as you are consistent throughout your paper.

When an abbreviation falls at the end of a sentence, only one period is used: He owned a hundred shares of A.T. and T.

## Numbers                                                    **17.2**

| | |
|---|---|
| **Num** | Correction: Follow conventional usage in using words or figures for numbers; be consistent in the treatment of numbers. |

There are few firm rules about using figures or words for numbers occurring in most writing. In general, books and magazines write out all numbers through one hundred and also larger numbers that can be written in two words *(six thousand, three million).* This style is usually appropriate for college papers and for most other kinds of general and formal writing. Newspapers and informal writing generally use figures for all numbers over ten, and some scientific and technical publications use figures exclusively.

**General and formal:** four, ten, fifteen, ninety-four, 114, 22,500, thirty thousand, five million [but usage varies]

**Informal:** four, ten, 15, 94, 114, 22,500, 30,000, 5,000,000 (or 5 million)

There are a few special situations (described in the section following) in which figures are always customary. In other cases, use the form that is appropriate not only for your audience but for your material. In general, write out all simple two-digit numbers and round numbers that can be easily read; use figures for numbers that cannot be written in two words and for series of numbers that are to be compared.

| Words appropriate | Figures appropriate |
|---|---|
| He shot three quail and one rabbit. | The next ship unloaded 3500 pounds of king salmon, 947 pounds of chinook salmon, and 200 pounds of crab. |
| Five votes were cast for the class president's proposal, twenty-one against it. | In Colorado 10,547 farmers voted for controls; in Indiana, 17,003; in Minnesota, 10,750. The nationwide total was 87.2% in favor. |
| If I had ten dollars for every time I've broken one of my resolutions, I would have at least a thousand dollars by now. | Dresses in the $15–$25 range were selling well, those from $26–$45 fairly well, and those over $46 hardly at all. |

Whichever form you use, be consistent. Don't change needlessly from words to figures or from figures to words in the same piece of writing:

**Inconsistent:** When I was 15, I thought anyone over thirty-five was old.

**Consistent:** When I was fifteen, I thought anyone over thirty-five was old.

Conventional uses of figures

Figures are customarily used in all the following situations:

1) Dates are always written in figures except in formal social correspondence, such as wedding invitations. The forms *1st, 2nd, 3rd,* and so on are sometimes used in dates, but only when the year is omitted:

October 10, 1967    Oct. 10, 1967    October 10    October 10th

2) Hours are written in figures before *a.m.* or *p.m.;* they are spelled out before *o'clock:*

| 7 a.m. | 1800 hours (military usage) | twelve noon |
| 11:35 p.m. | one o'clock | twelve midnight |

3) Mathematical and technical numbers, including percentages:

| 3.14159 | longitude 74°02′E. |
| 99.8 percent, 99.8% | .410 gauge shotgun |

Except in dates and street numbers, a comma is used to separate thousands, millions, etc., although it may be omitted in four-digit figures:

1,365 (or 1365) pounds    8,393,624    17,016

4) Page numbers and similar references:

| pp. 183–186 | page 12 |
| chapter iv | Genesis 39:12 |
| Ch. 19 | Act III, scene iv, line 28 (III, iv, 28) |

5) Sums of money, except sums in round numbers or, in formal style, sums that can be written in two or three words:

| **Figures** | **Words** |
| a bargain at $4.98 | Can you live on two thousand a year? |
| The British pound was once worth $4.85. | Coffee was then selling for about a dollar a pound. |

6) Street numbers (with no commas between thousands):

2027 Fairview North    Apartment 3C, 1788 Grand North

7) Statistics and series of more than two numbers, especially when the numbers are to be compared:

The survey showed that the class contained 24 Democrats, 18 Republicans, and 3 Socialists.

## Plurals of figures
The plural of a figure is written either with *'s* or *s:*

Six nines: six **9's,** six **9s**    By tens: by **10's,** by **10s**

## Numbers at the beginning of sentences
Numbers at the beginning of sentences are written out unless they are dates:

Two to 3% of loading and up to 10% is common and 20 to 30% in specially surfaced papers. . . .—"Paper Manufacture," *Encyclopaedia Britannica*

1960 was a year of devastating drought in China.

## Arabic and Roman numerals

Arabic numerals (1, 2, 17, 96) are used in almost all cases where numbers are expressed in figures. Roman numerals, either lowercase or capitals (i, ii, cxlvi; I, II, CXLVI), are occasionally used to number outlines, chapters, acts of a play, or formal inscriptions. They are almost always used to number the front matter of a book; a new pagination in Arabic numerals begins with the body of the book.

In Roman numerals a small number preceding a larger is to be subtracted from the larger (ix = 9, xc = 90). The following table shows the common Roman numerals (lowercase):

| | | | | | | | |
|---|---|---|---|---|---|---|---|
| 1 | i | 10 | x | 50 | l | 200 | cc |
| 2 | ii | 11 | xi | 60 | lx | 400 | cd |
| 3 | iii | 15 | xv | 70 | lxx | 500 | d |
| 4 | iv | 19 | xix | 80 | lxxx | 600 | dc |
| 5 | v | 20 | xx | 90 | xc | 900 | cm |
| 6 | vi | 21 | xxi | 99 | xcix | 1000 | m |
| 7 | vii | 30 | xxx | 100 | c | 1500 | md |
| 8 | viii | 40 | xl | 110 | cx | 1066 | mlxvi |
| 9 | ix | 49 | xlix | 199 | cxcix | 1962 | mcmlxii |

## Cardinal and ordinal numbers

Figures indicating number only are *cardinal numbers:* 1, 2, 3, 72, 135. The numbers indicating order *(first, second, seventeenth)* are *ordinal numbers.* Except in routine enumeration, ordinals should be spelled out rather than abbreviated to *1st, 2nd, 17th.*

Since the ordinals can be either adjectives or adverbs, the forms ending in *-ly (firstly)* are unnecessary and are now rarely used.

**Application: Using Numbers and Abbreviations**

1. Read the following sentences carefully, keeping in mind the principles stated in the preceding section. Do any of them use abbreviations or numbers in a way that would be inappropriate in college writing? Rewrite faulty sentences, making whatever changes are necessary. Since there are cases where there's a choice in usage, remember that one of the principles of using numbers and abbreviations is to be consistent.

a. When we arrived at the theater on 8th St., we found that the evening's performance would start an hr. late.

b. The University recently added 2 new members to its faculty—Jos. Blumenthal, MA, and Mary Persons, Doctor of Philosophy.

**c.** Six members of the OAS conferred recently with U.N. Representative Geo. H. Bush at his office in N.Y.

**d.** Fifty-five to 60% of U. of C. students approved the 2 o'clock curfew; about 30% were violently opposed.

**e.** His monument to St. Francis, a remarkable piece of sculpture, weighed over 2500 lbs. and rivaled his monument to Saint Peter.

**f.** P. 237 of the manual lists the home addresses of U.S. Senators & p. 298 lists their D.C. addresses.

**g.** On Dec. 23 CBS will dramatize the most celebrated Xmas story of recent times—"The Christmas Carol" by Chas. Dickens.

**h.** Dr. Roscoe Caries, D.D.S., reported that in an experiment involving two thousand and forty-four children, tooth decay was not significantly reduced.

**i.** Lee had 4 sisters (ranging in age from sixteen to 31 yrs.) and a widowed mother.

**j.** After 10 months the FBI agent finally tracked Groark to Ogden, Miss., where he found him suffering from d.t.'s in the barn of the Rev. John Gantry.

Application:
Using
Numbers
and
Abbreviations
**225**

# Part Two

Practices in Composition

# Discovering and organizing what you have to say 18

*. . . in time the good writer will acquire not only a sense of groping for but a sense of having groped to: he begins to know when he has finally reached whatever he was reaching for. —John Ciardi*

*Truth is not a lump of matter, decorated and disguised, but finally delivered intact; rather it is a web of shifting complexities whose pattern emerges only in the process of writing, and is in fact modified by the writing. . . . —Richard Ohmann, "In Lieu of a New Rhetoric"*

All of us have things to say. Most of us don't know that we have things to say. What we have to say is not always at the front of our minds, fresh, compelling, ready to be said. More often than not we have to find what it is, learn to know it, and watch it take first one shape, then another. This means exploring the world we're in, testing our personal resources, weighing our judgments and our whimsy, and evaluating our information.

From the start, whether you are in a composition course or doing some work that requires writing, you can expect to spend more time in thinking and hunting than you do in writing a complete draft of your paper. Of course there is no *requirement* that you do some thinking and hunting. It is possible to write without doing much exploratory thinking, but what often comes out then is a pale reflection of the thinking someone else has done. "Bad writing" is often bad because it is anonymous writing; it has no character. It is a gathering and reporting of conventional thoughts and conventional phrasings that do not *show* the writer; anyone might have written the same thing. Good writing begins to occur when you learn to accept and trust yourself as a source of delight, information, and insight for others, when you accept the responsibility of knowing yourself and learning to say what it is that uniquely connects you with a subject. Good writing begins to occur when you start taking over your experiences, learning all that they signify, and speaking out in words that you have made your own. Good writing begins to occur when you make what you write *yours*.

The first two sections that follow are about some of the

problems that are involved in exploring for a subject and making it your own. Section 18.1 includes some discussion of examining a situation for possible subjects, exploring a subject's potential, establishing a perspective for seeing the subject, and using resources to handle the subject. We've tried to suggest a number of different ways of finding a subject. It's unlikely that you would ever need to try them out in any single writing assignment. Section 18.2 is given over to an account of the relationship that exists among a writer, his subject, and an audience and to some of the ways of taking a subject to an audience. The third section, 18.3, discusses both formal and informal patterns for organizing material before you write.

**Plan**

**18.1**

## Finding and exploring what you have to say    **18.1**

Some years ago, C. Day Lewis commented on his own writing: "I do not sit down at my desk to put into verse something that is already clear in my mind. If it were clear in my mind, I should have no incentive or need to write about it, for I am an explorer, not a journalist, a propagandist, or a statistician." Later in the same passage he went on to say that "often I have gone some way with the poem before I am able to grasp the theme which lies hidden in the material that has accumulated." He is talking about writing poetry, to be sure, but what he says gives a clue to most other forms of writing as well. There's no reason to expect that you will already know everything you need to say when you sit down to write. You'll have to hunt for it. And when you find it, it may be a chameleon: it may change color while you look at it.

Ancient rhetoricians called this process of searching *invention,* and it's a good word to use. It comes from a Latin verb, *invenire.* Meanings given to this verb include (1) to come upon, or find; (2) to fabricate mentally, to create or devise in the mind. Both actions are important in the time before you write. *Invention* is a name for the processes by which you come upon, or *meet,* your own experiences, the things you know, and the things other people know; and you *make* something out of them in your mind by finding the way they mean something to you and by finding the way they fit together.

## Examining a situation for possible subjects

Often, of course, the situation you are in will determine what subjects you will write about. If you are in business, you must answer your correspondence. If you are in a laboratory, you must report your findings. If you are in a history class that requires three book reports on specified books, you must turn in the papers. Topics for writing may develop out of discussions in your composition class. Your composition teacher may assign a specific topic for you to write about. But even if you are given a specific topic to write about, your thinking hasn't been done for you.

**Plan**

**18.1**

The problem is that having a topic doesn't always make it possible for you to write, or give you a reason for writing. If you are assigned a topic such as "Why I Came to College" (and we hope that you won't be) or if you choose for yourself a topic such as "A Freshman Views the Ecology Movement," you still have to determine what you have to say and why it is worthwhile to say it. You still have to investigate the situation in which you and an audience are to come together. You still have to learn what the subject calls for from you and what kinds of resources are available for treating the subject. You still have to think about how the material can be most usefully presented to a particular audience, and about how you can be yourself, do justice to a subject, and meet an audience honestly. So, even if the topic is given, your thinking has not been done for you.

And if you're left free to choose for yourself what you will write about, a lot of thinking and searching is plainly still before you. Sometimes, given the freedom to choose their own topics, writers accept whatever ideas first come to mind, or use materials already available to them without thinking them through. Consider this essay, written in a freshman composition class:

### My Theater Experience

I worked at a theater before coming to college. When my parents started managing the drive-in, they drafted me to do the odd jobs there.

While working in the cafeteria, box-office, and the projection booth, I met many new people. I found that people come to a movie for different reasons. One man said that he came to get away from his wife and kids. Many boys and girls came to have dates. A few people, however, actually came to watch the movie.

Finding
and
exploring
what you
have to say
231

At the drive-in, I experienced different emotions due to the actions of my customers. One lady aroused my indignation when she claimed that her son, who was six feet in height, was under twelve years of age. A boy eleven years old does not have to pay admission; therefore her son was admitted free. I was amused when one boy tried to hide in the back floor of a car, under a quilt, while the driver drove into the theater. I am aware of such tricks, and the boy was caught. One girl caught her slacks on the barbed wire while climbing over the fence at the back of the theater. I helped her off the fence, and I sold her a ticket. She never came over the fence again.

I experienced new and enlightening experiences at the theater. At the drive-in, I found that real people are often more entertaining than people in the movies.

**Plan**

**18.1**

It's easy enough to see why a writer would decide to use this title and topic. Not everyone works in a drive-in theater; in fact, few do. Drive-in theaters have been at one time or another the butt of many jokes, the occasion for many stories about cultural patterns and practices among the young. A writer can safely assume that writing about work in a drive-in theater from firsthand experience is a subject not too many other writers are going to use. But even if a topic seems obvious and ready-made, it still deserves some searching and investigating. The author of this essay doesn't appear to value his own experiences very highly, or to have looked at things very closely. He hasn't shown the drive-in experience as it belongs uniquely to him. He hasn't explored his own experience, it seems, to share it with us. We're left wondering about what's *really* different about working in a drive-in, about who the "new people" are, about just exactly what makes people more entertaining than movies, about that girl hanging on the fence. We don't know what all of these things signify to the author; we don't know exactly how he sees them, or how they've entered his life. And we leave the essay thinking, too, that there are other things he could have told us from his unique experience: What does one learn about leisure from working in a drive-in, or about waste, or about dating practices? How does one learn to think about taste and manners from working there? The author of this essay hasn't yet "come upon" his subject and made something out of it. The essay needs more time spent in remembering episodes and practices and reflecting on what they mean.

When a topic is given to you, you still have exploratory work to do. If you are free to choose your own topic and if you choose a topic that seems to be obvious, you still have exploratory work to do. Likely to be still more troublesome are those occasions when you are free to write on your own topics, and no subject at all comes into your mind.

When that happens, you have the whole world before you, and that's sometimes the same as having nothing at all before you. There are so many possibilities that it's almost like having no possibilities at all. You're called upon, in this situation, to understand and write about your own private and unique view of some part of the world, and to combine multiple and varied impressions into a personal interpretation. What do you do? How do you get started?

### Keeping a journal

One thing you can do that may help you with all the writing you may need to do requires daily attention over a long period of time. Some composition teachers may require you to *keep a daily journal;* if your teacher doesn't, you might try on your own. What we're suggesting is that you commit yourself to make daily entries in some kind of journal. The entries may be words, phrases, sentences, paragraphs, essays, poems, bits and pieces. The point is to record in some way things that matter to you or puzzle you or cause you to wonder. Put down what you see and learn and feel and know. A journal can begin to get you in the habit of stating yourself on paper. To make it work as it should, you need to make daily entries: saving up for a week and writing a group of entries won't give you an account of what you were conscious of on *different* days. Don't be hesitant in making journal entries, and don't imagine that every entry should be something important. If a song you hear on the radio moves you, tell about the song and try to say why and how it moved you. If something goes sour in one of your classes, try to figure out what it is by recalling what different people said and did.

### Making abstractions concrete

A second thing you can do requires some practice, and could be a part of your journal. Try writing phrases and sentences that locate and embody ideas and impressions that come to you. The purpose in doing this is for you to get in the habit of putting your ideas and impressions into quite specific settings or quite specific terms, as in the following examples:

Finding
and
exploring
what you
have to say
**233**

**Ease and relaxation:** an unhurried visit to the Wagon Wheel Art Gallery in Colorado.

**Fear:** the whir of a rattlesnake when you can't see it; the taste of brass in your mouth after an out-of-control car just misses you.

**Comfort:** some good fresh pipe tobacco and some exciting books on a Friday evening with the weekend still ahead.

**Anxiety:** a message to call home without any indication of what it's all about.

Practice in creating particular scenes and terms to accompany ideas and impressions may help you to make what you know and feel concrete. It may also help you to avoid falling back on standard phrasings and clichés when you are trying to put yourself on paper. (See also §22.4, Concrete and abstract words.)

Neither the journal nor this practice in making knowledge concrete will guarantee that you always find good subjects to write about. Both may help by letting you see which way your thoughts and impressions are likely to run, which topics are likely to appear and reappear in journal notes, and which kinds of topics seem to matter to you most.

Seeing patterns and connections

There are some other things you can do to help locate what you're going to write about and to help in thinking about subjects that are assigned. The questions and observations that follow may help you to see patterns and connections in your own ideas and impressions:

1) Do you notice which things seem to recur in your experience? Actions, attitudes, phrasings, emotional reactions, and other experiences may never be *exactly* repeated, but there are likely to be recognizable likenesses among your experiences. If there are, the likenesses may help you to see a subject, or to see an assigned subject in a new way.

2) How do you look at your experiences? What do you focus on? How and when does your focus change? When you first entered your composition class, did you see and hear individuals, or did you respond to the pattern of the whole class? How do you look at it now? Shifting your focus from large range to close range, looking at a part, then at another part, then at both in relation to each other enables you to see and know what's around you, particularly if you know *why* your focus shifts.

3) How do your experiences differ from others? How varied is your experience? How do the things you are familiar with occur to other people? Answering questions like these may also help you understand your own ideas and impressions and learn what there is in them that has significance for you. Suppose, for example, that you are in a history class and that the professor always calls the roll at the beginning of class. Answering the questions above may help you see something of value in so minor an event. How does your professor's method of calling the roll differ from the methods other professors use? How does roll-calling change in form from one professor to another or from day to day? How does roll-calling in its various forms fit into a larger context? Is it a sign of a particular view of education or of students or of the professor's duties?

4) What can you learn about an idea, an event, or an experience by looking at it in three different ways? It has been suggested by some rhetoricians that each potential subject should be viewed as a *particle,* as a *wave,* and as a *field.* If you look at an experience as a *particle,* that means regarding it as something fixed so that you can examine its parts. If you look at an experience as a *wave,* that means regarding it as changing and dynamic so that you can see the relationships among the parts. If you look at an experience as a *field,* that means regarding it as part of a larger context so that you can see how it fits in the larger scene. Consider the history professor above who always called the class roll. Calling a class roll can be regarded as a complete act, so that you could examine its parts—the roll book or seating chart, the manner of calling names, the way of looking at each or some or none, and so on. At the same time, each of these parts may have some particular relation to other parts—as, for example, the professor's eyebrows' going up every day when certain names are called may signify some judgment he or she has made. And at the same time, calling a class roll may belong to a much larger context: it may be seen as part of a particular style of teaching, for example, or as part of a particular view of education.

5) What is there in your experience that can be shared with another? Can you find a way of presenting your experience that will make it possible for another to share? How can you

utilize the knowledge and values that others have so as to connect them with you and your subject?

Once again, we should note that asking and answering these questions will not guarantee that you can always find good subjects. They may help you to think about what you know and feel and to discover what's there that has significance. Without extensive exploration, it is possible for you to write competently. We think it's likely, however, that *good* writing will occur when something matters enough so that the writer feels the need to speak forth.

## Exploring a subject's potential

Even after you have discovered a subject, or after you have been given a subject, there is still good reason for asking what there is about a subject that most *needs* to be said and for asking where a subject's greatest *potential* lies. Any student, given an assignment to write a five-hundred-word theme and turn it in on Monday, can obviously argue that *something* needs to be said to satisfy the course requirements. But even the most routine subject ("My Summer Vacation," for example) given in a conventional assignment should be examined for its needs and possibilities. As you are thinking about topics assigned to you or about other possible topics, consider whether any of them can be developed into an essay that is *for* something, an essay that will involve you in working out a subject in the company of an audience. There is seldom any danger that the topic you select will be too narrow. It is the large subjects like "American Foreign Policy," "The Aims of Higher Education," and "The Role of Women in Contemporary Society" that lead to difficulty. On such ambitious subjects most writers can only repeat commonplace judgments and empty generalities, and after writing a paragraph or two, they find that they have nothing more to say.

Limit the topic you select so that you can develop it fully in the required number of words. Most college themes are short—even a thousand-word theme would fill only one newspaper column. Because even ten thousand words would not be enough to cover most large general subjects ("Justice," "Crime Prevention," "Forestry"), break down such subjects into topics you can handle. "TV Westerns," for example, might be limited to "The Effect of TV Westerns on Children." But since there are many children and several TV westerns, you might write a more interesting paper and offer more interesting judgments by focusing specifically on your little brother and TV westerns.

It's often helpful to concentrate on a single, well-defined aspect of the subject rather than on the subject as a whole:

| Too general | More specific |
|---|---|
| Voting as an obligation of citizenship | Arousing student interest in voting |
| Sportsmanship | How sportsmanship differs in tennis and baseball |
| Smog control | The effectiveness of smog control devices for cars |

As you gather information, your topic may change slightly — and it may continue to change through all the preliminary stages of your thinking. The important thing to remember at first is to keep the subject specific and to avoid falling back on a general subject.

There are some particular ways of thinking about subjects that may help you discover what is most interesting or useful or valuable in them. Some or all of the suggestions below may help you to recall relevant information that you already have about your subject, or call your attention to information that you need but do not possess; some may help you see some principle illustrated in your subject.

The first set of suggestions may be useful to you as you first begin thinking about your subject and also after you have developed a specific proposition or thesis and are seeking a way to explain it. The suggestions are borrowed from the works of both ancient and modern rhetoricians, who propose the following as ways of thinking about a subject:

1) What can you learn by *definition?* To what class does your subject belong? How does it differ from other members of the same class? Can definition help you to determine just what your main point is? If you have determined what your main point is, does definition give you a way of organizing your discussion?

2) Will *comparison* with something you know well help you to understand your subject? Can you detect similarities in your subject and one or more other things? Does detecting differ-

ences between your subject and a similar thing help you understand your subject? Does your subject differ in degree from similar things?

3) Studying *relationships* may tell you something about your subject and show you a way to organize your discussion. How is your subject connected with a cause? How and why did your subject come to be? Is your subject to be studied as an effect of some causes, or as a cause of later effects? What are the antecedents of your subject? What consequences are likely to follow from your subject? With what ideas or things is your subject incompatible? Are there ideas that are contradicted by your subject?

4) Is there expert *testimony* about your subject that you can call on? Are there laws, principles, precedents, or other kinds of testimony that will help you understand your subject and validate it to others?

Suppose, for example, that the general subject of *sportsmanship* interests you. Perhaps you're interested in athletics, or perhaps you've just seen an episode of bad sportsmanship, or perhaps you've simply wondered why people behave differently in games. The questions above may help you to discover how to go about discussing sportsmanship or to find what needs most attention. If you set out to define sportsmanship, a first step is to determine what class of things it belongs to. Is sportsmanship a *virtue,* a *mark of civility,* a *quality,* a *social disguise for aggression?* The problem of defining sportsmanship, in other words, may get to be so important that you decide that this is your subject and you don't have to look further. Each of the sets of questions above may give you a specific way of talking about sportsmanship.

Another set of suggestions lies in seven relationships that give coherence to discussions. If we put these relationships in the form of questions, they may give you some additional ways of inquiring into your subject:

1) With what is your subject *coordinate?* What can be linked to your subject by *and?*

2) From what is your subject *observably different?* What can be linked to your subject by *but?*

3) What can be cited as a *cause* for your subject? What can be linked to your subject by *for?*

4) What can be cited as a *result* of your subject? To what

Discovering
and
organizing
what you
have to say

238

conclusions does your subject lead? What can be linked to your subject by *so?*

5) What are the *alternatives* to your subject? What can be linked to your subject by *or?*

6) What can your subject be said to *include?* What examples, narratives, episodes can be linked to your subject?

7) What *sequences* exist within your subject? Is your subject part of a larger sequence?

These two sets of questions and suggestions can be used in two ways: first, as guides to thinking about your subject *before* you have settled on a central thesis you wish to develop, and second, as guides to developing and organizing your work *after* you have arrived at a central proposition.

## Locating a thesis

When you have gone far enough in your thinking and planning to select a specific topic, and you know pretty well what position you take toward it, it is often helpful (and sometimes necessary) to compose a *thesis statement.* This definite statement of the main point or central idea of your paper may help you see just where you are going and why, and it may also help you select the material you are going to use in the paper. Usually a single declarative sentence, the thesis sentence should normally be either a simple or complex sentence, though dependent modifiers can be added: if the thesis sentence has a *single* main clause (as in simple and complex sentences), then you're encouraged to keep one dominant idea at the center of attention in your paper.

The thesis sentence is not the topic of your paper or its title; it is a sentence that answers the question "What is the main idea that I am trying to present to the reader?" A statement of the central or controlling idea of a paper titled "The Honor System" might read "The honor system works only as well as the students want it to work" or "The honor system at this college is popular with the faculty but not with the students." In a paper explaining a process or activity, the thesis sentence might be "Learning to play the violin demands patience as well as talent" or "Performance is more important than appearance when you are buying a used car."

Writing a thesis sentence requires you to stop and think about the materials of your experience and to decide what is important or interesting. The essay "My Theater Experience" (see p. 231) might have been given direction and focus by a good thesis sentence. The author, with some thought and digging in his memory, might have written several essays about his theater experience. Consider some of the possibilities:

1) Since the writer indicates that he did many odd jobs around the theater, an essay could have developed on the behind-the-scenes operation of a drive-in theater;

2) The writer remarks that he "met many new people" and that "people come to a movie for different reasons"; an essay might have developed on the types of people who attend drive-in movies or on the reasons people have for attending or on the significance of drive-in movies in leisure living;

3) The writer "experienced different emotions"; an essay might have developed on the range of emotional responses theater workers experience and their problems in adjusting to them;

4) The writer might have written an informal essay on amusing episodes at a drive-in theater;

5) The writer might have developed an essay on the erratic, often unseemly behavior of people at drive-in theaters.

Suppose that a little thought leads the writer to choose the fifth possibility. Perhaps the first is so familiar to the writer that it is no longer very interesting. The possibilities listed second above probably require some interviews and some gathering of attendance statistics that the writer can no longer do. Perhaps the third and fourth possibilities don't seem important enough to tell about. But the fifth possibility is a good one, the writer thinks; here is a chance to write about the way people behave in the dark when they think no one is watching, at least no one they know ("People in the Dark," incidentally, wouldn't be a bad title). But just deciding on the fifth possibility doesn't give the writer a direction or focus. Writing a thesis sentence requires that the writer decide what the central thought is to be and say it in a single sentence. Consider some possible thesis sentences from the fifth suggestion above for a new essay on experience in a drive-in theater:

My experience working in a drive-in theater taught me that people behave differently in the dark, resorting to trickery, deceit, and foolishness.

I learned from my work in a drive-in theater that public manners and private manners are not the same.

Darkness seems to generate behavior in people that they would not dream of in the light.

At this point, a thesis sentence is still tentative, and further thinking and outlining may suggest changes. But each of these thesis statements suggests definite ways to get started on developing the paper.

## Using available resources

Two kinds of resources—what we might call *private resources* and *public resources*—should be considered in developing a paper. Some subjects require one, some the other, some both.

### Private resources

For some papers that you will write you already know enough to treat the subject well. Your own experience will provide subjects and material for many college themes: what you have done in school and out, the jobs you have held, your hobbies, the people you know, the places you have visited, the courses you are taking in college. Consider this brief list of topics and see how many you could write on from your own experience:

| | |
|---|---|
| Overcoming Self-Consciousness | Considerations in Buying a Car |
| A Job I Disliked | A Successful Amateur Play |
| Advice to a High-School Student About to Enter the University | The Perils of Teen-Age Marriage |
| | Building a Record Collection |
| Living Within a Budget | Hero Worship Among Teen-Agers |
| Baby-Sitters Earn Their Pay | |

You need not feel that a paper based upon your personal experiences will be boring to others. Some college freshmen, particularly when writing their first themes, are afraid that their own experiences have been too limited, or that their opinions and attitudes are too commonplace to be of interest to anyone but themselves. But much published material is based upon incidents and attitudes that are in no way unique or sensational ("Making Your Hobby Pay," "The Most Unforgettable Character I Have Met," "Diary of a City-Bred Farmer"). If you are interested in what you have to say, your readers probably will be too. A fresh and lively account of the experiences of a baby-sitter is more readable than a dull description of a journey up the Amazon. The problem in writing a personal experience paper, as demonstrated earlier by the analysis of the theme on "My Theater Experience," is to discover something worth writing about.

If you are far enough along in your thinking and planning to formulate a thesis, you will be able to tell whether or not your present knowledge, opinions, and attitudes are sufficient material. For papers based on personal experience, ask yourself as many questions as you can think of about the subject. If you are going to explain how a person should apply for a job, recall and analyze your own experiences in looking for work. How did you find out what jobs were available? How did you decide which jobs to apply for? Did you apply in person or by letter? If you were not hired, what were the probable reasons? What mistakes, if any, did you make either during an interview or in your letter of application? If you were going to apply for another job, would you go about it in the same way?

A similar analysis will help you gather material for papers presenting personal opinions or attitudes. If you decide to enumerate the qualities of a good teacher, think of two or three of your teachers who were outstanding and try to discover what qualities they had in common: a sound knowledge of their subject? a genuine interest in students? a willingness to help the slower students? fairness in grading? a sense of humor? You could extend your analysis by considering also one or two teachers who were definitely unsatisfactory, to see what qualities they lacked.

At this stage of thinking about your subject, jot down on paper every idea that occurs to you, whether you are sure you will use it or not. One idea often suggests another and better one, and may help you to reshape or clarify your thesis. After a reasonable amount of reflection, you will usually have more than enough material to write a paper of the assigned length.

Public resources

Not all papers can be written entirely from personal opinion or experience. Many subjects call for information that must be gathered by reading, by observation, or through personal interviews. Some subjects will demand thorough research and formal presentation. Others may require only the addition of your casual reading as support. Still others—such as some of the interpretive essays you will be asked to do in English

Discovering
and
organizing
what you
have to say
242

courses—may require that you gather additional information (for example, information about literary techniques), even though the paper is going to be an informal expression of your response to meaning in something you have read. It is perfectly permissible to use your reading casually for any subject that requires it—that is, not as in a formal report with documentation, but as the natural supplement to what you wish to say.

In using outside resources to develop material for a paper, read critically, and think about what you read. Be careful to distinguish between verifiable *facts* (the cost of living index in New York City and in Chicago) and opinions (the reasons why the Democratic Party lost the 1972 election). On controversial subjects, read and weigh the opinions on all sides of the question before arriving at a firm opinion of your own.

Make the effort to understand and assimilate material from published sources before using it in a paper. Instead of copying an author's words, think about the ideas he is expressing. Do you agree or disagree with them? Why? Proper acknowledgment should always be made for borrowed material—in a footnote if the paper requires formal documentation, or informally if the situation seems to warrant, as for the quotations opening the sections of this handbook. (See §28.8, Documenting the paper, for details on using materials from printed sources.)

## The meeting place of author, subject, and audience     18.2

*To say that the speaker must give himself with the truth adhering may sound pretentious, especially if you have the standard picture of the soapbox orator. But it is precise. The speaker and his message reach the hearer together. If the hearer finds the speaker repellent, the message hasn't a hope—it arrives discolored by, smelling of, the one who uttered it.—F. J. Sheed, "My Life on the Street Corner"*

Some kinds of writing you may do for your own sake—diaries, notes, and the like. Some kinds of writing you may do for the sake of the subject—laboratory reports, case histories, meditative explorations. Often, however, an audience of some kind is waiting, and you must find a just and happy balance among the material and arguments available on a subject, the interests, needs, and peculiarities of an audience, and your own character. You must be honest to yourself, do justice to a subject, and earn an audience. You can't be with your audience when they read what you have written. Your words on paper have to be your authentication and your testimony.

## The writer's position

If you imagine yourself, a subject, and an audience at the three points of a triangle, you'll be able to visualize some of the problems in determining where to stand. If you stand too close to your subject, you may forget the need of sharing it with an audience. If you stand too far from your subject, you may not see it clearly. If you stand too close to your audience, you may get to sounding too chummy. If you stand too far from the audience, you may seem remote and aloof.

It is possible—even common—for a writer to be so busy at winning the audience that the subject and even the writer are given scant service. Good writing, by contrast, requires honesty of the writer—an honest, serious approach to the subject and to the audience, and an honest critical understanding of his or her own capabilities. We are all *partial* when we write, since we cannot say all that there is to be said on any subject; the demands of space and time, the interests and patience of our readers, and the inadequacies of our own character and knowledge make it unlikely that what we write can ever express an entire truth. But that does not mean that our piece of writing is by definition a poor thing. Indeed, it is the character of good writing that it is a single, limited voice speaking in order to think things out.

To say that writers are necessarily partial and limited is not to say that they must be phony. They can *seem* to escape their incompleteness by resorting to standardized responses, stereotyped phrasing, and concepts uncritically accepted. And, in doing so, they can sometimes sound impressive: they can use elevated generalities, for example, or stereotyped impersonal language that allows them to pretend they are being totally objective. But it won't do.

Before you begin writing the first draft of a paper, you must discover where *you* stand with regard to your subject and to

Discovering
and
organizing
what you
have to say
244

your audience. Have you engaged yourself in the subject enough to make it interesting to others? Have you weighed it to give it worth? What position will you take toward your subject in presenting it to your audience? Must you address the audience in strictly logical and impersonal fashion? Or does the subject justify a more emotional presentation? Or should you concentrate rather on the impression of yourself that will emerge through your writing? Can you combine these tactics in such a way that you and your audience will come together and share an idea?

## Adjusting to the audience

As you are planning a piece of writing, you must keep in mind the interests and needs of your particular audience. It is easy, of course, to forget your readers and to think only about your subject in some of the writing you will do in college. The announcement of an assigned subject, as has already been suggested, does not necessarily give you a purpose for writing; but unless you *discover* a purpose and relate it to your audience, even a dutiful fulfillment of the assignment will amount to little. If you ignore your audience, your work is bootless, no matter how correct. It is difficult, when you are writing alone at night, for example, even to think of an audience. The easiest thing to do is to get the paper written without bothering about an audience. Still, each of us wants to be accepted as somebody real, a genuine person. We can extend the same gift to readers. When you write something, somebody real reads it. When you're writing for a class, it's easy to assume that your teacher is your only audience. Often it is better to write for your class, or for people who read habitually. One way to get in the habit of thinking about your audience, if your assignment permits it, is to specify a particular audience for what you are writing and indicate at the first of the paper who the audience is.

If the subject you are dealing with is controversial, and if both you and your audience are likely to have intense feelings about the matter, you may have particular problems in finding a living space where you and an audience can be together for a while. On matters we care deeply about, where feelings and emotions are taut — politics, ethical practices, conservation and ecology, personal relationships, social, professional, or

The meeting place of author, subject, and audience
245

sexual, for example—we have difficulty hearing each other, and we're not always likely to listen to logic. One reason for this, as Professor Carl Rogers has pointed out in his study of communication blocking and facilitation, is that we tend to react to value statements with more value statements. If one person says, "Oh, all the liberals want to do is tax us to death to take care of those lazy people on welfare," a second person who holds opposing views is likely to react with, "Why, that's not so, we need taxes for lots of things, and besides, people on welfare aren't lazy, they need help." When that kind of exchange occurs, and we think it does pretty often, the two speakers are in different worlds, and the logic of one won't persuade the other. The language that each person is likely to use in a heated value exchange is assertive language; it threatens the values of the other and causes him to become defensive and retaliatory. How can we meet an audience in such a situation? There is no easy way.

One thing you can do, if you find yourself in a context where you and an audience seem to be evaluating each other and threatening each other, is to move over into the shoes of your audience. You can begin by looking at the issue at hand from your audience's view, as Professor Rogers suggests:

Real communication occurs, and this evaluative tendency is avoided, when we listen with understanding. What does that mean? It means to see the expressed idea and attitude from the other person's point of view, to sense how it feels to him, to achieve his frame of reference in regard to the thing he is talking about.

You can still be authentically yourself and yet open to others. You can acknowledge opposing views and work to understand them. Most people don't plan to do evil, even those who disagree with us. If they disagree with us, it's usually because they see good in a different way, and we can try to see it as they do, without sacrificing our own views. It takes time and patience to search for the living space where you and an audience can be together, but that is a grace we owe each other.

Discovering
and
organizing
what you
have to say
246

## Organizing your material                    18.3

Before you begin to write, plan the order in which you intend to present your material. With some subjects the material itself will determine organization. For example, narratives (§27.4) and papers that describe personal experiences usually follow the order of events: first this happened, then this, then something else. An explanation of a process follows a similar step-by-step pattern of presentation. In descriptive writing ("Manhattan at Dawn," "A Trip Through the Carlsbad Caverns") the normal order may be from one point to another (entering the Caverns, going to the first level, arriving at the Big Room) or from a general impression to the specific details that give rise to it, arranged more or less in the order of prominence. (See §27.3, Description.)

The order of presentation may require more thought with other subjects, such as "A Criticism of Olivier's *Hamlet*" or "Repression and Rationalization as Defense Mechanisms." Whether you select the topic or your instructor assigns one, in most instances you will have to examine the material carefully to find the best order for your special purpose. (See §19.2, Developing your material, for suggestions about choosing a pattern of development.)

In organizing most papers, you will find it useful to make an outline. Four kinds of outlines are widely used: the scratch outline, the thesis-sentence outline, the topic outline, and the sentence outline. Sometimes your instructor will tell you which form to use. When you have no specific instructions, select the form that best suits your method of working and the kind of paper you are writing. In planning a long paper, especially one involving research, you will probably want to make a topic or sentence outline. For short papers and extemporaneous writing, informal notes or a scratch outline will generally serve the purpose. Even for long papers, you may find it useful to work informally for some time before committing yourself to a final, detailed plan. It is not uncommon, for example, for writers at work on long projects to draft key passages—an opening paragraph, a closing paragraph, a passage developing the central idea—and then to fit these bits of writing into a more formal plan, along with jotted notes, sentences, and other scraps of ideas. Whatever techniques you use, the important thing is to develop a plan that will guide you in writing your paper.

## Scratch outlines

A scratch outline is a series of notes—single words or phrases—jotted down to refresh your memory as you write. An outline of this sort is useful when time is limited, as when you are writing examinations or brief papers in class. The following is a sample scratch outline for a theme on the subject "The Value of Summer Jobs":

Earning money for clothes and school
Sense of responsibility
Learning to budget own time and money
Opportunity to learn about different kinds of jobs
Develop good work habits and maybe learn practical skills

The exact form of a scratch outline is not particularly important, since ordinarily you will be the only one who sees it. If the list is longer than five or six items, you may need to arrange the entries in some logical order (or number them) before beginning to write.

## Thesis-sentence outlines

If you have developed a thesis sentence (page 239), you may be able to use its parts as the terms of your outline. This can be especially helpful for short papers and essay examinations. Suppose, for example, that upon arriving in class you are given an assignment to write a short theme during the class period, and that one of the possible topics is "Campus Fashions." Suppose further that your experience and observation enable you within a few moments to jot down the following ideas on this general subject:

Something like hippie dress is fairly common
Standard fraternity-sorority dress is just as common
There are some variations
Most people dress pretty much alike
It's getting harder to tell the two styles apart

It is possible to arrange these notes as a scratch outline, as suggested above. Another moment's reflection, however, might enable you to exercise tighter control over your theme by formulating a thesis sentence such as this:

While there are some interesting variations in fashion here and there on campus, the dominant modified hippie and standard fraternity dress, which draw closer together every day, give our campus a near-homogeneous appearance.

If you can get this far quickly, you can use the thesis sentence as your outline. The sentence above, for example, could forecast a fairly brief, six-paragraph theme, each paragraph de-

Discovering
and
organizing
what you
have to say
248

veloping in sequence the structural units of the thesis sentence:

**Paragraph 1:** a brief introduction that ends with the thesis sentence
**Paragraph 2:** the interesting variations in fashion (this, judging from the form of the thesis, is an interesting but minor part of the theme)
**Paragraph 3:** the modified hippie style
**Paragraph 4:** the standard fraternity style
**Paragraph 5:** recent illustrations that show the two coming together
**Paragraph 6:** a conclusion on the homogeneity of style on your campus

One particular advantage of this method of organizing is that you can plan the shape and emphasis of your theme by planning the shape and emphasis of your thesis sentence. Your observation might lead you to revise the thesis sentence above in this way:

While the dominant modified hippie and standard fraternity dress (which draw closer every day) give our campus a near-homogeneous appearance, some very interesting variations have appeared here this year.

A short theme developed from this sentence would have a totally different emphasis from the one suggested above.

## Topic outlines

The topic outline, the most frequently used kind of formal outline, is helpful in organizing papers of more than five hundred words. It consists of brief phrases or single words (not sentences) that are numbered or lettered to show the order and relative importance of the ideas.

The first thing to do is to get all your ideas down on paper. On the subject "The Army as a Career for College Men and Women," your preliminary thinking might produce this rough, unsorted list of ideas:

Security
Promotion slow but steady
Many different branches appeal to different interests
Low pay
Depression won't bother you
Commissioned ranks open to men and women graduates
Can't be fired
Cost of uniforms
Discipline often annoying
Frequent moves hard on soldier's family
See interesting places and people

Social life restricted to small circle
Good retirement benefits
Annual vacation with pay
Military job training useful in civilian careers

### Determining the central idea

A quick glance at the list above reveals that some points stress the advantages of an army career; others, the disadvantages. The next step then is to divide the notes into two columns:

| Advantages | Disadvantages |
|---|---|
| Security | Low pay |
| Promotion slow but steady | Cost of uniforms |
| Many different branches appeal to different interests | Discipline often annoying |
| Depression won't bother you | Frequent moves hard on soldier's family |
| Can't be fired | Social life restricted to small circle |
| See interesting places and people | |
| Good retirement benefits | |
| Annual vacation with pay | |
| Commissioned ranks open to men and women graduates | |
| Military job training useful in civilian careers | |

In this form the relationship between the various ideas is not shown (What is the relationship between "Promotion slow but steady" and "Many different branches appeal to different interests"?) and there is no clear balance between the two columns (Is "Security" supposed to balance "Low pay"?). In analyzing the columns, however, you can see that there are two main ideas in each—the financial aspect of an army career and the living conditions that go with army life. You might then balance the notes in this way:

I. Financial aspect
   A. Disadvantages
      1. Low pay
      2. Cost of uniforms
   B. Advantages
      1. Security
      2. Promotion slow but steady
      3. Commissioned ranks open to men and women graduates
      4. Depression won't bother you
      5. Can't be fired

Discovering
and
organizing
what you
have to say
250

6. Good retirement benefits
7. Annual vacation with pay
8. Military job training useful in civilian careers
II. Social aspect
  A. Disadvantages
    1. Discipline often annoying
    2. Frequent moves hard on soldier's family
    3. Social life restricted to small circle
  B. Advantages
    1. Many different branches appeal to different interests
    2. See interesting places and people

When the notes are arranged in some system, decide on a main point you want to make in your paper. "The Army as a Career for College Men and Women" doesn't tell what you are going to say about the subject; it is a title, not a central idea.

At this stage you can see that there is more and stronger material on the financial advantages of a military career than on its disadvantages. On the other hand, the disadvantages of living conditions seem to outweigh the advantages. But assuming that you want to treat the subject fully and in a favorable light, you could frame a tentative statement of purpose: "Although there are definite disadvantages to an army career, the advantages outweigh them." This statement will now govern the reworking of the outline. At this stage it is still tentative and can be changed as the purpose becomes clearer in your mind.

Revising the outline
With the central idea as your guide, arrange the outline so that every part of it contributes directly to the purpose of the paper. Examine each heading to see if it needs to be strengthened or elaborated upon, if it repeats or overlaps another heading, or if it is unrelated to the central idea.

In the first part of the outline "Cost of uniforms" seems to be a weak point. Aren't officers given allowances for their uniforms? Possibly "Expense of frequent entertaining" is a stronger point, so substitute it for "Cost of uniforms."

The financial advantages of an army career seem to stand out, but looking at these entries closely, you will see that some overlap or are actually minor parts of other points. The heading "Security" obviously covers "Slow but steady promotion," "Commissioned ranks open to men and women graduates," and "Can't be fired." The fourth heading, "Depression won't bother you," is probably superfluous, since it really is part of "Can't be fired." Closer examination reveals that "Annual vacation with pay" is an aspect of living conditions rather than of finances; it should therefore be shifted to the second main heading.

Under "Advantages" in the second main heading, the first entry, "Many different branches appeal to different interests," seems out of place or else incorrectly phrased. Perhaps the point is that military people can find the jobs they like or are best fitted for.

As the plan now stands, the first part seems stronger. To make the argument more convincing, it would be a good idea to reverse the present order: begin with "Living conditions," and then end the paper on an emphatic note—the training that the army affords for success in other fields. After these changes have been made, and after some headings have been reworded to make them parallel in form, the final outline might be:

Thesis sentence: Although from the standpoint of finances and living conditions, there are some disadvantages to an army career for men and women, the advantages outweigh them.

I. Living conditions
   A. Disadvantages
      1. Discipline often annoying
      2. Frequent moves hard on soldier's family
      3. Social life restricted to a small circle
   B. Advantages
      1. Opportunity to find the job one is suited for
      2. Annual leaves with pay
      3. Chance to travel, to see new places, and to meet new people
II. Financial considerations
   A. Disadvantages
      1. Low pay
      2. Frequent entertaining expensive
   B. Advantages
      1. Security
         a. Slow but steady promotion, including commissions for men and women graduates
         b. Permanent employment
         c. Good retirement benefits
      2. Preparation for success in civilian careers after retirement

The outline now can be the basis for an orderly paper that makes a definite point.

## Sentence outlines

A sentence outline is developed in the same way as a topic outline, but the ideas are more fully expressed. Each heading is expressed as a complete sentence, usually consisting of just one main clause:

Thesis sentence: Although from the standpoint of finances and living conditions, there are some disadvantages to an army career for college men and women, the advantages outweigh them.

I. Living conditions are a major consideration in choosing a career.
  A. Army life has several shortcomings in this respect.
    1. The strict discipline imposed is often annoying.
    2. Frequent moves are hard on a soldier's family.
    3. Social life is usually restricted to a small circle of army families.
  B. On the other hand, there are certain advantages to life in the army.
    1. The military, with its wide range of occupations, gives one an opportunity to find the job he or she is best suited for.
    2. There are generous annual leaves with pay.
    3. Wide travel opportunities can introduce one to new places and people.
II. Financial considerations are also of major importance.
  A. Two disadvantages are apparent.
    1. Army pay is low compared to that in many civilian jobs.
    2. Officers are burdened with the cost of frequent entertaining.
  B. The advantages, however, are more striking.
    1. The army offers a high degree of job security.
      a. Promotions are slow but steady, with commissions open to men and women graduates.
      b. There is almost no danger of dismissal.
      c. Retirement benefits are good.
    2. An army career is an excellent preparation for success in civilian careers after retirement.

Each heading is a complete sentence, and only one sentence—not two or three. Each sentence is also in the form of a statement, not a question.

The chief advantage of a sentence outline is that the ideas will have to be clear and fully thought out before they can be stated in complete sentences. For that reason it is sometimes assigned for training in writing long formal reports such as the reference paper.

## Standard outline form

Numbering, indention, punctuation, and other physical aspects of outlines follow certain conventions, particularly when the outlines are to be read by someone other than the writer. When you are required to turn in an outline with your paper, use the type of outline your instructor specifies and put it in standard form.

## Numbering and indention

Make the numbering of your headings consistent throughout. This is the typical method for numbering and indenting a topic or sentence outline:

Thesis sentence: _____
_____ (Sentence statement)
I. _____ (Roman numeral for main head)
  A. _____ (Capital letter for subhead)
    1. _____ (Arabic numeral for second sub-
    2. _____ head)
      a. _____ (Lowercase letter for third sub-
      b. _____ head)
  B. _____
II. _____

The main heads (I, II, III . . .) are set flush with the left-hand margin. The subheads are indented four or five spaces in typed copy and about three quarters of an inch in longhand, or they may be indented so that they are directly under the first word of the preceding heading, as shown in this book.

When a heading runs over one line, the second line is indented as far as the first word of the preceding line:

I. The photoelectric cell, known as the "electric eye," has been put to a variety of practical uses.
  A. It is used in elevator floors to enable the elevator to stop at exactly the right level.

When you make an outline, avoid overelaborate and confusing systems. There is rarely any need to go farther than the third subhead (a, b, c . . .). Two levels of headings are often enough for a short paper.

## Punctuation and capitalization

In a topic outline, capitalize only the first letter of the word beginning the heading (and all proper nouns), and do not put any punctuation at the end of the entry, because these headings are not complete sentences.

I. Present need for physicists
  A. In private industry
  B. In government projects
  C. In colleges and universities

Punctuate every heading in a sentence outline just as you would punctuate the sentences in your paper: begin with a capital letter and end with a period or other end stop. Except for proper nouns, other words in the heading are not capitalized (a heading is not a title).

I. The advantages of specialization in college are numerous.
   A. Students can set goals for themselves.
   B. They can obtain more knowledge about their subjects.

Content of headings
Each heading in an outline should be specific and meaningful:

**Vague and useless**
The Profession I Want to Follow
  I. Introduction
 II. Why I prefer this work
III. What the opportunities would be
IV. The chances for success
 V. Conclusion

**Specific**
The Profession I Want to Follow
  I. Lifelong interest in veterinarian's work
    A. Grew up with animals on a farm
    B. Saw importance of veterinarian's work
    C. Worked with a veterinarian last two summers
 II. Many opportunities in veterinary work today
    A. In rural areas
    B. In cities
III. Worth-while and well-paid profession

Headings like "Introduction," "Body," and "Conclusion" aren't useful unless you indicate what material belongs in the sections. Instead of using general labels such as "Causes" and "Results," indicate what the causes or results are; it will save time later.

Putting headings in the form of questions or in statements that will have to be filled in later is not an efficient practice. The necessary information will have to be supplied when you write, so you might as well supply it in the planning stage.

**Indefinite**
I. The Wars of the Roses
  A. When they began
  B. Why?

**Definite**
I. The Wars of the Roses
  A. Started 1455
  B. Caused by rivalry between Houses of Lancaster and York

Dividing the material
Generally, if a heading is to be divided at all, it should be di-

vided into more than one part. When there is only one heading under a topic, it usually repeats what is in the topic and should therefore be included with it:

**Unnecessary division**
The Smithsonian Institution
I. Established by an Englishman
  A. James Smithson
    1. In 1846

**Accurate division**
The Smithsonian Institution
I. Established by James Smithson, an Englishman, in 1846

The main heads of an outline should represent equally important divisions of the subject as a whole.

**Unequal headings**
Growing Roses
  I. Preparing the soil
  II. Planting
  III. Growing the plant
  IV. Mildew
  V. Insect pests
  VI. Using a spray gun

**Equal headings**
Growing Roses
  I. Preparing the soil
  II. Planting
  III. Watering
  IV. Fertilizing
  V. Spraying

Similarly the subdivisions should designate equally important divisions of one phase of the main divisions:

**Unequal subheads**
I. Job opportunities in Wisconsin
  A. Raising crops
  B. White-collar work
  C. Dairy farms
  D. Factory jobs
  E. Breweries

**Equal subheads**
I. Job opportunities in Wisconsin
  A. Agriculture
  B. Business
  C. Industry

Headings of equal rank should not overlap: what is in *II* should exclude what is covered in *I; B* should be clearly distinct from *A.*

**Overlapping**
Ways of transporting freight
  I. Water
    A. Ships
    B. Freighters
  II. On the ground
    A. Trucks
    B. "Piggyback" in trucks
  III. Railroads
  IV. In the air

**Accurate**
Ways of transporting freight
  I. Ship
    A. Passenger ships
    B. Freighters
  II. Truck
  III. Railroad
    A. Loaded into cars
    B. "Piggyback" in trucks
  IV. Airplane

Discovering
and
organizing
what you
have to say
256

Making headings parallel

Headings in the same series are put in the same grammatical form. In a topic outline, if *I* is a noun, *II* and *III* are also nouns;

if *I* is a prepositional phrase, so are *II* and *III*. The same principle applies to subdivisions: when *A* under *I* is an adjective, *B* and *C* are also adjectives. A sentence outline should use complete sentences throughout and not lapse into topic headings. The following examples show how headings can be made parallel in form:

**Headings not parallel**
The Art of Putting
  I. The stance is fundamental
  II. The grip
III. Importance of the backswing
IV. Stroking the ball
  V. Follow through with care

**Parallel headings**
The Art of Putting
  I. The stance
  II. The grip
III. The backswing
IV. The contact with the ball
  V. The follow-through

## The outline in relation to the paper

The usefulness of an outline depends on the material in it. No matter how correct the form—in numbering, punctuation, and parallel structure—if the outline doesn't help in writing your paper, its main purpose has been defeated.

From the main divisions in a good outline you can estimate the number and the relative length of the paragraphs in your paper, although usually the paragraphs will not correspond exactly to the headings. You can frequently construct topic sentences for these paragraphs by rephrasing or expanding the headings. The divisions will show where transitions are needed within and between paragraphs and suggest the kind of development: contrast, comparison, additional illustration, summary, and so forth. (See §26.2, Patterns of paragraph development, and §19.2 Developing your material.)

An outline should be long enough to suit your purpose, and no longer. It should be no more complex than the material demands. The number of main headings for most papers ranges from three to five. A larger number of main heads for a thousand-word paper suggests that the division is haphazard or that the organization is faulty. The same principle applies to subheadings. Outlines that run from *A* through *J* or *K* need revision, for no single topic needs such minute subdivision. And except for very complex material, there is seldom any need to go beyond the third subhead.

When you are asked to submit an outline with your paper, it should represent the plan of the paper as it actually has been written, not as it *might* have been written. In other words, your outline serves as the table of contents. If you have found it necessary in writing the paper to depart from your original plan, make the corresponding changes in the final outline before handing it in.

## Applications: Material for Writing

**1.** Here is a list of general topics. Pick any *three* and make up an informal scratch outline for each, showing how you would turn a general topic into a topic specific enough for a 500-word theme.

*example: General topic:* Bias in news reporting
*Specific topic:* Do TV newsmen slant the news?
*Scratch outline:* 1. Many claim TV news misuses its power.
2. A former Vice President said, "controlled by Eastern liberals."
3. But many claim coverage is too conservative, based only on news conferences and press releases.
4. Problem: time is limited, can cover a few stories in depth or many superficially.
5. Bias may be in the eye of the beholder.

| | |
|---|---|
| Campus fashions | Population growth |
| College architecture | Study abroad |
| Prestige symbols | Student summer work |
| Modern heroes | Television standards |
| School discipline | Automobile safety standards |
| Academic freedom | Student power |
| Current music | Automation |
| Science fiction | Popular myths |

**2.** Every person is a storehouse of interesting ideas and experiences. Pretend that you are the only guest on a well-known 90-minute television talk show. Write out the questions the interviewer would ask (or that you would like to have asked!) about your life and opinions, and your answers to those questions. These answers could become the basis for many papers where the choice of subject is left up to you.

**3.** Each of the following topics has a thesis statement that can lead to an interesting paper, but some of the points listed don't have any bearing on the controlling idea and should be changed or eliminated. Arrange the ideas in groups that belong together, eliminating or changing them as necessary.

*Salmon Fishing:* Salmon fishing is a thrilling and inexpensive sport.
1) Requires skill
2) Prizes offered for biggest fish
3) Equipment need not be expensive

4) Boats can be rented cheaply
5) Salmon fight to the last breath
6) Columbia River and Puget Sound two of the best areas
7) Conservation efforts have paid off
8) Baked salmon is a delectable dish
9) How the Indians prepare salmon
10) No thrill equals that first strike

*Regulating Children's TV Habits:* Although some TV programs are undesirable, parents should not regulate what children watch.
1) There are some excellent educational programs
2) Developing good judgment depends on practice in choosing
3) TV often takes place of baby-sitter
4) Children want to watch what playmates watch
5) Some TV programs bad for immature minds
6) Children resent too much discipline
7) Outdoor exercise also important
8) Free play of curiosity develops intellect
9) Violence fascinates children
10) Overprotection in youth produces distorted ideas of reality

*Mexico and the United States:* Despite obvious differences, Mexico and the United States have much in common.
1) Both are in North America
2) Mexico has little industrial development
3) Populations are mixtures of many nationalities
4) Private enterprise basic to both
5) Mexico still not largely middle class, like U.S.
6) Poor transportation in much of Mexico
7) Both are republics with two-party systems
8) Mexico had great Indian civilization before Spanish conquest
9) Both provide extensive public welfare and free education
10) Great variety of natural resources in each

4. The following essay was written as an assignment for a freshman composition class. Write a critique of the essay with respect to the matters discussed in this section. Here are some questions to consider: Does it have a specific, manageable subject? Does the author seem to have a purpose in writing about it? What resources does the subject call for? Which has the author used? Would others have been better? What is the author's attitude? What is the approach to the audience? Is the manner of writing appropriate for the subject and the situation? Is it natural? How you consider these questions, and in what order, is another problem of planning for you.

### The Motion Picture Industry and Science Fiction

Science fiction has become stereotyped in the minds of the American public as juvenile and escapist literature through the greed of the Hollywood film industry.

Over the years, motion picture producers have flooded the coun-

Exer

Applications:
Material
for
Writing
259

try with a stream of "monster" and "space" movies. In so doing, they have created a distorted image of science fiction in the minds of most Americans, a conception of science fiction which causes the average person to assume that any book labeled as science fiction must be the story of a gigantic monster intent on destroying the world or that of a race of intelligent beings intent on destroying mankind.

The American public cannot be blamed for believing this to be a true picture of science fiction; for the great mass of evidence upon which they have had to base their judgment has been overwhelmingly of the trashy type. This is not to say that "monster" and "alien" movies must always be of this inferior type, but that they must remain so only so long as Hollywood can make two bad ones for the price of one good.

If we ignore the movies based, more or less, on the novels of Jules Verne and H. G. Wells because of their dated themes, we find that there have been very few films written by science fiction authors. I am personally familiar with only four such movies. "Voyage to the Bottom of the Sea," by Theodore Sturgeon was so unlike his usual style of writing as to cast doubt on his authorship. George Orwell's "1984" was terribly cut and rewritten for the screen. "Out of the Cold," by John Campbell, was retitled "The Thing" and was turned into an ordinary "monster" movie by Hollywood. Finally, Robert A. Heinlein's "Destination: Moon" was hailed by many people as the finest science fiction movie ever made.

The last of these four movies, "Destination: Moon," has been widely acclaimed, but it contained not a single monster or extraterrestrial creature and in addition won an Academy Award in one of the Academy's technical divisions. "Destination: Moon" should have shown Hollywood that science fiction movies could be more than just another "monster" movie. A glance at today's movie listings which contain an advertisement for "Ghidrah, the Three-Headed Dragon" will show that even concrete evidence cannot shake the Hollywood mentality.

Because of this unreasoning attitude, only the power of the dollar can ever force Hollywood to produce science fiction films that deal with man's destiny and the problems that will confront him in the years to come instead of its usual fare of monsters and aliens. This could only be brought about by action on the part of the general public, but because the public has been convinced it knows all about science fiction, this is impossible. Science fiction readers thus faced with an insoluble problem are reduced to a vague and uncertain hope that the future will bring a change for the better. The movie industry has prevailed, and science fiction must remain stereotyped.

5. Write a scratch outline on any one of the following topics that appeals to you, or choose your own. When you have jotted down all your notes, frame a thesis sentence and put the notes in the

Discovering
and
organizing
what you
have to say
260

form of a topic outline. Finally write the first and last paragraphs
of the paper.

Why People Watch Excavations      Speaking in Public
Should Physical Education         Unusual Place Names
   Be Required in College?         Forecasting Election Results
Income Is Not the Primary         I Prefer Bach
   Goal of Education              Our Local Parking Problem

6. Check the following outlines from the standpoint of effective and
useful planning. Then state specifically what you consider to be
the unsatisfactory aspects of each one, in form and content. Revise the outlines accordingly.

**a.** Types of American schools
   I. Schools open to everyone
      A. Elementary schools
      B. There are many colleges and universities
      C. Secondary or high
      D. Providing technical instruction
      E. Private schools

**b.** Why everyone should be able to swim.
   I. Everyone should learn to swim.
      A. As early as possible.
         1. Children have been taught as young as three years
   II. The ability to swim may save your life.
      1. never swim alone
      2. don't show off in the water
      3. Many schools require students to pass swimming tests.
         a. my experiences
         b. Red Cross lifesaving test.

**c.** Increasing automation in industry presents many problems.
   I. Unemployment
      A. Permanent layoffs
      B. Shorter working hours
      C. Decreases job opportunities
   II. What is automation?
      A. Definition
      B. Uses
         1. Where it cannot be used
      C. There are many advantages to automation
   III. Increased leisure time
      A. Recreation
         1. Hobbies
         2. Traveling
         3. Adult education classes
   IV. New skills are required.
      A. Trained technicians
      B. The unskilled workers are laid off.
         1. Providing government benefits
         2. Providing added training
   V. Is automation here to stay?

# Writing the first draft

*. . . The great thing is to last and get your work done and see and hear and learn and understand; and write when there is something that you know; and not before; and not too damned much after. Let those who want to save the world if you can get to see it clear and as a whole. Then any part you make will represent the whole if it's made truly. The thing to do is work and learn to make it.* — Ernest Hemingway, Death in the Afternoon

**Draft**

**19**

When you are reasonably well satisfied with your preparations and your plans for organizing your material, it's time to begin the actual writing. You probably shouldn't expect to be *completely* satisfied with your preparation and planning. Even with long and careful preliminary work, you won't always have a good sense of all that you are going to say until you do the writing itself. Sometimes, when you have studied a subject and thought it out, you'll be able to lay out a plan for a piece of writing that has in it everything you wish to say in the order you wish to say it, and your own attitude toward your subject matter will already be clear. If that happens, the actual writing may be easier than usual: you may have little to do but complete your outline or plan by adding illustrations and transitions. Often, however, even when you have thought your subject through and have a good, thorough, workable plan, you still won't have a good sense of all that's to be said — you still won't know exactly which illustrative material you may need to use to fill out parts of your plan, and your own attitudes toward the material may not be clear until you have found the words for them. It has often been remarked that we do not always know what we think until we hear what we say. Thinking and planning are not always over when you've developed a plan for your writing.

For this reason, when you are composing papers outside the classroom, it is usually best to write them out in rough draft first. Revising and copying can come later. No matter how certain you are about the material and the order of presentation, a complete first draft is important if the final paper is to represent your best work.

Up to this point you have been dealing with ideas in abbreviated or shorthand forms as notes or outline headings, though you may have written bits and pieces in complete form. Now you are ready to put it all down in full sentences and paragraphs, to see the whole paper as your reader will, and to make whatever changes may be necessary for continuity and effectiveness.

## Getting started 19.1

Begin writing the first draft as soon as you have decided on the content and organization of the paper. Don't wait for "inspiration" or the proper mood—write while the ideas and information are still in your mind; an outline that you put away for three hours or three days can look cold and unfamiliar if your mind isn't still turning in the same way. For almost everyone writing is work, and you must often begin writing when you would much prefer to do something else. If you wait until the last minute, your first draft may have to serve as your final paper, and the cracks and loose screws in it will show.

The beginning of a paper is often the most difficult part to word effectively. If you can't think of a good opening sentence, begin with some other part; if the wording of a good first paragraph doesn't come to you at once, start with a part that comes more easily. You shouldn't waste time trying to get an ideal opening; as you work, a good start will often occur to you. Many beginnings are written last. (See §19.4, Opening paragraphs.)

Once you have broken the ice by writing two or three sentences, you'll often find it easier to go on, even without that elusive "inspiration." Writing, like many other activities, calls for a warm-up, and you may have to do a few laps and some wind sprints before you're ready to go.

As a rule, write the first draft as rapidly as you can. Your paper will have more life if you put your ideas down one after the other without pausing to worry about correctness. At this stage you should concentrate on getting down the gist of what you have in mind. You are the only one who will see your first draft, and matters of spelling, punctuation, and wording can be taken care of in revision. (See §20.1, Revising the first draft.)

Plan to spend at least an hour at uninterrupted writing. When you are working on a paper that is too long to be written in one sitting, stop in the middle of a paragraph or a passage that is going easily and well, perhaps even in the middle of a sentence. This ordinarily makes it much easier to get started again when you come back to your work. Take time to read over what you have already written before you begin writing again.

Leave plenty of space in the first draft for making corrections and changes. There should be ample margins on both sides of the page and space between lines for insertions and corrections.

## Developing your material    **19.2**

Make the first draft as complete as possible. Write down more than you will probably use in your final paper; be generous with explanations and illustrative examples. It is much easier to cut out material in revision than it is to look for more to satisfy the requirements of length or completeness of presentation. Papers that are heavy with material added at the last moment always seem disjointed. Those that have been pruned down from, say, fourteen hundred to a thousand words are likely to be more compact and to the point.

Put in any good ideas that occur to you when you are writing the first draft, even though they may not have appeared in the original plan. In this stage an outline does not need to be followed down to the last minor subdivision. Frequently a sentence written on paper will bring to mind an aspect of the topic that you overlooked when your material was in the form of notes. If the new idea turns out to be irrelevant, it can be omitted in revision; but if it is important, you can alter your outline to include it.

### Kinds of development

As the full paper grows from the organization plan you have decided on, it should follow the form of development that best suits the subject and that will be clearest to the reader. If you have made an unusually complete plan for your paper, the plan itself may tell you how to develop and amplify each part. Often, however, an outline or some other kind of plan will tell you what is to be in each part of your paper, not what to do with it, or how to write it out. The patterns of development discussed in the section on paragraphs (§26.2) may be useful to you in developing whole papers, though adequate development of a whole paper may require a combination of different kinds of paragraphs. Which kind predominates is determined by the needs of the paper. These are some of the most commonly used types of order:

1) **Time:** describing events in the order of their occurrence. This is appropriate in narrative writing (the story of a hike, a report of an athletic contest, an account of an incident in history) or in describing a process (the construction of a log cabin, the application of stage make-up, stages in the development of a frog).

2) **Space:** describing objects as they exist within a certain area, often used in expository writing (a description of a city from outskirts to center, of a ship from bow to stern, of a mural from left to right).

3) **Increasing complexity:** beginning with the simple or familiar and proceeding to the more complex or unfamiliar (discussing wind instruments beginning with the toy whistle, continuing to simple flutes, and ending with orchestral instruments like the oboe and bassoon).

4) **Comparison and contrast:** discussing all the features of one idea or situation, then all the features of another, and ending by drawing a conclusion about the two ("Television and Newspapers As Sources of News," "Popular Heroes of Two Generations," "Public Schools and Private Schools"). If such a plan seems to make the paper break in the middle, present a sequence of comparisons and contrasts on each major point — not all the features of public schools and then of private schools, but some order like this: 1. Cost of attendance, 2. Curriculum, 3. Facilities.

5) **Support:** beginning with a general statement or impression and then supporting it with specific examples, details, reasons. This method is useful for such topics as "The Value of Studying Foreign Langages," "The Problems of Increasing Automation," "Freshman Composition Courses Should Be Abolished."

6) **Climax:** beginning with a specific fact or situation and unfolding the subject until it stands completed at the end. A

paper about the development of the polio vaccine might begin with the need for the vaccine, then take up the problems facing researchers, go on to explain how solutions were found, and end with the production of an effective vaccine.

7) **Cause to effect or effect to cause:** beginning with an analysis of causes, culminating in a statement of effect, or stating the effect first, then moving to the analysis of cause. The subject should determine which pattern is better: if you are writing about your city's traffic mess, for example, you might want to describe that problem briefly at the beginning as an effect already known, then proceed to an analysis of the causes, which are probably less well known.

The working outline should represent the kind of development most appropriate to your subject. For example, the topic outline for the paper on the army as a career (p. 252), with its grouping of advantages and disadvantages, lent itself naturally to the comparison-and-contrast method. Often two kinds of development are used in combination: a narrative could follow both the order of time and that of climax; the method of support might be used effectively with comparison or climax. The essential thing is that you present your material in some sensible order.

## Using sentences to control direction

One way to get into your draft and develop your meaning—especially if you are having trouble starting your paper or a particular section of it—is to use a sentence to direct the development. In your opening, for example, you can use your thesis sentence to forecast the development of your theme as a whole. (See §18.3.) And in the body of your paper, you can similarly work with sentences to direct the development of each section.

Suppose that you have developed this topic outline as the basis for a paper:

The Profession I Want to Follow

Thesis sentence: I want to become a veterinarian because of my lifelong interest in veterinary work, because of the many opportunities it offers, and because it is a worthwhile and well-paid profession.

I. Lifelong interest in veterinarian's work
  A. Grew up with animals on a farm
  B. Saw importance of veterinarian's work
  C. Worked with a veterinarian last two summers

II. Many opportunities in veterinary work today
   A. In rural areas
   B. In urban areas
III. Worthwhile and well-paid profession

The thesis sentence is a guide, directing the development of the outline and the theme. It could be used, for example, to forecast a climactic development that places increasing stress on the series of three factors.

The separate sections of the theme could also be directed by opening sentences. For example, we can assume that Section I will require at least three paragraphs. To control the relationships among them, the writer could introduce the section like this:

Although I grew up with animals on a farm and saw the importance of the veterinarian's work, I didn't really understand all that a veterinarian does until I worked with one the last two summers.

This sentence, which might be used to open the first paragraph of the first section or might be used alone as an introduction, shows how the ideas in Section I are related and gives the writer a direction: there is a time sequence which suggests that the three paragraphs might be narrative; the last paragraph should probably get the dominant stress.

The first section closes with the idea that the writer is aware of the value of the veterinary profession. Section II, then, might open with a sentence like this:

The needs for veterinary work are great in the country and surprisingly varied in the city.

This sentence, which makes the rural and urban needs coordinate, could forecast a balanced treatment by the method of comparison. The section would probably be developed in two paragraphs. Section III might then be directed in this way:

Because the needs for veterinary medicine are great, the work is worthwhile; because the work is needed, the pay is good.

This balanced introductory sentence could lead the writer into a balanced, judicious paragraph stating an effect—the causes having been analyzed in Sections I and II.

## Using paragraphs to control direction

Sometimes a writer can also use particular patterns of paragraph development (§26.2) to determine a means of expanding the material. For example, given the thesis sentence and outline just discussed, it might be helpful to think of the three paragraphs of Section I as statements of cause. All three paragraphs could then be developed by illustration, one of the methods for explaining cause. The same thing could be done with Section II. There would then be five illustrative paragraphs stating causes; the paper could then culminate in a final paragraph stating the effect. By planning a theme in this way, a writer can know beforehand what should be accomplished in each paragraph.

Using paragraph patterns can be especially helpful in writing short themes. Suppose you arrive in your composition class some Monday morning to find an assignment on the blackboard for an in-class theme. One of the suggested subjects invites your response to the idea of an honor system. If you are familiar with the patterns of paragraph development, you might be able very quickly to settle on a design, a means of developing your paper. Not everyone has participated in an honor system; not everyone knows what it is. You might therefore decide that the purpose of your paper would be to explain what an honor system is. Knowing the pattern of definition, you could develop your explanation like this:

**Paragraph 1:** entirely **illustration,** describing an honor system in action

**Paragraph 2: comparison** of honor system with similar things, such as codes of behavior in clubs

**Paragraph 3: contrast,** an account of how honor system is unlike other codes

The sequence of three paragraphs forms a definition: the first by illustration identifies the *term;* the second by comparison puts the term in a *class;* the third by contrast shows how it *differs* from other members of the same class. With this three-paragraph definition, you might then be able to write a fourth, concluding paragraph of evaluation.

## Relating paragraphs in sequence  **19.3**

As you write your first draft, remember that you are going to have to take a reader with you. Your individual paragraphs should represent a progressive development of the subject. If there is too wide a gap in ideas between the end of one paragraph and the beginning of the next, the reader may not be able to follow your line of thought.

## Showing the connection between paragraphs

Link paragraphs together by connecting the topic of a new paragraph with the topic of the preceding one. This is not as hard as it may sound; usually it's easy—and natural—to phrase the opening statement of a paragraph so that it grows out of what you have just said. This method of gaining continuity is illustrated in the following sentences from the first six paragraphs of an essay that explores some current problems of communication (linking words are in heavy type and explanatory notes are in brackets):

| | |
|---|---|
| . . . This is less a matter of vocabulary range than of vocabulary control. It has to do with the entire **process** by which an individual organizes his thoughts for purposes of transmission. | Last two sentences of paragraph 1 |
| The prime element in **this process** is sequence. . . . | Opening of paragraph 2 |
| . . . But it does rule out ungoverned circling and droning, reminiscent of buzzards hovering and swooping over a victim until he drops. | Last sentence of paragraph 2 |
| It contributes nothing to a conversation to have an individual interrupt himself in order to insert sudden thoughts. [Here the author begins to illustrate what he means above by "circling and droning."] | Opening of paragraph 3 |
| The abuse is compounded when these obtrusive thoughts are invaded by yet others so that nothing is complete, neither the sentence, nor the paragraph, nor any of the vagrant incidents or ideas that are strewn around like fragments of an automobile wreck. | Last sentence of paragraph 3 |
| The following quotation is a **fair approximation** drawn from a recent conversation. . . . [There are no specific linking words, but | Opening of paragraph 4 |

"fair approximation" introduces a quotation that will illustrate how "nothing is complete" in the "circling and droning."]

" . . . you know, nothing in any of the newspapers can tell us what it is like, especially if you want to know what the real facts were. . . ." — Close of quotation ending paragraph 4

He was at least two hundred words and three minutes beyond his topic sentence, and I had yet to hear the title of the book. **The passage quoted** is not a parody. [Refers to the quotation in the preceding paragraph] — Opening of paragraph 5

. . . Oral communication in our society comes close to being a complete bust. — Close of paragraph 5

Let me be a little crotchety at **this point**. . . . [Refers to tentative conclusion that ends the preceding paragraph] — Opening of paragraph 6

Norman Cousins, "Are You Making Yourself Clear?"

As this example shows, paragraphs can be connected by a variety of methods and transitional devices: paragraph 2 repeats a key word, *process;* paragraph 3 amplifies a point made at the end of paragraph 2; paragraph 4 illustrates the point made in paragraph 3; paragraph 5 refers to the illustration in paragraph 4, with *The passage quoted;* paragraph 6, with *this point,* refers to a conclusion drawn in paragraph 5. (These same methods can be used to link sentences within a paragraph; see §26.3.)

### Showing the relation to the topic of the paper
Whenever possible, show the relation between the paragraph and the topic or thesis of the paper. This is a good way to keep your paragraphs going in the same direction. For example, in this discussion of the games played by primitive peoples, the author begins each paragraph by introducing a different kind of sport:

Wrestling is probably universal. . . . — Paragraph 1
(four sentences follow)

| Races are far more common. . . . | Paragraph 2 (three sentences follow) |
| Ball games are also widespread, but vary greatly in type. . . . | Paragraph 3 (six sentences follow) |
| Frequently the ball games are played in a more elaborate way. . . . | Paragraph 4 (fourteen sentences follow) |
| In the Plains and Southwest of our country the "hoop and pole" game enjoyed great popularity. . . . | Paragraph 5 (six sentences follow) |
| Compared with such sports rope-skipping seems simple, but the Australian Euahlayi make an art of it. . . . | Paragraph 6 (two sentences follow) |
| Polynesians lead in aquatic sports. . . . | Paragraph 7 (four sentences follow) |
| Maori stilt-walkers raced one another across streams, and also tried to upset one another's balance. . . . —Robert H. Lowie, *An Introduction to Cultural Anthropology* | Paragraph 8 (two sentences follow) |

## Transition paragraphs

For major transitions, such as from one main section of a long paper to another, a brief self-contained paragraph will often serve to prepare the reader for what is coming next. This is a typical transition paragraph:

No such startling change in the habits of a people could have taken place without far-reaching social effects. Let us glance at a few of them. — Frederick Lewis Allen, *The Big Change*

Ordinarily the subject matter of successive paragraphs is so closely related that separate transition paragraphs are not needed, and in short papers they are usually out of place.

## Opening paragraphs                                           **19.4**

The first paragraph of a paper has two functions: to introduce the subject and to arouse the reader's interest. Plan your paper so that you can get into your subject as quickly as possible. Don't begin too far back: if your topic is the assassination of Lincoln, there is no need to start with an account of

Lincoln's early career or even of his presidency. The shorter the paper, the more direct your beginning should be.

If, after finishing your first draft, you find that you have written an obviously weak beginning, see if the second or third sentence, or even the second paragraph, may not provide a better starting point. Often the first few lines of writing are simply a warm-up for the writer, and the paper actually begins a few sentences later.

### Effective openings

No matter what you are writing about, the beginning of your paper should catch the reader's interest and get him into the subject. Some of the ways to accomplish this are discussed below:

### A statement of purpose or point of view

This should not be a mechanical statement ("In this paper I am going to give you my reasons for majoring in political science.") or a flat rewording of the assignment, but a natural lead into the topic:

When I decided to enter the university, like most freshmen I had only the vaguest notion of what subject I intended to major in. But now after two quarters of haphazardly chosen course work, and after a good deal of self-analysis, I have decided that **there are at least four good reasons why I should major in political science.**

If your purpose is to discuss one aspect of some general topic, the first paragraph can make the limits of your paper clear:

The Great Lakes are one of the major lake systems of the world. Through the centuries many large cities have grown up along their perimeter as people recognized their value for inland navigation, water supply, and recreation. Pollution of their waters by industrial wastes has also inevitably increased through the years, until now it presents a serious threat. **The pollution problems in Chicago are typical of those of the Great Lakes area as a whole.**

### A definition

If your paper deals with some subject which has a variety of meanings for different readers, it is good to make your definition clear at the outset. There is no need to start with a flat and stereotyped statement like "According to Webster, a hobby is 'an engrossing topic, occupation, or plan, etc., to which one habitually returns.'" Give a definition that fits your own approach to the subject:

A hobby, as I see it, is an activity that takes up most of your spare time and all of your spare money. At least that has been my experience since I became interested in photography. . . .

## An important fact

One of the quickest and clearest ways to open a paper is with the statement of an important fact that will lead to the general topic. This is a natural opening for a narrative and can also be good for a discussion of ideas:

There have been two downright attempts by government to curb freedom of the press in America since Plymouth Rock. The first took place when John Peter Zenger, a New York publisher, was jailed in 1735 for criticizing the British colonial governor, but through a brilliant defense by Andrew Hamilton, a salty old Philadelphia lawyer, was acquitted. In the second instance, 63 years later under our own young Constitution, the accused was less fortunate.—Alvin Harlow, "Martyr for a Free Press," *American Heritage*

Publishers estimate that there are approximately 800 books-only bookstores in the entire United States. This is the rough equivalent of the number of bookstores in the city of London alone.—Marya Mannes, "Empty Bookstores Equal Empty Minds," *Fort Worth Star Telegram*

## A reference to personal experience

If your subject is one with which you have had some personal experience, a reference to your connection with it provides an appropriate beginning. In an essay on the complex problems of leading a university, for example, the author, a university president, begins in this way:

Before Clark Kerr went through the revolving presidential door at Berkeley, he defined the modern multiversity president's job. It was, he said, to provide "sex for the students, football for the alumni, and parking for the faculty." Eight years later, after my own maiden year as president of the University of Cincinnati—whose 36,104 students make it the largest urban multiversity in the country after New York City's—I can report: The parking problem is worse. College football is being energetically chased by man-eating tigers (in our case the Bengals). Sex is so taken for granted as to rate no priority.—Warren Bennis, "The University Leader," *The Saturday Review*

## A lively detail or illustration

A good way to arouse the reader's interest and curiosity is to begin with a lively detail—perhaps with an anecdote, an apt quotation, or an allusion to some current topic. Such material should of course be related to the subject of the paper, as is this beginning of an article on the conservation of natural resources:

There may be more truth than humor in the cartoon of two cave men wearily dragging the carcass of a saber-toothed tiger to the mouth of the home cave, surrounded by a number of drooling cave babies. One provider is saying to the other, "They get further and further away each year, and scarcer and scarcer." Certainly the impact of man upon nature has been recognized from earliest times.—Samuel Ordway, Jr., "Plunder or Plenty?" *The Saturday Review*

## Openings to avoid

The opening paragraph should mark the actual beginning of the paper and be clearly related to the subject. If it does not create interest in the subject or get it under way, it probably does not belong in the paper. These common mistakes make poor beginnings:

### Beginning too far back

If you are discussing the organization of the United Nations, there is no need to begin with the reasons for the failure of the League of Nations, nor is there any reason to begin a paper on Nixon as President with an account of his legislative career. The shorter your paper, the more direct should be your beginning. A statement of your purpose or a rewording of your central idea is the simplest way to begin a paper written in class.

### An apology or a complaint

A statement such as this is discouraging to most readers: "Being a mere freshman, I'm afraid that what I have to say on this topic won't be of much value. . . ." Complaints are also better left unwritten: "Before I started to write this theme, I thought I could find some interesting material on it in the library, but there wasn't any. . . ." Remember that readers are interested only in the ideas that you present, not in the difficulties or disappointments you may have had while writing the paper.

### Too broad a generalization

"Science in the last fifty years has made more progress than any other branch of knowledge" is a generalization far too sweeping to explain or prove in a five-hundred-word or even a five-thousand-word paper. Statements such as this are likely to be more impressive to the writer than they are to the reader. Wherever possible, begin with a specific statement: "Though smaller than your thumb, an electronic device called the transistor has had a tremendous effect on radio and television sets."

### A self-evident statement

Avoid starting a paper with a remark so obvious that it need not be mentioned: "America has a great number of resorts and parks situated in many scenic localities." And resist the temptation—it's good exercise, anyway, once in a while—to open your paper with some commonplace observation that gives no hint of your subject: "It has been said that the only thing constant in life is change." If you have started your paper with a self-evident remark, see if the sentence immediately following is a good beginning for your paper. There is a place in writing for such self-evident remarks as that shown above: you may sometimes find them, for example, as openings for works that are leisurely and meditative, where the authors wish to move slowly from familiar ground to new territory.

## Closing paragraphs 19.5

The beginning and ending of your paper—the point at which you meet your readers and the place at which you leave them—should be among the most interesting and forceful parts of your paper. Make the ending definite and emphatic, if possible—unless, of course, you are writing a paper that specifically calls for another tone, reverie, whimsy, or whatever. Otherwise, plan your paper so that it won't trail off or leave your reader up in the air. The final paragraph should round out your discussion in such a way that the reader will know you have said all you intended to say and that you have not stopped because you were tired of writing or because time ran out. Remember that the total effect of your paper may depend largely upon the way you end it.

### Effective conclusions

Your final paragraph should tie together the ideas you have been developing and emphasize the main point of the paper. Some suggestions for effective conclusions follow:

### A climax

Make your final paragraph the culmination of the ideas you have been developing, or save the most important idea for the last. The concluding paragraph thus becomes the climax of the paper. A student paper of about a thousand words, which has described in detail the operation of a large used-car lot, brings all the details to a focus in this conclusion:

> This used-car lot was sponsored by an organization which sells over a million cars a year, so it was by no means a fly-by-night affair. Although no sloppy repairs were done, and no highly crooked deals were tolerated, there was just a slight suspicion that the company was getting the best of every customer on every deal. This company, however good or bad, is representative of many similar organizations in the United States.

### A suggestion for action

**Draft**

**19.5**

If you have been criticizing some situation (parking on the campus, the price of textbooks, daylight saving time), end your paper with a positive suggestion for action. Make the statement definite, as in this ending of an article about gambling laws:

> The underworld is thriving on our hypocrisy and stupidity. So long as we persist in our efforts to end gambling by prohibitory legislation, we promote police corruption. Police honesty can never be a relative matter. Police corruption erodes the average citizen's respect for the law and makes him cynical about all law enforcement. We cannot continue to tolerate a partnership that invites corruption. And, yes, we owe it to the judiciary to end the existing judicial farce.—John Murtagh, "Gambling and Police Corruption," *The Atlantic Monthly*

### A summary statement

Longer and more formal papers are sometimes concluded by restating the main points of the discussion. This final paragraph, for example, sums up the author's assessment of the problems caused by fires in urban areas:

> Fire as a wasteful, destructive force in human affairs presents a host of problems. They include financing the fire departments, promulgating codes and standards, training firemen, devising strategy and tactics for fire fighting, providing insurance and obtaining the technical and scientific facts that underlie many of the decisions that must be made. Since fire strikes without warning, the fireman and the fire-protection engineer must do the best they can with the knowledge available at the moment. It will take many specialists in many fields, working many years, to provide all the knowledge and data required to make the urban environment fire-safe.—Howard W. Emmons, "Fire and Fire Protection," *Scientific American*

But for most papers written in composition courses, it is seldom necessary or advisable to summarize what has been said. The result is often a weak and mechanical ending.

Tying in the ending with the beginning

The final paragraph may repeat, in different wording, the opening idea. This method is particularly useful for longer papers, both to remind the reader what the main subject is and to give it final emphasis. Or it may return to some figure of speech or point of view used to introduce the subject. For example, an article surveying changes in education begins and ends with the same analogy:

Anyone who attempts to survey the effects of five years of change on American public education must feel great kinship with the photographer who attempts a snapshot of a moving subject, because the changes are unceasing. My survey was predictably outdated before its results could be received, tabulated, and published. . . .

With all the shortcomings of the box-camera approach, one must still draw the conclusion that, if another type of photograph were possible — an aerial shot of the entire American public school system — it would show perceptible and generally consistent activity everywhere, a scurrying directed toward augmenting the "product" of public schools in quantity. and especially in quality. — Richard Kleeman, "Five Years of Change," *The Saturday Review*

Draft

19.5

Endings to avoid

Avoid unemphatic, inconclusive, or contradictory endings. Here are some typical pitfalls to avoid in your closing paragraphs:

An apology

Ending a paper with an apology for its shortcomings only serves to emphasize them:

I am sorry this paper is so short, but I always have a difficult time putting my ideas on paper.

If you carefully work out your ideas before writing and then present them as effectively as you can, you will not need to apologize for your efforts.

A qualifying remark

If the last sentence of a paper is an exception or a qualifying remark, it weakens everything that has been said before:

Although I haven't answered why some people refuse to face facts, I have come to the conclusion that not facing facts may be a natural part of human nature. Of course this can be carried to extremes.

There may be two sides to every subject, but when the purpose or scope of your paper is limited to the arguments for one side only, don't suddenly shift to the other side in your conclusion. If, for example, you have been presenting every argument you can think of in favor of price controls or strict ecological legislation, don't end like this: "Of course, there is much to be said for the other side also." If you feel such a qualifying statement is necessary, make it earlier in the paper.

Minor details or afterthoughts

A paper describing the role of the pitcher in baseball shouldn't end with a remark about other aspects of the game:

Baseball is one of America's favorite sports, and to spend an afternoon at Sox Park or Wrigley Field watching two great pitchers battling for a victory is an exciting experience. What I have said about pitching gives you an idea what a pitcher must keep in his mind while out there on the mound, or as a substitute on the bench. **There are eight other players on the team besides the pitcher and the same can be written about each individual player and his position.**

Some concluding statements make a reader wonder whether the writer actually finished his paper or abandoned it in the middle of an idea:

I could go on and on for pages and pages describing the other interesting people I met on the ship, but the length of this paper doesn't permit it.

Instead of putting a sentence such as this at the end of your paper, round out the description fully, or if the topic is already developed sufficiently, see if the next to the last sentence wouldn't make a respectable conclusion.

## Framing a title    19.6

Word the title of your paper so that it gives a definite and accurate idea of the subject matter in as few words as possible. A title need not mystify or startle the readers, although it may perhaps arouse their curiosity or appeal to their sense of humor. Interesting titles are always appreciated, but one that is brief, simple, and exact will serve the purpose.

A title should not suggest more than the paper actually covers. If you are discussing your tastes in music, avoid such sweeping titles as "Modern Jazz" or "Music of Today"; use instead "Music I Like" or "Why I Prefer Paul Simon." A report on the experiences of a baby-sitter scarcely deserves the title "Child Psychology" or "The Care of Infants"; "Experiences of a Baby-Sitter" will be good enough if you cannot think of a better title.

Unnecessarily long titles are not satisfactory, especially those that merely repeat the assignment: "An Experience in Childhood That Left a Lasting Impression on Me." The thesis sentence of your paper is not intended to serve as a title. Instead of writing "Reading Taught by Sound Should Replace Sight Reading," name the subject: "Reading by Sound."

The title is not part of the paper, and it should not be referred to by a pronoun in the first sentence. If you want to mention the title in your opening, rephrase it slightly.

| **Unsatisfactory** | **Satisfactory** |
| --- | --- |
| Becoming a Citizen | Becoming a Citizen |
| This is not a difficult process in the United States. . . . | It is not difficult for an immigrant to become a citizen of the United States. . . . |

**Applications: Developing and Writing Your Paper**

1. Finding the most appropriate pattern of development for your topic will make your paper more effective. This chapter suggests that there are at least seven different ways in which a paper or portion of a paper may be developed (*time, comparison and contrast,* etc., p. 265). Below is a series of topics; each has a suggested pattern of development listed after it. Write out five sentences to show how you would develop each topic according to that pattern.

   *example: topic:* New artists change our musical tastes. *pattern:* time
   1. In the mid-1950's, Elvis Presley changed the direction of pop music with "Blue Suede Shoes" and other hits.
   2. By the early 1960's, folk musicians like Bob Dylan and the Kingston Trio brought different sounds to the attention of the nation.
   3. The Beatles took the spotlight in the later '60's, and spawned an entirely "new" sound, which many other groups imitated.
   4. The early 1970's found a new and "slicked-up" country sound which brought country music onto the popular music charts in a big way.
   5. Many singers and groups have come and gone in the past twenty years, but it is interesting that artists like Presley and Dylan have not only been able to change with the times, but they have also helped shape and change our musical tastes.

   a. *topic:* Building a new shopping center downtown. *pattern:* space
   b. *topic:* Opinion is divided on the harmfulness of marijuana. *pattern:* comparison and contrast
   c. *topic:* The discovery that the world is round changed both science and everyday life. *pattern:* cause to effect

2. A good beginning to a paper at the very least tells the readers what they are going to read. The best beginnings do that and also

**Draft**

**19.6**

Applications:
Developing
and
Writing
Your Paper
**279**

arrest the readers' attention. Revise the following openings so they are at least good—but try to make them great.

*example:* In your modern world of today, personal hygiene has become very important for success in the modern complex world of business.

*good:* These days, if you want to get ahead, it probably helps to look good and smell good.

*great:* Each year, Americans spend billions on creams, deodorants, after-shaves, soaps, and other products designed to make them look and smell good. It is a sad reality that one's success in the world is probably determined as much by grooming as it is by talent.

**a.** There are many topics of importance in the news these days. One of the many important topics is how we are going to control inflation.

**b.** I have always liked certain kinds of hobbies. One of the most interesting hobbies I enjoy writing about is training pigs, which is a very interesting hobby.

**c.** The abolishment of capital punishment and the reasons why I favor it is the subject of this paper.

**d.** The morning was dark and gray. A fog enshrouded the dormitory, and reflected my mood as I approached the delicate topic of required physical education.

**e.** "There are two sides to every question," says the proverb. This is not so in the case of the controversy over whether or not to register handguns. Only one opinion can be substantiated with facts. According to my dictionary, a handgun is a "gun which can be held in one hand easily, usually a pistol."

**3.** It is always easier to "stand off" like the Monday morning quarterback and see how someone else's writing can be improved than to actually do a better job. Criticizing and revising are important skills to sharpen, however, especially when they concern your own writing. Below are five sample beginnings and endings from student papers. For each one, write two or three sentences criticizing the writing. (Point out effective writing, too.) Then, pick two from the five and rewrite them yourself.

*example: Beginning paragraph from a paper called "Good Neighbors or Bad"*
   Since I myself have never been outside of the United States, it may be foolish of me to think I can make any useful suggestions about our Latin American policy. However, I have read about recent events in the Caribbean and South America with great interest, and, if you will bear with me, I would like to comment at some length on our present policy.

*critique:* (1) Writer doesn't really complete his thesis statement until the last two words of the paragraph. (2) Writer needlessly emphasizes his own weaknesses, which turns off the reader.

*rewrite:* Recent events in the Caribbean and South America have stirred up a great deal of interest in the press about our neighbors to the south. It seems to me that we should take this opportunity to reexamine our country's role in these events, and perhaps our entire Latin American policy in general.

**a.** *Beginning paragraph from a paper called "The Utility of Cats"*
When the California Gold Rush was at its height, grain supplies were so devastated by rats that prospectors eagerly paid $100 and up for cats. One enterprising merchant is said to have made a fortune by bringing a shipload of stray cats from New York to San Francisco via Cape Horn. Although the cat has not always been so highly prized, its usefulness to man has been recognized since the days of the Pharaohs. Its continuing popularity in the United States is certainly due to its utilitarian as well as to its decorative qualities.

**b.** *Beginning paragraph from a paper called "Modern Chicken Farming"*
The world today is not what it was fifty years ago. Just think of all the amazing technological changes that have taken place. The automobile has replaced the horse and buggy; radio and television have revolutionized communications; modern medicine has conquered disease. And in 1945 the atomic age was born. Chicken farming, too, has changed drastically from what it was in 1920. I would like to describe some of those changes in the pages that follow.

**c.** *Closing paragraph from a paper called "What a Liberal Education Means to Me"*
But the greatest value of a liberal education is a personal one; it goes beyond politics and economics. Besides helping the individual to live in his world, it helps him to live with himself. Liberal studies stimulate a love of reason and a flexible, inquiring attitude toward the great questions of mankind. They keep the mind strong and alert and stimulate a well-rounded intellectual development which is as essential to a full life as physical development. A liberal education, in the deepest sense, is an education for life.

**d.** *Closing paragraph from a paper called "The Population Explosion"*
All the statistics indicate that the future is bleak for the human race if the population explosion is not checked. Food, water, and other essential resources are even now inadequate. Living space is dwindling fast. Of course the picture may not be as dark as it looks. Maybe science will find a solution before long, or maybe the explosion will just taper off.

**e.** *Closing paragraph from a paper called "Population Pressures"*
An architect recently suggested that cities could be built in the sea to house the extra millions. They would consist of concrete buildings like silos attached to pontoon islands, and could extend as far below the water as they do above. People who lived on the lower levels could then watch the fascinating underwater world through their living-room windows! Man has never even begun to exploit the sea and knows very little of its hidden wonders.

*Do not be afraid to seize whatever you have written and cut it to rib-
bons; it can always be restored to its original condition in the morning, if that course seems best. Remember, it is no sign of weakness or
defeat that your manuscript ends up in need of major surgery. This is
a common occurence in all writing, and among the best writers.—E. B.
White,* The Elements of Style

**Rev**

**20.1**

When you have finished the first draft of a paper, put it aside
for a while before revising it. Most people find it difficult to
look at their own writing carefully while the ideas they have
tried to express are still running about in their minds. For this
reason, the first draft should be written as early as possible,
so that you can wait a day or two (or at least several hours)
before examining it. If the assignment gives you time to write
a draft and put it aside for a *week or two,* you may be aston-
ished to discover how perceptive a critic you are when you
return to it for revision. The purpose of revision is to check
major as well as minor matters: to tighten and improve the
organization, the content, and the expression, as well as to
correct the mechanics of your writing.

## Revising the first draft     **20.1**

You may save time and improve the quality of your writing by
going over the first draft systematically looking for specific
flaws. A hit-or-miss approach to revision is likely to be a
waste of time, since you may catch only the most glaring
faults.

Your papers will usually be evaluated on the basis of the following points. Keep them in mind when you revise:

1) **Content:** the ideas, facts, examples used to support the
central point of your discussion
2) **Organization:** the pattern by which your ideas are developed, from beginning to end
3) **Wording:** the way in which ideas are expressed, including
grammar, word choice, sentence structure, and general effectiveness of expression
4) **Mechanics,** or conventions, of writing: spelling, punctuation, division of words at ends of lines, and so forth

No one seriously expects that you will re-read your paper four times to check for each kind of fault. The four categories overlap; usually, for instance, content and organization can be checked at the same time. The purpose of a systematic method of revision is to help you concentrate on your individual problems.

## Checking the content

Read the first draft thoughtfully to make sure you have put in enough material to make the subject clear, convincing, and interesting to your readers. Here are five questions that may help you judge the effectiveness of the material:

1) Are more (or better) details, examples, or illustrations needed?
2) Is the information sufficiently clear so that the reader who knows little or nothing about the subject can readily understand it?
3) Are there general statements that need to be supported by facts? If you say, for example, that Texas has the best flying weather in the United States, have you presented facts and figures to support this idea?
4) Do the opinions or attitudes you have expressed represent your own convictions on the subject, or have you merely repeated what you have read or have heard other people say? It is easy to use the expression "the American way of life"; it is much more difficult to explain what it means.
5) Have you included any statements that do not have direct bearing on the subject you are discussing? If so, remove them in revision.

## Checking the organization

Study the first draft to see if the subject advances from one section to the next and if the emphasis falls where you want it to. As you revise the paper, ask yourself these questions:

1) Is it clear from the beginning (or near the beginning) what the paper is about? Avoid wordy and irrelevant introductions.
2) Does each paragraph advance the subject, or is there some skipping back and forth?
3) Do the important ideas stand out clearly from the minor points and details?
4) Will the ending leave the reader with the impression that you want to make?

## Checking the wording

Read your paper aloud (or have someone else read it to you) to see if it sounds the way you intended it to sound. If you read at an easy, normal tempo, you'll catch most of your unnecessary or awkward repetitions, balky or confused constructions, and unnecessarily involved sentences. Even if you don't know immediately what is wrong, your ear will at least locate spots where there is trouble.

1) Are there any words whose meanings you are not quite sure of? In case of doubt, consult your dictionary.

2) Have you used any technical term or unfamiliar expression that needs explanation?

3) Do you notice any unnecessary repetition, either of individual words or of ideas, that should be omitted?

4) Is the level of usage consistent throughout? Watch for any unintentional lapses from one variety to another, as from formal to informal usage.

5) Are any of the sentences too involved? If you stumble over a passage while reading it, revise it for greater clarity.

## Checking for accuracy

Most of the common errors marked on student papers (spelling, punctuation, fragmentary sentences, omission of words, and so forth) result from carelessness or haste. You can eliminate many such mistakes from your writing by looking carefully for the specific kinds of mistakes that have occurred most frequently in past papers.

If you aren't quite certain about the spelling of a word, don't trust to luck or rely on a friend's opinion; find the correct spelling in your dictionary. If fragmentary or run-on sentences give you trouble, take time to analyze any sentence you suspect may be incorrectly punctuated. If you have used too many commas in previous papers or have failed to paragraph properly, study the sections in this handbook that deal with these matters.

## Manuscript form

**20.2**

> **MS**  Revision: Be sure the manuscript is in the form specified.

Make a neat and accurate copy of your revised paper to submit to your instructor. Follow the directions he or she gives you for the form: the size and the kind of paper; margins and spacing; numbering of pages; endorsement. Typical manuscript form is described in the following pages.

## Typed papers

If you have a typewriter and know how to use it, it is a good practice to type all papers written outside class. Typed manuscript is easier to read than most handwriting and is generally preferable for written work in all college courses.

In typing your final draft, use unlined white 8½ by 11 inch paper, but not onionskin that lets the type show through.

Type everything double spaced except long quotations and footnotes. These should be set off appropriately and single spaced, as shown in the sample reference paper (p. 487).

Follow standard conventions in typing. For the figure 1 use lower case l (not capital I). For a dash use two hyphens with no space between the words and the dash:

    The book--a first edition--was missing.

Before you hand your paper in, check it carefully for typographical errors. Uncorrected typing mistakes are usually considered to be errors.

## Handwritten papers

If you cannot type, you need not worry that your grade will suffer. With reasonable care, handwritten papers can be made just as acceptable as those that are well typed.

Use lined white paper 8½ by 11 inches, with lines at least one half inch apart. Themes written on closely lined paper are hard to read and difficult to correct. Do not use pages torn from spiral-bound notebooks, because their rough edges stick together. Use black or dark blue ink.

Handwritten papers should be easy to read. If a word looks misspelled or is difficult to decipher, it may be marked as an error. Handwriting that is too small puts an unnecessary strain on the eyes of the reader; handwriting that is excessively large is no less difficult to read. Try to strike a happy medium in size. If you have developed what you consider to be an individual style of penmanship, make certain that it will be as legible to others as it is to you.

## Margins and spacing

Leave ample margins on both sides of the page. An inch and a half on the left and an inch on the right are customary margins in handwritten and typed papers. Leave at least an inch and a half at the top and an inch at the bottom of every page.

Indent paragraphs uniformly. Five spaces from the left-hand margin is an acceptable indention for typed papers, and about an inch for those written in longhand. Don't indent any line that is not the beginning of a paragraph, even though it is the first line on a page. The last line on a page should not be left partly blank unless it is the end of a paragraph.

Don't crowd your writing at the bottom of a page. Start a new page, even if it will contain only a line or two.

## Division of words

| | |
|---|---|
| **Div** | Revision: Divide the word marked according to the syllabication given in a reliable dictionary. |

If you leave plenty of room at the right-hand side of your page, you will not have to divide many words at the ends of the lines. It is a good idea to divide words only if writing them out or putting them on the next line would make the lines conspicuously uneven.

Words of one syllable should not be divided at all: *through, played, bright.* Also avoid breaking a word if a single letter will be left at the beginning or end of a line. There is no point in dividing a word like *a-lone;* the single letter at the end of the line is less attractive than leaving space and carrying the whole word over to the next line. See §21.2, p. 304, Spelling and word division.

Words spelled with a hyphen *(mother-in-law, self-confidence)* should be divided only at the hyphen.

## Form of the title

The title appears on the first page of your paper. On unlined paper, place it in the center about two inches from the top of the page; on lined paper, write the title on the top line. Leave a blank line between the title and the first line of the text.

Capitalize the first and last words in your title and all others except short words like *and, the, a, an,* and prepositions less than six letters long.

Breaking and Training a Horse    How Not to Become Overweight
The Art of Making Friends    Strength Through Community

No period should be put after a title. However, if the title is expressed as a question or as an exclamation, it should be followed by the proper end punctuation.

Why not UMTC?    Man Overboard!

Titles are not enclosed in quotation marks. Even when familiar quotations are used as titles, no marks are needed:

Blood, Sweat, and Tears    The Home of the Brave

## Numbering pages

The first page of a manuscript is not numbered. Begin with the second page, using Arabic numerals (2, 3, 4 . . .) for paging. Numbers are customarily put at the top of the page in the right-hand corner or in the center. Make certain that the pages of your paper are in the right order before you turn the paper in.

Long tables, diagrams, charts, and other material supplementary to the words of the text are usually put on separate pages, placed near the part that refers to them, and numbered consecutively with the other pages.

It is not necessary to write "more" at the bottom of each page or to put "Finis" or "The End" at the conclusion.

## Endorsing the paper

Sign your papers as your instructor directs. Include all the information he or she asks for, and put it in the right order. Clear and uniform endorsement is a real convenience to the teacher who must handle the papers.

Ask your instructor how the papers should be submitted, whether folded, flat, or otherwise. Sheets should be held together by paper clips or by staples, but not by pins, bobby pins, or string. Use binders only for longer papers.

## Proofreading

When you finish your final draft, put it aside for a while and then proofread it carefully before handing it in. No matter how perfect the finished product may appear, it will pay to give it one final check. Errors somehow creep into even the most careful writing. To find them, you will have to get away from the paper for a time so that you can look at it with a fresh eye.

MS

20.2

Look for slips of the pen or typing errors, for the omission of words and marks of punctuation. And look particularly for the kind of mistakes that have been marked on your previous papers.

## Making corrections in the final copy

Changes and corrections should be kept to a minimum, particularly on important papers. When you have to make major changes in the final copy (rewording sentences, revising paragraphs), do the page over. For minor changes (spelling, punctuation, adding or striking out a word), make the corrections neatly and according to standard practices.

To add a word, use a caret (∧) and write the missing word directly above it:

Manuscript should *be* easy to read.

To strike out a word, draw a straight line through it (don't use parentheses or brackets):

Final copy should be as ~~as~~ accurate as possible.

To indicate the beginning of a new paragraph where you have failed to indent, write the symbol ¶ immediately before the first word of the new paragraph:

So ended my first day away from home. ¶ The second day. . . .

To correct a misspelled word, draw a line through it and write the correct form directly above. This makes a neater and more legible correction than an erasure:

Quality is more important than ~~quanity~~ *quantity*.

To indicate in typed copy that two letters should be reversed in order (transposed), use a curved line:

be⁀tween          re⁀cieve          Smith⁀'s novel

## Submitting manuscript for publication

Manuscript that is to be submitted for publication, in a campus magazine or elsewhere, should be typed and should follow the directions already given.

The writer's name and full address should be typed in the upper left-hand corner of the first page. A stamped, self-addressed envelope should be enclosed for the possible return of the manuscript. A short covering letter should be included to provide information about the sources of the material used, its accuracy, or possibilities for illustration.

## Revising a corrected paper 20.3

In composition, as in other areas of experience, you often learn by making mistakes. No matter how conscientiously you have applied yourself to a written assignment, you may find that the instructor has marked a number of corrections on the returned paper. To improve your writing skills, you must give serious attention to these corrections. Many instructors require their students to revise all corrected papers and resubmit them. But even if the instructor does not ask for revisions, it is worth your time to make a careful analysis of all correction marks and to revise or rewrite the paper accordingly. A cursory glance down the margins is not enough—if errors and weaknesses are not studied and corrected they will no doubt recur in other papers.

Some papers, of course, may contain only minor errors, requiring the change of a few words or punctuation marks on the original. Often, though, a satisfactory revision means sentences or even whole paragraphs must be rewritten or rearranged. For passages that require extensive changes, experiment with different versions. Then read the revisions through several times to determine which is the best one.

In correcting a paper, it is important to understand *why* the corrections are necessary. If the instructor's mark is not immediately clear to you, consult the correction symbol key at the back of this handbook and then read the relevant section in the text, noting the examples and comparing them with the passage marked.

Compare the original and corrected versions of the student paper reprinted on pages 290–293. This paper was used because it exhibited a variety of faults. (The most serious fault was pointed out in the instructor's overall comment: "Your general approach is vague and unrealistic. What do you actually *do* when you are studying your best?") Study the instructor's marks on the original version and determine their meaning. Then examine the changes (underlined) made in the corrected paper. In working out the revision, the student has learned such things as the following:

## Good Study Habits

It is important for every college student to develop good
study habits. A lucky few have already developed them in
high school, but for the majority of students the greater
demands of college work requires some adjustment. Good
study habits consist primarily of two things: a mature mental
attitude and appropriate physical techniques.

Everyone should remember that being a college student is a
demanding full-time job, and they should be prepared to spend
about forty-five or more hours a week at it. Like any other
job, it requires effort and concentration. Some students are
indifferent toward required courses, which they feel are
uninteresting or cannot see how they are related to their
chosen course of study. Students should remember that if
colleges require certain courses, usually of a general
nature, this means that they present basic knowledge that
every educated person is expected to acquire while in college. If you are indifferent to such courses, you are
condemning yourself to a lopsided intellectual development,
which you will probably regret later on in life.

Whether attending class or studying at home, full
concentration is essential. Students sometimes complain that
they do poorly in courses even though they spend many hours
studying everyday. "Studying" means inattentively running
their eyes over a page between frequent distractions from the
radio, conversing with their roommates, and daydreams. Five
hours of this kind of studying is worth less than an hour of
uninterrupted concentration on the material. A student who
goes to a lecture without having done the assigned reading
and without having reviewed his notes from the last lecture
is not really in a good mood to acquire new information and
relate it to what he already knows.

An erratic and undisciplined approach to study is usually
disasterous. Many students ignore course assignments until
just before an examination. Then they frantically do all the
required reading in one or two nights, try to decipher
sloppy, disorganized notes, and stay up all night over black
coffee cramming hundreds of facts into their heads. The
result is usually that he comes to the examination fatigued
and stupefied by a plethora of chaotic data. All of this
could have been avoided if the student had kept up with his

Good Study Habits

It is important for every college student to develop good study habits. A lucky few have already developed them in high school, but for the majority of students the greater demands of college work <u>require</u> some adjustment. Good study habits <u>are</u> <u>based</u> <u>on</u> two things: a mature mental attitude and appropriate physical techniques.

Everyone should remember that being a college student is a demanding full-time job, and <u>he or she</u> should be prepared to spend about forty-five or more hours a week at it. Like any other job, it requires effort and concentration. Some students are indifferent toward required courses <u>because</u> <u>they</u> <u>consider</u> <u>them</u> <u>uninteresting</u> <u>or</u> <u>unrelated</u> <u>to</u> <u>their</u> <u>chosen</u> <u>field.</u> <u>They</u> should remember that <u>such</u> <u>courses</u> <u>are</u> <u>required</u> <u>because</u> <u>they</u> <u>provide</u> <u>general</u> <u>knowledge</u> <u>expected</u> <u>of</u> <u>every</u> <u>col-</u> <u>lege</u> <u>graduate.</u> <u>Students</u> <u>who</u> <u>neglect</u> <u>these</u> <u>courses</u> <u>are</u> <u>limiting</u> <u>their</u> <u>intellectual</u> <u>growth</u> <u>and</u> <u>usually</u> <u>regret</u> <u>it</u> <u>later.</u>

<u>Full</u> <u>concentration</u> <u>is</u> <u>essential</u> <u>both</u> <u>in</u> <u>the</u> <u>classroom</u> <u>and</u> <u>in</u> <u>the</u> <u>study</u> <u>room.</u> Students sometimes complain that they do poorly in courses even though they spend many hours studying <u>every</u> <u>day.</u> <u>But</u> <u>to</u> <u>many</u> <u>of</u> <u>them</u> "studying" means inattentively running their eyes over a page between frequent distractions from the radio, <u>conversations</u> with their roommates, or daydreams. Five hours of this kind of studying is worth less than an hour of uninterrupted concentration. <u>The</u> <u>same</u> <u>principle</u> <u>applies</u> <u>to</u> <u>class</u> <u>attendance.</u> A student who goes to a lecture without having done the assigned reading and without having reviewed his or her notes from the last lecture <u>is</u> <u>not</u> <u>concentrating</u> <u>on</u> <u>acquiring</u> new information and <u>relating</u> it to what he or she already knows.

An erratic and undisciplined approach to study is usually <u>disastrous.</u> Students with poor study habits ignore course assignments until just before an examination. Then <u>they</u> frantically do all the required reading <u>in</u> <u>a</u> <u>day</u> <u>or</u> <u>two,</u> try to decipher <u>their</u> sloppy, disorganized notes, and stay up all night over black coffee cramming hundreds of facts into <u>their</u> heads. The result usually is that they come to the examination <u>not</u> <u>only</u> <u>exhausted</u> <u>but</u> <u>also</u> <u>confused</u> <u>by</u> <u>a</u> <u>mass</u> <u>of</u> <u>unrelated</u> <u>facts.</u> <u>They</u> <u>could</u> <u>have</u> <u>avoided</u> <u>all</u> <u>this</u> <u>by</u> <u>keeping</u> <u>up</u> <u>with</u> <u>their</u> <u>assignments,</u> <u>making</u> <u>orderly</u> <u>notes,</u> <u>and</u>

**Cor**

**20.3**

**Awk** assignments and had gotten into the habit of taking neat, orderly notes which <u>were reviewed by him</u> regularly.  Studying **Pass** for an examination should involve only glancing over his notes and readings and planning how to organize related facts to answer the questions most likely to be asked.

**Inf** A student should not be afraid that his <u>room mates</u> and friends will <u>call him a square</u> if he sets aside regular times for daily study and refuses to be interrupted.  On the

**Log** contary, most good students are respected by their fellow students and popular because they devote more time to social activities than students with poor study habits.

| | |
|---|---|
| **MS** | Titles of papers are not enclosed in quotes or underlined. They should be set off from the body of the paper by extra space. |
| **Agr** | Blind agreement should be avoided. Despite intervening words, subject and verb must agree: *demands* (S) *require* (V). |
| **WW** | Words should be chosen for their exact meaning. |
| **Agr** | Pronouns must agree in number with their antecedents. *Everone* is singular and should be referred to by a singular pronoun (*he* or *she* rather than *they*). |
| **//** | Constructions joined by coordinating conjunctions should be equivalent in rank and meaning. |
| **Wdy** | Ideas should be expressed as directly and economically as possible. |
| **Ref** | Pronouns should refer clearly to a definite antecedent. The pronoun *they,* marked for faulty reference in the original version, might seem to refer to *colleges* or *students* as well as to *courses.* |
| **Div** | A word should be divided at the end of a line according to the syllabication shown in a dictionary. |
| **Shift** | Shifts in person (*they* to *you* in the second paragraph, *they* to *he* in the fourth paragraph) should be avoided. |

reviewing <u>their</u> <u>notes</u> <u>regularly.</u>   Studying for an
examination <u>then</u> <u>would</u> <u>involve</u> <u>no</u> <u>more</u> <u>than</u> <u>glancing</u> over <u>the</u>
<u>material</u> <u>and</u> <u>mentally</u> <u>organizing</u> <u>it</u> <u>in</u> <u>terms</u> <u>of</u> <u>the</u> <u>questions</u>
<u>most</u> <u>likely</u> <u>to</u> <u>be</u> <u>asked.</u>

 Students should not be afraid that their <u>roommates</u> and
friends will <u>make</u> <u>fun</u> <u>of</u> <u>them</u> if they set aside regular times
for daily study and refuse to be interrupted.   On the
contrary, <u>good</u> <u>students</u> <u>are</u> <u>usually</u> <u>respected</u> <u>for</u> <u>their</u>
<u>scholastic</u> <u>achievements</u> <u>and,</u> <u>because</u> <u>they</u> <u>use</u> <u>their</u> <u>time</u> <u>more</u>
<u>efficiently,</u> <u>are</u> <u>usually</u> <u>freer</u> <u>to</u> <u>participate</u> <u>in</u> <u>social</u>
<u>activities</u> <u>than</u> <u>are</u> <u>students</u> <u>with</u> <u>poor</u> <u>study</u> <u>habits.</u>

**DM**   The sentence should include the word to which the modifier refers.

**¶ con**   The relationships among ideas in a paragraph should be made clear to the reader.

**No ,**   Subject and verb should not be separated by a comma: *A student* (S) *is* (V).

**Awk**   Awkward passages should be smoothed out when revising a first draft.

**Big W**   Stilted, unnecessarily heavy language is out of place in all kinds of writing.

**Pass**   The awkward use of the passive voice should be avoided, especially an unnecessary shift to passive from active.

**Inf**   Writers should be consistent in their level of usage. The informal *call him a square* is probably out of place in this relatively formal paper.

**Log**   The logic of a statement must be made clear to the reader. Devoting a large amount of time to social activities does not necessarily make a student popular; neither do good study habits. The writer's intended meaning is made clear in the revision.

Revising
a
corrected
paper

Whenever you write a paper, your *last* paper is a valuable resource, if you are willing to take the time to use it seriously. If your teacher has marked it thoroughly, his or her marks and suggestions may let you see what kinds of mistakes you are likely to make, where your attention is likely to wander, what you are likely to omit, what you are likely to include unnecessarily. The author of the paper shown above should probably be particularly concerned about the instructor's general comment on the importance of dealing directly and realistically with the subject matter. Even the corrected version of this paper, although it eliminates most of the specific faults in the original version, is still pretty conventional and not too interesting.

**Cor**

**20.3**

In correcting this paper, the student should also have observed that there are two large categories of weaknesses in his or her writing: faulty diction and awkward sentence construction. The instructor has called the student's attention to poor word use in four instances: the inaccurate *consists of;* the vague and inappropriate *a good mood;* the inflated *fatigued and stupefied by a plethora of chaotic data;* and the colloquial *call him a square.* In addition, the passages marked for sentence economy (Wdy) and awkwardness (Awk) are marred by poor word choice as well as faulty sentence construction. The student author hasn't shown skill in selecting accurate, appropriate, and forceful language to express his or her ideas. If the writer wants to avoid word errors in future papers, he or she will have to read the text sections on diction thoroughly, become more alert to other writers' use of words, consult the dictionary frequently, and study his or her own first drafts critically to eliminate wordiness and pretentiousness.

The instructor has also marked several passages for sentence and paragraph weaknesses. The second paragraph concludes with two long, clumsy sentences (Wdy). The third paragraph lacks continuity (con), because the student has omitted certain words and expressions necessary to indicate connections and transitions between ideas. The fourth paragraph contains two jumbled, awkward sentences (Awk). In the corrected version, the student has made each of these passages more clear and direct, and has gained valuable practice in expressing the ideas as economically as possible. To avoid sentence weaknesses in future papers, he or she should practice reading the sentences and paragraphs aloud to see whether they are difficult to follow, repetitious, or ambiguous. And to assure continuing improvements, the student should become more alert to sentence patterns used by other writers, particularly in published material.

All students who analyze their errors and revise their papers as carefully as the writer of the sample paper did will soon find that even their original drafts are improving.

## Application: Editing and Revising

One of the best ways to learn is by doing. The following is a student theme entitled "The Farmers and Food Prices." Pretend that you are an English instructor and mark up the theme with all of the marks such as "awk" and "big W" that you can legitimately defend (see the chart on pp. 292–293). When you have finished, write a helpful terminal comment to the student and assign the paper a grade. Comparing your suggestions and evaluations with others' is a useful activity, either in or out of class.

**Cor**

**20.3**

"The Farmers and Food Prices"

When people complain about high food prices, the blame always ends up in the farmer's lap. "Those farmers are making a fortune and we're almost starving!" I hear people say. Well, I can tell you that the farmers do not make a fortune, and that compared to any other workers, farmers are overworked, underpaid, and have jobs with the most risk and least security.

Labor unions have decreed that laborers can work no more than forty hours a week without being paid overtime, which is time-and-a-half. And if you ask a laborer to work on Sundays or holidays, they get double-time. But the farmers have to work every day, often from sunup to sundown (which in the summer is over fourteen hours). Cows must be milked everyday, Sundays and holidays included. And when the crops are ripe, the farmer's must work to harvest them seven days a week until all are in. There is no forty-hour week, no overtime, no double-time, for farmers.

Laborers have unions which negotiate wage contracts for them. Members of the most powerful unions get longevety and cost-of-living raises yearly. But farmers get paid what the food processors feel like paying them. They cannot strike

for higher wages. The only thing they can do is withhold
their crops from the market until the prices rise to where
they think they should be. But if they do that, people think
their just being greedy, when really their only doing what
laborers are doing, trying to get a living wage.

If you asked a laborer to work at a job where all the
products he works on, through no fault of his own, can
disintegrate over night and where he will get no pay if this
happens, he will just laugh at you. But farmers do just
that. They must work to get out a product which may or may
not materialize, depending on purely outside influences,
particularly inclement weather. If there is a too-wet
spring, they cannot plant in time. If there is a too-wet
fall, the harvest is delayed or sometimes even ruined. If
there are shortages of gasoline or fertilizer, farm work will
be held up. The farmers are at the mercy of the elements
and the various chemical shortages that can happen at any
time.

So, its not the farmers who make a killing while your food
bill goes up. Any money they make can never fully pay them
for the risk they take and the hard work they do day in and
day out, year after year.

Exer

*There was a time when the meaning of language presented no problem, when it was a simple matter, upon being challenged as to meaning, to call to witness the dictionary. But in our age of universal skepticism, we have come to know that dictionaries are not depositories of eternal meanings of language. Dictionaries are made by ordinary human beings, who have collected data from—of all people—you and me, the general users of the language.—James E. Miller, Jr.,* Word, Self, Reality

While it probably is more reliable than any single one of us, a dictionary is not a supreme authority that can be quoted to settle all arguments about words and their meanings. Rather, it is a record of the ways in which language is actually used, and any dictionary is an incomplete record. The pioneer lexicographer Samuel Johnson concluded long ago that it was foolish for a man to attempt to "embalm his language." But the notion still persists that a dictionary is—or should be—a code of law for language use.

For this reason there has been considerable debate, and some heated argument, in the past generation about whether a dictionary should *prescribe* or *describe* language use. Some people want a dictionary to tell us which pronunciation is right, which meaning is proper, which use of a word is legitimate. They have some good reasons for wanting these things. When we see a real estate company advertising *ranchettes* for sale (actually half-acre plots) or a toy company advertising an electric train set that has *manumatic* switching controls (actually a small lever that the owner moves by hand), we may all for a moment at least long for a dictionary to declare that such words are not only deceitful, but also rude, crude, and unacceptable. Other people, including the editors of many dictionaries, declare that dictionaries are not intended to rule our use of language. They too have reason on their side. Almost any rule that a dictionary could offer to govern pronunciation or definition would have originated in observation of how people at some particular point in the past actually pronounced and defined. In other words, if a dictionary sets out to be a system of law, what that means is that the editors are converting the *habits* of some past time into *rules* for the present.

The editors of many dictionaries that have been recently published did not wish to do this. They wanted to *register* how the language is used. To that end, many offered a variety of acceptable pronunciations for many words, and some made no effort to dictate what was "best." Some editors began to quote more modern writers to illustrate meaning. Some editors, too, have begun to omit usage labels (which declare that some words are *colloquial* or *vulgar* or *erroneous*) on the ground that the correctness or appropriateness of a word can seldom be determined out of context.

Contexts, the situations in which words are used, change, and language changes. The changes are not always good, and it's understandable that we might sometimes wish for an authority to stop changes that are not good. In the course of generations of usage, for example, the word *dilapidated* lost a precise meaning that was possible. If we had retained its root meanings from Latin, we could now use the word only to speak of *stone* structures (houses, buildings, and the like) that have fallen into disrepair and decay. Through customary usage, however, the word lost any specific meaning and is now used to refer to anything that has fallen into disrepair. Changes often *are* good: our language has for centuries, for example, been enriched and enlarged by the addition of words from other languages. Such additions give us ways of talking that we did not have before. *Canyon* and *mesa,* for instance, both relatively recent borrowings from Spanish and both now common English words useful in accounts of certain landscapes, have no exact equivalents in English. Written use of *mesa* is recorded as early as 1775 in an account of a Florida landscape; no other written use is recorded until 1859, but the word has since become common enough, as has *canyon,* which first appeared in writing, as far as records can tell, as recently as 1861.

Since language changes—sometimes for the worse, probably more often for the better—a dictionary cannot control, but simply record the way it is actually used. The standards for determining what good language is rest in other hands (see Introduction).

## Selecting a dictionary        **21.1**

A good dictionary, though not a final authority, is an indispensable reference tool for every college student. Dictionaries answer questions about the meanings, spellings, origins, and pronunciations of words. They also give a good deal of information about the forms of words (plurals, past tenses) and idiomatic constructions (what preposition, for example, is commonly used with a particular noun or verb). One of the most valuable habits a student can acquire in a college composition course is checking a dictionary for the meaning and spelling of words.

Dictionaries differ in size and purpose, but certain criteria apply in evaluating any dictionary for general use. First of all, it should be up to date. New words and expressions are continually coming into the language *(acrylic, ambience, apartheid, brainstorming, psychedelic)* and old words are always being used in new senses (a *crash* program, a publicity *handout*). Even spelling and pronunciation can change with time *(catalog, catalogue; ab'də mən, ab dō'mən)*. In addition, most dictionaries are somewhat encyclopedic, including information about prominent people and places. There are always new names to be added *(Kosygin, Zaire)* and new facts to be recorded.

In an effort to keep their entries up to date, most dictionaries make limited changes every year or so. Check the copyright dates before you buy a dictionary to find out when it was last revised. You might also want to look up some words that have recently come into use to see if they are included.

In evaluating a dictionary you should also consider the quality of its editing. A good dictionary of current English is not simply an updating of earlier word books; it reflects the research and judgment of a large staff of experts who record and analyze hundreds of thousands of examples of words in actual use. It is the responsibility of the lexicographer to make certain that the language has been sampled adequately and that all the most common uses of even uncommon words have been found. Then all these raw materials must be carefully gone through, some discarded and some reworked. Eventually the result should be a concise yet accurate description of the words that constitute the great bulk of our language. Whatever "authority" a dictionary has, then, depends on the scholarship, discrimination, and judgment of its editors.

**Dict**

**21.1**

## Dictionaries for general use

The most complete descriptions of contemporary English are to be found in the various unabridged dictionaries. Though not practical for desk use, these large dictionaries are invaluable for reference, and at least one of them is available in every college library:

*New Standard Dictionary of the English Language* (Funk & Wagnalls)

*The Random House Dictionary of the English Language* (Random House)

*Webster's Third New International Dictionary* (G. & C. Merriam). The most complete record now avaliable.

*World Book Dictionary* (Field Enterprises)

Two older dictionaries continue to be very useful:

*The Century Dictionary and Cyclopedia* (The Century Company). Although this ten-volume work, the most comprehensive dictionary ever published in the United States, has not been reprinted since before World War I, it contains much information not available in more recent dictionaries. *The New Century Dictionary* (Appleton-Century-Crofts) is basically an abridgment of this work.

*Webster's New International Dictionary of the English Language* (G. & C. Merriam). The second edition of the unabridged Webster, first published in 1934, is no longer in print but remains available in most libraries.

For everyday use, the most practical dictionary for a student to own is one of the shorter "college" dictionaries listed below. Your instructor may recommend that you buy a particular one, or leave the choice to you. Each of these dictionaries has its own special strengths, but all are well edited and adequate for college use:

*American Heritage Dictionary* (American Heritage and Houghton-Mifflin)

*Random House Dictionary*, College Edition (Random House)

*Standard College Dictionary* (Funk & Wagnalls; text edition published by Harcourt, Brace & World)

*Webster's New World Dictionary of the American Language* (World Publishing Company)

*Webster's New Collegiate Dictionary* (G. & C. Merriam)

Sample entries from some of these dictionaries, showing the organization of their entries and some of their distinctive features, are reproduced on pages 306–307.

## Special dictionaries

The general dictionaries—abridged and unabridged—are supplemented by a number of specialized word books which occasionally need to be consulted for material not to be found in general works.

### Historical dictionaries

Good dictionaries for general use are based in part upon scholarly dictionaries made over long periods of time. *The Oxford English Dictionary* (twelve volumes and a *Supplement,* 1888–1928) is a historical dictionary of the words and idiomatic phrases of the English language. It traces the various forms and meanings of each word, giving the date of its first appearance in recorded English and illustrative quotations from writers to show its typical use at various times in its history (a dozen or more columns are sometimes devoted to a single word). In many kinds of study it is a basic source for research. *The Shorter Oxford English Dictionary* (two volumes) is an abridgment of the larger work and somewhat easier to use; recently the entire work has, by virtue of miniaturized print, been published in two volumes that come with a magnifying glass.

*The Dictionary of American English* (four volumes), made on the same plan as the *Oxford,* gives the history of words as they have been used by American writers from 1620 to 1900. *A Dictionary of Americanisms* (two volumes) gives the history of words that originated in the United States and brings the record of American English down to 1944. Periodicals like *American Speech* and *PADS* (Publications of the American Dialect Society) regularly publish regional and occupational vocabularies.

### Dictionaries in special subjects

Dictionaries of slang and other specialized languages are available, and most special fields have dictionaries of their specialized vocabularies. It is a good idea to know the titles of those in any fields you are going to work in. The following list merely suggests the range of such books. Most of them are revised from time to time.

Ballentine, J. A., *Law Dictionary*
*Chambers's Technical Dictionary*
Clark, D. T., and B. A. Gottfried, *Dictionary of Business and Finance*
Dorland, W. A. N., *American Illustrated Medical Dictionary*

English, H. B., *A Student's Dictionary of Psychological Terms*
Good, C. V., *Dictionary of Education*
Hackh, I. W. D., *Chemical Dictionary*
Henderson, I. F. and W. D., *Dictionary of Scientific Terms*
Rice, C. M., *Dictionary of Geological Terms*

## Learning to use your dictionary                          21.2

Dictionaries differ not only in the information they include but in the way they present it, and the best dictionary in the world will be of little value to you unless you know how to read and interpret the information it provides. Before using a new dictionary, read the front matter carefully. It will explain the organization of entries, the method of indicating pronunciation, the use of restrictive labels, and the meaning of abbreviations and symbols used in the definitions and etymologies. Then look carefully at a page of entries to see how words and phrases are handled. Test your understanding of the pronunciation guide by using it to pronounce some familiar words. Look through the table of contents to see what sections of information your dictionary provides in addition to the main alphabetical list of words. You may find a short grammar of the English language, a discussion of punctuation, a table of signs and symbols, a list of colleges and universities in the United States, and a guide to the preparation of manuscript copy.

A little time spent in learning to use your dictionary can make it immensely useful to you. The following sections describe the kinds of information found in most dictionaries, and pages 306–307 illustrate the way this information is presented in four good college dictionaries. The exercises beginning on page 311 will give you some practice in the actual use of your own desk dictionary.

### Spelling and word division

Develop the habit of using your dictionary to check the spelling in your papers. If you are unable to find a word because you are uncertain of one of the beginning letters, try to think of other possible spellings for the same sound. (Is it *gibe* or *jibe*?) Remember that dictionaries give the spelling not only of the base form of a word but also of distinctive forms—the principal parts of verbs, the plurals of nouns, the comparative and superlative forms of adjectives and adverbs—that are in any way irregular.

Your dictionary may give two spellings for a word when usage is divided *(hemoglobin—haemoglobin; although—although).* Use the spelling that the editors have indicated is the more common one. (The method of listing variants will be explained in the front matter.) Avoid spellings labeled British (such as *colour, gaol*) in favor of the usual American spelling.

Dictionaries divide words into units (usually corresponding to spoken syllables) by means of small dots or spaces: *de·mar·ca·tion, de light ful.* This device will enable you to see each part of the word clearly and to notice if you have omitted or transposed any letters. In writing, divide a word at the end of a line only where your dictionary shows a division. The word *reorganization,* for example, might be divided at the end of a line in any one of five places: *re·or·gan·i·za·tion.* Not all dictionaries divide every word in exactly the same way, but by following the practice of any good dictionary you will avoid such careless blunders as dividing *bedraggled* into *bed-* and *raggled.*

See also §15, Spelling, and §20.2, Manuscript form.

## Pronunciation

Because English spelling is not consistently phonetic (there are over 250 ways to spell the forty-odd sounds in English), dictionaries use a system of special symbols to show how words are pronounced. The word *bamboozle,* for example, might be respelled this way after the entry word: *băm boo' zəl.* The pronunciation key at the bottom of the page will illustrate, with familiar words, the sounds represented by the symbols *ă, ōo,* and *ə.* Since the consonants *b, m, z,* and *l* have no special marks over them, you may assume that they are pronounced in the usual way. The accented syllable in *băm boo' zəl* is indicated by a heavy stress mark. Phonetic spellings also indicate secondary stress, when appropriate, usually by a lighter mark (') but sometimes by a different symbol. Since the system for showing pronunciation varies somewhat from dictionary to dictionary, you should study carefully the explanatory notes in the front of your own book before attempting to use its pronunciation key.

# Sample entries from college dictionaries
## Funk & Wagnalls Standard College Dictionary

**ad·vance** (ad·vans′, -väns′) *v.* ·vanced, ·vanc·ing *v.t.* **1.** To move or cause to go forward or upward. **2.** To offer; propose: to *advance* a suggestion. **3.** To further; promote: to *advance* the progress of science. **4.** To put in a better or more advantageous rank, position, or situation. **5.** To make occur earlier; accelerate. **6.** To raise (a rate, price, etc.). **7.** To pay, as money or interest, before legally due. **8.** To lend: Can you *advance* me some money? **9.** *Law* To provide an advancement for. — *v.i.* **10.** To move or go forward: The armies *advance* on all fronts. **11.** To make progress; rise or improve: The stock market *advanced*. — *adj.* **1.** Being before in time; early: an *advance* payment. **2.** Being or going before; in front: the *advance* guard. — *n.* **1.** The act of going forward; progress. **2.** Improvement; promotion. **3.** An increase or rise, as of prices. **4.** *pl.* Personal approaches; overtures: His *advances* were rejected. **5.** The supplying of goods, money, etc., on credit. **6.** The goods or money so supplied; a loan. **7.** The payment of money before it is legally due: He requested an *advance* on his salary. **8.** *U.S.* The front or foremost part. Abbr. **adv.** — **Syn.** See PROGRESS. — **in advance 1.** In front. **2.** Before due; beforehand: to prepare for lunch *in advance*. [ME *avauncen* < OF *avancier* < L *ab ante* from before < *ab-* away + *ante* before; the initial *a-* was later altered to *ad-* as if from L *ad-* to, toward] — **ad·vanc′er** *n.*

## The Random House Dictionary

**ad·vance** (ad vans′, -väns′), *v.,* -vanced, -vanc·ing, *n., adj.* —*v.t.* **1.** to bring or send forward. **2.** to present for consideration, as an opinion. **3.** to further the development or prospects of. **4.** to promote, as to a higher rank. **5.** to increase (a rate or figure). **6.** to accelerate. **7.** to furnish or supply (money or goods) on credit. **8.** *Archaic.* to raise (a banner, flag, etc.). —*v.i.* **9.** to come or go forward. **10.** to make progress or show improvement. **11.** to increase in price, value, quantity, etc. —*n.* **12.** a forward movement. **13.** a noticeable progress or improvement. **14.** a promotion, as in rank or status. **15.** Usually, **advances. a.** attempts at forming an acquaintance, reaching an agreement, etc., made by one party. **b.** actions or words intended to be sexually inviting. **16.** an increase in a rate or figure. **17.** *Com.* **a.** a sum of money or quantity of goods furnished on credit. **b.** the act of furnishing this sum or quantity. **c.** the total number of sales, as of tickets to a play or of an item of merchandise, made before a play begins its run or the item is available. **d.** the sum of money collected through such sales. **18. in advance, a.** in front (often fol. by *of*). **b.** beforehand. —*adj.* **19.** before all others: *an advance section of a train.* **20.** made beforehand: *an advance booking of tickets.* **21.** issued beforehand: *an advance copy.* [ME *avaunce(n)* < OF *avanc(i)e(r)* < VL *abantēāre* = LL *abante* away before (see AB-, ANTE-) + *-āre* v. and inf. suffix; *ad-* by confusion of prefixes] —**ad·vanc′er,** *n.* —**ad·vanc′ing·ly,** *adv.* —**Syn. 2.** adduce, propound; offer. **3.** forward, promote. **6.** quicken, hasten, speed up. **7.** loan. **9.** ADVANCE, PROCEED imply movement forward. ADVANCE applies to forward movement, esp. toward an objective: *to advance to a platform.* PROCEED emphasizes movement, as from one place to another, and often implies continuing after a halt: *to proceed on one's journey.* **15.** overture, proposal. —**Ant. 1, 2, 9.** withdraw. **9.** retreat. **11.** decrease.

## Webster's New Collegiate Dictionary

¹**ad·vance** \əd-'van(t)s\ *vb* **ad·vanced; ad·vanc·ing** [ME *advauncen*, fr. OF *avancier*, fr. (assumed) VL *abantiare*, fr. L *abante* before, fr. *ab-* + *ante* before — more at ANTE-] *vt* **1 :** to bring or move forward **2 :** to accelerate the growth or progress of **3 :** to raise to a higher rank **4 :** to supply or furnish in expectation of repayment **5** *archaic* **:** to lift up **:** RAISE **6 a :** to bring forward in time; *esp* **:** to make earlier <~ the date of the meeting> **b :** to place later in time **7 :** to bring forward for notice, consideration, or acceptance **:** PROPOSE **8 :** to raise in rate **:** IN-CREASE <~ the rent> ~ *vi* **1 :** to move forward **:** PROCEED **2 :** to make progress **:** INCREASE <~ in age> **3 :** to rise in rank, position, or importance **4 :** to rise in rate or price — **ad·vanc·er** *n*

**syn 1** ADVANCE, PROMOTE, FORWARD, FURTHER *shared meaning element* **:** to help to move ahead *ant* retard, check
**2** see ADDUCE

²**advance** *n* **1 :** a moving forward **2 a :** progress in development **:** IMPROVEMENT <an ~ in medical technique> **b :** a progressive step <the job meant a personal ~ forward> **3 :** a rise in price, value, or amount **4 :** a first step or approach made **:** OFFER <her attitude discouraged all ~s> **5 :** a provision of something (as money or ●oods) before a return is received; *also* **:** the money or goods supplied — **in advance :** BEFOREHAND — **in advance of :** ahead of

³**advance** *adj* **1 :** made, sent, or furnished ahead of time <an ~ payment> **2 :** going or situated before <an ~ party of soldiers>

## Webster's New World Dictionary

**ad·vance** (əd vans′, -väns′) *vt.* **-vanced′, -vanc′ing** [ME. *avancen* < OFr. *avancer*, to forward < VL. *\*abantiare* < L. *ab-*, from + *ante*, before: spelling *ad-* by association with L. *ad*, to, forward] **1.** to bring forward; move forward [to *advance* a chessman] **2.** to raise in rank, importance, etc.; promote **3.** to help or hasten the success or completion of; further [to *advance* a project] **4.** to put forward; propose **5.** to bring closer to the present; specif., *a)* to cause (a future event) to happen earlier *b)* to assign a later date to (a past event) **6.** to raise the rate of; increase [to *advance* prices] **7.** to pay (money) before due **8.** to lend —*vi.* **1.** to go forward; move ahead **2.** to make progress; improve; develop **3.** to rise in rank, importance, etc. **4.** to rise in price or cost; increase —*n.* **1.** a moving forward **2.** an improvement; progress [new *advances* in science] **3.** a rise in value or cost **4.** [*pl.*] approaches to get favor, become acquainted, etc.; overtures (*to* someone) **5.** a payment made before due, as of wages **6.** a loan —*adj.* **1.** in front [*advance* guard] **2.** beforehand; ahead of time [*advance* information] —**in advance 1.** in front **2.** before due; ahead of time —**ad·vanc′er** *n.*
**SYN.—advance** is used to describe assistance in hastening the course of anything or in moving toward an objective; to **promote** is to help in the establishment, development, or success of something [to *promote* good will]; **forward** emphasizes the idea of action as an impetus [concessions were made to *forward* the pact]; **further** emphasizes assistance in bringing a desired goal closer [to *further* a cause]—**ANT. retard, check**

Dictionaries often list two or more pronunciations for a word when usage is divided (as shown in the entries for *advance* on pages 306–307). Although the first pronunciation is usually the more common one, it is not necessarily "preferred," and you should use whichever pronunciation is customary in your own community. *Webster's Third New International Dictionary* provides a comprehensive survey of American usage in pronunciation, as does Kenyon and Knott's *A Pronouncing Dictionary of American English,* available in most college bookstores.

## Meaning

Dictionaries are perhaps most important for what they tell us about the meanings of words. To a reader, a dictionary is useful for finding the meanings not only of unfamiliar words but also of familiar words used in new senses. To a writer, dictionary definitions are most useful for checking the meanings of words there may be some doubt about—words, perhaps, such as *ubiquitous* or *officious.* Were these words used with their exact meaning in the first draft? In revising, the writer should check the dictionary to make sure.

Dictionaries begin each definition, or group of definitions, with an abbreviation showing whether the word is being defined as a noun *(n.),* adjective *(adj.),* transitive verb *(v.t.),* intransitive verb *(v.i.),* or other part of speech. This information is important, for words usually have different meanings in different grammatical contexts. Sometimes the meanings are closely related (for example, the meanings of *advance* as a verb, a noun, or an adjective) but sometimes they are completely different (the meanings of *fly, plant,* and *court* as verbs or as nouns).

In looking for the meaning of a word in context, therefore, you must ordinarily isolate the right group of definitions before you can find the particular meaning you are looking for. Then you should look over all of the definitions included in that group. Some dictionaries give the oldest meaning first and other dictionaries the most common one. Often you will want neither of these but a more specialized meaning that comes late in the entry. At the end of the entry, or at the end of a group of definitions for one part of speech, you may also find one or more idioms listed—notice, for example, the idiom *in advance* under the entry for *advance.*

In using dictionary definitions, you should keep two general principles in mind:

1) A dictionary does not *require* or *forbid* a particular meaning or use of a word; it merely *records* the most common ways in which a word has actually been used. Therefore you must exercise judgment in deciding whether a particular word will be appropriate in a particular context.

2) A dictionary definition is for the most part a record of the *denotation,* or specific meaning, of a word; at best, it can only suggest the *connotation,* or suggestive qualities, which varies with context and with use. (See §22.1) In general, it is better not to use a word until you have heard it or read it and know at least some of its connotations.

## Areas of usage and special labels

Some words (or particular meanings for some words) are labeled in a dictionary as *dialectal, obsolete, archaic, foreign, colloquial, slang, British, United States,* or are identified with some particular activity or field—*medicine, law, astronomy, music, sports, manufacturing, electricity.* Both kinds of labeling are illustrated in the sample entries on pages 306–307. One of the college dictionaries *(American Heritage)* even includes a separate section on usage. Words unlabeled in a dictionary are considered part of the general vocabulary.

Usage labels can serve as rough guides, but you should bring your own observation to bear on individual words. Certainly you would ordinarily avoid words marked *obsolete* or *archaic,* but many words that carry no label *(albeit, perforce)* would be equally out of place in most college writing. On the other hand, many words marked *Dial.* or *Colloq.* (such as *highbrow*) might fit perfectly well into both informal and general English. The label *colloquial,* which many people mistake to mean nonstandard, simply suggests that a particular usage is more characteristic of speech than it is of writing. The label *U.S.* means that the usage is found in the United States but not in other parts of the English-speaking world.

Most dictionaries of the English language include frequently used words and expressions from foreign languages. Some dictionaries indicate that such terms are generally considered foreign by listing the language in parentheses: *(It.), (Fr.).*

Some also use an identifying mark, such as a dagger or an asterisk, before all foreign-word entries. Such labels are useful because they help distinguish between foreign words that are now considered part of the English vocabulary *(chalet, aria, mesa)* and those that are still considered distinctly foreign *(dolce far niente, Weltanschauung, enceinte)* and must be underlined in a paper. (See §14.4, page 188, Italics for foreign words.)

## Synonyms and antonyms

Most dictionaries list words of similar meaning *(synonyms)* with the basic or most comprehensive word of a group and explain how these various related words differ slightly in meaning, especially in connotation. The entries reproduced on pages 306–307, for example, compare the meaning of *advance* with the meaning of such related words as *promote, forward, further,* and *proceed.* One of the dictionaries refers the reader to a synonym study that relates the meaning of *advance* to that of *progress.* Sometimes the entry for a word will also list an *antonym,* a word of opposite meaning, as *cowardly* would be an antonym for *courageous.*

There are several specialized books containing lists of related words: *Webster's Dictionary of Synonyms,* Fernald's *Standard Handbook of Synonyms, Antonyms, and Prepositions,* Soule's *A Dictionary of English Synonyms,* and Roget's *Thesaurus.* The *Thesaurus* is probably the most widely used book of synonyms, but since it does not give definitions, its chief use is to remind a writer of words he recognizes but does not use regularly.

## Etymology

A dictionary not only tells how a word is used and pronounced but also gives its origin, or *etymology.* Sometimes the etymology is merely a notation of the language from which the word was borrowed (as *decór* is from French and *Gestalt* is from German) or a statement of how it was coined. But often the etymology is fairly complicated; the development of the word *advance,* for example, is traced back through Middle English to Old French and finally to Latin. The explanatory notes at the front of your dictionary include a discussion of etymology and a key to the abbreviations and symbols used in tracing a word's origin.

Knowing how a word originated will often help you understand and remember it. Knowing that *philanthropy,* for example, comes from the Greek words *philein* (to love) and *anthropos* (man) may help fix its meaning in your mind. Beyond this, it may help you figure out other unfamiliar words by analogy *(philology, anthropocentric).*

Etymologies often illustrate how word meanings have changed from their original to their present use and are interesting as records of human thought and experience.

### Applications: Practical Use of the Dictionary

1. This assignment will pay you dividends in learning to use dictionaries and in your writing if you do it diligently. Write a 500–800 word paper in which you compare and contrast three related words in modern English. You may pick any three words, but you may find that you want to drop one and add another as you go along. Examples of words to use are *nice–lovely–good* ("nice" may surprise you), *mad–lunatic–insane, land–shore–beach, host–guest–motel.*

   Your paper should include, of course, an introduction and a general conclusion. It should also include the origins of each word, how the meanings have changed over the years, the modern definitions of each word, and the interrelationship among the words. Remember to put the information in your own words—don't plagiarize, and don't simply copy the articles from the dictionaries. Consult at least *two* dictionaries (the *O.E.D* mentioned on p. 303 is a good place to start). Feel free to try out different combinations of words. An important part of your task as writer is to make the paper more interesting reading than the dictionaries you consult.

2. To help you familiarize yourself with your dictionary, write out the following information about it, for discussion in class or to be handed in.

a. The title, the name of the publisher, and the most recent copyright date. This date may be found on the back of the title page.

b. A list of the sections following the introduction and preceding the dictionary entries (such as "How to Use the Dictionary," "A Guide to Pronunciation," "Usage Levels").

c. A list of the material in the appendix (if any), such as "Signs and Symbols," "Biographical Names," "Colleges and Universities in the United States."

d. Do the words appear in one alphabetical list or in separate lists (for biographical names, geographical names, abbreviations, etc.)?

e. Are derived forms (*cynical* and *cynicism* from *cynic,* for example) listed separately as main entries in the alphabetical list, or are they listed under the base word?

f. Do the etymologies come at the beginning or at the end of an entry?

**g.** The order of the definitions of the words. Does the older meaning or the current meaning come first in words such as: *bibulous, cute, ghastly, shrewd, liquidate, souse* (noun), *recession, fulsome?*

**3.** What information do you find in your dictionary on the spelling of these pairs of words? Are the spellings interchangeable? If so, which form would you use and why?

aesthetic — esthetic  
carat — karat  
catalog — catalogue  
catsup — catchup  
criticise — criticize  
draft — draught  
encyclopaedia — encyclopedia  

favor — favour  
fiber — fibre  
gaol — jail  
gray — grey  
licorice — liquorice  
sac — sack  
traveling — travelling  

**4.** To familiarize yourself with the pronunciation key in your dictionary, write out the following exercises:

**a.** What pronunciations does your dictionary list for each of these words? Is the first pronunciation given the one you hear most frequently? If not, tell how it differs, including the stress (accent):

| | | | |
|---|---|---|---|
| address | creek | greasy | pianist |
| adult | decadent | herb | poinsettia |
| Celtic | drama | impotent | research |
| coupon | gibberish | leisure | Oedipus |

**b.** How is each of these words pronounced when used as a noun? As a verb?

| | | | |
|---|---|---|---|
| confine | escort | impact | misuse |
| conflict | exploit | import | refuse |
| consort | ferment | | |

**5.** Answer the following questions by referring to the definitions given in your dictionary:

**a.** Would a professor be flattered if you called him a *pedant?*

**b.** Where does a *Yahoo* live?

**c.** Is a *ladybird* a female bird?

**d.** In what kind of writing would it be appropriate to use the word *gimmick?*

**e.** Would you be likely to find the word *lackaday* in contemporary writing?

**f.** In what profession would the word *dolmen* most likely be used?

**g.** What dialect uses of the word *fetch* does your dictionary give?

**h.** Where would you be most likely to hear the word *legato?*

**i.** When a man *rests on his laurels*, what is he doing?

**j.** Which of the following expressions would be underlined in a paper to indicate they belong to a foreign language?

Realpolitik   de facto   sarong   savoir-faire   toccata   vice versa

**6.** Consult your dictionary and choose the best definition for the italicized word in each of these sentences:

**a.** At ten he became a printer's *devil.*

**b.** The university allowed considerable *latitude* in dress.

**c.** A *shingled* bob framed her small face.
**d.** His *fellowship* expired at the end of the year.
**e.** Luther objected to the sale of *indulgences*.
**f.** The entrance fee was *fixed* at twenty dollars.
**g.** She has extremely *catholic* reading tastes.
**h.** Aristotle thought of virtue as the *mean* between two excesses.
**i.** A shift in the *fault* may cause a severe earthquake.
**j.** They soon discovered that the resort was a *white elephant*.

**7.** Answer the following questions by consulting the *grammatical information* given in the dictionary entry for each word:
**a.** What is the past participle of *shear*?
**b.** What is the past tense of *bear* in the sense of *carry*?
**c.** What does *feign* mean when it is used intransitively?
**d.** What does *gull* mean when followed by a direct object?
**e.** What is the plural of *ghetto*?
**f.** What is the plural of *stratum*?

**8.** Consult the *etymologies* in your dictionary to answer the following questions:
**a.** What is the origin of these words?

| | | |
|---|---|---|
| fedora | Hellenic | orangutan |
| feral | lacquer | robot |
| gerrymander | lampoon | sandwich |

**b.** Which of the following words have retained most or all of their original meanings? Which have retained some? Which none?

| | | |
|---|---|---|
| bigot | fiasco | pilot |
| curfew | miscegenation | silly |
| fecund | pedigree | tragedy |

**9.** The following questions can be answered by finding the special information they require in the dictionary. In some cases it is attached to the regular word entry; in others special sections at the back or front must be consulted.
**a.** Distinguish between the following similar words:
deviate – digress – diverge – swerve
slim – thin – slender – skinny
fictitious – legendary – mythical
giggle – titter – snicker – chuckle
latent – potential – dormant
**b.** Give antonyms for the following words: *authentic, chaste, devout, futile, venial.*
**c.** Who was John Huss? When did he live?
**d.** Where are the Carpathian Mountains?
**e.** How large is a lemming?
**f.** Is Mexico City smaller or larger than Paris in population?
**g.** Where is Miami University? Can a woman enroll there?
**h.** How long is a furlong?
**i.** What does the symbol B/L mean in business and commerce?
**j.** What does the sign ∴ mean in mathematics?

*Respect for the word is the first commandment by which [we] can be educated to maturity—intellectual, emotional, and moral.*

*Respect for the word—to employ it with scrupulous care and incorruptible heartfelt love of truth—is essential if there is to be any growth in society or in the human race.*

*To misuse the word is to show contempt for man. It undermines the bridges and poisons the wells. It causes Man to regress down the long path of his evolution.—Dag Hammarskjold,* Markings

We usually take for granted that we know the meanings of the words we use, except when there is a question of accuracy *(infer* or *imply?)* or of appropriateness *(boss* or *supervisor?).* But if you are to use the words that will best convey your meaning, you need to do more than simply accept and use the first words that come to mind. You need to take an active interest in words as words. What gives a particular word its special meanings in different situations? In what different ways can a word be used? How will others take the words? Words have many possible meanings. If you are to choose those that best serve your purpose, you need to know first what the choices are.

**Mng**

**22.1**

## Words in context and situation 22.1

Words do not actually have "meaning" until they are used in speaking or writing. Then their meaning derives partly from the *context,* or the words around them, and partly from the *situation* in which they are used, which involves the attitudes and purposes of either a speaker and listener or a writer and reader.

It is easy to see how the context limits the meaning of a word. A word like *deck, run, fly,* or *match* can be used in several senses, but usually in a particular sentence it can have only one meaning:

Tomorrow we'll take a **run** up to the lake.
You will have to **run** to catch the train.
Frowning, she noticed the **run** in her stocking.
Aaron scored the third **run** after there were two out in the seventh.

When the store opened on the morning of the sale, there was a **run** on piece goods.

The situation in which a word is used also helps clarify its meaning. The word *bill* in "The bill is too large" would mean one thing if the speaker were trying to identify a bird and another if he were discussing family finances. A writing situation includes at least a topic of discussion, a writer, and the potential audiences. If the writer's and the readers' experiences of the topic under discussion are similar, they can communicate with some ease. If their experiences are different, space separates them. Writer and reader seem then to inhabit different worlds, and each may seem alien to the other. Then the writer has a larger chore: to find ways of bringing readers into the world he or she occupies, or at least to find ways of enabling readers to see and understand the writer's world. To do this may take special pains; it means taking particular care to use words that will help the reader know the writer and see the writer's world.

## Denotation: the core of a word's meaning

Words are arrangements of sounds or letters that we use to bring our ideas, attitudes, notions to another person's attention. These may be objects or "things" *(typewriter, Golden Gate Bridge)*, qualities *(excellent, hard)*, relationships *(without, hers)*, actions or conditions *(running, homesickness)*, or ideas *(democracy, truth)*.

When we think first about the meaning of words, we usually think of their *denotation*, what they have come to represent as a result of the ways they have been used. This is the meaning that dictionaries record and try to describe for us. The thing that a word refers to or suggests is called its *referent*.

Some kinds of words have more definite denotations than others because their referents are more limited or more exact. Depending on their definiteness, words may be classified into three groups:

1) **Concrete words,** words that name specific people, places, or objects, are the most exact in meaning: *Walt Whitman, Lake Erie, my bicycle, the library, reindeer, a Boy Scout knife.*

2) **Relative words,** words that describe qualities, are less definite than concrete words and frequently depend for their meanings on the situation or on the writer's past experience

with a term: *hot, pretty, honest, angry, silly, impossible.* In New York City, a *tall* building might mean any structure over twenty stories, but in a city with no skyscrapers, *tall* might refer to any building higher than five stories.

3) **Abstract words,** words that refer to general concepts— acts, situations, relationships, conditions—are the least definite: *reasoning, citizenship, education, intelligence, culture, objectives, art.* Since these words have a range of reference (think of all the activities that may be included in *education,* for example), rather than a specific referent, they are more difficult to use exactly than concrete words. (See also §22.4, Concrete and abstract words.)

## Connotation: the suggestion of words

Most words have been used by so many different people in such different circumstances for such different purposes that they have acquired associations and suggestions that go beyond their denotation. The qualities that words have acquired from their expanded use are called *connotation.*

Very often the chief difference between words of closely related denotation is in their connotation. Both *inexpensive* and *cheap* refer to low price, but *cheap* may also connote poor quality; *average* and *mediocre* both refer to the middle of a range, but *mediocre* suggests dispraise; *belief, faith, creed, dogma* all refer to ideas held, but they differ widely in suggesting how they are held. It is easy to see why some students of language say that there are no true synonyms.

Dictionaries try to suggest the shades of meaning that words may have, but the best way to find the exact connotations of a word is to observe how it is actually used in current writing and speech. The connotative value of a word often changes over time. *Sly,* for example, once meant *skillful,* but as it is generally used now it would fit into the same context as *devious* or *tricky;* it may even suggest *criminal* or, sometimes, *lecherous.* Words like *genteel* and *bucolic* have lost their favorable connotation as the values they represent have lost much of their appeal. Certain words, usually those whose referents arouse widely ranging responses, are extremely variable in connotation: *pop art, radical, socialism, jazz.* When you use such words, be cautious, making sure that your attitude is clear to your reader and that you are being fair to your subject. Words with high connotative value, like words that are associated with prickly controversies, may create special problems for you. The art of the whittler who sat in the town square may be useful to you here.

The whittler, a man widely known for his uncannily realistic carvings of birds, when asked how he managed to achieve such realism in his carvings, said, "Well, I just whittle off all the wood that don't look like a bird." When you use words that have high suggestive power, you may have to whittle off all of the meanings that you do not want to express. This may mean taking the time to define, to set limits to what you are trying to say, to establish clearly how you want to use the words. Any potential readers you have are real people, too, and they are at liberty to take your words in any way they wish unless you have shown them the limits of meaning that you have in mind. If you refer to a coeducational dormitory, for example, some people will hear a reference to free sex and a scandalous decline in moral character, *unless* you take pains to declare the nature of a coeducational dormitory as you wish them to see it.

## Fair words and slanted words    22.2

The problem is that there is space between us. Your readers are over *there;* you are over *here.* Your readers are not in your shoes, and they don't have your history. They don't see things as you see them, or know them as you know them, just as you don't see and know things as they do. If you want your readers to see and know things as you do, at least for a moment, you have to show them where you are, how you have positioned yourself. Words chosen carefully for their connotative value can help you show your readers what your attitude is toward your subject. An honest and fair representation of the position you have taken toward your subject is entirely proper and fitting. Sometimes, however, writers assault their audience—intentionally or accidentally—by using words weighted in their favor. Such writing is often called *slanted writing.*

## Words used fairly for effect

It is not possible to speak or write in completely neutral, objective language about anything that has fully engaged our interest. To write well about a subject, we must care about it enough to take a position or make a judgment concerning it.

In factual as well as in imaginative writing, interest, liveliness, and effectiveness depend greatly on the successful use of connotation. Our awareness of all the values that words have enables us to represent our subject precisely, to address our audience with a varied and appealing language, and to show where we stand in relation to our material. Honestly used, words with high connotative value give *shape* and *texture*—as opposed to *slant*—to what we say.

The following passage, obviously part of a campaign that seeks action, is emphatic and persuasive because of the connotation of many of the words. Phrases such as *generous twinges* and *conventional charities* hit at our complacency, and many others *(slumlords, loan sharks, and clubhouse politicians)* are calculated to suggest the burden of poverty. The passage does not represent unfair slanting because we know from the writer's style that his argument is to be taken as opinion and evaluated on the basis of the evidence given and the reader's own experience.

While most Americans have occasional generous twinges and dutifully support the conventional charities, by and large they have no exposure to the actual experience of the poor. It is hard for them to realize that there are fellow Americans today who are still being denied the right of suffrage by intimidation, fraud, and mayhem; who are suffering the condescensions of the prosperous in order to get and keep servile jobs; who are enduring the importunities of slumlords, loan sharks, and clubhouse politicians who profiteer off the poor; and who are always being admonished to patiently wait for a better day—which is virtually certain not to come if awaited patiently. Poverty in America is to be unwelcome, unwanted, and apparently unneeded in the society of one's own citizenship and birthright. It means the despair of any human hope that something will happen in the discernible future that might significantly change the day-to-day existence of those men, women, and children who are poor.—William Stringfellow, *Dissenter in a Great Society*

## Slanted words

The story is told of a harvester of enormous appetite who shortened the legs of the dining table on the side where he sat so that the food would slide toward him for instant availability. By exploiting the suggestive power of words, writers can similarly tilt arguments and meanings in their favor.

Sometimes slanting occurs only because writers, in their enthusiasm, allow words that are too intense to intrude in statements presented as fact. To say "All television programs are designed for the twelve-year-old mind" is allowing a personal distaste for television programing to make the writer careless. Often *all* or *most* should be *many,* or a superlative should be reduced to a less extreme word, or *only* or *nothing but* should be changed to allow for other possibilities.

Much unfair slanting occurs in statements of opinion where a writer, knowingly or not, assumes that he or she is the only reliable resource. There is nothing slanted in a simple statement of one's likes or dislikes ("I can't stand these weirdos with their long hair"). But the same opinion stated as a general fact in slanted wording ("Long hair and fanciful clothing are signs of decadence") implies that the writer expects the reader to share that opinion without thinking about it.

Just as writers who unfailingly trust themselves as the only reliable resource are likely to slant their writing, so are writers who, in their enthusiasm for their own position, fail to consider more than one possibility. The following passage is from an essay in which the author argues that destroying the wilderness and its resources is a perfectly natural and appropriate human activity:

> The trumpeting voice of the wilderness lover is heard at great distances these days. He is apt to be a perfectly decent person, if hysterical. And the causes which excite him so are generally worthy. Who can really find a harsh word for him as he strives to save Lake Erie from the sewers of Cleveland, save the redwoods from the California highway engineers, save the giant rhinoceros from the Somali tribesmen who kill those noble beasts to powder their horns into what they fondly imagine is a wonder-working aphrodisiac?
>
> Worthy causes, indeed, but why do those who espouse them have to be so shrill and intolerant and sanctimonious? What right do they have to insinuate that anyone who does not share their passion for the whooping crane is a Philistine and a slob? From the gibberish they talk, you would think the only way to save the bald eagle is to dethrone human reason. — Robert Wernick, "Let's Spoil the Wilderness"

Unexamined assumptions (wilderness lovers are hysterical) and unsubstantiated assertions (they speak gibberish) are the source of much slanting. For this reason, many of the most serious instances of slanting come in writing on social or political problems, especially when the words reflect prejudice. This type of slanted writing can be objected to on at least four grounds: it doesn't accurately represent the situation being discussed; it suggests that the writer is at the very least careles of what he or she says and more probably willing to distort the facts for his or her own purposes; it stands in the way of an intelligent and constructive approach to problems that affect the public interest; and it is likely to antagonize the reader (unless similarly prejudiced) and so prevent clear communication.

Not all slanted writing uses obviously weighted words. The picture that emerges in the following passage depends upon seemingly innocuous phrases (such as "impeccably groomed lawns" and "waiting to be courted by promoters and gladhanders"):

The spectators wander among the fifteen impeccably groomed tennis lawns, pausing at times in the gardens and terraces where the champagne and Pimm's Cup flow and the strawberries are served with clotted Devonshire cream. The athletes relax in blue wicker chairs in the airy players' tearoom, enjoying a commanding view of the grounds and waiting to be courted by promoters and gladhanders from around the world. Even the luxuriant grass at Wimbledon is nursed, humored and tended with the utmost respect by solicitous groundsmen. Not surprisingly, the over-all effect of all this pampering of people and things is greater than the sum of its parts: tennis at Wimbledon generates the heady sensation that something very special is happening at almost every moment of the tournament. — Pete Axthelm, "The Wimbledon Way," *Newsweek**

It is not enough to use words cleverly to achieve an effect. In choosing words for their connotative value, remember that you have a responsibility to deal fairly with both your subject matter and your audience.

Choosing the right word

**22.3**

> **WW**  Revision: Replace the wrong word marked with one that accurately conveys your intended meaning.

In the relatively factual prose of most college writing, words should be used in their established forms and senses; if they are not, the reader may be misled or confused. An expression such as "The scene *provoked* his imagination" (in which *provoked*, commonly meaning "angered," is inaccurately used instead of *stimulated*) interferes with communication. In revising your papers, check any words that you are unsure of, especially those that are not part of your regular vocabulary. Be particularly alert to words that are easily confused.

## Distinguishing words of similar spelling

In English there are many pairs of words that closely resemble each other in sound or spelling but have quite different meanings: *moral* and *morale, personal* and *personnel, historic* and *histrionic.* When writing hastily, you may accidentally substitute one word for another, but you can easily eliminate such errors by proofreading your work and by referring to a dictionary when necessary. When words of identical pronunciation, called *homonyms,* are confused in writing, the mistake may be called a spelling error *(bear* for *bare; there* for *their).* But your instructor is likely to label it WW (wrong word) if he or she suspects that you may not know the difference in meaning *(principal* for *principle; affect* for *effect).*

The following words are frequently confused in college papers. Learn to distinguish their spellings and meanings:

accept—except
adapt—adopt
affect—effect
allusion—illusion
censor—censure
cite—site
complement—compliment
conscientious—conscious
credible—creditable—credulous

detract—distract
formally—formerly
human—humane
imply—infer
persecute—prosecute
precede—proceed
principal—principle
respectful—respective
stationary—stationery

## Distinguishing words of similar meaning

Word errors most frequently occur because the writer has failed to distinguish between words of similar meaning. A synonym is a word of *nearly* the same meaning as another:

angry—annoyed—indignant
frank—candid—blunt
multitude—throng—crowd—mob
strange—peculiar—quaint—bizarre

A few words have identical meanings and are therefore interchangeable *(flammable—inflammable; ravel—unravel; to-*

*ward—towards)*. But most synonyms, while they refer to the same idea or object, differ somewhat in denotation or connotation and thus cannot be substituted for each other without affecting the sense or tone of the statement. One term may be more formal than another *(coiffure—hair-do);* more concrete *(tango—dance);* more exact *(charitable—kind);* or more personal *(dad—father).*

Usually it is not the more subtle distinctions between closely related words that cause trouble *(necessary—indispensable; intrinsic—inherent)*, but the failure to distinguish between common words in different contexts:

The mysteries of the unknown arouse curiosity that must be **fulfilled.** [for **satisfied**]

We may expect food consumption to increase everywhere because of the **growth in people.** [**increase in population**]

The only way to avoid such errors is to notice how words of similar meaning are used in various contexts. Connotation as well as denotation should be considered. Notice, for example, how unexpected the last word in this statement is:

In the 1870's, Dodge City was a lawless gathering place for gun-toting cowboys, professional bad men and killers, and other **scamps.**

*Scamps* might be quite appropriate in referring to mischievous children, but the term is conspicuously out of place in this company of desperadoes. Some synonyms are too heavy or too flippant for the context:

The water was rougher past the next bend, and we had **difficulty circumventing** the rapids. [too formal: had **trouble getting around** would be more appropriate]

I enjoyed studying Plato, because among other things I **got the lowdown on** what is meant by a Platonic friendship. [too informal: **learned** would be better]

But remember the principle of appropriateness. There are special situations in which such incongruities might be useful. Mark Twain and Will Rogers, for example, could sometimes, by mixing different kinds of language, get comic effect from the incongruity.

Writers sometimes use strings of fanciful synonyms to avoid repeating the same expression for an idea or object *(cats, felines, furry beasts, tabbies, nine-lived creatures)*. Such "elegant variations" are pretentious and are usually more annoying than simple repetition. Readers expect key words to be repeated when they cannot be replaced by pronouns *(cats . . . they)*. Factual synonyms *(these animals)* are also unobtrusive and will seldom strike the reader as repetitious.

## Distinguishing words of opposite meaning

Some words that have contrasting or wholly opposite meanings are frequently confused, probably because the writer associates them mentally but has reversed their meanings. Among the most common antonyms or near antonyms are the following. Make sure that you know their meanings.

| | |
|---|---|
| concave — convex | inductive — deductive |
| condemn — condone | physiological — psychological |
| explicit — implicit | prescribe — proscribe |
| famous — notorious | subjective — objective |
| former — latter | temerity — timidity |

Confusing such pairs may result in your saying the very opposite of what you intend. Half-knowing a word is often more dangerous than not knowing it at all.

## Learning new words

Although many word errors are caused by confusion or carelessness, it's easy to use the wrong word (or settle for the almost-right word) simply because you do not know another one. College papers are likely to deal with complex ideas and precise distinctions that may demand a larger vocabulary than the writer has needed in the past.

It has been estimated that children enter first grade knowing about 25,000 words and add 5000 every year, so that they leave high school with a vocabulary of perhaps as many as 90,000 words. The average vocabulary for college graduates is approximately twice this size. These figures are for *recognition* vocabulary, the words that we understand when we read or hear them. Our *active* vocabulary, the words we actually use in writing or speaking, is considerably smaller.

Most people use only about a third as many words as they recognize. Thus, an obvious way for you to enlarge your working vocabulary is through conscious exercise. In making an effort to say precisely what you mean you should search not only among the words in your active vocabulary, but also among those you have learned to recognize. Frequently we find new words in reading *(cybernetics, rhetoric, apartheid)* and learn their meanings from the context or from a dictionary. Using these words in writing or speaking helps to make them more readily available for future use.

It is sometimes possible to guess the meaning of a word by knowing its parts. Many scientific words, for example, are formed with suffixes and roots from Greek or Latin:

| | | |
|---|---|---|
| mono- (one) | -graph (writing, written) | poly- (many) |
| bi- (two) | bio- (life) | macro- (large) |
| tele- (at a distance) | photo- (light) | micro- (small) |

Since the combined meanings of the parts may only approximate the meaning of the whole, however, it is usually safer to use a dictionary and learn the entire word.

Ordinarily we learn and remember words not for their own sake but for the meanings they represent. We have a good stock of words in the fields that interest us because facts and ideas are retained chiefly in verbal form. Thus, anything that extends the range of your ideas or experiences will help to enlarge your vocabulary. The typical college course, for example, adds to a student's vocabulary several hundred new words and new meanings for familiar words.

When you meet a new word that is likely to be useful, learn it accurately at the start—its spelling and pronunciation as well as its usual meaning. Students often have trouble in their college courses because they only half know the specialized words essential to a subject. Using these words in conversation, when they are appropriate, or in reviewing course work with another student will fix them in your mind so that you can use them easily and accurately in examinations, papers, and class discussions.

## Concrete and abstract words     **22.4**

Words can be classified according to the nature of their referents as *abstract* or *concrete* (p. 315). Abstract (general) words refer to ideas, qualities, acts, or relationships. Concrete (specific) words refer to definite persons, places, objects, and acts. This list demonstrates the differences between the two kinds of words:

| Abstract (general) | Concrete (specific) |
|---|---|
| institution | Austin College |
| labor | running a ditching machine |
| men's organization | Lion's Club |
| a politician | the senator from Kentucky |
| food | cheesecake |
| an educator | my history teacher |
| creed | Westminster Confession |

Often a word cannot be labeled as abstract or concrete until it is read in context:

| Abstract | Concrete |
|---|---|
| Honest labor never killed anyone. [a generalization about all labor] | In the GM contract dispute, labor seeks a five-cent per hour wage increase. [in the context, a specific reference to the United Automobile Workers] |

## Effective uses of concrete and abstract words

Concrete words are essential in discussing situations, incidents, and processes that are based upon personal experience or direct observation: impressions of people or places, discussions of plans for the future, explanations of the writer's attitudes or interests. Abstract words, on the other hand, are usually necessary in discussing general ideas ("The Intangible Values of Education"), for summarizing facts or stating opinions, or for analyzing theoretical problems ("    Specialization in Education Undesirable?").

Abstract words are more characteristic of formal than of general or informal English and are best used by writers with a good deal of experience in handling ideas. In this passage, for example, the writer uses very few concrete words, yet the meaning is clear to anyone who is interested in jazz:

Some of the most brilliant of jazzmen made no records; their names appeared in print only in announcements of some local dance or remote "battles of music" against equally uncelebrated bands. Being devoted to an art which traditionally thrives on improvisation, these unrecorded artists very often have their most original ideas enter the public domain almost as rapidly as they are conceived to be quickly absorbed into the thought and technique of their fellows. Thus the riffs which swung the dancers and the band on some transcendent evening, and which inspired others to competitive flights of invention, became all too swiftly a part of the general style, leaving the originator as anonymous as the creators of the architecture called Gothic. — Ralph Ellison, "The Charlie Christian Story"

But broad ideas can also be discussed in concrete terms. For example, this discussion of evolution and the laws of nature, a fairly abstract notion, begins in language that is quite specific:

> Over the radio the weatherman talked lengthily about cold masses and warm masses, about what was moving out to sea and what wasn't. Did Benjamin Franklin, I wondered, know what he was starting when it first occurred to him to trace by correspondence the course of storms? From my stationary position the most reasonable explanation seemed to be simply that winter had not quite liked the looks of the landscape as she first made it up. She was changing her sheets.
> Another forty-eight hours brought one of those nights ideal for frosting the panes. When I came down to breakfast, two of the windows were almost opaque and the others were etched with graceful, fernlike sprays of ice which looked rather like the impressions left in rocks by some of the antediluvian plants, and they were almost as beautiful as anything which the living can achieve. Nothing else which has ever lived looks so much as though it were actually informed with life. — Joseph Wood Krutch, "The Colloid and the Crystal"

Generalization is appropriate—even necessary—when a writer must summarize a large body of facts. This is frequently done in short papers on general subjects, where the writer's primary concern is to survey briefly the available facts and explain their significance. The important thing in such cases is to choose general words that *accurately* summarize the specific details examined, without distortion or unnecessary vagueness. A student writing a paper on conservation, for example, might run across this passage:

> In the seven years from 1883 to 1890 the New South Wales Government was forced to spend not less than £1,543,000 in its attempt to control the scourge, and today rabbit control both in Australia and in New Zealand is a financial load upon every community. Many methods of eradicating this pest have been attempted. In Western Australia more than 2000 miles of fencing was erected at a cost of almost £500,000, but after it was all up it was found that some rabbits were already on the other side of the fence! Unfortunately, incidental to the compulsory use of poison for rabbits, there has been a very great destruction of wildlife as well as livestock, and phosphorus poisoning, employed for rabbit control, has been one of the principal causes of death among the marsupials and native birds. — Fairfield Osborn, *Our Plundered Planet*

In writing the paper, the student might effectively generalize from these facts as follows:

Attempts to limit the rabbit population in Australia and New Zealand have been costly and destructive of other animal life.

It is perfectly proper to use abstract words when the material calls for them, if they can be used accurately and clearly. But writing on almost any subject gains force through the use of specific words. It is usually more convincing to generalize at the beginning or end of a paper, on the basis of a number of specific facts, than it is to pile up generalities throughout.

## Excessive use of abstract words

> **Abst**   Revision: Replace the abstract expression marked with one that is more specific.

The most common fault in the wording of many student papers is a fondness for abstract terms where concrete words would be more meaningful and certainly more interesting. Even if an assigned topic is so worded that it seems difficult to discuss in specific terms ("The Importance of Education," "What Democracy Means"), a paper can be reasonably factual, concrete, and convincing if it is written in words that represent the writer's own experiences and beliefs.

Some students make the mistake of believing that the more general the expression, the more convincing and impressive it is. Others mistake the use of abstract words for intellectual discipline. The use of a general or indefinite expression where a concrete one would fit is annoying to readers:

I think that this quarter's work has helped me to form new physical actions and has broadened my mental ability.

If the writer means that he has learned *to swim,* or *to play baseball,* or *to dance,* he should say so; and he might also indicate just how the quarter's work has broadened his "mental ability." Has it helped him to concentrate? Taught him better study habits?

The excessive use of abstract words can become an unfortunate habit in writing. Some students never take *physics, history, economics,* or *French;* instead, they encounter *various interesting courses of study;* rather than going to a specific college, they attend *an institution of higher learning;* they do not play *golf, bridge, tennis,* or *baseball,* but *participate in various recreational activities.* Few traits of style are less convincing than the unnecessary use of vague, abstract terms for ideas that could better be expressed concretely. Here is H. W. Fowler, writing in *Modern English Usage,* on "abstractitis":

The effect of this disease, now endemic on both sides of the Atlantic, is to make the patient write such sentences as *Participation by the men in the control of the industry is non-existent* instead of *The men have no part in the control of the industry; Early expectation of a vacancy is indicated by the firm* instead of *The firm say they expect to have a vacancy soon; The availability of this material is diminishing* instead of *This material is getting scarcer; A cessation of dredging has taken place* instead of *Dredging has stopped; Was this the realization of an anticipated liability?* instead of *Did you expect you would have to do this?* And so on, with an abstract word always in command as the subject of the sentence. Persons and what they do, things and what is done to them, are put in the background, and we can only peer at them through a glass darkly. It may no doubt be said that in these examples the meaning is clear enough; but the danger is that, once the disease gets a hold, it sets up a chain reaction. A writer uses abstract words because his thoughts are cloudy; the habit of using them clouds his thoughts still further; he may end by concealing his meaning not only from his readers but also from himself. . . .

## Applications: Working with Words

1. The meaning of a word very often depends on the context in which it is used. Each of the italicized words in the following paragraph on Roman architecture could mean something entirely different in another context. Write a brief definition of what each of these words means in the context in which it is used, and then write a sentence illustrating how each of the words would have a different meaning in another context.

The result is that the whole of *living* Rome is a surprisingly *contemporary* city. How many of us who photograph the Spanish Steps *realize* that the birthplace of George Washington is older? *Masons* were working on the Trevi *fountain,* into which we throw coins to *acknowledge* our nostalgia to return, while Benjamin Franklin was in London presenting the tax grievances of the *Colonies* to the British government. The great Piazza del Popolo, below our Pincian *lookout,* did not even exist when Jackson was fighting the Battle of New Orleans—it was still a blueprint in the *studios* of Giuseppe Valadier. We can find an American *parallel* even for Alexander Borgia. When the bells of Valencia were ringing out for his *elevation* to the throne of Saint Peter, the bells of Palos, in Spain, were still vibrating in the ears of the sailors aboard the little caravels *pitching* westward under the command of Columbus. And if we visit the magnificent church of Santa Maria Maggiore and look up at its gleaming, *coffered* ceiling we are sure to be told that this was the first gold brought back from the Americas.—Sean O'Faolain, "A Pontifical Splendor," *Holiday* Magazine

2. The connotative value of words is very important in determining their use: for example, you might say "I am *plump;* you are *heavy;* he is *fat*"; three different pictures emerge. Arrange the following groups of words into columns, according to their connotation: favorable, neutral, or unfavorable. Supply missing words wherever necessary.

a. student, scholar, bookworm
b. stubborn, firm, pigheaded
c. average, mediocre
d. counterfeit, replica, copy
e. racy, obscene, blue
f. unusual, bizarre, unique
g. tolerant, flexible, wishy-washy
h. caustic, penetrating, sharp
i. egghead, intellectual
j. reserved, aristocratic, snobbish
k. simulated, bogus
l. buffoon, wit, comic
m. officer, policeman, fuzz
n. svelte, skinny, thin
o. literary artist, hack, writer

3. While it is true that there is no such thing as purely objective writing, it is true that there are times when information should be presented as objectively and factually as possible. The following news story is an example of slanted writing; rewrite it so that, if it appeared in a reputable newspaper, both sides in the dispute would feel fairly treated.

## Activist Group Disrupts County Board Meeting

Members of the upstart group ACT (Aware Citizens Together) disrupted a meeting of the Fairview County Board last evening protesting the Board's plan to change the present floodplain building restrictions. Local civic groups have endorsed the change, which would permit building construction on the floodplain of the Wolf River.

ACT's founder, Ralph Mendez, says that ACT was formed to protect the citizens whose homes, he claims, will flood each time the Wolf River rises if the floodplains are used as construction sites. Plans for a library and a senior-citizens' recreational center will have to be scratched if Mendez and his fellow protesters have their way, as these are among the buildings proposed for construction on the now-vacant property.

Mendez, who has had several arrests for rioting and disorderly conduct, was a founder and officer of the Students for a Democratic Society (SDS). He has also been closely associated with several citizen activist organizations. The usual tactic of these organizations is to involve well-meaning but naive or uninformed citizens around seemingly valid issues of concern, and eventually to condition these citizens to distrust, dispute, and even agitate against the legitimate functions of government.

4. The first word that comes to mind is not necessarily the best one, even if it means *approximately* what you intend. Read each of the following sentences carefully and choose the word in parentheses that most *exactly* expresses the intended meaning.

a. He found after he had paid his tuition that he hadn't the money (requisite, necessary) to buy his dinner.
b. The latest statistics (dispute, refute, rebuke) his claim that the economy is expanding.
c. In time Einstein (convinced, persuaded, showed) most physicists that his theory was correct.
d. I admired her (poise, coolness, refinement) under the stress of a difficult examination.
e. Most states have laws that (stop, deter, prohibit) gambling.
f. We stopped in our stroll on lower Main Street to (give, donate, contribute) some money to a blind man.
g. Perhaps if you (heed, obey) the Dean of Men in this, he will relent in that.
h. No sooner had he got his own private office than he had conceived a (plan, design, scheme) to become president.
i. My instructor did not report me to the Dean, although he made it clear he did not (accept, condone, tolerate) my behavior.
j. The remarks at the end of his speech (implied, inferred, insinuated) that he had some financial support for his plan.

5. Examine the diction in the following sentences to determine whether some words are misused. If so, rewrite the faulty sentences, supplying more exact or more appropriate words. Be prepared to explain why you made each change.

a. Within the next few days the assassin gained considerable renown.
b. If there was any morale to the story, I did not find it.
c. I do not like to be around him, for his perpetual pessimism aggravates me.
d. A student who is writing a research paper should compulsively read through the leading works devoted to his subject.
e. How can a teacher instigate his class to write better?
f. My mother has always been a zealot of bridge and canasta and other trivial amusements.
g. If we adopt the plan, how will the changes in procedure effect the goals?
h. The course has made me familiar with new ideals in the study of genetics and things like that.
i. I found this poem extremely obtuse, and even after struggling over it for hours with a dictionary and an encyclopedia I could not decipher many of its illusions.

**j.** I have never been very adapt at tennis, so when the rest of the crowd wanted to go out to the courts I abstained.

**6.** The larger your vocabulary, the easier it is to choose the best word when you write and understand what you read. Classify by number the words in the following list as (1) words you now use in speaking and writing; (2) words that you understand but do not generally use; (3) words that you believe you have seen before and might understand in context; (4) words totally unfamiliar to you. Look up the words that you number 3 or 4 in a dictionary. Which of these words might be useful to you?

| | | | |
|---|---|---|---|
| anthropomorphic | fetish | lobotomy | sacrosanct |
| bibliography | feudalism | madras | scrimmage |
| brigantine | galaxy | malevolent | sediment |
| buff | gauche | metamorphosis | semantics |
| cabal | genocide | meteorology | shanghai |
| caisson | graffito | nadir | spondee |
| celibate | hedonist | neolithic | staccato |
| codicil | hoecake | opaque | tangent |
| context | iconoclast | paltry | tare |
| crustacean | ignis fatuus | parthenogenesis | teetotaler |
| decadent | illiterate | pedant | tovarich |
| deciduous | improvise | piston | tranquilizer |
| demitasse | kilometer | quixotic | Uncle Tom |
| duenna | larva | quantum | venal |
| eclectic | libido | recant | versatile |
| ellipse | limbo | rococo | whimsy |

**7.** Concrete words add liveliness and interest to writing. The following paragraph is from a paper describing the advantages of living in a big city. Underline all expressions that seem to you too general, vague, or otherwise ineffective. Then rewrite the paragraph, making the language as concrete and direct as possible.

Individuals who live in an urban metropolis can engage in more leisure activities. There are many cultural institutions where they can observe wonderful artistic productions or historical artifacts; most of these require no financial contribution on their part. Then there are the commercial enterprises that present dramatic or musical arts and other interesting activities. They also have the opportunity to become acquainted with the cultural differences in the various areas surrounding them as they explore both desirable and undesirable environments within the metropolitan context. Such explorations can affect their intellectual growth and toleration. To people who come from a background limited in such knowledge, these experiences are factors of great importance.

**8.** Assume that you are writing a short information paper on Prohibition and wish to incorporate the information given below. How can you effectively *generalize* from the material without citing the specific illustrations? Write out your generalization.

**Exer**

To meet all these potential threats against the Volstead Act, the Government appropriations provided a force of prohibition agents which in 1920 numbered only 1,520 men and as late as 1930 numbered only 2,836; even with the sometimes unenthusiastic aid of the Coast Guard and the Customs Service and the Immigration Service, the force was meager. Mr. Merz puts it graphically: if the whole army of agents in 1920 had been mustered along the coasts and borders—paying no attention for the moment to medicinal alcohol, breweries, industrial alcohol, or illicit stills—there would have been one man to patrol every twelve miles of beach, harbor, headland, forest, and riverfront. The agents' salaries in 1920 mostly ranged between $1,200 and $2,000; by 1930 they had been munificently raised to range between $2,300 and $2,800. Anybody who believed that men employable at thirty-five or forty or fifty dollars a week would surely have the expert technical knowledge and the diligence to supervise successfully the complicated chemical operations of industrial-alcohol plants or to outwit the craftiest devices of smugglers and bootleggers, and that they would surely have the force of character to resist corruption by men whose pockets were bulging with money, would be ready to believe also in Santa Claus, perpetual motion, and pixies.—Frederick Lewis Allen, *Only Yesterday*

*Words constitute the ultimate texture and stuff of our moral being, since they are the most refined and delicate and detailed, as well as the most universally used and understood, of the symbolisms whereby we express ourselves into existence. We became spiritual animals when we became verbal animals. The fundamental distinctions can only be made in words. Words are spirit. Of course eloquence is no guarantee of goodness, and an inarticulate man can be virtuous. But the quality of a civilization depends upon its ability to discern and reveal truth, and this depends upon the scope and purity of its language.—Iris Murdoch, "Salvation by Words,"* New York Review of Books

Words occur in sentences, and sentences occur in paragraphs and compositions. If they are to yield to a reader the meaning that you want, words must be used accurately in context. They should be appropriate to the purpose and tone of the composition: the individual words should fit the subject, they should sound like the writer, and they should reach the intended reader.

Because you can't judge the effect of words out of context, you must rely on your own judgment in choosing words that will tell your meaning and reveal your attitude toward your subject. A dictionary is a useful guide to meaning, but it is of little help when it comes to putting proper words in proper places.

In the absence of specific guidelines, there are three things you can do to help make your word choice more effective. First, you can choose more thoughtfully from the range of your own present vocabulary the words that best suit your purpose. A good part of the time when we are writing or speaking, many of us just accept and use the first words that come along. Often we already own words that would be more precise and appropriate than the first ones we think of. Second, you can sharpen your judgment by paying closer attention to the language around you—the language of your classmates, your instructors, your parents, the people you hear speak on television and radio—and noticing the differences in usage that you hear and read. Third, you can read widely to familiarize yourself with the range and variety of writing. All written English is a bank you might draw on.

We may call a piece of *writing* formal, even if its vocabulary is largely from the range of general English, when its sentences are unusually complex, its organizational patterns tight and demanding. We call *vocabulary* formal if it ranges much beyond the characteristic spoken vocabulary, from words slightly more characteristic of writing than of speaking to such specialized words as *moribund, educand, genotype,* and *ailurophobe.*

## Appropriate use of formal words

In using formal language, you run the risk of sounding remote from your subject and from your reader. Unless you are at ease with formal words, you also run the risk of seeming affected. But some situations demand and deserve the precision of good formal usage. Some things cannot be said easily, or at all, otherwise. If the nature of your subject requires a tough vocabulary, as the following passage seems to illustrate, use it:

> Semantic aphasia is that numbness of ear, mind and heart—that tone deafness to the very meaning of language—which results from the habitual and prolonged abuse of words. As an isolated phenomenon, it can be amusing if not downright irritating. But when it becomes epidemic, it signals a disastrous decline in the skills of communication, to that mumbling low point where language does almost the opposite of what it was created for. With frightening perversity—the evidence mounts daily—words now seem to cut off and isolate, to cause more misunderstandings than they prevent.
>
> Semantic aphasia is the monstrous insensitivity that allows generals to call war "pacification," union leaders to describe strikes or slow-downs as "job actions," and politicians to applaud even moderately progressive programs as "revolutions." Semantic aphasia is also the near-pathological blitheness that permits three different advertisers in the same women's magazine to call a wig and two dress lines "liberated."—Melvin Maddocks, "The Limitations of Language," *Time,* March 8, 1971

Formal words are appropriate to writers and speakers who use them easily and naturally and to situations that require them for precision. College students should increase the number of formal words in their active vocabulary, but these words should be the necessary ones for discussing ideas, reflecting an actual growth in intellectual scope, not an attempt to translate ordinary matters into "big words."

Big W

**23.1**

The
effect
of
words
**334**

## "Big words"—stilted language

In *Modern English Usage* H. W. Fowler remarks that sometimes "We tell our thoughts, like our children, to put on their hats and coats before they go out." Noting that "the less of such change there is the better," he adds, "there is nothing to be ashamed of in *buy* or *see* that they should need translating into *purchase* and *observe;* where they give the sense equally well they are fit for any company and need not be shut up at home."

"Big words," as the term is used here, are any and all expressions that are too heavy or too formal for the situation. Such words sound stilted, whether they are short or long, common or uncommon. A typical fault of inexperienced writers is the use of big words in a misguided effort to sound profound:

It is difficult to filter out one specific cause for a social problem. Most often there are many minute factors interrelated and closely correlated. Our conception of a social problem today possesses more magnitude than that of two or three decades ago. We now consider the world as a unit rather than an aggregation of component entities.

Ideas are easier to understand and are more convincing if the wording is natural. It should be exact, not inflated beyond the requirements of the subject or the expectations of the reader. The language of the sentences just cited, for example, might be simplified as follows:

A social problem can seldom be traced to a single, specific cause. Today we are much more aware of the complexity of social problems than we were twenty or thirty years ago, for we have come to see that all societies are interrelated.

Students are most likely to use stilted language in papers written near the beginning of a composition course, when they aren't certain what attitude they should take toward their material or toward their readers. They may use inflated diction because they wrongly believe that a paper written for a composition course should be as formal and impersonal as possible, or that big words will impress the reader, or that inflated diction is humorous ("a fair damsel garbed in the mode

**Big W**

**23.1**

Formal
words
**335**

of the moment" instead of "a fashionably dressed young woman").

An extreme use of big words is sometimes called *gobbledy-gook*—inflated diction that seems to have lost all contact with the matter being discussed. Writing full of such jargon is often found in print today, especially in specialized journals and government publications, but this does not make it good English. Here is what James Thurber had to say of such language:

Great big blocky words and phrases bumble off our tongues and presses every day. In four weeks of purposeful listening to the radio and reading the newspapers I have come up with a staggering list, full of sound and fury, dignifying nothing: "automation," "roadability," "hummature," "motivational cognition" (this baby turned up in a series of travel lectures and was never defined), "fractionalization," "varietism," "redesegregation," "additive," "concertization" (this means giving a concert in a hall, and is not to be confused with cinematization or televisionization). . . . Ization is here to stay. It appeals to bureaucrats and congressmen because of its portentous polysyllabification. Politicians love it the way they love such expressions as "legislativewise." Lord Conesford, stout defender of the Queen's English, recently paraphrased Churchill's "Give us the tools and we will finish the job" by Washingtonizing it like this: "Supply us with the implements and we will finalize the solution of the matter."—James Thurber, *Alarms and Diversions*

The remedy for too many big words is simple: Read aloud what you have written, preferably some time after you have written it; if you find the language markedly different from what you would use in conversation, look at the words carefully to see whether you can find simpler substitutes.

## Technical words

In writing intended for a general audience, unfamiliar terms not made clear by the context should be defined or explained. Technical terms or unfamiliar expressions that often need explaining include:

1) Scientific terms *(isotope, lobotomy, gneiss)*, and other expressions restricted to a specialized activity *(a cappella, heroic hexameter, escrow, chiaroscuro, farinaceous, binary).*

2) Words used in special senses rather than in the usual way (the *spine* of a book, to *justify* a line of type, the *recorder* as a wind instrument, a *frog* as a fastener for a jacket).

3) Foreign words and phrases not customarily used by most people *(lex talionis, pourboire, eisteddfod, Walpurgisnacht).*

You should not use an inexact or wordy expression in place of a necessary technical term. If, for instance, the subject of a paper is "Mountain Climbing," it is better to define and use a word like *piton* than to say "those little metal gadgets that they tie ropes to." Do not use unfamiliar words just to show off, but use and explain those that are essential to your subject.

Often a simple definition or explanation can be worked into the sentence where the technical term is introduced, as in the following examples:

The ability of the heart to function depends primarily on the state of the heart muscle, or myocardium, as it is technically known.

In the study of rhetoric we are first to consider *inventio,* or what we now refer to as the problems of pre-writing.

In cold weather the Eskimos wear mukluks (fur boots) and parkas (short fur coats with fur hoods).

As a rule, do not simply quote a dictionary definition, which may be too narrow, but compose one that fits the style and scale of your own paper. Compare a dictionary definition of *oligarchy* with this description of the term:

I mean by "oligarchy" any system in which ultimate power is confined to a section of the community: the rich to the exclusion of the poor, Protestants to the exclusion of Catholics, aristocrats to the exclusion of plebeians, white men to the exclusion of colored men, males to the exclusion of females, or members of one political party to the exclusion of the rest. A system may be more or less oligarchic according to the percentage of the population that is excluded; absolute monarchy is the extreme of oligarchy.—Bertrand Russell, *The Impact of Science on Society*

The crucial thing in defining a term is to give an adequate description of the way *you* are using it, with details and concrete illustrations to clarify the meaning.

## Informal words 23.2

Informal words include those marked *colloquial* in dictionaries and most of those marked *slang.* They are part of general English but may not be appropriate to all kinds of writing.

### Appropriate use of informal words
Informal words are often appropriate in discussions of sports,

informal situations, and humorous material. They are also sometimes fitting in discussions of more important topics, especially by young people, where the language otherwise is typically general English. You will find such words used, without apology or quotation marks, in many of the most reputable publications. Note the boldface words in this paragraph:

What happens to the child who is treated as an adult is that he **gets fresh** — becomes impertinent, disobedient, whiny, and a pest. Nobody enjoys him much any more, beginning with himself. Even to his loving mother he sometimes **gives a stiff pain in the neck.** But if she has read a book . . . she knows that this is because he feels anxious and insecure. Therefore she controls her impulse **to warm his tail** and send him to bed without supper; she treats him, instead, with monumental patience and slightly forced demonstrations of affection. **Daddy,** who comes home from the office pretty tired, in need of a drink and some peaceful home life, is likely to be less long-suffering. He may even raise the possibility of **cracking down.** — Helen Eustis, "Good-By to Oedipus," *Harper's Magazine*

If you are tempted to apologize for informal words by putting them in quotation marks, ask yourself whether they are genuinely appropriate. If they are, use them without apology, but if not, replace them with words from the general vocabulary.

## 23.2 Inappropriate use of informal words

> **Inf**  Revision: Change the informal expression to one that is more general.

It is disconcerting to a reader to encounter an informal expression in relatively formal writing:

The displaced persons in Europe experienced many **tough breaks** after the end of the war. [more appropriate: **hardships**]
The natives believe that they can expiate certain offenses against tribal customs by **throwing a feast.** [better: **giving a feast**]

In formal writing, informal words not only indicate a shift in variety of usage but may also suggest that you've grown careless toward your subject:

When Desdemona failed to produce the handkerchief, Othello began to suspect that she **wasn't on the level.**

Be particularly careful about certain expressions so widely used that you may not realize (until the slip is called to your attention) that they are considered informal rather than general usage:

The
effect
of
words
**338**

Plays of this sort are seldom seen **in our neck of the woods.**
Faulkner had **a funny habit** of writing long, rather complicated sentences.

## Live words and death masks                      **23.3**

Good writing, whether factual or fictional, captures a reader's interest and holds attention; other writing, concerned with similar facts or ideas, may strike a reader as lifeless and boring. In either instance the wording may be correct enough, but in the more enjoyable and memorable reading the words are fresh and direct:

> Then a tremendous flash of light cut across the sky. Mr. Tanimoto has a distinct recollection that it travelled from east to west, from the city toward the hills. It seemed a sheet of sun. — John Hersey, *Hiroshima*
>
> Supper was a young squirrel who had nevertheless achieved an elder's stringiness, roasted in foil on the embers, and a potato baked in the same way. — John Graves, *Goodbye to a River*

The search for fresh and direct expression does not require that you should strain obviously for effect, by searching for unusual expressions or words, any more than it requires that you should use eccentric punctuation or unconventional sentence structure. It does mean that you should take an interest in the freshness of your expression and that you should take sufficient time and thought to put aside *death masks* in favor of live words.

We have used the expression *death masks* as a general name for several kinds of words and expressions, including worn-out terms, euphemisms, incongruous figures of speech, or currently overworked expressions. A *death mask* is a casting made of someone's face just after death — and that seems to have little to do with words. But two ideas are brought together in the term that together describe the effect of some words: they are dead — they lack vitality and freshness; they hide or mask meaning. A euphemism, for example, is lifeless language, and it hides the writer's meaning, masking it as something else. Several varieties of death masks are discussed in the following sections.

## Old-fashioned words

We naturally use words that are current. In fact there is a temptation to resort too easily to "vogue words" *(bottleneck, breakthrough),* to allude to current activities *(getting off the launching pad),* or to add the fashionable suffix *-wise* to words that are in good use as they stand ("The play was a success *profitwise*" for "The play made a profit").

On the other hand, some writers mar their papers with old-fashioned expressions which, although they may not be obsolete or archaic, seem incongruous in contemporary writing. They may think that such words sound impressive or elegant; the reader, however, is more likely to consider the writing affected or foolish:

One may relax on the **greensward** of a Sunday and listen to a rousing band concert.

The game seemed to have been won, but **alas!** we failed to gain the necessary three yards in four tries.

Little schooling was required in **days of yore** to get along in life.

**Trite**

**23.3**

Here are some old-fashioned expressions with their present-day equivalents:

| | |
|---|---|
| amidst — among | deem — think, consider |
| befell — happened | supped — ate, dined |
| brethren — brothers | twain — two |

The best way to detect old-fashioned words is to read the passage aloud and decide whether you would use such an expression in ordinary conversation.

## Trite expressions

> **Trite** Revision: Replace the trite expression with one that is fresher or more direct.

Trite expressions, or clichés, are pat phrases so familiar that, given the first words, we can usually finish the expression without thinking:

This is going to hurt me more _____
He is down but not _____
Gone but _____
It isn't the heat but _____

The effect of words

340

Try to avoid the following overworked expressions that occur with relentless frequency in student papers:

| Cliché | Comment |
|---|---|
| according to Webster | Did Webster write the dictionary you are using? |
| history tells us | A dubious personification, one that often leads to empty generalizations. |
| the finer things of life | Name two or three. No matter what they are—a good pipe, a Beethoven quartet, a cheesecake—they'll be more convincing to the reader than this nebulous phrase. |
| last but not least | Is the last item or fact *never* of least importance? |

The problem with trite expressions is that you can use them without thinking. They are there in the air, and you can fill a gap on your page by plucking one. They are part of a community language; using them easily becomes habitual. But when you use trite expressions, they replace your own words and thoughts, and so they mask your own meaning.

Figurative language (§23.4) adds interest to writing when it is fresh and appropriate, but stale comparisons and personifications only serve to bore the reader. It will not make anything seem cooler, hotter, or neater if you describe it as *cool as a cucumber, hot as a two-dollar pistol,* or *neat as a pin.* Here is a short list of trite figures of speech; you can probably think of many similar expressions:

quick as a wink
lost in thought
sly as a fox
rotten to the core
white as snow
in a nutshell
darkness overtakes us
commune with nature
the rat race

at the drop of a hat
a watery grave
run like a deer
like a shot from a cannon
brave as a lion
Mother Nature
spreading like wildfire
bull in a china shop
the crack of dawn

Similarly, many quotations have lost their vividness through overuse:

a sadder and wiser man
stone walls do not a prison make

all the world's a stage
water, water, everywhere

So thoroughly are quotations from Shakespeare woven into our daily speech that some people, when they read or see a

**Trite**

**23.3**

Live words
and
death masks
**341**

play such as *Hamlet* or *Julius Caesar* for the first time, are surprised to find that they have been "talking Shakespeare" all their lives:

to be or not to be        lend me your ears
uneasy lies the head        not wisely, but too well
something rotten in the state of Denmark

There are many fresh, vivid lines from less-quoted sources — in modern poetry, for instance, and in Shakespeare, too — if you wish to enliven your writing with quotations.

When you find yourself using overworked expressions, look at them closely to see if they actually mean anything to you; usually you will decide that they really mean very little, and you will make your point another way.

## Euphemisms

Trite

23.3

A euphemism is a polite and often affected expression used in place of a more common term which the user fears might be offensive. Euphemisms are often used in conversation out of consideration for the listener's feelings: a teacher might tell a mother that her child is *slow* or *exceptional* rather than *dull* or *stupid;* a saleswoman is more likely to tell a customer that she has a *problem figure* than that she is *overweight* or *fat.* But although euphemisms are often necessary in social situations, they ordinarily sound evasive or affected when they are used in writing.

| Euphemistic expression | Direct expression |
|---|---|
| a reconditioned automobile | a used car |
| underprivileged, disadvantaged | poor |
| senior citizens | old people |
| halitosis | bad breath |
| unmentionables | underwear |
| expecting | pregnant |
| pass away | die |
| lay to rest | bury |
| our statement apparently has escaped your attention | you haven't paid your bill |
| preferred customer | customer who pays his bills regularly |

## Specialized euphemisms: machine-tooled and scientific

"In the present century," H. W. Fowler notes, "euphemism has been employed less in finding discreet terms for what is indelicate than as a protective device for governments and as a token of a new approach to psychological and sociological problems." What is especially interesting and revealing about much current euphemistic language is its origin. A large variety of euphemistic, disguising words come from presumably objective, scientific attitudes. They mask what may be relatively simple, perfectly ordinary, occasionally brutal actions, but in doing so they reveal writers' and speakers' impulses to show themselves as precise and totally efficient.

For example, the recent habit of making verbs by adding -*ize* to other words apparently grows out of a belief that the -*ize* verb is more thorough. "To make a final decision" might be taken as an arbitrary action, but "to finalize the decision" presumably is meant to suggest that the speaker is going to "wrap it all up," take all the necessary steps, pursue the process logically, and arrive at an end. The speaker who replaces *ugly* in a description of a city scene with *deleterious to the visual planning of the urban landscape* may be trying to get several different effects; one apparent purpose is to rid the statement of the messy emotional reactions and judgments implied by *ugly* and to suggest instead the neutral, controlled judgment implied in the "safe" language of the euphemism. A similar motive seems to be at work when writers use the passive voice unnecessarily—*it is thought* instead of *I think, it is felt* instead of *the family feels, it is believed* instead of *the committee believes*. Writers apparently decide sometimes that *it is thought* is somehow more dispassionate and disciplined and rational than *I think*. A large number of words used to describe social interactions appear to be intended to show us as more efficient and controlled than we are. Some people never have friendly *chats* or *informal talks;* they have *dialogues* or *unstructured conversations;* some committees are organized so as to give each member *ample opportunity for verbal elaboration of subjective intent,* while others let the members have *a a chance to explain their views.* When a government agency substitutes *termination with extreme prejudice* for *execution* the effect is not just to mask a brutal act but also to let the act be seen as part of a logical sequence of decision-making. When in Vietnam military officials would speak of destroying *structures,* instead of *houses* or *buildings,* they not only masked the precise nature of the act, but also gave the act, with the noncommittal *structures,* a sense of unimpassioned objectivity.

In the last few years we have frequently heard and seen words that, though originally associated with machines, especially computers, are now being used in accounts of other activities. The trouble is, the words don't lose their machine associations even when they are used in other contexts. When speakers talk about *software* when they mean *paper, print-outs* when they mean *published results,* or *input* when they mean *information* gleaned from outside sources, then they are making machine talk, giving ordinary acts and objects the appearance of a splendid, computerlike efficiency. Other expressions have become common: *at this point in time* replaces *now, that time-frame* replaces *then,* and *zero-defect system* replaces *perfection.*

The peril in these and other forms of euphemism is that the words get farther from the things they refer to. In most instances, if you are tempted to use a euphemistic expression, don't. In most instances, if you have already used a euphemistic expression, revise it.

**Fig**

**23.4**

## Figures of speech 23.4

Figures of speech are expressions of comparison, personification, or association that are used to intensify statements or to make them more expressive and vivid, usually by shifting from the ordinary uses and meanings of words. This is a literal, nonfigurative statement:

The fewer words a man uses, the more quickly his meaning will be understood.

The same idea can be expressed in a more memorable way by a well-chosen figure of speech:

. . . meaning is an arrow that reaches its mark when least encumbered with feathers. — Herbert Read, *English Prose Style*

Notice how the use of well-chosen figures of speech enlivens this description of a summer morning in New York:

Heat has an effect on sound, intensifying it. On a scorching morning, at breakfast in a cafe, one's china cup explodes against its saucer with a fierce report. The great climaxes of sound in New York are achieved in side streets, as in West 44th Street, beneath our window, where occasionally an intestinal stoppage takes place, the entire block laden with undischarged vehicles, the pangs of congestion increasing till every horn is going—a united, delirious scream of hate, every decibel charged with a tiny drop of poison.—E. B. White, *The Second Tree from the Corner*

The use of figurative language is not limited to purely descriptive passages or to "literary" subjects. You will find figures of speech used freely and effectively in such diverse material as financial articles, literary criticism, advertising copy, sports writing, and political discussions.

## Types of figurative language
Early texts in rhetoric and composition classified many figures of speech (Richard Sherry's *A Treatise of Schemes and Tropes,* published in 1550, catalogs about three hundred), but these are the ones most widely used in current writing:

*Hyperbole* (deliberate exaggeration for interest and emphasis):

It was a day **to end all days.**
He's the **greatest** little second baseman **in the world.**

*Irony* (use of a word to signify the reverse of its literal meaning):

For Brutus is an **honourable man.** . . .
That's just **great.** [expression often signifying disgust]

*Litotes* (deliberate understatement, often calculated to magnify the impact of what we say by its incongruity and restraint):

Hemingway was not a **bad** writer.
Golly, what a **gully!** [a description of the Grand Canyon]

*Metaphor* (implied comparison between unlike things that, perhaps unexpectedly, have something in common):

Out, out, brief candle!

**Life's but a walking shadow,** a poor player
That struts and frets his hour upon the stage
And then is heard no more. . . .

*Metonymy* (substitution of an associated word for what is actually meant):

But most by **numbers** judge a poet's song;
And smooth or rough with them is right or wrong. . . .

Suited to the **plow,** he sought to live by the **pen.**

**Fig**

**23.4**

*Onomatopoeia* (use of words to create a sound appropriate to the sense):

It was a hot day in late July when I sat with Uncle Miles at Belting beside the **strippling ream.** The deliberate Spoonerism was Uncle Miles's, and it did seem to express something about the stream that rippled beside us as we sat on the spongy grass. To say strippled rather than rippled conveyed something about the movement of the water, and ream instead of stream suggested that large bream waited in it ready to be caught.—Julian Symons, *The Belting Inheritance*

*Oxymoron* (coupling contradictory terms):

At eleven, she **enjoyed the fright** of reading **Dracula.**

*Periphrasis* (substitution of a descriptive phrase for a name, sometimes of a name for a descriptive phrase):

Be true to the **red, white, and blue.**
For two consecutive holes, plus a drive on the third, he was **Arnold Palmer;** then came disaster.

*Personification* (attribution of human qualities to nonhuman or abstract things):

They turned and waved, and then the jungle **swallowed** them.

*Simile* (stated comparison between two unlike things that, perhaps unexpectedly, have something in common):

My mistress' bosom is **as white as the snow, and as cold.**

*Synecdoche* (substitution of a term for another to which it is related in a system of classification, as in naming a part when a whole is meant, naming a whole when a part is meant):

**Wisconsin** meets **Oregon** in the Rose Bowl.
The poor man had twelve **mouths** to feed.

## Effective figures of speech

**Fig** Revision: Change the figure of speech marked to an expression that is more appropriate to your subject and your style; avoid inconsistent figures.

Although figures of speech, if they are fresh and perceptive, clearly have an appeal, they are *not* mere ornaments. Indeed, when they seem to be ornaments, we can usually conclude that they are used unnaturally and ostentatiously. If they are vivid and natural, they make writing attractive, but they can accomplish much more than this.

Each kind of figurative language has its special uses. Metaphor and simile, for example, can enlarge our perception and understanding of a subject, and can say much in little space. If a writer says, "The old cowpuncher's parenthetical legs were covered by worn brown chaps," we gain from the metaphor a pretty clear picture of the cowboy's shape; some notion of his age and the amount of time he has spent on a horse; and some insight into his character and the writer's attitude toward him (the choice of metaphor suggests a familiar, even comic treatment). We can learn something about a subject in one area by the light cast on it from language of another area, much as we do in reading parables and allegories, which in a sense can be considered extended metaphors.

Figures of speech can help us to understand the writer's attitude toward his subject and toward his audience. Appropriate personification and periphrasis, for example, are signals of a writer's emotional involvement in his subject, and perhaps of his wish to make an emotional appeal to his audience. Litotes, hyperbole, and simile, because they show us something about the way a writer sees things, can enable an audience to know what kind of person addresses them, how perceptive he is, and how reliable he may be.

**Fig**

**23.4**

For these reasons it is obvious that figurative expressions should be in keeping with your subject and your style, and that they should be accurate enough to contribute to the meaning. Expressions that are too strong or that strive too hard to be picturesque only confuse or irritate the reader:

As fall comes in with its gentle coolness, Mother Nature **launches her chemical warfare,** changing the leaves into their many pretty colors.

My grandfather's barn was **like a medieval fortress shrouded in legend.**

Straining for unusual expressions seldom results in effective writing. The figures to use are those that actually come to mind when you are trying to give an exact account of the subject. They should be fresh, if possible, but, even more important, they should fit their context and sound natural.

## Consistent figures of speech
A figure of speech should not begin with one kind of picture and switch to another wholly unrelated one. These *mixed*

*metaphors,* as they are usually referred to, often present a ludicrous picture instead of the fresh insight the writer intends:

The nineteenth century **became a door** opened by some of the braver authors, through which many of the earlier ideas of writing for children, which had been **crushed or discarded, again sprang to blossom,** and spread into the many branches of children's literature that we have today.

If you can look at your own writing with some degree of objectivity, you can usually determine whether a figure is consistent or not. Sometimes an expression that seemed very vivid at the moment of writing proves, upon rereading, to be confusing or even ridiculous.

### Applications: Using Words Effectively

1. Most of us are impressed when a writer or speaker uses "big words" effectively. A large and powerful vocabulary is generally taken as an indication of intelligence and education, and it is worth your while to work on building your vocabulary. On the other hand, to *misuse* a "big word" makes you sound foolish instead of intelligent. Almost as bad is to use terms that are unnecessarily obscure when simpler ones might be clearer. It is seldom that you will want the reader to laugh *at* you, as we might laugh at the speaker in an old movie who said, "Boy, what a walk! You should have seen her *osculating* down the street!" In the following passages, words are not used effectively or appropriately for their purpose. Rewrite them into clear and effective English.

   a. *From a student composition:* Our high school was eminently well equipped for various recreational pursuits. For those of sportive inclinations, there was the capacious gymnasium, which resounded to multitudinous roars whenever our champions engaged a challenging contingent. Here, too, were held gala affairs; as the strains of melody reverberated to the dome, the floor was inundated by swirling taffeta and a phantasmagoria of colored illuminations.

   b. *From a professional journal for teachers:* This film demonstrates the progress of an idealized date, from the ideational impetus to the request, acceptance, the dating experience itself, and the final leave-taking, in the process raising some significant questions regarding dating and suggesting partial answers as discussional guides. Such questions as "How does one say good night?" aid in stimulating class discussion of the dating process and the problem areas inherent in it.

   c. *From a sermon delivered to a predominantly middle-class congregation:* In like manner Our Lord dignifies a really simple activity of

Fig

**23.4**

His disciples, as we have read in the pericope from The Gospel of a fishing expedition. We cannot ignore the fact that most of us live our life in the simplicities of it; the few things that come along as profundities (which we sometimes see as milestones) are not our escape from the realities, but our confirmation of these.

**d.** *From a letter to the editor:* Is the love of monetary remuneration such that it acerbates all else into obliviousness? Can we not conjure into our configurations and substratums of consciousness some other destination than the all-mighty dollar? Man has pilgrimaged too long after the bread and has forgotten his ultimate ontogeny. The interface at this juncture needs must be between flesh and spirit, not body and buck.

**2.** One way television writers can always get a laugh is by sending an ordinary person dressed informally into a very fancy French restaurant to order a hamburger or a bowl of chili. This inappropriateness of dress and behavior is the same thing as a writer using too-informal words when writing about a serious or formal subject, as the writer of the following theme on Henry David Thoreau's "Civil Disobedience" did. Rewrite the theme so that the words are more appropriate to the subject.

Exer

To me, Thoreau seems to be basically a live-and-let-live sort of person. He doesn't think you should let the government do your thinking for you or con you into going along with something you think is wrong. In fact he comes right out and says the best idea would be no government at all, if people were ready for that kind of setup. Since most of them aren't, he thinks we ought to make the best of what we have. As for himself, Thoreau thought the Mexican War and slavery were wrong, and to beef up his complaint he refused to pay his taxes. Of course this meant getting locked up, but he figured that by making a sort of model of himself he could get other people to back him up and put some pressure on the boys in Washington. I guess this isn't really as featherbrained as it sounds, because it worked O.K. in India when Gandhi tried it, even if Thoreau didn't get anywhere with it in the U.S.A. Anyway, he was mainly a sort of out-of-doors person and probably liked camping and things like that better than mixing in politics.

**3.** We all use clichés and trite expressions in our writing, but good writers use more fresh and direct expressions and fewer clichés than bad writers. In any case, we need to be aware of figurative language so that we can manipulate it effectively. Sometimes a worn-out statement can be improved by a simple direct statement of the idea; other times it is worth a little thought to mint a new comparison.

*example: cliché:* She worked her fingers to the bone on that job.
*direct statement:* On that job, the hours were long and the work was hard.

Applications:
Using
Words
Effectively
**349**

*figurative language:* She said that the job was harder than a petrified egg.

Now try your hand at rewriting the following sentences. Indicate which of your sentences are direct and which are figurative.

**a.** If he wins the election—and he may—we are all up the creek without a paddle.
**b.** Silence reigned supreme among us as the principal gave us a piece of his mind.
**c.** When he got to the campus post office and found his draft notice, it was a bitter pill to swallow.
**d.** Armed to the teeth with notes and No-Doz, he started to work on his research paper.
**e.** The chairman nipped the squabble in the bud and got the discussion down to brass tacks.
**f.** Each and every man should take out life insurance so that his loved ones will be well provided for when he goes to his eternal reward.
**g.** I told him straight from the shoulder that his work was no longer acceptable.
**h.** If it didn't mean showing my hand too soon, I would tell the newspapers that I intend to throw my hat in the ring.
**i.** A teacher is called upon to render services beyond the call of duty time and time again. His unselfish devotion to the youth of America goes a long way toward making this a better world to live in.
**j.** The investigators didn't leave a stone unturned in their relentless search for the fugitive from justice.

**4.** The critic I. A. Richards has speculated that we use figurative language more than we are aware. He maintains that we can barely get through three sentences without it. Try checking out this claim in any magazine you have handy. Go through an article or two, copying the figurative language that you find. Try classifying it according to the ancient "schemes and tropes" listed on p. 345. This process may heighten your awareness of figurative writing, and help make your own writing richer.
*example:* There were nine *hands* on the ranch (synecdoche) who tended the cattle and also the fields of wheat that *rippled like waves* (simile) in the wind.

PARAGRAPHS
SENTENCES
AND
DOUBLE LETTER SCORE
TRIPLE WORD SCORE
TRIPLE LETTER SCORE
DOUBLE WORD SCORE

# Sentence length and economy

*A writer of bad prose, to become a writer of good prose, must alter his character. He does not have to become good in terms of conventional morality, but he must become honest in the expression of himself, which means that he must know himself. There must be no gap between expression and meaning, between real and declared aims. . . . Prose style is the way you think and the way you understand what you feel.* — Donald Hall, The Modern Stylists

Good sentences are varied in length and in pattern. Sometimes they are leisurely, unfolding slowly and gradually rounding out an idea; sometimes they are direct and emphatic. They may be balanced, or curt, or loose. They may be accumulating, piling up facts or ideas or observations to achieve a meaning, or they may be discriminating, distinguishing grammatically among facts and ideas and observations to state a meaning. In other words, they are as different as people.

The stylistic qualities of sentences are matters of choice rather than of rule. You can write short, grammatically correct sentences almost indefinitely, but if you wish to say what cannot be said in that way — to expand your meaning or to vary it — then you must choose from among the various correct grammatical constructions the forms that will be effective for your situation. Remember that reading first-draft sentences critically and revising them can be extremely important to you in developing a good style.

This chapter is about the stylistic features of sentence *length,* including economy of wording. Chapter 25 considers the variety of forms, or *patterns,* that sentences may take to communicate meaning.

## Sentence length as a matter of style

Written sentences may vary in length according to your purpose, the way in which you typically express your ideas, and the type of material you are presenting. Longer sentences generally occur in rather formal discussions of complex ideas, shorter ones in rapid narrative, easy exposition, and other general writing.

Sentence length varies somewhat according to the fashion

of the times. Early nineteenth-century writers built their ideas into sentences that averaged thirty to forty words. Current writing uses somewhat shorter sentences, averaging between twenty and thirty words. These figures are only averages, of course; the individual sentences may vary greatly in length.

There is no special virtue in either long sentences or short ones. More important is the total effect of a passage in which the sentences are characteristically long or short. In the following paragraph by a well-known scholar and teacher, the sentences are considerably shorter than the average for professional writers. Yet the form is appropriate because the statements—many of them directives or suggestions for action—are intended to be emphatic. (The one long sentence near the middle varies from the pattern, but it is itself a series of brief statements):

Concentration must be learnt. It should be learnt in school. A good teacher can teach it to his pupils. It should not be imagined as nothing but an effort of the will. Concentration is also an intellectual process. It is choice. Take the same boy who reads his book slowly, grudgingly, five lines at a time, and increase the urgency of his study—somehow, anyhow—make the choice clearer to him, and the importance of his study paramount—put him to work on the prize essay—and then watch. "Turn that radio off!" he shouts. He clears the table, except for one photograph. He sits fixed in one position till he is cramped. Sometimes, when he is really intent, he will miss meals and forget about sleep. All this because he has chosen one aim and discarded others. And that, after all, is what we learn to do throughout life.—Gilbert Highet, *The Art of Teaching*

But in another work, Highet uses a longer, more complex and leisurely sentence pattern, appropriate both to the subject matter and to the kind of audience he is addressing:

Are these shadows on so many of our horizons the outriders of another long night, like that which was closing in upon Sidonius? We cannot yet tell. But modern scholars must regret that they have to work during a time when instead of that general supranational comradeship which helped to build the learning and culture of the sixteenth and nineteenth centuries, it is becoming more and more difficult to exchange opinions across the world, to bring from distant countries books where new and vital points of view are freely expressed, to carry on many-sided correspondences with far-off scholars and encounter no difficulties other than those involved in the common search for truth, and to feel oneself part of a worldwide structure of art and learning, greater than all the things that divide mankind: nationalities and creeds, fear and hate.
—Gilbert Highet, *The Classical Tradition*

The problem of length in most student sentences is seldom a matter of the average number of words per statement. More often it is variety and appropiateness: the ability to use the form, long or short, that best suits your purpose and your material and that will give variety and liveliness to your writing.

Sometimes, especially when you first start writing in college, you may be tempted to keep sentences short. It's safe: punctuation errors and other troubles may be less likely to show up in short sentences. The world around you may sometimes seem to show you evidence that short statements are the characteristic form of human utterance. The opening lines of newspaper stories are often filled with short sentences. Radio disc jockeys often speak a staccato rhythm of short sentences. Television commercials and magazine ads and billboards depend almost exclusively on short, presumably punchy statements. Some, indeed, on occasion do not use sentences at all: Volkswagen advertisements in magazines have for some time been treating short phrases and sometimes single words as if they were whole sentences and punctuating them as such.

Don't be too cautious, and don't be too quickly convinced by the apparent evidence for short statements. There are some things that you can't say briefly. There are some times when a leisurely accumulation of insight and observation in a sentence will let you be more thorough, more honest. John Erskine, the novelist, remarked some time ago that "When you write, you make a point, not by subtracting as though you sharpened a pencil, but by adding." In *Notes Toward a New Rhetoric,* Francis Christensen, too, says that "composition is essentially a process of *addition.*" As you add to sentences, more often than not they become more specific. Start with a base sentence, for example:

The girl sat in the chair.

The statement is generalized. The girl is given no identity, nor is the chair; the manner of sitting is not specified. But consider what happens when we add to the statement:

1) The small girl sat in the big chair.

2) Quiet and thoughtful, the small girl sat curled in the big, brown, high-backed chair.

3) Quiet and thoughtful, the small girl sat curled in the big, brown, high-backed chair, her legs tucked under her, a book in one hand, a cup of coffee in the other.

4) Quiet and thoughtful, lost in what she was reading, the small girl sat curled in the big, brown, high-backed chair by the record player, her legs tucked under her, a book in one hand, a cup of coffee in the other.

With each addition, the scene is more clearly specified.

Just here, an interesting paradox occurs: *by adding you take away.* If you write the sentence *The girl sat in the chair,* since you give no identity or distinguishing marks to the scene, readers are at liberty to see the girl and the chair according to *their own* experiences. As you add specifying details to the sentence, making it more clearly a scene from *your* experience, you gradually subtract from your readers' visualization of the scene and make it possible for them to see it as you do. With each addition, the texture of detail in the sentence becomes richer. Many ways of adding to your basic sentences are open to you:

1) you can make the subject, the verb, or the complement compound;

2) you can insert appositives into the subject – verb – complement structure;

3) you can use verbals or verbal phrases;

4) you can use noun clauses for the subject or the complement;

5) you can use adjective clauses to modify the subject or the complement;

6) you can use adverb clauses to modify the verb;

7) you can add adjectives, adverbs, or prepositional phrases.

With each addition – and there are others that you can devise by reviewing the section on the grammar of sentences – it is also possible to begin rearranging the sentence.

## Sentence length and meaning 24.2

> **SL**  Revision: Rewrite the passage marked to eliminate choppy or stringy sentences and to show the relationship of ideas.

Appropriate sentence length is determined less by the number of words in a sentence than by what a sentence contributes to the total meaning of a paragraph. Self-evident or extremely obvious statements contribute nothing to writing:

These scientific theories came into being only after definite steps had been taken.

Of course definite steps were taken. This statement is so general that one could substitute for *scientific theories* almost anything that comes to mind—the Brooklyn Bridge, the United Nations, a college dance, or a term paper.

## Choppy (too short) sentences

Some sentences say too little because a simple idea has been broken up unnecessarily into two or more statements, as in this example:

I took my first course in mathematics at Riverdale High School. This was first-year or elementary algebra.

Most readers will not feel any need to invest their time in these individual sentences, which might better be combined:

I took my first course in mathematics, elementary algebra, at Riverdale High School.

A succession of very short sentences tends to give a piece of writing a halting, jerky effect. Such sentences also impede the flow of thought, for they fail to show how ideas are related:

We arrived at the induction center that afternoon. We were divided up. We were sent to barracks. They were reserved for draftees. The barracks were old. The floors were scrubbed almost white. Vague scars of cigarette burns marked them. I wondered how many wars had brought draftees here.

The choppy movement of this passage gives an effect the writer did not intend. The passage could be made smoother by combining related statements:

When we arrived at the induction center that afternoon, we were divided up and sent to the old barracks reserved for draftees. The floors were scrubbed almost white, but the vague scars of cigarette burns marking them made me wonder how many wars had brought draftees here.

Short sentences are useful in various writing situations—in dialog, for emphasis, for creating a feeling of rapid action or of tension—but you must exercise judgment if you are to use them successfully. In the following passage, for example, the writer's intention was probably to convey a feeling of excitement, but the breathless style defeats this purpose because it is continued too long, with no break in sentence pattern:

It was my senior year in high school. Our basketball team had won the trophy the year before. This year the team was considered even stronger. Nearly every member of the pep club was seated. It was the final game. We had come all the way through the tournament without a defeat. This game would determine which team would be the champion. I looked toward the end of the gym. The referees were talking. They, too, were excited. Would that starting gun never go off! My hands were clammy. My cheeks burned.

Examine closely any passage in your own writing that contains a noticeable number of consecutive sentences under eighteen words. Try reading the passage aloud to see whether it conveys the effect you intended or whether the writing is simply hasty.

## Stringy sentences

Avoid stringing together (with *and, but, so, and then*) statements that should be written as separate sentences or as subordinate elements. Sentences carelessly tacked together in this manner are not only monotonous to read but lose all their emphasis because every idea seems to be of equal importance:

About fifty feet away I saw a buck deer running for safety **and so** I kneeled on my right knee **and then** I brought the rifle to my right shoulder. He was still running, **so** I fired one shot at him, **but** I missed, **but** he stopped and looked at me, **and then** I had a much better target to shoot at.

Reading such sentences aloud should reveal their weaknesses and help you to revise them for better organization:

About fifty feet away I saw a buck deer running for safety. Kneeling on my right knee and bringing the rifle to my shoulder, I fired once, but missed. He stopped to look at me, providing a much better target.

Stringy sentences often result from linking too many main clauses together *(Most people know that our productive system is the world's best and they have grown to expect great things from this system, and they should)*. The cure lies in cutting down the number of coordinating conjunctions *(and, but, so)* and in subordinating ideas of lesser importance.

## Relating ideas clearly

Avoid combining unrelated ideas in the same sentence. If there is a relationship between the ideas, so that they can reasonably be combined, show what it is. Don't leave it to your reader to puzzle out:

As Byron is the poet of youth, it is appropriate that the new and completely reset edition of his poems should be published on March 1. [What is the relation between **youth** and the date of publication?]

Nassau has a delightful climate that attracts hundreds of tourists every year, and some historians think that Columbus landed in this area in 1492. [If there is any relationship between Nassau's climate and Columbus, it should be stated.]

Sentences that are haphazard or contain contradiction can be improved by clarifying the intended relationship:

| **Haphazard** | **Revised** |
| --- | --- |
| There is no evidence to support the fact that her marriage to another writer may have had some influence on her style. | Although her marriage to another writer may have had some influence on her style, there is no evidence to support this. |
| I consider *The Old Man and the Sea* one of the literary masterpieces of our time, but many people have disliked Hemingway's other novels. | Even those who have disliked Hemingway's other novels are likely to enjoy *The Old Man and the Sea,* which I consider one of the literary masterpieces of our time. |

A sentence should be constructed so that the most important idea receives greatest emphasis; the relationship of other ideas can usually be shown in subordinate constructions.
See also §25.2, Subordination to control and clarify meaning, and §25.4, Sentence emphasis.

Avoiding wordiness                                    **24.3**

> **Wdy**  Revision: Make the sentence or passage marked less wordy and more direct; avoid unnecessary predications.

Sentence economy means wording statements so that their meaning can be grasped by the reader without unnecessary effort. No one likes to listen to a speaker who talks too much and says too little, and no reader likes to cut his way through a tangle of useless words or constructions to get at a relatively simple idea. Phrases, clauses, or other constructions that use many words to say what can be said more directly are called *circumlocutions.*

Practicing sentence economy doesn't mean that you should

strip your sentences down to the bare minimum, as you might in composing a telegram or writing a classified ad. The shortest words and simplest constructions are not always the most economical, for they may fail to convey your exact or complete meaning. Economy of expression requires rather that you state your ideas in the most accurate and direct way possible.

Often it is possible to make a statement more direct by reducing a complete predication (a sentence or a clause) to a shorter construction (a phrase or a single word):

**Sentence: The snow lay like a blanket.** It covered the countryside. [two predications]

**Clause:** The snow, **which lay like a blanket,** covered the countryside. [two predications]

**Phrase:** The snow covered the countryside **like a blanket.** [one predication]

**Word:** The snow **blanketed** the countryside. [one predication]

Since each clause you use increases the number of predications, one way to tighten sentence form is to eliminate unnecessary and ineffective verbs and their modifiers:

| Two predications | Reduced |
|---|---|
| He crawled slowly over the river bank, looking for the flint chips which would mean that he had found a campsite. | He crawled slowly over the river bank, looking for flint chips marking a possible campsite. |

The two verbs that can most frequently be eliminated without any loss of meaning are *be* in its various forms and *have:*

| Excessive predication | More economical |
|---|---|
| **He is a native of the plains** and knows the value of water conservation. | **A native of the plains,** he knows the value of water conservation. |
| A few of the fellows **who were less serious** would go into a bar **where they would** have a steak dinner and a few glasses of beer. | A few of the **less serious** fellows would go into a bar **for** a steak dinner and a few glasses of beer. |
| **There** is only one excuse **that is acceptable,** and **that is** "I have a class this hour." | **Only one excuse is acceptable:** "I have a class this hour." |

If a large number of your sentences begin with *There,* see if some of them couldn't just as well start with another word:

| Wordy | More direct |
|---|---|
| **There are two plays in our anthology** and I like them both. | I like both plays in our anthology. |

| There is a suggestion box in almost all big business houses where employees may put ideas. | Most big business houses provide suggestion boxes for their employees. |
|---|---|

While a writer's style and the general movement of his or her sentences determine to a large degree whether shorter or longer constructions are more appropriate, the careless habit of consistently using two or more statements where one would be just as effective should be avoided in all styles of writing.

## Removing deadwood                                    24.4

> **Dead**  Revision: Revise the sentence or passage marked to eliminate deadwood.

*Deadwood* is a term for a particular kind of wordiness: lazy words and phrases that clutter up a statement without adding anything to its meaning.

Anyone acquainted with violin construction knows that the longer the wood is seasoned, the better **the result will be as far as** the tone of the instrument **is concerned.**

Empty expressions like those in boldface above are excess baggage and do nothing to further communication. They often find their way into first drafts because they come so handily to use, but you should take care to prune them out in revision. Eliminating deadwood will make a statement neater and more direct without changing its meaning in the least, as these examples illustrate (deadwood in boldface):

Every thinking person these days seems to agree **with the conception** that the world has gone mad.

Because **of the fact that** she had been ill, she missed the first two weeks of classes.

After a delay of forty-five minutes, the audience **got to the point that it** became restless and noisy.

The wordy formulas that serve as fillers in casual conversation are more noticeable and annoying in writing than they are in speech. Roundabout expressions should be replaced in revision by terms that say the same thing more directly:

| | | |
|---|---|---|
| **get in touch with** | *means* | **call** or **see** |
| **due to the fact that** | *means* | **because** or **since** |
| **in this day and age** | *means* | **now** or **today** |
| **at the same time that** | *means* | **while** |

Certain words, generally in stereotyped phrase combinations, account for much of the deadwood found in student writing. This list, while not exhaustive, illustrates phrases built upon the most common of these words:

| Word | As deadwood | Deadwood eliminated |
|---|---|---|
| case | **In many cases** students profit from the research paper. | Many students profit from the research paper. |
| character | Her gossip was **of a sordid and ugly character.** | Her gossip was sordid and ugly. |
| exist | The crime conditions **that existed** in Chicago became intolerable. | The crime conditions in Chicago became intolerable. |
| fact | In spite of **the fact that** he is lazy, I like him. | In spite of his laziness, I like him. |
| factor | Speed is also **an important factor.** | Speed is also important. |
| field | Anyone interested in **the field of** American history should take his course. | Anyone interested in American history should take his course. |
| instance | **In many instances,** students write their papers just before the deadline. | Often students write their papers just before the deadline. |
| line | He always thought he would be successful **along agricultural lines.** | He always thought he would be successful in agriculture. |
| manner | He glanced at her **in a suspicious manner.** | He glanced at her suspiciously. |
| nature | She seldom talks on any subject **of a controversial nature.** | She seldom talks on any controversial subject. |
| seems | **It seems that** we have not lost a daughter, but gained another icebox-raider. | We have not lost a daughter, but gained another icebox-raider. |
| tendency | When I am supposed to be working, I **have a tendency to** clean my pipes and dawdle. | When I am supposed to be working, I clean my pipes and dawdle. |
| type | His father had an executive **type of** position. | His father had an executive position. |

These words have definite meanings in some expressions (a *case* of measles, a minor *character* in the play, a *field* of clover, and so forth), but as used here, they are meaningless and unnecessary deadwood.

> **Rep** Revision: Eliminate the ineffective repetition of
> words, meaning, or sound.

Unless repeated for a definite reason, a word or a phrase should not be made conspicuous by too frequent use in the same passage.

### Effective repetition

Sometimes repetition is essential for meaning or for sentence structure:

Try as we may, we cannot, as we write history, escape our **purposiveness.** Nor, indeed, should we try to escape, for **purpose** and meaning are the same thing. But in pursuing our **purpose,** in making our **abstractions,** we must be aware of what we are doing; we ought to have it fully in mind that our **abstraction** is not perfectly equivalent to the infinite complication of event from which we have **abstracted.** — Lionel Trilling, *The Liberal Imagination*

Intentional repetition may also be effective for emphasis:

There is no way of becoming **inaccurate** by industry, and if you deliberately try to be **inaccurate** you fail. **Inaccuracy** is perhaps the most **spontaneous** and the **freest** of **gifts** offered by the Spirit to the wit of man. It is even more **spontaneous** and more **free** than the **gift** of writing good **verse,** or that rarer **gift** which I have also written of here — the **gift** of writing abominably **bad verse;** exceptionally **bad verse;** criminally **bad verse;** execrable **verse.** — Hilaire Belloc, *On*

Some kinds of words must of course be used over and over again: articles *(a, an, the),* conjunctions *(and, but, or),* prepositions *(of, in, at),* and pronouns *(it, that, my, which).* Because their purpose is strictly functional, these words are usually not noticed.

### Useless repetition

Unintentional, unnecessary, and ineffective repetition of words is illustrated in these passages:

The bonfire was sparkling and **gay.** Here and there the light from the fire showed a **gay** homecoming pennant. Then the cheerleaders dashed through the crowd, their **gaiety** infecting everybody.

When I was in high school, I would take a book home once or twice a week and maybe read it two or three hours at a **time. Most of the time** I would read **most** of my homework just in **time** to have it ready before class began. It was very easy **most of the time** to read the assignment and have it prepared when my **time** came to be called upon for recitation.

Repetition of this kind is weak and ineffective, for it focuses attention on words rather than on ideas. It also suggests that the writer may be careless and unconcerned with what he or she is saying.

Repetition of words

Repeat words in a passage only when you have good reason for doing so. Key words (such as the subject) may sometimes be repeated for clarity or emphasis, but less important terms should not be used more often than necessary.

| Careless repetition | Revised |
|---|---|
| The **problem** of feeding its ever-increasing population is one of India's most acute **problems.** | Feeding its ever-increasing population is one of India's most acute problems. |
| Many people think **that** if a **product** is endorsed by a prominent person **that** it is a good **product** to buy. | Many people think that a product endorsed by a prominent person is a good one to buy. |

Especially to be avoided is repetition of the same word in two different meanings:

| If I **run,** I'll get a **run** in my stockings. | If I run, I'll **tear** my stockings. |
|---|---|
| Astrology is so popular in Hollywood that many movie **stars** won't sign a contract unless the **stars** are favorable. | Astrology is so popular in Hollywood that many of the movie stars won't sign a contract unless their **horoscopes** are favorable. |

It is not always possible to correct careless repetition by striking out a word or substituting another of similar meaning. When a passage becomes badly cluttered like this one, complete rewriting is the only way to clear it up:

| Annoying repetition | Revised |
|---|---|
| There has been a **theory** advanced that the Vikings were here long before Columbus. As time goes on, more evidence is found to substantiate this **theory.** After reading several **articles** about **this,** I ran across some **articles** on the first discovery of America by people other than the Vikings. **This** interested me greatly, and I decided to investigate **this** as my topic for the research paper. | I began looking for a topic by reading several articles on the discovery of America by the Vikings, a theory that is being substantiated by increasing evidence as time goes on. Then, more or less by accident, I found that the Vikings may not, after all, have been the first people to visit America. This idea interested me greatly, and I decided to make it the topic of my research paper. |

## Repetition of meaning

Adding an expression that repeats the meaning of another (called *tautology*) is one of the most common forms of unprofitable repetition. The **boldface** expressions in the following sentences are a form of deadwood (§24.4). They should be omitted because they merely repeat ideas that are sufficiently expressed in other words in the sentences:

In the modern world **of today,** time has a meaning different than it had when transportation was slower.

It is believed that the age of the earth is about two billion years **old.**

She decided to trim the family room in bright red, but the **resultant** effect was not what she had anticipated.

Words like *color, size,* and *shape* often needlessly repeat a meaning that is already clear:

| **Unsatisfactory** | **Revised** |
| --- | --- |
| His hair was brick red **in color.** | His hair was brick red. |
| **The length** of the locks is about two thirds of a mile **long.** | The locks are about two thirds of a mile long. |
| Behind the house was an enclosed court which was rectangular **in shape.** | Behind the house was an enclosed rectangular court. |

The abbreviation *etc. (et cetera)* means "and so forth." To write "*and* etc." is equivalent to saying "and and so forth." Avoid this nonstandard expression.

## Repetition of sounds

A sound should not be made conspicuous by careless repetition. The cumulative effect of certain suffixes like *-ly, -ment,* and *-tion* may be unfortunate:

The concept of such sanctua**ry** immuni**ty** unquestionab**ly** predominant**ly** influenced the enemy to enter into the conflict.

Written permis**sion** of the administra**tion** is required for reregistra**tion** of those students who are on proba**tion.**

Alliteration—the repetition of the same sound at the beginning of words in a series—is out of place when it attracts attention to the words at the expense of the ideas:

I am looking for a shop that still has **p**leated **p**ants for **p**oor and **p**aunchy **p**rofessors.

He then made himself comfortable in a **r**ather **r**ickety **r**attan **r**ocker.

Even though your papers are not usually written to be read aloud, you should try to avoid unintentional sound patterns that may be momentarily irritating or distracting to a reader who has a well-tuned ear:

The enemy was reported to have seized this important **port,** and reinforcements were hurrying up in sup**port.**

### Applications: Working with Sentence Length and Economy

1. It's not too hard to write short sentences, but longer ones may require you to practice some. Five basic sentences appear below. To each one add the following constructions: one appositive, one verbal or verbal phrase, one adjective clause, one adverb clause, two adjectives, two prepositional phrases.

   *example:* The singer looked surprised.
   *appositive added:* The singer, *a woman of indeterminate years,* looked surprised.

   **a.** The third baseman hit a double.
   **b.** Mrs. Merriwether took the job.
   **c.** The book is interesting.
   **d.** The class inspired her.
   **e.** Joe fell.

2. The following paragraph is awkward and difficult to follow because it is composed of stringy and sprawling sentences. Rewrite it so that its ideas are clearly related in sentences of appropriate length.

   One of the rare cases in which public opinion has succeeded in influencing the quality of mass entertainment is that of comic books which are sold by the millions to young children. At one time, most of these books were filled with material that was highly objectionable and it was growing steadily more violent and gruesome to the point that even the more hardened adults who examined them were shocked and had fears that they might be dangerous to young, unformed minds. Some of these books depicted nothing but a long succession of sadistic crimes that were pictured in great detail, and on several occasions it was found that delinquents who had committed crimes admitted that they deliberately imitated brutalities they had seen in comic books which obsessed them. Finally parents and educators decided that the situation was a dangerous one and had to be brought under control before it became a permanent threat to the community and to the mental health of young Americans, whose early ideals influence their adult lives.

3. Examine the following passages and be prepared to discuss them from the standpoint of meaning and effectiveness of communication. Write a short criticism of each one; is the meaning obvious? ambiguous? contradictory? Wherever possible, suggest revisions that would make the meaning clear.

**a.** My high-school days are over and I realize I cannot turn back time, so I must now make the best of my future. Now that I am continuing my education, I am also trying to improve on the mistakes I made in high school. One by one I am ironing out the deep wrinkled problems and solving them.

**b.** There is a lot of evidence that great scientific discoveries do not happen by chance, but usually involve thinking on the part of the scientist.

**c.** There are two major factors that help a person mature, heredity and environment. Although my heredity was good, my environment was a different matter. The friends I had were by no means juveniles, nor were they scholars. Since I spent most of my spare time with my buddies, I adopted the same habits they had concerning studying. We did not excel or fail in school, but we could have done a lot better.

**d.** As time passes, many complexities in our environment result from scientific and technological advancements which create new branches in every field of activity, thus causing the youth of today to seek out a more thorough education.

**e.** The body goes through certain changes between youth and old age, whether a person realizes it or not.

**4.** Rewrite the following paragraph, tightening it wherever possible by substituting words and phrases for clauses; eliminate all unnecessary words.

There were so many things to do and the summer was so short. We could go and chase rats in the barn, which was a dangerous and slightly sickening enterprise; we could teach a kitten how to play circus. We could climb to the roof of the corridor where we could watch the ducks file out to the pond, and crack dry mirthless jokes to one and another. We could help with the cider press, where all the apples with a rotten spot, those that had been claimed and contended for by the yellow jackets, disappeared into the hopper and gushed out the sides in a seethe of liquor that was brown and bubbly. There were so many things to do and the summer was so short.

**5.** Read the following sentences carefully, looking for roundabout expressions and deadwood. Then rewrite them into direct and economical statements.

**a.** In college one must put away the childish thoughts of her girlhood and begin thinking of the future that lies ahead with adult ideas and responsibilities.

**b.** Throughout my previous school days I have been the type of person who hasn't had to study a great deal to get grades above those obtained by the average student.

**c.** One of my bigger excuses was the fact that I claimed there were too many social activities currently in progress.

**d.** The method used to detect the approach of other ships is radar.

Exer

**e.** One lady aroused my indignation when she claimed that her son, who was six feet in height, was under twelve years of age.

**f.** Habits can be classified into two distinct types: one is the useful, progressive, uplifting kind while the other is of the nature that deteriorates character and often damages the physical body.

**g.** My scholastic averages show, in my opinion, a rather distorted picture of my true knowledge.

**h.** I have chosen this road of higher education to reach my goal, which is that of teaching children.

**i.** To reach this goal I must be well educated and have a thorough understanding of my subject.

**j.** The income from the tourist business is an important source of revenue for people who own businesses in Florida.

**6.** Revise the following sentences to eliminate careless or ineffective repetition of words, meaning, or sounds. If the repetition in any statement seems intentional and effective, explain what purpose it serves.

**a.** The hazy figures in the background are vague and indefinite, and they add a sinister note to the painting.

**b.** The advantage of getting a broader perspective through travel is only one of the advantages of spending a summer traveling through the United States.

**c.** Many people live so compulsively by the clock that they have a fixed time for eating, a fixed time for bathing, and a fixed time for everything but enjoying life.

**d.** An application of lotion to the area of inflammation should relieve the pain.

**e.** Concrete and steel have both been used successfully in skyscraper construction, but buildings of concrete must have much thicker walls at the lower levels than those of steel. On the other hand, concrete has a far greater decorative potential than steel.

**f.** The shock of discovering that someone you trust is not worthy of your trust can have a traumatic effect on the mind that lasts for years.

**g.** Most reasonable teachers are rational and do not grade papers on the basis of personal feelings or emotions toward the students.

**h.** In a serious discussion, the participants cannot let unimportant matters interfere with subjects they must discuss thoroughly and seriously.

**i.** When Bob went to a party, his mother brought him and his mother picked him up. When he had a homework problem, his mother solved it. And if he failed an exam, his mother called on the teacher personally.

**j.** In 1967 he led an expedition to Sumatra to study sacred rites seldom witnessed by outsiders.

# Sentence variety, control, and emphasis        **25**

*There is a natural emphasis in his style, like a man's tread, and a breathing space between the sentences.* —Henry David Thoreau, Walden

You can write without making choices, just by putting down the words, phrases, and sentences that come to mind most easily, but it may not be possible to write *well* without making some choices. Good writers don't always accept the first words that come to mind, or the first sentences that take shape on their papers. Because the construction of sentences can be arranged and rearranged, you can gain some control over the sentences you write and emphasize your meaning to insure your reader's understanding.

## Sentence variety        **25.1**

> **Var**  Revision: Vary the sentence patterns in the passage marked to avoid monotony or to make your meaning clearer or more emphatic.

When reading good writing we are usually unaware of the pattern of the sentences; it is only when the pattern becomes monotonous, either in length or in arrangement, that it forces itself to our attention. Consider these two paragraphs, the first a rephrasing of the second:

We hear that Russia emphasizes foreign language and so we have suddenly increased our own offerings in these fields. Our schools have not analyzed our needs, though. There is one school that has re-established Latin and another school that has introduced conversational French for infants. These schools haven't asked whether Latin or conversational French are as imperative as knowledge of Moslem customs or religion. The same schools haven't asked what languages are needed and for what ends.

Hearing that Russia emphasizes foreign language, we have suddenly increased our own offerings. But too seldom have our schools analyzed our needs. One school has re-established Latin; another has introduced conversational French for infants. Seldom have they asked whether Latin and French are as imperative as knowledge of Moslem customs or religion, or what languages are needed and for what ends. —Lou LaBrant, "The Dynamics of Education"

The ideas in both versions are identical; so too are most of the words. What makes Mr. LaBrant's original paragraph more readable, more understandable, is the movement of the statements—a movement casual and natural, with variety in sentence structure. In the first version, the five sentences all begin with the subject (*there* delays the subject in the third sentence); the length of the sentences ranges from eight words to nineteen words. In the original version, the four sentences begin, in order, with a verbal, a conjunction, a subject, and an adverb; length ranges from nine words to twenty-seven words. In the first version, all five sentences form a series of assertions. In the original version, the first is an observation from experience; the second, opening with the conversational conjunction, states a critical reaction, which is amplified by illustration in the third. The last affirms the criticism and forecasts a proposal.

## Varying sentence beginnings

When several consecutive sentences begin the same way—with a noun subject, for example—the passage is likely to be monotonous and to lack impact:

**Meteorology** has made many advances in recent years. **Weather observation balloons** have been developed to gather data from the upper stratosphere. **Time-lapse photography** has improved the study of cloud formations and patterns. **Barometric instruments** of greater sensitivity are widely used. **Radar** is useful in detecting the approach of storms and precipitation.

Sentence beginnings can be varied and made more interesting by occasionally starting with a modifier—a word, phrase, or clause—as in this passage from an essay on the Grand Canyon:

**We** have almost come full circle. **Once** those who had seen the Canyon thought of it as useless. **Then came** those who thought it might be useful because of the river which flowed through it. **They** were in turn followed by men like Theodore Roosevelt, who saw the Canyon as a precious heritage of wonder and beauty. **Now, today,** it is threatened again by men interested only in exploitation, men who unfortunately have the means to destroy what no age before ours was "technologically advanced" enough to transform and mar.

**"Human needs come first"** is the all too specious slogan of those for whom the words of Theodore Roosevelt carry no weight. **They** do not like to admit that those primary needs in which they happen to be interested are the "human needs" of temporary economic advantage. **That the Grand Canyon, the sublime "great unknown" of John Wes-**

Sentence
variety,
control,
and
emphasis
370

**ley Powell,** might fall victim to the manipulations of sloganeers should be unthinkable; that it is not unthinkable should be our shame.
—Joseph Wood Krutch, "The Eye of the Beholder"

To begin sentence after sentence with the same kind of modifier is no less monotonous, of course, than to begin every sentence with the subject. Deliberately inserting or shifting modifiers to gain variety is a makeshift or affected practice, hence an ineffective one. The emphasis you wish to make and the general movement of the passage should determine your sentence beginnings. Professor Francis Christensen has noted that professional writers place an adverbial modifier or other secondary element before the subject in about 20 percent of their sentences.

## Varying S–V–O order

A less common means of varying sentence patterns is changing the usual order of subject-verb-object or subject-verb-complement in declarative statements. This is called *inversion:*

Supplementing the guitars and drums are a solo cello, a ragtime piano, an Indian sitar, sound effects of barnyard animals, and a complete symphony orchestra. —Peter Schrag, "Facing the Music"

Except in questions and requests, inversion should ordinarily be used only when the words put first really deserve special emphasis by withholding the subject. Inversion used solely for variety may have painful results, as in this reversal:

A garden city, with one of the most delightful climates in the world, is Victoria.

## Loose and periodic sentences

Sentence patterns may also be varied by using both loose and periodic sentences.

### Loose sentences

In a loose sentence the main statement comes first, followed by subordinate elements that explain or amplify its meaning. This pattern is the one most commonly used both in conversation and in writing, for we characteristically make our points by building up meanings. Notice especially the last sentence:

I looked hard for that old hotel I had known, which then housed the headquarters to which I had to report. Perhaps it was the empty building, once a hotel, on the rue Gambetta, across from the courthouse and a block from the market. One could only guess. I took the car up to the heights above the city to the citadel on the Montagne du Roule, which had been built by Napoleon. Now the great stone walls enclose a museum of the disembarkment and of the liberation, one of a string stretched all along the Norman coast, at Arromanches, at Utah Beach, and at Ste.-Mère-Eglise, where the paratroops came down like confetti the night before the landings. — Horace Sutton, "A la Recherche of an Old War"

One particular kind of loose construction, called *prolepsis* in early rhetoric texts, can be useful. *Prolepsis* is the expression of a general statement, which is then followed by amplifying details:

Once on the mound, he was a most unlikely looking pitcher, slouching, tangle-footed, absent, with the aspect of a lost goose.

Modern homes have lost a tempo they once had — urban activities speed them up, television governs some hours, and separation from relatives and neighbors leaves them alone.

Such a construction can set the subject for a paragraph or short essay, determine its content, and act as an outline. The second sentence above, for example, could be amplified in an essay that had three key parts, each fully illustrating one of the three factors listed.

Loose, or *accumulating,* sentences are standard fare. Common in both speech and writing, they are an interesting reflection of the writer. As you add to a sentence, amplifying and specifying your meaning, you show yourself in the *process of thinking.*

Periodic sentences

A periodic sentence, however, is more often than not the statement of *completed thought.* Much less common in speech and in writing, a periodic sentence is one in which the main statement is not completed until the end or near the end of the sentence:

And around the sunken sanctuary of the river valley, stretching out in all directions from the benches to become coextensive with the disc of the world, went the uninterrupted prairie. — Wallace Stegner, "Quiet Earth, Big Sky"

Although periodic sentences were characteristic of much writing before this century, they are now much less common than loose sentences. They require planning beforehand and are more typical of a formal than of a general style. The very fact that periodic sentences are not widely used, however, gives the pattern all the more value as a means of achieving emphasis.

When you are framing a periodic sentence, make certain that the suspension is not awkward or unnatural, as it is in this example:

The reader will probably agree after reading this essay **that Pearl Buck's example** of the woman who, after being married for a number of years and raising a family, gradually loses interest in most of her former outside activities, **is true.**

## Varying kinds of sentences

If you discover in scrutinizing your first draft that you have written an essay in which most of the sentences have the same kind of clause structure, you should consider combining, dividing, or reshaping your sentences. Quite aside from the question of variety, different kinds of sentences — simple, compound, complex — are ordinarily necessary for meaning and for emphasis.

Sometimes a question or directive makes an effective variation from the usual declarative sentence:

Only by resurrecting our own memories can we realize how incredibly distorted is the child's vision of the world. **Consider this, for example. How would Crossgates appear to me now, if I could go back, at my present age, and see it as it was in 1915? What should I think of Bingo and Sim, those terrible, all-powerful monsters?** I should see them as a couple of silly, shallow, ineffectual people, eagerly clambering up a social ladder which any thinking person could see to be on the point of collapse. I would be no more frightened of them than I would be frightened of a dormouse. — George Orwell, *Such, Such, Were the Joys.* . . .

Questions and commands can be effective if they serve a legitimate purpose, but like other sentence patterns they should not be used solely for the sake of variety. Unless the answer is self-evident ("Who would trade freedom for tyranny?"), don't raise a question without answering it. Never conclude a paper with a pointless, blunt question such as "What do *you* think?"

## Subordination to control and clarify meaning  **25.2**

**Sub**  Revision: Show the intended relationship between ideas by using appropriate subordination, or correct the faulty subordination.

By bringing related ideas together, you give continuity to your writing and signal the direction of your thinking to your reader. But even when ideas are so closely related that they belong in the same sentence, they do not necessarily deserve equal weight. You must decide, in every case, how contributing ideas can best be arranged around a major idea, or how minor points can best accumulate to help make a major point. This means that every sentence should be *composed*.

An indiscriminate clustering of ideas in a sentence or paragraph is a disservice to the writer, to the subject, and to the reader. Ideas are *not* all the same: some are antecedents to others, some are conditions of others, some are less important than others. If you fail to show the relationship of one idea to another—whether in a single sentence or in a series of sentences—you may be informing your readers, in effect, that all your ideas are equally important or that you are too lazy to bother making your meaning clear:

**Failure to subordinate in a single sentence**

I worked hard and I turned out a first-rate manuscript, and I missed my deadline and my publisher was angry.

**Ideas effectively related**

Although I worked hard and turned out a first-rate manuscript, my publisher was angry because I missed my deadline.

**Failure to subordinate in a series of sentences**

That, I think, is our ancient mission. Sometimes we have deserted it. Then we have failed. You must help us. Then there will be no desertion. I do not want to mislead the people. I would rather lose the election. I do not want to misgovern the people. I would rather lose the election.

**Ideas effectively related**

That, I think, is our ancient mission. Where we have deserted it we have failed. With your help there will be no desertion now. Better we lose the election than mislead the people; and better we lose than misgovern the people.—Adlai Stevenson, Speech accepting the Democratic nomination for President, 1952

Subordination serves writers in several ways. You can put minor ideas into grammatically dependent constructions in order to stress your major point in an independent construction. And at the same time, if you are judicious, you can precisely relate the major and minor ideas. The key statements in the following passage occur at the first of each sentence. Because the author does not move slowly toward his main points but chooses to announce them bluntly at the start of each sentence, they form a dramatic list of predictions for the future:

**Houses will be the natural environment,** not formally specified, since there the individual will want to express himself. **Normal multistory residence buildings will need much greater areas per floor** so that a whole community will be able to operate at each level—a community with its shopping center, playgrounds, and public squares. **Automated factories will be placed within the earth,** especially in hills and mountains.—C. A. Doxiadis, "The Coming Era of Ecumenopolis"

In each sentence in this passage, contributing points follow the major statement. In the first two sentences they are arranged to establish cause-effect relationships.

Thoughtful subordination also allows you to move easily from sentence to sentence, using dependent constructions as transitions. Notice, for example, the subordinate clause introducing the last sentence of this passage:

When you write, you make a point, not by subtracting as though you sharpened a pencil, but by adding. When you put one word after another, your statement should be more precise the more you add. **If the result is otherwise,** you have added the wrong thing, or you have added more than was needed.—John Erskine, "A Note on the Writer's Craft"

Because grammatical constructions are important signals of meanings, you should make certain in checking your first draft that you have not put major ideas into minor constructions, or minor ideas into major constructions—a fault known as inverted or "upside-down" subordination.

See also §3, Subordinate clauses and connectives, especially §3.5, Faulty subordination.

**Paral**

**25.3**

## Parallelism                                           25.3

> **Paral (II)** Revision: Make the sentence elements marked parallel in form.

Ideas of equal value in a statement can be made *parallel*—that is, they can be expressed in the same grammatical form. Putting coordinate ideas in parallel constructions helps the reader see in which direction the statement is going and makes for smoother writing, since it helps prevent unnecessary shifts in person and number and in the tense and mood of verbs.

## Elements in series

Words, phrases, and clauses in series are best stated in parallel form. The boldface words in the following sentence are parallel because each is the object of the preposition *with:*

His mind was filled with artistic **projects, schemes** for outwitting his creditors, and vague **ideas** about social reform.

The compound predicates in this sentence are also parallel:

His dramatic attempt to take over the conduct of his own case **alienated** him from his counsel, almost **broke up** the trial, and probably **helped** to cost him his life.—Joseph Kinsey Howard, *Strange Empire*

When coordinate ideas are not stated in parallel form, the statement is likely to seem awkward and unpolished:

| Not parallel | Parallel |
|---|---|
| We were told **to write** in ink, **that we should** use but one side of the paper, and **we should** endorse our papers in the proper manner. [an infinitive phrase and two clauses] | We were told **to write** in ink, **to use** but one side of the paper, and **to endorse** our papers in the proper manner. [three infinitive phrases] |

A preposition or a conjunction should be repeated between the items of a series when necessary for clarity:

| Preposition not repeated | Clearer |
|---|---|
| These problems are currently of great concern **to** the school system, teachers, and many parents. | These problems are currently of great concern **to** the school system, **to** teachers, and **to** many parents. |

| Conjunction not repeated | Clearer |
|---|---|
| The opposing citizens argued **that** the increased tax rates were exorbitant and the commissioners should find some other way to raise the money. | The opposing citizens argued **that** the increased tax rates were exorbitant and **that** the commissioners should find some other way to raise the money. |

## Elements being compared or contrasted

Elements that are compared or contrasted through the use of pairs of conjunctions such as *either . . . or, neither . . . nor, not only . . . but* (or *but also*) are usually clearer and more emphatic when they are stated in parallel constructions:

It is not always easy to select, at your bookshop or library, the particular book which will best serve your purpose, but if, before deciding, you give a little attention to certain points, you are less likely **either to**

**buy one** which will not give you full return **or to take home** from the library one which will cause you disappointment, delay or inconvenience. — Lionel McColvin, "How to Use Books," *The Wonderful World of Books*

This is the life of a musician in which are recorded **not only the events** of his life, **but also details** of all his works, which are analyzed and described fully. — Ibid.

Since readers expect similar constructions to follow pairs of conjunctions, they may be momentarily confused or sidetracked if the pattern is shifted:

| **Shifted** | **Parallel** |
|---|---|
| You may go to the ski jump either **by special train** or a **chartered bus may be taken.** | You may go to the ski jump either **by special train** or **by chartered bus.** |
| He admired the Senator not **for his integrity,** but **because of his political cunning.** | He admired the Senator not **for his integrity,** but **for his political cunning.** |

Making related ideas parallel is one of the jobs of revision. Similar forms for similar ideas help hold a sentence together.

## Balanced and antithetical sentences

When parallel constructions, especially clauses, are noticeably equal in length and similar in movement, the sentence is called *balanced.* Balance is useful for emphatic statements, for comparing and contrasting ideas:

Abbé Dimnet, in *The Art of Thinking,* was teaching the American how to think in a few easy lessons, just as ten years later Mortimer J. Adler was to teach him how to read in a few somewhat harder ones. — Leo Gurko, *The Angry Decade*

The best model of the grand style simple is Homer; perhaps the best model of the grand style severe is Milton. — Matthew Arnold, *On Translating Homer*

When contrasting clauses occur in parallel constructions in a single sentence, the sentence is called *antithetical.* Such a construction fittingly emphasizes a striking or important contrast:

You may eat without danger our canned food, fresh and hot from your own campfire, but you will drink in peril the dirty water, polluted and foul from the nearby stream.

Antithetical sentences can easily be overused, but they are occasionally effective to mark turning points in an essay — the first half of the sentence pulling together what precedes, the contrasting second half forecasting what follows.

> **Emph**  Revision: Rewrite the passage marked so that the position and expression of the ideas will show their relative importance.

In composing your sentences you should help your reader to see your ideas in the same relative importance as you do — to distinguish among the most important, the less important, the incidental. Although the emphasis given to particular ideas depends in large part upon the way the whole paper is put together, from the beginning to the final paragraph, individual sentences can weaken or strengthen this effect. The sentences in the following paragraph, for example, are unemphatic because they are haphazardly constructed. They are wordy, the beginnings are weak, and each ends in a flabby construction:

There are some interesting points about contemporary American life in "The Mobile Society" by Herman Matthews. Some of the things he notes are the paradoxes in it. The way a person often reduces his independence by relying more on mechanical devices is one example the author gives. A man may actually become the machine's slave instead of its master, as he thinks he is.

To make the statements more forceful and concise, the writer might have revised the sentence structure in this way:

In his essay "The Mobile Society," Herman Matthews points out some of the paradoxes in contemporary American life. He notes, for example, that increasing reliance on mechanical devices often reduces a person's independence. Thinking he is the machine's master, he may actually become its slave.

## Emphasis by position in the sentence

Important ideas can be stressed by putting them in emphatic positions in the sentence. In longer statements the most emphatic position is usually at the end, the next most emphatic position at the beginning:

If it was the workings of our democracy that were inadequate in the past, **let us say so.** Whoever thinks the future is going to be easier than the past **is certainly mad.** And the system under which we are going to have to conduct foreign policy is, I hope and pray, **the system of democracy.** — George F. Kennan, *American Diplomacy, 1900 – 1950*

Sentences — particularly those that introduce or sum up the

Sentence
variety,
control,
and
emphasis
**378**

main points of a topic—should end strongly. Statements that are qualified by a phrase or a word at the end are usually weak:

**Unemphatic**
The work at the mill was hard and often dangerous, but the mill hands didn't complain, **or at least very seldom.**

**Improved**
The work at the mill was hard and often dangerous, but the mill hands seldom complained.

These songs are dull and unoriginal, **with few exceptions.**

With few exceptions, these songs are dull and unoriginal.

Because the main statement is not completed until the end, periodic sentences are frequently more emphatic than loose sentences:

**Loose**
Sociology 101 should interest every thoughtful student with its discussion of the theoretical as well as the practical aspects of human behavior.

**Periodic**
Sociology 101, with its discussion of the theoretical as well as the practical aspects of human behavior, should interest every thoughtful student.

A particular kind of periodic sentence, the *climax* sentence, directs the reader through phrases and clauses arranged in ascending order to the most important element at the end:

We shall fight on the beaches, we shall fight on the landing-grounds, we shall fight in the fields and in the streets, we shall fight in the hills; we shall never surrender.—Winston Churchill, Speech following Dunkirk, 1940

Sentences that begin with *There is* or *There are* tend to be unemphatic as well as wordy; frequent use of these constructions will make your writing seem flat and uninteresting.

**Flat**
There were several people who objected to the commission's plan.

**Improved**
Several people objected to the commission's plan.

## Emphasis by separation
Ideas can be emphasized by setting them off from other parts of the sentence with strong internal punctuation—semicolons, colons, or dashes (§12 and §13):

It is one thing to read *Time;* it is another to pronounce the words correctly.—E. B. White, *Quo Vadimus?*

The northern Maine wilds were cloaked by a thick haze on my arrival, and when I flew out a week later there was a mountain-hugging fog.

**Emph**

**25.4**

Within that span there was rain, more fog — and a bear called Lonesome George. — Lew Dietz, "The Myth of the Boss Bear," *True*

When the ideas warrant it, the most emphatic separation is into individual sentences:

Adolescence is a kind of emotional seasickness. Both are funny, but only in retrospect. — Arthur Koestler, *Arrow in the Blue*

### Emphasis by repeating key words

Statements can be made emphatic by repeating important words or phrases:

These and kindred questions **need** discussion, and **need** it urgently, in the few years left to us before somebody presses the button and the rockets begin to fly. — George Orwell, *The Orwell Reader*

His highest hope is to **think** first what is about to be **thought,** to **say** what is about to be **said,** and to **feel** what is about to be felt. — Bertrand Russell, *Unpopular Essays*

In your reading you will sometimes see a word or phrase repeated deliberately for effect at the beginning of consecutive clauses or sentences:

I believe this government cannot endure permanently half slave and half free. **I do not expect** the Union to be dissolved — **I do not expect** the house to fall — but **I do expect** it will cease to be divided. — Abraham Lincoln, "House Divided" speech, 1858

**The light** has gone out, I said, and yet I was wrong. For **the light** that shone in this country was no ordinary light. **The light** that has illumined this country for these many years will illumine this country for many more years, and a thousand years later **that light** will still be seen in this country and the world will see it and it will give solace to innumerable hearts. — Jawaharlal Nehru, Speech on the death of Gandhi, 1948

The Declaration of Independence illustrates this same kind of repetition. Occasionally you will also see a word or phrase repeated at the end of consecutive clauses, as in Psalm 136, where each verse concludes "for his mercy endureth forever." In the hands of a skilled writer, these techniques can be highly effective, but they should be used very sparingly, and only when a serious subject can be honestly and appropriately conveyed in the deliberate manner they suggest.

Effective (and intentional) repetition should be distinguished from careless repetition, as discussed in §24.5.

### Emphasis by mechanical devices

The least effective way to emphasize ideas is by underlining or capitalizing words, by setting them off in quotation marks, or by using emphatic punctuation marks (!!!). Certain kinds of advertising rely heavily on such devices:

"Oh, of course," you may reply, "it's just a matter of calories." But IS it? Suppose you had to choose between a larger glass of orange juice and half a sirloin steak? You would probably reach for the orange juice. Actually, *the steak would give you 15 times as many ENERGY-stimulating calories. Yet the total number* of calories in each is roughly the same! So, you see, it ISN'T "just a matter of calories." It's the KIND of calories that makes the big difference.

In college writing, mechanical devices for emphasis should ordinarily be avoided; the wording of the statement or its position in the sentence should give it the emphasis it deserves.

### Applications: Sentence Variety, Control, and Emphasis

1. The two basic sentence types, *loose* and *periodic,* can serve as powerful tools to make your writing much more interesting to read. The loose sentence (often called the "cumulative sentence") can be compared to a freight train: in its basic form, it consists of a simple sentence to which thoughts are coupled on—much as freight cars can be attached to an engine. Below is a sample "freight train," followed by five simple sentences or independent clauses for you to add at least 3 "cars" to.

*example:* It was a depressing day: + black clouds obscured the sun. + a cold wind whistled through the trees, + and even the birds seemed to be in hiding.

   **a.** This house is your dream house +
   **b.** The eastern third of China is the core of the nation +
   **c.** Oil played an important part in building America +
   **d.** The college's student council listened attentively +
   **e.** "Liberation" can mean a lot of different things +

The periodic sentence has a different effect than the loose sentence, since the main idea (or independent clause) is postponed until the end. The periodic sentence can be compared to a firecracker in its effect: you light the fuse and wait for the explosion. This kind of sentence is very good for building up suspense. Consider the "firecracker" below; then expand the following clauses to make five of your own.

*example:* After he found the candlestick on the rug, + and after he ascertained that the fingerprints were not those of the dead woman + and after he found the scratches on the lock of the patio door, + the inspector became convinced that *this was a case of murder.*

   **f.** When the sun went down +
   **g.** After finals were over for the seniors +
   **h.** Although regular class attendance is important +

**i.** While others might need lots of money +

**j.** If you have followed the map carefully up to this point +

2. Related elements that should be parallel but aren't will confuse the reader, at least for a moment or two. Rewrite the following sentences, eliminating unnecessary words and making related elements parallel in form.

**a.** To touch the heart of his mystery, we find in him one thought, strange to the point of lunacy: the thought of duty, the thought of something owing to himself and to God and his neighbor: an ideal of decency, to which he would rise if it were possible; a limit of shame that he will not stoop below if possible.

**b.** I wrote because it amused me, and I enjoyed correcting the work, too.

**c.** I told him to report to the principal's office and that he was to bring me a note from his mother.

**d.** The town turned out to be hard to reach, a bore, and very chilly in the evening.

**e.** The squirrel in our front yard is a playful sort, and who mocks us from his tree.

**f.** He trudged his way through his homework, and finished off his notes, then turning on the TV.

**g.** The house was charming and a real buy, but it was not near enough public transportation nor quite large enough for our family.

**h.** People who haven't been to Alaska ask questions about the prices, how cold it gets in winter, and what is worth seeing.

**i.** I am tall and bald and have an ungainly gait.

**j.** This report is exceptionally complete and a fine example of concise writing.

3. We have all had the experience of saying something very dramatically and then realizing we couldn't really live with our words. When this happens in writing, the result can be a sentence that is at best ineffective, and at worst comical. Other times, we cover up the important point when we don't want to. Revise the sentences below so that the important points receive neither too much nor too little emphasis.

*example:* I am all in favor of big families—unless of course the parents don't want lots of children, or can't feed and clothe the children properly.

*revised:* As long as the parents have both the desire for children and the means to support them, I see nothing wrong with large families.

**a.** Television programs today are very adolescent in content, at least most of them.

**b.** There were two magnificent volcano peaks which towered over the valley.

**c.** Theoretically, the plan seemed flawless; its results, however, were disastrous.

Sentence
variety,
control,
and
emphasis
382

**d.** Students on the campus were completely unaware that under the abandoned stands of Stagg Field scientists had produced, through concentrated day-and-night effort under rigid security precautions, the first controlled atomic chain reaction.

**e.** There is something the average voter doesn't realize—that his ONE vote really *can make a difference;* in fact, it can change the outcome of the WHOLE ELECTION!

**f.** Thumbing frantically through his catalog and clutching his registration cards in his sweaty hands while he stands in line is the typical freshman.

**g.** Sculpture is an excellent hobby, although it can be expensive and not everyone has the skill to pursue it.

**h.** Outside his office there were several customers waiting and they insisted there were other matters they had to attend to.

**i.** The recent civil defense drill—like all the preceding ones—showed that public apathy toward survival methods is immense.

**j.** Many juvenile delinquents (you'd be surprised *how* many) have parents who refuse to try to *understand* them.

**6.** *Review exercise on sentence effectiveness.* Read the following passage through carefully, keeping in mind all the sentence weaknesses discussed in §24 and §25. Then, without changing its content or organization more than is necessary, revise the passage so that the sentences are economical, varied, and generally effective.

Countless are the beauties and wonders of nature, and also countless are the pleasures that I have experienced in the study of nature. With a feeling of awe for the principles of geometry, I have examined the intricate design of a snowflake. Caught in the curved arm of a stem, a violet's perfect grace has been a source of wonder to me. While studying an ant lion's method of survival, I have gained a new respect for nature's skilled engineering. With a feeling of envy I have watched a monarch butterfly in soaring flight, or in a tranquil seance on a sunlit leaf.

The respect and admiration I have felt for nature have been important parts of my thinking since childhood. As an explorer in my grandmother's garden, I was delighted by the feel of damp corn silk against my cheek, and hypnotized by the rhythmic movements of a dirt dauber building its mud cocoon. Never failing to check for tonsils, I was ecstatic over each snapdragon's rainbow-hued throat.

Applications:
Sentence
Variety,
Control,
and Emphasis
**383**

*. . . besides saying, asking, or commanding something, each sentence in any paragraph accomplishes—or should accomplish—an identifiable task, a piece of work, in cooperation with the sentences that surround it. It affects our understanding of those other sentences; it interacts with them, and in so doing helps to shape or control the idea that the reader takes from the paragraph. To put the matter metaphorically, most paragraphs (except extremely short or transitional paragraphs) disclose or represent an action that took place within the writer's mind.—Richard L. Larson, "Sentences in Action: A Technique for Analyzing Paragraphs"*

A paragraph can be taken as a form of punctuation. The indention of the first line of a paragraph tells your reader that you're taking a new step, shifting attitude, turning to a new feature of your subject, looking at some part of your subject in a different way. If a piece of writing shows a mind at work, then paragraph indentions are the major signs that let a reader follow the mind's movement. But at the same time that it separates units of thought for reading ease, a good paragraph is clearly and smoothly related to the paper as a whole and sometimes serves the paper additionally by providing transition or by emphasizing key points. These features of paragraphs are explored in Section 19, "Writing the first draft," which discusses the use of paragraphs to control the direction of a paper, techniques for relating paragraphs in sequence, and the special character of paragraphs that open or conclude a paper. This section is concerned with the general problems of paragraph development and paragraph continuity.

**¶ dev**

**26.1**

## Paragraph development and length  26.1

> **¶ dev**  Revision: The paragraph marked is not adequately developed. Add enough explanation or illustration to make the central idea clear and complete.

In a well-developed paragraph the central meaning is clear and complete. Some ideas can be fully expressed in a few simple statements; others may require from a hundred to two hundred words or more of explanation or illustration in order to be complete.

## Underdeveloped paragraphs

The effect of underdeveloped paragraphs is illustrated by the following student narration of a trip:

Two years ago I took my first trip to Alaska. On this particular voyage there were only forty-five passengers. I learned from the steward that the usual number of weekly passengers ranged from seventy-five to two hundred.

The fruit basket in each cabin was filled daily with apples, oranges, and other kinds of fruit. Since meals were included in the price of the ticket, we could choose anything we wanted from the menu without worryng about the price.

We arrived at our first port, Sitka, on a rainy day. We were told that the ship would be there for about four hours unloading cargo and that we could go ashore if we so desired. After taking a good look at the town, I decided that I would very much prefer to be on board ship.

These paragraphs don't work well because they raise questions that the writer fails to answer: Why were there so few passengers on this trip? (This should be explained in the first paragraph or else not mentioned.) What is the point of the second paragraph, which jumps so abruptly from the introductory statements? the abundance of food? how cheap it was? how much the writer enjoyed it? Some statement is needed at the beginning of this paragraph to link it with the preceding one and to express the main idea ("Because there were so few passengers, we were offered more food than we could eat. . . ."). The third paragraph leaves the reader wondering what Sitka looked like, what unpleasant things the writer saw that made him prefer to stay on his ship. Three or four explanatory sentences would have cleared up this point and would have made the paragraph more interesting.

The following paragraph is similarly underdeveloped. It is too brief to convey adequately the writer's ideas:

People have been faced lately with many different ideas and systems of government. Each has tried to win the majority to its side, frequently by force or by unscrupulous propaganda. Each person thinks of himself or herself as being representative of the majority.

This paragraph could be improved by listing some specific examples after the second sentence (Russia? China? Spain?) and by using a separate paragraph to explain the third sentence.

¶ dev

**26.1**

Paragraph
development
and
length
**385**

A good way to avoid underdeveloped paragraphs is to explore all your ideas fully in the first writing, putting down everything that occurs to you. If the paragraph turns out to be too long or to contain irrelevancies, it is easy enough to trim it in revision. To do the reverse—to fill out an underdeveloped paragraph with details and explanations—takes much more time. (See §19, Writing the first draft.)

## Typical content of paragraphs

No rule exists that says a paragraph *must* do this, or that, or the other. Paragraphs may have one sentence or many. One paragraph may state a point and amplify it with explanation and illustration. Another paragraph may be nothing but illustration of a point made in a preceding paragraph. A whole series of paragraphs may contain only episodes and illustrations to explain an earlier point.

Still, it is probably reasonable to say that *most* fully developed paragraphs are composed of three kinds of statements:

1) *General statements* in a paragraph may range from attitudes and opinions (This is the better plan; You are wrong) to large generalizations (Everyone needs some form of artistic expression; College curricula are in desperate need of reform). General statements may also appear as *restatements,* where a general statement is put into different words for clarification; *summary statements,* where ideas already introduced are brought together, and *conclusions,* where material previously presented leads to a new judgment.

2) *Specific statements* are generally subtopics of a general statement. In a paragraph opening with the general statement "This is the better plan," the specific statement that followed might be something like "It has three particular advantages." Specific statements may often be used for one of the following purposes:

**to expand,** where a sentence amplifies and explains a general idea already expressed;

**to define,** where a sentence gives the meaning of a word or words in another sentence;

**to qualify,** where a sentence restricts the meaning of a general statement already made;

**to concede,** where a sentence acknowledges facts or ideas contrary to a statement already made;

**to refute,** where a sentence introduces some kind of evidence contrary to a statement already made;

**to evaluate,** where a sentence makes some judgment about a statement already made;

**to identify a cause or result,** where a sentence states what produced the event described in a previous sentence, or what resulted from it.

In this, and in what follows just below, we are indebted to Professor Richard L. Larson's study of paragraphing.

3) *Details* are particular observations and facts (He is eleven years old; This violet is a Blue Akey; In two years the city's population increased by 11,460) and summaries of facts (All day the planes had been running late). Details may be offered for several purposes:

**to particularize,** where sentences give the specific facts or details implied in a more general statement;

**to exemplify,** where sentences illustrate what is meant by a previous statement;

**to describe,** where sentences give details to help the reader visualize an object, person, or scene;

**to narrate,** where sentences show actions or events in series, in order to particularize a previous statement;

**to support,** where sentences offer evidence for a previous statement;

**to compare or contrast,** where sentences explain something already said by comparing it or contrasting it with something else.

Generalizations and statements of opinion are most convincing when supported by details, because details can usually be checked for accuracy. Most effective writing, in fact, is made up largely of *details,* with occasional *general statements* to hold them together and show their meaning, and with occasional *specific statements* to direct the reader's attention. The following short paragraph contains all three of these elements:

| | |
|---|---|
| There are not many good critics for an art, but there have been almost none for the modern theatre. | General statement |
| The intellectuals among them know little about an operating theatre and the middlebrows look at plays as if they were at a race track for the morning line- | Specific statement to expand |
| up. It is a mixed-up picture in many ways. | General statement |
| One critic who wrote | Detail to support |

Right margin:

¶ **dev**

**26.1**

Paragraph development and length

**387**

that *The Little Foxes* was a febrile play later called it an American classic without explaining why he changed his mind. — Lillian Hellman, "Theatre," *Pentimento*

Whatever the purpose of a paragraph is, its full development often depends on adequate use of both details and general statements. An *expository* paragraph, for example, is a unit of facts (details) and ideas (general statements) *to explain*. This is the way a doctor begins an explanation of coronary thrombosis, a term unfamiliar to many readers:

The diagnosis of "heart disease" is feared by all of us, and not without reason. As long as the heart beats there is hope, but we all realize that if the heart stops beating we will die.

The ability of the heart to function depends primarily on the state of the heart muscle or myocardium, as it is technically known. Our existence, therefore, depends largely on the state of the blood vessels that bring nourishment to the myocardium — the coronary arteries. The heart can, of course, be damaged by other disease processes. For instance, the heart may fail because it is irreparably damaged by an infection as in rheumatic heart disease, or by poisons, or toxins, as in diphtheria. — William A. R. Thompson, M.D., "Coronary Thrombosis," *Today's Health*

The first paragraph makes contact with the reader's common knowledge and concern. The second begins the actual exposition, explaining the meaning of the technical word *myocardium* and rapidly adding other facts that expand the reader's understanding of coronary thrombosis.

An *argumentative* paragraph is a unit of facts (details) and ideas (general statements) to *persuade*. The following paragraphs open an argumentative essay that calls for changes in our colleges by pointing out present weaknesses. The first paragraph begins with a general statement that is explained by the details following. The second paragraph contains two general statements — the first announcing the existence of problems, the second announcing more clearly the nature of the problems. The third paragraph opens with a question that guides the development of the paragraph, which is filled with details:

It is understandable that there should be so little fundamental criticism of our colleges and universities. Most original thinking still comes from them, but this is less because they are such good places for it than because there is hardly any place else with even the minor advantages they afford. Few students are unbiased or competent critics. Journalists too often today reproduce others' views rather than develop their own — and the views they would reproduce on colleges and universities would be naturally of the "expert" — presidents and admissions officers and professors. Perhaps most important, most people are too worried about getting their children into college to be concerned much about what goes on once they get there.

But there are extremely serious problems in the colleges. And despite the millions of dollars now being spent on research in higher education, we are not doing much to make college education much more than a huge boondoggle — which is what most of it is today.

From where do I draw my evidence for this view? Aside from my own experience as a student (City College in New York, the University of Pennsylvania, Columbia University), I have been a college teacher: I taught sociology for a year at the University of California in Berkeley, a year at Bennington College in Vermont, a half-year at Smith College — a crude sampling of our better universities and colleges. I have lectured or engaged in research at a half-dozen more colleges and universities, and have friends with whom I have talked about teaching and its problems at almost every important university in the country. Of course I am aware of exceptions, but I am confident that my general conclusion about college holds. — Nathan Glazer, "The Wasted Classroom," *Harper's Magazine*

Developing paragraphs by full use of details removes a frequent worry of student writers — "getting the required length." An assignment of "about six hundred words" means that the students are to take a subject and select from their information and thinking about it what can be conveyed in about that number of words. The bulk of the space in most papers should be taken up with specific details, with occasional general statements to interpret or summarize their meaning. A final test question for either a paragraph or a paper is "Have I put in enough of what I know and believe about this subject to lead a reader to see it as I do?"

## Topic sentences

Both the clarity and completeness of a paragraph can often be enhanced by stating its main idea in what is called a *topic sentence:* a key sentence to which the other statements in the paragraph are related. The topic sentence typically comes at the start of the paragraph, as in this example:

**All the while, in other parts of the world, the terrors of the second World War were being foreshadowed by a series of ominous and bloody events.** In the north of Spain, a revolt of the Asturian miners was being ruthlessly suppressed through the importation of Moorish

¶ dev

26.1

troops from Africa. Hitler was carrying out his "blood purge" against a cadre of former associates. Dollfuss, after slaughtering the socialist working class of Vienna, in February, was himself murdered by the Nazis in July. In October, King Alexander of Yugoslavia and Foreign Minister Barthou of France were assassinated by Croatian terrorists in the pay of Mussolini, and in December, Kirov, a close associate of Stalin, met a similar fate on a street in Leningrad. Meanwhile, in the Chaco jungles far to the south, the unpublicized but sanguinary war between Bolivia and Paraguay was dragging on without headlines and seemingly without end. — Leo Gurko, *The Angry Decade*

Another method is to work *toward* the topic sentence, using it as a summary or a conclusion for the details in the paragraph, as in this passage from an argumentative work:

Behold the fowls of the air: for they sow not, neither do they reap, nor gather into barns; yet your heavenly Father feedeth them. Are ye not much better than they? / Which of you by taking thought can add one cubit unto his stature? / And why take ye thought for raiment? Consider the lilies of the field, how they grow; they toil not, neither do they spin: / And yet I say unto you, That even Solomon in all his glory was not arrayed like one of these. / **Wherefore, if God so clothe the grass of the field, which to day is, and to morrow is cast into the oven,** *shall he* **not much more** *clothe* **you, O ye of little faith?** — Matthew 6:26–30

The purpose of a topic sentence is twofold: (1) to help the writer focus his or her ideas on one central thought to which every statement in the paragraph is directly related, and (2) to make it easier for the reader to see what the paragraph is about, by specifically stating its controlling idea. Topic sentences are most typically found in expository and argumentative writing, but often even in descriptive paragraphs a single sentence will state a dominant impression that is borne out by the remaining sentences. (See also §26.2, page 393, Inductive and deductive development.)

## Appropriate paragraph length

Remember that a fully developed paragraph should embody a clear-cut division of the topic. A paragraph indention is a mark of separation, indicating to the reader that one stage in the development of the topic has been completed and that another is about to begin.

A paragraph that attempts to cover more than one stage of the topic should be divided:

About three years ago when I started my junior year in high school, a neighbor who was the captain of the local National Guard unit paid me a visit. He started talking about the wonderful possibilities the Guard had to offer—training in radio, electronics, and other technical subjects. Evidently he must have been a good recruiting officer, for after he talked for an hour, I fell for his argument and joined, thinking I might learn something. I did. **[Next sentence starts a new stage of the topic.]** After attending a few drills, I was able to draw some conclusions about this outfit and my place in it. All the fancy talk I had heard was just propaganda, for as soon as I got my uniform, they hustled me down to the anti-aircraft installation. From then on, for two and a half years, I spent most of my weekly drills wiping the guns while the NCO's stood around talking baseball and women to each other. Occasionally they would look busy when they saw an officer coming, but most of the time they loafed while I worked.

Since the discussion of recruiting clearly stops with "I did," the next sentence should begin a new paragraph.

Perhaps a more common fault of inexperienced writers is breaking up related statements into too many paragraphs. This distracts the reader and gives the writing a choppy effect:

> The day of the game finally arrives and the first thing you do is look out the window to check on the weather.
> As the paper predicted, it is a beautiful sunny morning with very little wind—real football weather. You try to pass the morning by reading about the game, while you are counting the hours and the minutes until the game starts.
> Finally you start for the game, only to find the nearest parking lot over a mile from the stadium. You begin the long walk across the campus, joining the thousands of people all as eager as you are, all hurrying in the same direction.
> As you pass the impressive Gothic buildings, memories of your college days come back to you, and you wish for a moment at least that you were back in school again.

The first two paragraphs concern the morning of the game and should be written as one; the last two paragraphs also deal with one topic—the trip to the stadium—and should similarly be combined.

To get an idea of how your paragraphs compare in length with those of experienced writers, examine some articles in several recent publications. Students beginning a writing course generally write paragraphs averaging from forty to seventy-five words, but as they learn to develop their ideas more fully their paragraphs approximate those in books and magazines—seventy-five to a hundred words. Paragraphs in newspapers are usually considerably shorter, but they are deliberately abbreviated for fast reading and are not typical of general writing. Ordinarily if there are more than two or three indentions on a single page of one of your papers, you should look at your writing carefully to determine whether or not you have separated things that belong together in the same paragraph.

This does not mean that a short paragraph is automatically a poor one: even a one-sentence paragraph can sometimes be used to good effect. In the following passage, for example, a single short sentence conveys a dramatic moment and hence deserves to stand alone as the second paragraph:

> And it was wild. The wind, whistling out of the south at 25 knots, the most that *Tinkerbelle* could stand up under reefed main, built up menacing seas that threatened to bowl her over on her beam ends. She had to be swerved around periodically to meet the biggest of the cross waves almost head-on or she'd have gotten into serious trouble. Yet on we swooshed like the proverbial scalded cat, reeling off a fraction less than two nautical miles every fifteen minutes.
> "England, here we come!" I yelled at the stars.
> But it was no time for exuberance; we were perched too precariously on the thin line between maximum speed and minimum safety. To remain on that perch demanded senses tuned to their greatest receptivity. It called for unwavering alertness, instant detection of the slightest change in conditions, and swift, appropriate responses. A moment's inattention could be disastrous. — Robert Manry, "Crossing the Atlantic in a 13-foot Sailboat," *Harper's Magazine*

¶ **dev**

**26.1**

In the next example, so much is packed into a single long sentence that it too fully deserves to stand as a paragraph:

> But to bring us entirely to reason and sobriety, let it be observed, that a painter must not only be of necessity an imitator of the works of nature, which alone is sufficient to dispel this phantom of inspiration, but he must be as necessarily an imitator of the works of other painters: this appears more humiliating, but is equally true; and no man can be an artist, whatever he may suppose, upon any other terms. — Joshua Reynolds, *Discourses upon Art,* No. 9

Single-sentence paragraphs that serve as transitions between one part of the discussion and another are fairly common in papers that have several main divisions. The sentence below follows a four-paragraph introduction and clearly forecasts the development of the rest of the essay:

> There are, I found, three main sources of waste in college teaching: the classroom system, the examination system, the departmental system. — Nathan Glazer, "The Wasted Classroom" *Harper's Magazine*

The real test of paragraph length is not the number of words or lines but rather the answer to these questions: Why was indention necessary? Should any one of the paragraphs be written as two, for clarity and emphasis? Are two so closely related that they should be combined? Appropriate paragraph length follows almost automatically from effective paragraph development.

## Patterns of paragraph development      **26.2**

Much of the labor of writing consists in managing general statements and details, arranging them in sequences that move toward a point, or support a point, or move toward a transition, or achieve some other effect.

### Inductive and deductive development

The two basic patterns for developing the main idea in a paragraph are *deductive development,* supporting a main point made at the beginning of the paragraph, and *inductive development,* moving toward a main point at the end. Deductive and inductive development are often referred to as the methods of *support* and *climax.*

In the following paragraph, inductive in pattern, the early sentences provide the data on which the conclusion—the last sentence—is based:

Puffing heavily, I flopped into the cockpit and lay clutching the handhold above the compass as my breathing slowly returned to normal. The situation, to state the case mildly, could have been a lot worse. I had been given a bad scare and was soaked through, but nothing really calamitous had happened. *Tinkerbelle* was still right side up and clear of water, and neither she nor I had suffered so much as a scratch. And, best of all, I now had evidence of exactly how stable she was. That one piece of empirically gained knowledge transformed the whole harrowing experience into a blessing in disguise. There would be no more torturous nights in the cockpit; from now on I would sleep in comfort in the cabin, even in the foulest weather, with the assurance that my boat would remain upright. No longer did I need to fear being trapped there by a capsize. This discovery made the remainder of the voyage immensely more enjoyable than it would otherwise have been.—Robert Manry, "Crossing the Atlantic in a 13-foot Sailboat," *Harper's Magazine*

The more common deductive pattern, illustrated in the following paragraph, has the primary assertion or main point first, followed by supporting details:

> On the earth, the original crust had long since been obliterated by volcanoes, convection processes, erosion, ice ages. Cooked again and again in the volcanic fires of a seething interior, earth landscapes appeared and disappeared; mountains rose and were eroded by wind and water; land masses broke up and drifted apart. Primeval rocks vanished. The scars of early meteoritic bombardment, which must have cratered the early earth as well as the moon, were erased on the restless, turbulent earth.—Richard Lewis, "The New Moon, in the Light of Apollo," *Saturday Review/World*

Notice that the central thought in both of these paragraphs is focused in a topic sentence, its position depending on the pattern the writer has used to develop his main idea.

## Other patterns of development

Some texts spell out a number of specific "methods" for developing paragraphs. The catalog of methods usually includes deduction (support) and induction (climax) as well as these patterns:

1) **Illustration,** ordinarily another name for the overall method of elaborating a general statement by illustrative details

2) **Definition** (frequent in exposition and argument), the explanation of a term by logical definition, that is, by assigning the term to an appropriate species or class and then distinguishing it from other members of the class

3) **Comparison** and **analogy,** the explanation of a particular subject by pointing out its similarities to another subject, usually one that is better known or more easily understood

4) **Contrast,** the explanation of a particular subject by pointing out how it differs from another subject

5) **Cause-effect,** the arrangement of a paragraph according to cause-effect sequence, such as beginning a paragraph with a general statement giving a cause and filling out the paragraph with specific effects, or beginning a paragraph with a series of specific statements naming separate causes and concluding with a general statement that gives the effect

6) **Classification,** the explanation of a subject either by putting it into the class it belongs to and then examining the characteristics of the class, or by dividing the subject in order to consider its individual parts

7) **Chronological order** (characteristic of narrative writing and of expository writing concerned with explaining a process), the arrangement of events in temporal order

8) **Spatial order** (probably most characteristic of descriptive writing), the arrangement of objects in some systematic spatial sequence, as near to far, far to near, high to low

It is possible to write good paragraphs by deliberate use of any one of these patterns, and you can probably find examples of each in the magazines you read. The pattern of development in the following paragraphs is indicated in the margin:

### Development by definition

I am interested in driving as a sort of art, a challenge to my wit and abilities. By driving I do not mean knowing how to shift from first to second or how to turn around in the back yard or how to get over a stretch of deserted country road. I am talking about the sort of thing you do if you try to make good time between, say, New York and Boston or between Kansas City and Seattle, running around forty to sixty miles an hour on the open road and pushing through lines of traffic as quickly as common sense will let you. Nothing that I write will apply to the snail-paced progress in a traffic-jammed city street. Let's consider a few simple truths about getting from here to there in a car.—Lincoln Dryden, "How to Drive a Car," *Harper's Magazine*

First step of definition: **driving** classified as **art**
Negative distinctions

Differentiation: driving specified as distinct from other members of the class

Negative distinction

Transition to following paragraphs

### Cause-effect development

Overpopulation would drive wildlife to the wall; the eagle and the elk would become memories; the smell of pine already is synthesized and marketed in pressurized cans for use in deodorizing our apartments and—who knows—perhaps someday our cities. Many would eat fish-flour, but few would know the taste of

Single cause stated: **overpopulation**
Effect No. 1
Effect No. 2

Effect No. 3
Effect No. 4

brook trout or fresh-caught salmon. — Stewart L. Udall, "Our Peril-
ous Population Implosion," *The
Saturday Review*

All of these methods, or patterns, of development are good,
but they are no more relevant to paragraph development than
to writing sentences or long papers. A single sentence may
state a complete analogy, and an entire paper may be struc-
tured as a definition. The methods are really no more than
characteristic ways of thinking, operations we go through as
we mull things over and work them out.

## Combining patterns of development

You should notice too as you read that the various methods
or patterns of development often converge in a single paragraph. For example, the paragraph below depends on the
contrast stated in the sixth sentence *(At no place, however,
. . .),* the comparison in the seventh sentence *(these planners
are like generals),* and the implied contrast in the last sentence (progress *should* come from urban planners, but instead it has come from two other sources):

> One is appalled by the lack of historical dimension in so much mod-
> ern sociology as well as urban studies. This is particularly true of the
> American Institute of Planners' conference. Often they express them-
> selves with warm-hearted rhetoric. They know slums and ghettos ex-
> ist and that they should not. They realize the social tensions of cities,
> the hatred and fear between the rich and the poor: the splendor of
> the former's environment, the ugliness of the latter's. At no place,
> however, does the conference discuss the nature of political action
> required to effect change. In many ways these planners are like gen-
> erals deep in the tactics and strategy of war without an army to fight
> it. Social progress and the improvement of cities have been due to
> two fundamental processes: one, technological advance, which could
> be quickly exploited for private profit; the other, radical political pro-
> test. — J. H. Plumb, "The Future Without the Past," *The Saturday Re-
> view*

The following short paragraph illustrates three patterns of
development: By *defining* a conventional internal combustion
engine in the first sentence, the writer is then able to *contrast*
the diesel engine with it. The explanation of the diesel engine
is then further developed by telling in *chronological order*
how it works:

> The conventional gasoline engine functions by drawing a vaporized
> mixture of gasoline and air into itself, compressing the mixture, ignit-

ing it and using the resulting explosion to push a piston down a cylinder. In the cycle of the diesel, only air is drawn in; the air is then very highly compressed so that it heats up naturally. In the next stage, a very accurately timed and measured quantity of fuel is injected into the cylinder, and because of the heat of the air, the mixture explodes spontaneously, which is why the diesel is sometimes referred to as a compression-ignition engine.—Tony Hogg, "That Old-time Ignition," *Esquire*

A paragraph, like a full paper, should follow the form of development that best suits the subject and that will be clearest to the reader. See also §19.2, Developing your material.

## Paragraph continuity                26.3

> **¶ con**   Revision: Rewrite the paragraph marked to make the relationships between ideas clear.

A paragraph represents a chain of thought; it is a series of statements that are associated in your mind and that you want the reader to see in the same relationship. The elements in most paragraphs should be related as closely as the elements in a sentence, where presumably the parts fit each other to make a whole. In the following paragraph, notice that the pattern is deductive: a general statement (the topic sentence) opens the paragraph and is followed by specific statements clearly developed from the general statement. Note, too, that the opening sentence illustrates the same kind of relationship, its second clause developing out of its first *(If . . . , then)*.

¶ con

26.3

If the scheme of things is purposeless and meaningless, then the life of man is purposeless and meaningless too. Everything is futile, all effort is in the end worthless. A man may, of course, still pursue disconnected ends, money, fame, art, science, and may gain pleasure from them. But his life is hollow at the center. Hence the dissatisfied, disillusioned, restless spirit of modern man.—Walter T. Stace, "Man Against Darkness," *The Atlantic Monthly*

In the paragraph below, the relationships between successive statements are shown in the margin:

| | |
|---|---|
| Have you got termites? In your house, I mean. It is the newest | Three sentences presenting the subject |

and most fashionable house disease. It used to be called "ants" and no one was interested. Also sinus used to be called catarrh. But "sinus" made the old disease under another name popular. Last summer in the fashionable country places the talk was all about termites. How so and so suddenly stepped on her floor and went right through. And, my dear, they had to call an exterminator and it cost hundreds and hundreds of dollars to get rid of the things; the whole house was almost torn apart and they had to treat the floors with the most awful smelling stuff! If you hadn't termites, you just weren't in Society.—Roy Chapman Andrews, *This Amazing Planet*

Contrast
Comparison

Repetition of idea in third sentence
Example of the "talk"

Example continued

Repetition of idea in third sentence

It is not so important to be able to name the relationships as it is to make sure that they will be clear to your readers. They should not have to "read between the lines" to supply missing connections.

## Methods of showing continuity

The most common ways of showing continuity between statements are: (1) *repetition* of an important word from a previous sentence, (2) use of a *synonym,* a different word of much the same meaning as one already used, (3) use of a *pronoun* referring to a word or idea in the preceding sentence, (4) use of a *connecting word,* an adverb or a conjunction that points out the thought relationship. These signs of the relationship between statements are emphasized and labeled in brackets in the following paragraph:

An instructive example of the failure of a people to take advantage of available materials is afforded by the Onas of South America. **In this respect** [synonym: failure to take advantage of available materials] **they** [pronoun: the Onas] may be contrasted with the Eskimos. **Here** [adverb: connecting with preceding two sentences] are **two peoples** [synonym: the Onas and the Eskimos] living in cold environments, the one to the north, the other to the south. **The Eskimos** [repetition] have made a most satisfactory adjustment to their environment. **They** [pronoun: the Eskimos] have good houses and a complete wardrobe. **Indeed** [adverb: connects and emphasizes], **the latter** [pronoun: a complete wardrobe] surpasses that of most civilized peoples of the past. **The Onas** [repetition], **on the other hand** [connective: shows contrast with preceding statements], go practically naked, and lacking adequate shelter, seek unsuccessfully to keep warm before an open fire. **Yet** [connective: contrast] **the Onas** [repetition] hunt the guanaco, the skin of which is suitable for clothing. In trying to account for the backwardness of **these people** [synonym: the Onas], **then** [connective: result], geographic conditions are not be emphasized. — William F. Ogburn and Meyer F. Nimkoff, *Sociology*

The thought of this paragraph is a unit, and each statement follows the other clearly. You cannot start reading it after the first sentence without realizing that something has gone before. (The sentence "The Eskimos have made a most satisfactory adjustment to their environment" could start a paragraph, but if it did, the paragraph would be about Eskimos, not about Eskimos and Onas.)

We are inclined to overlook the absences of guides to the reader in our own writing, because the relationship of ideas is already clear to us, but we notice immediately when other writers forget to show the connection between ideas. Consider how the following unconnected paragraph is improved by showing the relationship between the statements:

**Unconnected version**

Many people today believe that objectionable movies should be censored by federal or local agencies. The recent emphasis in American films on immorality and violence is outrageous. They are undermining our nation's morals and our prestige abroad, according to many people. There may be some truth here. I agree with the diagnosis, but I cannot accept the cure. Censorship poses a greater threat to a democracy, in my opinion.

**Relationships shown**

Many people today believe that objectionable movies should be censored by federal or local agencies. **These critics** have been outraged by the recent emphasis in American films on immorality and violence. **Such films,** according to **them,** are undermining our nation's morals and our prestige abroad. **This** may be true. **However,** although I agree with **their** diagnosis, I cannot accept **their** cure. It seems to me that censorship poses a greater threat to a democracy **than objectionable entertainment.**

¶ con

26.3

## Eliminating irrelevant ideas

Paragraph continuity is damaged by the introduction of irrelevant and unrelated ideas. These break the chain of thought and make a paragraph seem ragged:

Among the oddities of the plant world, Venus's-flytrap is one of the most interesting. **Venus is the mythological goddess of love.** It is a carnivorous plant that catches and devours insects and occasionally even small birds. This is done by means of paired lobes that resemble the halves of an oyster or clam, **scientifically known as bivalves.** When the lobes are open, they expose a colorful interior that attracts insects in search of nectar. Once it is disturbed, the powerful lobes snap shut, and strong digestive juices go to work to break down and assimilate the body. **Some people have successfully grown these plants in their homes.**

The boldface statements in this example are not directly related to the subject of the paragraph, and in revision they should be omitted or transferred to another paragraph. The last sentence above, for example, might be appropriate in a paragraph telling how to grow Venus's-flytrap, but it is out of place in a description of the plant's physical qualities.

## Continuity in descriptive paragraphs

The details in a descriptive paragraph should give the reader a clear, unified impression. Descriptive writing is more than simple enumeration. You need to choose the most effective details and arrange them so that the more important ones stand out. The following paragraph illustrates a lack of selection and focus. Too much attention is given to minor details, and as a result no single impression emerges:

We entered the Roundup Room through a curtained entrance just past the check room on a right turn. The Roundup Room was a long ell-shaped affair with the end of the ell angling off to the left. It was about two-hundred feet long and probably fifty feet wide. Along the wall on the left ran a long bar made of dark wood. Behind the bar five bartenders were busily filling orders and giving them to a dozen or so waitresses ranging in age from about twenty to forty-five. Above the bar mirror on the wall were paintings of western scenes and cartoons, like those I described on the outside of the building. Down the aisle in front of us there seemed to be a beehive of activity, with couples coming and going to the small dance floor. I say "small" because it couldn't have been more than twenty-five feet square. On our right were small tables, all filled with customers, and on the right wall, farther down, were a number of small booths. We threaded our way through the smoky haze to an empty table.

If the writer intended to emphasize the overcrowding and confusion in this room, he should have concentrated on those features and omitted or briefly summarized such unnecessary details as the shape and dimensions of the room, the paintings above the mirror, and so on.

¶ con

26.3

In writing a descriptive paragraph, decide what main impression you want to achieve; then arrange your material so that all the statements contribute to this central impression. See also §27.3, Description.

## Continuity in narrative paragraphs

When you are relating an experience, describing an incident, or summarizing the plot of a story or play, keep the action moving in one direction and avoid unnecessary interruptions. The boldface sentences in the following paragraph destroy the continuity of the narrative because they stop the action:

It was the seventh of August 1973. My friend and I were hitchhiking from a small town in the northern part of the state. Unlike most adventurers I did not notice the sky nor did I feel the impending danger. **I guess I don't make a very good hero. Now I must get back to my story.** After waiting by the side of the road for some time, we were picked up by two men in an old Chevy.

Later events in this narrative should show whether or not the writer is "a very good hero." This unnecessary remark not only slows down the story, but also suggests the outcome of the incident before it is unfolded.

The connection between statements in a narrative paragraph is usually simple, since it is controlled by time. Events follow each other as they happened in time or as they are imagined to have happened. The verbs usually carry this movement, and the continuity is made stronger by the repetition of the same grammatical subject from one sentence to another. Time may be emphasized and made more obvious by adverbs—*then, next, before, soon, later, presently*—or by adverbial phrases or clauses: *When he got to the corner . . . , After the last dance. . . .* The boldface verb forms and adverbs of time in this passage show how large a part words of action and time play in giving continuity to a narrative paragraph:

They **ran** for three hours. **Finally, avoiding** hummocks and **seeking** low ground, they **intercepted** the rain squall. **For ten minutes they ran** beneath the squall, **raising** their arms and, **for the first time, shouting** and **capering. Then** the wind **died** and the rain squall **held** steady. They **were studying** the ground. **Suddenly** one of them **shouted, ran** a few feet, **bent forward** and **put** his mouth to the ground. He **had found** a depression with rain water in it. He **bent down,** a black cranelike figure, and **put** his mouth to the ground. — Eugene Burdick, "The Invisible Aborigine," *Harper's Magazine*

To maintain continuity in narrative paragraphs, keep the tense of verbs consistent. If you start with one tense—the past or the present—don't shift without reason to another. See also §27.4, Narration.

### Applications: Developing Effective Paragraphs

1. As you have just read, there are many different ways to develop, or "build," a paragraph. Francis Christensen has pointed out that one commonly used method is to have each sentence in the paragraph refer back to the topic sentence. Examine the model below, which follows this pattern, and then develop similar paragraphs from the topic sentences provided.

   *example:* topic sentence: One popular linguistic myth is that people living in technologically unsophisticated cultures speak primitive languages. / But the languages of native American Indians such as the Hopi, the Navajo, or the Washoe of Nevada are as complex in syntax and phonology as English or German. / The many languages of Africa, also, are just as rich and complicated as any language in the Indo-European family. / Even the Ainu—one of the most primitive people discovered thus far—prove to have a language that is capable of expressing the most subtle thoughts and needs of the speakers. / If there is such a thing as a "primitive" human language in existence anywhere on earth, the burden of proof now rests with those who glibly equate mechanization with linguistic superiority.

   a. I can think of five reasons why I should be elected President.
   b. A car is still a necessity in our society.
   c. What do students want from a college education?

2. Another common method for developing paragraphs is for each sentence to carry on, or build upon, the previous thought, as in the model below. Using the following topic sentences, write paragraphs following this model.

   *example:* Lots of Americans talk about "getting in shape," but few do much about it. / By "getting in shape" I *don't* mean taking a walk now and then or wearing a girdle. / There is only one way to get in shape, and that is with regular exercise. / And regular exercise means setting aside some time of the day, *every day,* for strenuous physical activities. / Among the useful activities are jogging, push-ups, and sit-ups.

   a. The road to riches is usually a muddy path, not a freeway.
   b. The registration system at this college is incredibly complicated.
   c. Without the "missing link," evolution remains a theory.

3. Each of the following three paragraphs lacks continuity. Rewrite them, making whatever rearrangements, additions, or omissions are needed to make the continuity clear.

**a.** My grandparents still follow many of their national customs. They have lived in the United States for almost forty years. The traditional ceremony of the eggs begins on the night before Easter, when my grandmother prepares a dozen elaborately decorated eggs. Despite her age, she still has a very firm hand. The eggs are passed from hand to hand around the table, where the whole family has gathered. My grandfather chants a prayer meanwhile. The eggs are taken outside and buried in the garden, and everyone goes to bed for the night. Then everyone takes the candle he has left lighted in his window and returns to the garden. As dawn is breaking, the eggs are dug up and placed in a basket decorated with flowers. There is a sumptuous breakfast to celebrate the successful recovery, and man's redemption by Christ has been acted out.

**b.** By 1937 Americans began to grow aware of the menace of fascism. The United States government extended the Neutrality Act to cover the war in Spain. This prevented the republicans from getting American guns and supplies. Up until 1937 Americans had paid more attention to domestic than to foreign problems because they had not been dramatized. But tensions were mounting in Europe, and the Spanish Civil War attracted a great deal of interest. A Gallup poll taken in 1937 showed that 65 percent sided with the republican forces against the fascist Franco. It was 75 percent in 1938. Of course Hitler represented fascism at its worst, as we all know.

**c.** When I got about thirty feet out into the lake, I saw that the water was rougher than I had thought. Several large breakers hit me full in the face, and I took in too much water for comfort. There are techniques good swimmers use to avoid getting swamped by breakers, but I had never learned them because I didn't think it was important at the time. I decided to head back toward the rocks, but I couldn't see the flat shelf where I had entered. In desperation, I headed toward a jagged group of rocks nearby. Just as I got close to it and was groping for a foothold, a large breaker threw me against a sharp edge and knocked me breathless. Being thrown against rocks in rough waters is a danger many inexperienced swimmers overlook.

**4.** Assume that the following list is a collection of notes you have jotted down on the subject of land problems in the Mediterranean area. Incorporate the information into an orderly, unified piece of writing, using appropriate paragraph divisions. Add whatever words or phrases are necessary to make the relationships between ideas clear.

Mediterranean countries were once prosperous.
Their population is rising fast.
Many trees were cut down in past centuries.
The Mediterranean basin used to be the center of Western civilization.
The land is becoming less productive every year.

Much of the land today is arid or semi-arid.
The United Nations has started a project there to improve land use.
Grass and trees help water soak down into the soil.
Poverty is widespread in Mediterranean countries.
Desert areas cover 1.25 billion acres and are increasing every year.
Trees are essential to prevent erosion.
Restoring all the forests would take too long.
The United Nations is financing increased fertilization.
The land has been overgrazed, so that much grass and forest have been destroyed.
The topsoil is being washed away.
Floods are becoming widespread.
The United Nations wants to restore balanced land use.
Irrigation would be a help.
The sizes of grazing herds must be reduced.
Agriculture and animal husbandry must be integrated.

5. Pick a topic from the sentences below, and write *two* different paragraphs from the same sentence. Choose two of the patterns discussed in §26.2, Other patterns of development.

a. Much of the flavor of a nation comes from its quaint customs.
b. With the coming of the railways, life on the prairies changed rapidly.
c. Movies are worse than ever.
d. Suppose the telephone had never been invented.

**Exer**

*. . . a word spoken in due season, how good is it!*—Proverbs 15:23

*A word fitly spoken is like apples of gold in pictures of silver.*
—Proverbs 25:11

The long and short papers that you will write for your composition course are not so different from the reports and term papers that you will write for your other college courses, and these in turn are not so different from the practical, business, or technical writing that you may do outside of college. A letter of recommendation, for example, is both informative and persuasive. It offers information about a person's past (usually narrative) and about his present (often descriptive) in order to make an argument for his future. The argument may be developed by any of the methods you might use in developing an argumentative paper in your composition class. An answer for an essay examination will probably be developed in much the same way as an expository essay for a class paper. And a letter in which you apply for a job is a kind of specialized personal essay, not remarkably different from some personal writing you will do in your composition class except that in the letter of application you may pay closer attention to your audience.

All that has been said in the preceding sections of this handbook about planning and writing papers for a composition course applies, then, to most of the writing you will do in or out of college. The possibilities that are open to you and the needs of your writing chores will vary with changes in your subject, your audience, and in the occasion for which you are writing. It may be useful, before discussing some particular forms of writing, to think about what is possible and what may be required in various situations.

One way to see the nature of different kinds of writing is to start with a simple diagram representing the chief elements in writing. (In the following paragraphs we are calling on the work of Professor James Kinneavy in *A Theory of Discourse* for help in differentiating among different kinds of writing.) We'll put these chief elements in connection with each other so as to suggest their interaction in writing:

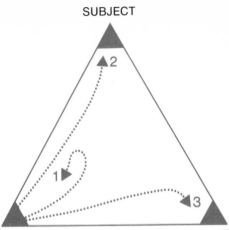

SUBJECT

AUTHOR

AUDIENCE

The triangle connects the chief elements—author, subject, audience. The pointing lines inside are meant to suggest something about the nature of different kinds of writing, as we'll see.

In many kinds of writing the author is dominant; the writing is by the author and, in many ways, for the author. As line 1 in the diagram shows, this kind of writing leaves the author and returns to the author. It may be called *expressive writing,* for the author's need to express appears to be the primary motive in such writing. You should note two things about *expressive writing.* First, there are many different kinds of *expressive writing.* Personal letters, diaries, and journals oftener than not seem intended chiefly as personal expression; some descriptive writing is the author's account of learning to see. Some expository and argumentative writing turns out to be *expressive writing* when the author, instead of seeking to explain or to persuade, uses the occasion for meditative purposes to work out personal thoughts about a subject. Second, expressive writing offers some opportunities and sets some limits that other kinds of writing don't. You are probably free, for example, to write more informally than you might otherwise and to use looser forms of organization. On the other hand you may not be free to enter into a technical discussion of something that has taken your interest. You are your own prime object of attention in this kind of writing; you must first of all be honest with yourself.

But in other kinds of writing the subject deserves primary attention, and you must get out of the way. As line 2 indicates, some writing is focused on the subject, with the author and any possible audience fading into the background. Kinneavy calls this kind of writing *referential writing;* it refers to something outside the author. Many business letters—letters, for example, that make sales transactions, or memoranda that discuss organizational problems—are *referential writing,* as are most reports, including book reports, laboratory reports, and other class reports. Most answers on essay examinations and most writing about literature are forms of *referential writing.* You don't have the same kind of freedom in this kind of writing that you might with *expressive writing;* the subject must be dealt with, and that may require tighter organization, a more technical language, and a close control of your own opinions. But you need not think of *referential writing* as only limiting; sometimes it is a great advantage to get outside yourself and plunge into the exploration of a subject.

In other kinds of writing, which Kinneavy classifies as *persuasive writing,* the audience seems to be the proper target of attention. Many forms of writing wish not to express an author's views or to explain a subject, but rather to move or to persuade an audience. Sermons belong to this group, and so do letters of recommendation, critiques, all forms of argument, and some kinds of public letters, for example, letters of protest. Writing in this class may make particular demands on you; it may require close, lucid reasoning that an audience can easily follow, and sure, specific evidence that will support assertions. Most troublesome of all—it will require you to be believable in a way not demanded by *expressive writing* or *referential writing.*

We'll not try to classify fiction, poetry, and drama here. In those forms, author, subject, and audience mingle and interact, and the written works usually have no other end in view except to be what they are. A poem, in other words, probably exists not just to express its author's views, or to explain something, or to persuade an audience, but just to be a poem; it is its own justification, much as a song is.

The particular writing tasks you will face both in school and out of school may each have special needs, forms of organization, and styles. This general scheme of organization— *expressive writing, referential writing,* and *persuasive writing* — is a reminder that the language you use, the style you use in sentences and paragraphs, the forms of organization you depend on, the relationship you establish among yourself, your subject, and your audience, may vary according to what the writing you are doing needs to do. It makes a difference in the way we talk and write whether we are talking about ourselves, some subject outside ourselves, or to an audience. Speakers and writers sometimes go astray when they forget what they are supposed to be doing. We've all been in classrooms where teachers have become so involved in their subject (referential discourse) that they have forgotten their audience of students (requiring persuasive discourse). We've all heard salesmen and politicians so intent on selling themselves to us (persuasive discourse) that they have forgotten to know very much about their subject (requiring referential discourse).

The particular techniques you will use may vary, too, depending on your immediate, practical goals. This section will consider some of the special problems involved in different kinds of writing: exposition, argumentation, description, narration, answers to essay examinations, reports, literary analyses, and letters.

## Exposition

The purpose of exposition is to *inform* your readers, to carry their knowledge of something beyond its present point, to help them understand a situation or a process, to give them information about an idea or belief. It ranges from the explanation of small personal matters ("How to Select a College Wardrobe") to complex scientific treatises ("The Effect of Ultraviolet Light on Steroids").

Skill in exposition is essential in all college work. You will probably do more expository writing, where you inform your reader or explain a point of view, than any other kind of writing. Most of the reading required in college, except in literature courses, is also expository. Increasing skill in expository writing, then, is a major aim of beginning composition courses.

**Exp**

**27.1**

Writing
in and out
of
college
**410**

Most of the suggestions about writing in §18, Discovering and organizing what you have to say, and §19, Writing the first draft, are especially relevant to exposition. You will also find it helpful to study §26.2, Patterns of paragraph development. Definition, comparison, contrast, and the other methods of development discussed there are useful, even necessary means of explanation.

## Gathering information

Whatever your subject and whatever the length of your paper, you will have to exercise judgment in deciding what resources to use and in gearing your information to your particular audience and situation. (See §18.2, Using your resources.) Some of the short expository papers you will be assigned in college can be based entirely on your own knowledge and experience. Other papers will require that you gather and evaluate information from various sources in order to develop your subject adequately.

Even when you base your paper on a personal experience, such as building a boat or working in a drive-in theater, you may find it useful to add to your information by reading in the library or by talking to people who have had similar experiences. It is a good idea in planning such a paper to make a list of points about which your memory is hazy or about which you lack adequate information. Then, to fill in the gaps, you can extend your observations or read what others have reported about the subject.

For typical information papers on subjects such as "The Electoral College" or "Devices for Controlling Air Pollution," you will usually need to consult a variety of printed sources — books, magazines, newspapers — to find information you cannot gather first-hand. Some of these sources may be course textbooks or assigned outside readings which provide basic facts and figures to use as a nucleus for the paper. Others may be books of your own that supply information on subjects that interest you, like sports, hobbies, or history. Or you may find relevant information in current magazines and newspapers, either those you subscribe to or those in the college library.

## Relating specialized information to your reader

In gathering and selecting additional facts to use in an expository paper, be particularly careful to consider your audience. If you are writing a paper for a group of bridge fanciers, you probably need not define terms like *point count* and *slam* or explain how a *finesse* is made, since your readers would be familiar with such fundamentals. But if you are writing on bridge for an English class, you cannot expect the typical student to have this knowledge; to make sure that your audience understands, you must take the time to insert brief explanations. If you omit them, the whole paper may be puzzling or even incomprehensible to general readers. Remember that you are writing the paper in hopes of telling them something new, of adding to their knowledge in an area where they do not have your background. Put yourself in their place: what words or ideas might be unfamiliar to them? How can you explain these things so that they will understand them?

The following passages show effective and ineffective ways of relating specialized information to general readers:

**Ineffective**
There are various ways to bridge the gap from one solo to the next. The trumpeter may play a series of riffs accompanied only by the rhythm section. This is probably the most common method.

If the bleeding becomes severe or there is a chance of infection, you may have to cauterize the wound.

**Effective**
There are various ways to bridge the gap from one solo to the next. Probably the most common method is for the trumpeter to play a series of short, conventional jazz phrases, called "riffs," accompanied only by the rhythm section—piano, bass, and drums.

If the bleeding becomes severe or there is any chance of infection, you may have to cauterize the wound by searing it with a piece of metal that has been held over a flame until it is red-hot.

Exp

27.1

Writing
in and out
of
college
412

## Documenting your information

When your own observations form the basis of the paper, be sure to tell the readers why you consider your statements to be fairly authoritative. Otherwise they may not be sure how much value to attach to them. Somewhere near the beginning of the paper, state the circumstances under which you gathered your facts:

Since I was sixteen I have spent my summer vacations working in a local department store, first as a stock clerk and later as an assistant display manager. During that time, I have become familiar with the typical organization of a large retail store. . . .

My home is only nine miles away from the Menominee Indian reservation, and I have had frequent opportunities to meet and talk to members of the Menominee tribe. . . .

In gathering examples for this paper, I spent ten hours listening to radio programs featuring rock-and-roll records and copied down the lyrics of a dozen of the current favorites. . . .

When you incorporate published material into your paper, be sure to reproduce it accurately and to credit the sources, whether you quote them directly or not. It is not fair to present someone else's experiences or observations as if they were your own. In a research paper, credit is given formally by means of footnotes (§28.8, Documenting your paper), but in a general paper mention may be made informally. The following are some typical examples of how such acknowledgments can be handled:

Franklin Soames, the author of *Zapotec Culture,* found that. . . .

At a recent medical convention, H. L. Matthews, the noted urologist, was quoted as saying. . . .

But according to Jean Lafontant, in a recent article in *Saturday Review/World.* . . .

Sources which have been used extensively may be given in a note at the beginning or at the end of a paper:

Much of the material for this paper was taken from C. D. Darlington, *The Evolution of Man and Society* (New York: Simon and Schuster, 1969).

## Argumentation 27.2

Whereas the purpose of exposition is to *inform* your readers, the purpose of argumentation is to *convince* them. The two kinds of writing have much in common, and both are based on facts or impressions gathered from various sources. But expository writing simply *presents* information, while argumentative writing *uses* it to support or test a belief. A paper describing current fashions in clothing, the social habits of bees, or the history of the slave trade invites the readers to share the writer's knowledge of the subject; a paper attacking campus rules for dress, on the other hand, expresses an opinion and tries to convince the reader of its validity. Like exposition, argumentative writing ranges widely, from matters close at hand ("Down with Large Classes") to those of major public concern ("Let's Get Rid of the Electoral College").

## Locating the argument

An argumentative paper *proposes* something. Whether it calls for action or simply asks for the recognition of a point of view, it centers on a proposition that the writer must be prepared to prove.

An argument from a proposition, as Professor Edward P. J. Corbett has said in *Classical Rhetoric for the Modern Student,* is similar to a factual report in that it can ordinarily be judged as true or false; but a statement of fact is not in itself an occasion for argument, since presumably facts can be checked. An argument is also similar to a statement of opinion, in that it represents a judgment the writer has made; but an opinion is not an occasion for argument unless it is based on *facts* instead of mere preference, for only then can its validity be proved.

In planning a persuasive paper, you must take the time to formulate your proposition carefully. As your thesis statement, your proposition gives direction and unity to your argument. Ordinarily it needs to be simple—composed ideally, perhaps, of a single subject and a single predicate. If you argue, for example, that "County government must be put into new hands on election day and reformed to keep state and federal agencies from encroaching on local authority," you have, by using a double predicate, introduced two arguments, both of which must then be proved.

You should find the suggestions in §18.1, Discovering a subject, helpful in formulating an arguable proposition.

## Using resources and evidence

When we state our opinions in informal situations, we often give little or no evidence to support them: "John is a reckless driver"; "The cost of living is going up every day"; "Divorce is the main cause of juvenile delinquency." This does not mean that we have no good reasons for believing as we do, but simply that our reasons are usually known and accepted by our listeners. On occasions when our opinions are questioned, we may attempt to support them with facts drawn from our experience and reading: "John had two accidents

**Arg**

**27.2**

Writing
in and out
of
college
**414**

last month, and he always drives too fast." "Steak is up sixty cents a pound, and a refrigerator costs almost twice as much today as it did six years ago." "Psychologists say that emotional stability depends on a secure family life." Such evidence is considered acceptable or even convincing in informal situations, usually because the listener's personal regard for the speaker lends some weight to the evidence.

In writing, however, the relationship with your audience is far more impersonal; authority must rest much more on the facts themselves. Readers who know neither John nor you will want to know what kind of accidents John had and who was at fault; they will wonder whether "too fast" means in excess of speed limits; they may suspect that "always" is an exaggeration. Before accepting your opinion in regard to the relation between divorce and delinquency, they may want to hear what psychologists say in their own words, to be sure you are not misinterpreting their remarks or ignoring opposed opinions.

The more facts supporting your opinion that you can gather from experience or from the written statements of others, the more reason you can give your readers to accept that opinion. You will probably not be able to present absolute *proof,* but the greater the weight of your evidence, the more probable it will seem to them that your belief is the best one.

## Types of arguments

Some traditional kinds of argument may suggest certain ways of thinking about your material that will lead you to the evidence you need. One is the *argument from nature.* Not long ago on a college campus a young man who wished to call attention to inadequacies in the campus guidebook petitioned to have his name placed on the ballot in an election for homecoming queen. He maintained that he was eligible on the grounds that the guidebook stipulated only that candidates should be students under twenty-one; sex was not mentioned in the body of the rules. The young man's petition was denied through an argument from nature. Pointing out that the rules came under the heading "Eligibility requirements for homecoming queen," his opposition seized on the meaning of the word *queen* — by nature a female — to deny his eligibility. An argument from nature may be developed by a number of techniques: by defining the nature of a thing; by studying the meanings attached to the key words in a proposition; by classifying the subject in order to establish a frame of reference in terms of which it can be discussed.

People cannot always agree on the nature of things, of course, and for that reason they have often turned to other kinds of argument. The *argument from analogy* brings a subject and argument into a reader's knowledge by suggesting its similarity to something better known, as in the fairly common—but usually ineffective—analogy of government and business. The evidence you bring to this kind of argument must show that the comparison is both meaningful and accurate.

The *argument from consequence* enforces a proposition by examining cause and effect, antecedent and consequence. This is a useful kind of argument, but it is limited by the fact that human affairs are not ordered by certain laws of causality. Poverty *sometimes* breeds crime; prolonged tyranny *frequently* leads to revolution; honesty is *occasionally* rewarded. Before expressing an opinion about the outcome of some course of action, or about the cause of some event, make sure that the weight of evidence lends probability to your statement.

The *argument from authority* depends upon the testimony of respected persons, the authority of institutions, the weight of important documents. This is probably the least popular of the traditional kinds of argument, for most audiences prefer to feel that the truth is *discovered* in the course of an argument, rather than that it has been *pronounced* by authority.

## Taking the argument to your audience

Whatever kind of argument you use, and those above are only samples, remember that your readers have some confidence in their own intelligence and judgment and are likely to resent a writer who attempts to make up their minds for them. (See the discussion of author-audience relationships in §18; note especially the commentary on Rogerian approaches to argument.) State your facts as specifically as possible—so that your readers can check them for themselves if they want to—and give your reasons for whatever conclusions you draw. Compare the following statements for effectiveness:

**Arg**

**27.2**

Writing
in and out
of
college
416

| Vague | Specific |
|---|---|
| A couple of years ago, the president of a big corporation said that taxes were too high. | In a speech to the Toledo Chamber of Commerce on April 14, 1972, Oscar Winslow, president of the Winslow Steel Corporation, said, "Corporation taxes today are so high that they are destroying business incentive." |
| In many of his newspaper articles, H. L. Mencken made slighting references to democracy. Anyone can see that he despised it. | In his articles for the Baltimore *Sun,* H. L. Mencken frequently referred to democracy in terms such as these: "the domination of unreflective and timorous men, moved in vast herds by mob emotions" (July 26, 1920); "it may be clumsy, it may be swinish, it may be unutterably incompetent and dishonest, but it is never dismal" (July 14, 1924). |

In trying to persuade readers to accept your opinion, you will naturally want to gather facts that will support your position. It is not fair to your readers, however, to suggest that *all* evidence reinforces your belief. They may be familiar with contrary evidence; even if they are not, its absence may make them suspect that you are stacking the deck in your favor. In a court of law, an attorney who deliberately suppresses evidence damaging to his or her case may be disbarred from future practice. The consequences to writers are usually not so serious, but they may also lose the case.

When you come across facts that do *not* support your opinion, give them as careful consideration as those that do. Is their source authoritative and relatively free of bias? Do they offer serious and relevant reasons to question your present opinion? Do they outnumber the facts you can find to support it? It may be that you will want to alter or modify your proposition after taking opposing facts into account. You may decide that your original opinion was wrong; many writers are unaware of the flimsy basis of their beliefs until they begin trying to substantiate them.

Even if the facts you gather do not change your opinion, it is unfair to simply discard those that fail to support it. In fact, it will strengthen your position in the readers' eyes if you frankly admit unfavorable evidence along with your reasons for being unpersuaded by it. Remember that the readers are your jury. If you have arrived at an opinion by weighing opposing evidence sensibly, they should be able to do the same.

## Testing the argument

One way to test your argument, or to examine the argument of another writer or speaker, is to scrutinize it for flaws in reasoning and in the use of evidence. Probably the most common flaws are these:

### Hasty generalization

In informal situations, we often overgeneralize from the facts: "She's *never* on time"; "Advertising is *only* a pack of lies." A little consideration shows us that in reality all-or-none, black-or-white situations are rare; reality is more accurately described in terms of finer shadings and degrees. Most readers are aware of this, and although they will accept and make statements like the above uncritically enough in conversations, they are suspicious of them in writing.

Be especially cautious in using terms like *all, always, everybody, nobody, never, none, only,* and *most.* Before making such all-inclusive statements, make sure that they are justified. If there are any exceptions to some assertion you make, modify your language to make it more accurate. Don't say that *all* young people want a home and family: *some* or *many* might be more accurate. Before you say that *most* early marriages end in divorce, ascertain from some reliable source whether more than 50 percent actually do; otherwise you are not justified in using *most.* Keep in mind that the English vocabulary provides you with a wealth of qualifying terms (*some, few, often,* to name only a few) and choose those that most accurately describe the number, extent, and frequency of the facts you are asserting. Compare these two statements for precision of expression. Both are based on the same facts (of the delinquents in the State Training School, 75 percent come from low-income families, 45 percent have used narcotics at some time, and 20 percent have IQ scores over 100):

**Overgeneralization**
Almost all delinquents in the State Training School come from homes **on the verge of starvation. Most** of them are dope **addicts,** and **very few** are **brilliant.**

**Accurate statement**
**Three out of four** delinquents in the State Training School come from **low-income homes. Almost half** of them have **at least experimented with narcotics. A significant minority** are **above average mentally.**

## False analogy

Comparison and analogy are effective means of arguing, but only if there is really a basic similarity between the compared terms. If, for example, a university administrator sets out to argue for new rules and economies in his school on the basis that it should be run like a business, we should probably reject his argument on the grounds that his analogy is not valid, for similarities between a business and a university seem only incidental, not essential.

## Post hoc, ergo propter hoc

This fallacy (literally, "after this, therefore because of this") is the fairly common one of assuming that two events or things are causally related simply because they are related in time. The young man who gets a raise a week after acquiring a new deodorant probably owes his success to something else.

## Non sequitur

The label *non sequitur* ("it does not follow") applies to errors of reasoning in which the conclusion does not follow from the evidence presented. Sometimes a step in reasoning has been omitted, and the fallacy can be corrected by supplying the missing link. But sometimes the conclusion is drawn from evidence that has no bearing on the issue: that Bart Starr uses a particular shaving cream has nothing to do with its quality; that a man does not beat his wife has nothing to do with whether he is a good husband; that the army teaches useful skills has nothing to do with the wisdom of sending troops to other countries.

## Begging the question

This term applies to an argument that assumes the truth of what needs to be proved. A politician who argues "Our feeble county government, desperately in need of reform, must be placed in new hands on election day" is begging the question unless he *proves* that the present government is feeble and in need of reform.

## Ignoring the question

This is a broad term that applies to all arguments that are irrelevant, as when a governor argues that his administration is not corrupt because the state budget is balanced. Another way he might ignore the issue would be to resort to an *argumentum ad hominem* ("argument against the man"), attacking the integrity of his opponents rather than the charge of his own corruption. Or he might use *glittering generalities* such as "my devotion and dedication to the fine people of this great state" to draw his audience into acquiescence by the weight of good words. All arguments that use emotional means to persuade an audience to arrive at a judgment without examining the evidence are ways of ignoring the question.

When you have finished the first draft of an argumentative paper, examine it carefully for flaws. Have you weighed the available evidence? Are your generalizations supported by fact? Are your inferences valid? Make sure that your argument is both honest and sound.

## Description                                    **27.3**

The purpose of descriptive writing is to enable a reader to see an object, person, or scene as you have seen or imagined it. This requires an eye for significant details as well as a knack for putting sense impressions into words. Description is often written for its own sake, as a form of artistic expression, and it may also be an important part of other kinds of writing, from long research papers to technical reports and case histories.

### Seeing your subject clearly
To make a description vivid to a reader, you must first of all know where you stand, physically and mentally, in relation to the thing you are writing about. How did you see your subject? From what angle? Under the weight of what mood? How can you define your subject, distinguishing it from similar things in the same class? What makes this particular sunset, for example, different from all others?

Descriptive writing succeeds only when you show your audience the specific, identifying details of object or scene. This requires that you see it clearly yourself, that you understand what you see, and that you say *precisely* what you see, as the writer has done in this passage:

I know how a prize watermelon looks when it is sunning its fat rotundity among pumpkin vines and "simblins"; I know how to tell when it is ripe without "plugging" it. I know how inviting it looks when it is cooling itself in a tub of water under the bed, waiting; I know how it looks when it lies on the table in the sheltered great floor-space between house and kitchen, and the children gathered for the sacrifice and their mouths watering. I know the crackling sound it makes when the carving knife enters its end and I can see the split fly along in front of the blade as the knife cleaves its way to the other end; I can see its halves fall apart and display the rich red meat and the black seeds, and the heart standing up, a luxury fit for the elect. — Mark Twain, *Autobiography*

No two persons look at a scene in exactly the same way. What makes one writer's description more vivid than another's is the kind of details selected and the way they are arranged.

## Selecting and arranging details

Good descriptive writing is precise. If in describing a person you write "I first noticed this lady because she was wearing a funny hat," your description won't mean much to the reader because there are many kinds of funny hats. State in specific terms what the hat looked like: perhaps it was a black velvet beret covered with sea shells or perhaps it was a miniature merry-go-round.

Notice how lifeless the description is in this paraphrase, from which the specific expressions have been removed:

After Lincoln became a lawyer, he started to pay more attention to his appearance. But even though he wore his hair in the accepted fashion of the time, he still wasn't well dressed. As a result, he acquired the reputation of being one of the most careless dressers in town, along with another local man, who was a judge, and who was equally careless about the way he looked.

By way of contrast, compare the description as it was written:

And though Lincoln had begun wearing broadcloth and white shirts with a white collar and black silk cravat, and suggestions of side-burns coming down three-fourths the length of his ears, he was still known as one of the carelessly dressed men of Springfield, along with Stephen Logan, who wore unbleached cotton shirts and had sat two years as a circuit court judge wearing an unbleached cotton shirt with no cravat or stock. — Carl Sandburg, *Abraham Lincoln: The Prairie Years, I*

Being specific in descriptive writing doesn't mean that you should overload your sentences with adjectives and adverbs. While such words are used to "describe" or qualify other words, too many of them can be disastrous to any piece of descriptive writing. To refer to the Grand Canyon as "*absolutely* the *most marvelous* sight I have *ever* seen in my *entire* life'' may give your readers some hint about your emotions, but it won't tell them much about the Canyon or help them re-create your impression of it.

The details you select for a descriptive passage should contribute to a central impression. (See §26.3, page 400, Continuity in descriptive paragraphs.) Often a few well-selected details will give a sharper picture than a large number of ill-assorted ones:

In the spring, Tipasa is inhabited by gods and the gods speak in the sun and the scent of absinthe leaves, in the silver armor of the sea, in the raw blue sky, the flower-covered ruins, and the great bubbles of light among the heaps of stone. At certain hours of the day the countryside is black with sunlight. The eyes try in vain to perceive anything but drops of light and colors trembling on the lashes. The thick scent of aromatic plants tears at the throat and suffocates in the vast heat. Far away, I can just make out the black bulk of the Chenoua, rooted in the hills around the village, moving with a slow and heavy rhythm until it finally crouches in the sea. — Albert Camus, ''Nuptials at Tipasa''

If you are writing a character sketch, remember that what a person does or says may be more revealing than physical details. This brief paragraph tells the reader more about what kind of person Mrs. Hopewell is than would a good many lines of purely personal detail:

Nothing is perfect. This was one of Mrs. Hopewell's favorite sayings. Another was: that is life! And still another, the most important, was: well, other people have their opinions too. She would make these statements, usually at the table, in a tone of gentle insistence as if no one held them but her, and the large hulking Joy, whose constant outrage had obliterated every expression from her face, would start just a little to the side of her, her eyes icy blue, with the look of someone who has achieved blindness by an act of will and means to keep it. — Flannery O'Connor, ''Good Country People''

To give focus to a description, you may find it useful to adopt one of the methods for developing material discussed in §19.2. For example, a spatial arrangement that takes you from left to right in picturing your subject, or from high to low, or from near to far, or from far to near, may help you to create order in your description. Professor Leo Rockas has said in *Modes of Rhetoric* that description is writing that aspires to be painting—its order is determined by space. Professor Rockas suggests, indeed, that when writers set out to enliven description with active verbs (part of a time order), they convert it into narration.

Often objects attract attention to themselves and deserve to become subjects for description because of some special impression they make. Thus, an interesting way to organize description is to focus attention on the dominant impression, subordinating all else. In the following passage the impression of quiet laziness, idleness, dominates the scene:

After all these years I can picture that old time to myself now, just as it was then: the white town drowsing in the sunshine of a summer's morning; the streets empty, or pretty nearly so; one or two clerks sitting in front of the Water Street stores, with their splint-bottomed chairs tilted back against the walls, chins on breasts, hats slouched over their faces, asleep—with shingle-shavings enough around to show what broke them down; a sow and a litter of pigs loafing along the sidewalk, doing a good business in watermelon rinds and seeds; two or three lonely little freight piles scattered about the levee; a pile of skids on the slope of the stone-paved wharf, and the fragrant town drunkard asleep in the shadow of them.—Mark Twain, *Life on the Mississippi*

Good descriptive writing demands restraint and discrimination. It also takes practice to get the exact effect that you want. One way to get additional practice is to study published examples of descriptive writing that appeal to you, observing what kinds of details the writers use and how they present them.

## Narration

The purpose of narrative writing is to re-create an experience or event, usually without expository comment. Like description, narration depends upon particulars, but unlike description, it moves through a time period:

It was almost midnight when they slipped between the frigate *Emerald* and the southern tip of Prudence Island. Close to the shore, they suddenly heard horses running. As his men weighed their oars, Barton had the chilling thought that he had been decoyed into a trap. But the sound died away; it was apparently nothing more sinister than a few horses frolicking in a pasture. Running ashore in the cove, Barton left a man to guard each boat while the five squads made their way up the gulley.—Leonard Falkner, "Captor of the Barefoot General," *American Heritage*

### Point of view
The particulars of narrative writing are reported to an audience selectively through a given point of view. Ordinarily it is

neither possible nor desirable to present every action in a sequence of events. Rather, you should focus on those aspects of an experience that, from your point of view, make it worth preserving.

Most of the narrative writing you do will be presented as the narrative of either a first-person observer or participant or of a third-person observer. Personal narratives and autobiographical sketches are ordinarily told in the first person, but it will depend on the story you tell whether you present yourself as participating or observing. In historical writing, reports, and case histories, you will ordinarily present the action in the third person, letting the events speak for themselves.

Whether you report an action as a participant or observer, try to focus attention directly on what went on. In the following passage the narrator draws attention to *himself* rather than to the event he is narrating:

I was riding with a friend late one night, returning from a long weekend trip. I was extremely tired, and I am sure he was too, and as a result we weren't very observant about traffic lights. I did notice in the distance one very red blinker light, though. I also saw a car directly in front of ours, like a slow moving ship in a submarine's sights. I knew immediately that we were going too fast to stop, so my natural reaction was to brace myself for a crash. It seemed to me that I could hear the tires squealing for minutes before anything happened. I was surprised to find during those actually few short seconds that I was seeing a variety of vivid colors that I hadn't even noticed before. I was aware of the yellow dividing strip of the highway, and still off in the distance, the brilliant red flashes of the traffic signal. There were also the browns and grays and whites of the surrounding buildings, that I hadn't seen a few moments before, but now were things of sharp beauty.

This narrative could be tightened up, and the *I*'s made less conspicuous, by revising some of the sentences:

Late one night I was riding with a friend. We were both extremely tired after a long weekend trip and not very watchful of the traffic lights. But I was dimly aware of one very red blinker light in the distance. Suddenly a car loomed up in front of us, like a slow moving ship seen through a submarine's sights. We were going too fast to stop, and instinctively I braced myself for the crash. Our tires squealed for what seemed minutes. Actually only a second or two passed, but in that brief instant, all the color of the scene jumped into view—the bright yellow dividing strip of the highway, the brilliant red flashes of the traffic light, the browns, grays, and whites of the nearby buildings. For one sharp moment everything took on a strange and fearful beauty.

**Nar**

**27.4**

Writing
in and out
of
college
**424**

A reader will understand your experience more clearly if you concentrate on the events as they happened instead of on your feelings about them.

## Use of tenses

In narrative writing events are typically written down in chronological order, with verbs and adverbs controlling the movement:

... **After a long half hour,** the rain **eased** a bit and the clouds **rose.** I **relaxed** a little. I **was showing** them that a rookie **could get through. Just then,** the engine **stopped** cold. As a rule, **when** an engine **fails,** it **will give** some warning. The water temperature **will rise,** or the oil pressure **will drop,** or there **is a knocking or clanking.** Even if it **is only for a minute or two,** it **gives** the pilot a chance **to look around** and **head for** a field or open place. However, **when** the timing gear in a Liberty engine **failed, one second** it **was roaring along** even and strong, and **the next** there **was** a tremendous silence. I **quickly twisted** all the knobs and gadgets in the cockpit, but there **was** no response, and the engine **stayed** dead. **While** my hands **were trying to restart** the engine, my neck **was stretching** and my eyes **searching** for some sort of field **to land in.** I **was surrounded** by heavily forested, sharply rolling hills. To my left **was** a cuplike basin with a small clearing. It **was** downwind, but my gliding radius **didn't allow** much choice. I **went** for it. — Dean C. Smith, "Flying by Guess and by God," *The Atlantic Monthly*

Most narrative writing uses the past tense, but the present (or "historical present") is sometimes used to create a sense of events actually happening, as in this paragraph:

Our ship is hooting for all she's worth. An important last-minuter comes surging up. The rope hawsers are being wound clankily in. Seagulls — there are never very many in the Mediterranean — seagulls whirl like a few flakes of snow in the upper chill air. Clouds spin. And without knowing it we are evaporating away from the shore, from our mooring, between the great *City of Trieste* and another big black steamer that lies like a wall. . . . — D. H. Lawrence, *Sea and Sardinia*

Whether a narrative is written in the present or past, one tense should be kept throughout. This paragraph illustrates unnecessary and confusing tense shifts:

As I **hop** [present tense] on the city transit that will take me to the University, I notice that as always the bus is filled past capacity. As I **turned** [past] around, I saw a blind man sitting directly behind me with a dog lying at his feet. I **watch** [present] the dog, sitting there perfectly still, looking through the glass doors. Suddenly the dog **got up** [past], nudged his master, who pulled the cord above his head and with no difficulty got off the bus and proceeded up the street. I **won-**

**dered** [past] how a dog could be trained to know when to get off the bus, when to cross the street, and when to wait for a signal. Dogs seem to have more sense than some humans.

### Pacing a narrative

Because it moves through a time sequence, narration presents some problems not found in description. Foremost among these is the problem of pacing. Whether a series of events that you are narrating covers three years, three weeks, or three hours, you cannot reproduce the entire sequence— nor should you want to, for much of the time in any sequence of events is filled with action that has no particular bearing on the experience you are relating. The problem is to pace the telling of your story so that thorough attention goes to the significant actions and less attention to actions that have less immediate impact for your narrative.

If you study any example of effective narrative writing you will see, as Professor Rockas has noted, a balance of "remote" narration and "minute" narration. We *do* something just about all the time, but it may be that only a small portion of our doing is directed toward an end that is central to the experience we are trying to preserve in narrative. Still, if the significant actions that warrant narration are to have any context and continuity, they must be seen as part of a continuing stream of events. What you must do, then, is find a way to suggest a considerable amount of time in a relatively short space (remote narration) and so create a context for your slower, more detailed account of the significant actions (minute narration). If you are a reader of comic strips, you will remember that in a strip such as *Steve Canyon* or *Mary Worth* the cartoonist-narrator will occasionally use a picture or two to show the heroes at their regular work; but when some dramatic episode nears its climax, he may use the full strip for several weeks to present a single, climactic action. Similarly in a television program such as *Gunsmoke,* we sometimes get brief glimpses of the hero going about his daily routine, but the dramatic action demands most of the time.

### Including adequate details

If your narrative is to come alive for your reader, you must include enough details to make it interesting and understandable. Avoid any statement that might leave the reader wondering "What?" or "Why?" or "When?" or "Who?" In this paragraph, for example, the narrator fails to tell *what* his teacher said or *why* "the results of the contest were disappointing":

On the night of the final judging, I was so nervous I could hardly move my fingers. As I waited backstage for my turn to appear, I was sure I had forgotten the opening notes of my number completely. I began thinking of ways to escape; maybe I could faint or pretend to be violently ill. But then at the last minute my piano teacher came by to wish me luck and **said something that suddenly changed everything.** When my turn came, I played with ease and confidence. **Although the results of the contest were disappointing,** I was pleased that I had conquered one of my major enemies — stage fright.

In selecting details, choose those that illuminate or enliven significant actions. A narrative should not be loaded down with minute and unimportant details. You can usually make your point and still keep the action moving by selecting two or three lively incidents, as in this example:

Grandmother didn't need reasons for fussing at Grandpa. She told everyone that he wouldn't chop wood or carry water for her. If he did bring wood to her, she would throw it out the window, stick by stick, not caring where it landed. If he brought her water, carrying it from the spring, several hundred feet away, she would pour it out — over him, if possible. Then she would take the empty pail and her cane, and trudge painfully down the long slope to the spring and back again, though it might take her half the morning, the time depending upon her mood and strength. "If I want fresh water, I have to carry it myself, because George is walkin' to Marionville or sittin' on his behind somewhere," she would say to anyone she chanced to see. "And if I want wood, I have to get my boy Jake to come over and chop it for me." — Bertie Johnson, "The Never-Ending Time," *The New Yorker*

See also §26.3, page 401, Continuity in narrative paragraphs.

## Essay examination answers 27.5

Answering an examination question in essay form is similar to writing a short expository or argumentative paper. In studying for the course, you have become familiar with a fairly wide range of information; to answer a specific question you must recall the relevant material, organize it, and present it in essay form.

# Reading the questions

Because most examinations have a time limit, students often begin writing feverishly after no more than a glance at the questions. The results of such frantic haste are usually disappointing. You can use the allotted time far more profitably if you take a few minutes at the start to read all the questions and directions. If a choice is offered, decide which question you are best prepared to answer and cross out the others. If the questions have different values, plan the amount of time to spend on each: a question worth 10 percent, for example, should not take up 30 percent of your time. Try to save a few minutes at the end to check your answers.

Before beginning to write, be sure to read the question thoroughly. Many answers are unsatisfactory simply because students misinterpret or forget the question in their hurry to fill the paper with words. The instructor has deliberately planned the questions to test your knowledge in specific areas; he or she is not asking you to improvise and answer questions of your own making. Examine each question carefully and decide what kind of answer it requires. Don't misread or overlook key words. Notice in the following questions how a change in one word would affect the whole question:

Explain the effect [causes] of the Spanish-American War.
Describe the reproduction [digestion; development] of the frog.
Discuss the structure [sources; significance] of *Moby Dick.*

Since the verb often determines the nature of the answer, take particular care to interpret it properly. Here are some of the verbs instructors commonly use in essay questions.

**analyze:** give main divisions or elements, emphasizing essentials
**classify:** arrange into main classes or divisions
**compare:** point out likenesses
**contrast:** point out differences
**criticize:** give your opinion as to good and bad features
**define:** explain the meaning, distinguish from similar terms
**describe:** name the features in chronological or spatial order
**discuss:** examine in detail
**evaluate:** give your opinion of the value or validity
**explain:** make clear, give reasons for
**illustrate:** give one or more examples of
**interpret:** give the meaning or significance
**justify:** defend, show to be right
**review:** examine on a broad scale
**summarize:** briefly go over the essentials

Exam

27.5

Writing
in and out
of
college
428

To make sure that in writing you do not stray from the question, repeat its key word or words in your opening sentence.

## Writing the answers

Before beginning to write an answer to a question, remember that the instructor expects you to demonstrate *specific* knowledge on the subject. A succession of vague generalities will not be acceptable. Even if you are discussing a fairly broad general topic, support whatever generalizations you make with specific illustrations. Do not omit essential particulars because you assume the *instructor* is familiar with them already; the main purpose of the examination is to find out what knowledge *you* have acquired.

A scratch outline (§18.3, page 247) of the main points you plan to develop in your answer may be useful as a guide in writing. But whether you make an outline or not, make a concentrated effort to set your thoughts down in some logical order: all the sentences should relate to the question asked, and each should lead to the next in an orderly fashion. Many essay answers are unsuccessful because students, although well-informed, present information in a haphazard, unrelated fashion, giving the impression that they are thoroughly confused on the subject. Remember that the *length* of the answer is not the criterion of its worth: choosing the right facts and organizing them sensibly will impress the reader far more. Avoid throwing in unrelated material just to demonstrate your knowledge or to disguise your ignorance of more pertinent information. Since the time you have to write your answer is limited, you should confine yourself strictly to what you know about the specific question asked. Your instructor is not likely to give you much credit for a short essay on the wrong subject, no matter how good it may be.

Examination answers should be written in acceptable general English. Although instructors do not expect an essay written in class to be as fully developed and as polished in style as one written at home, they do expect it to be adequate in grammar, usage, and the mechanics of writing. Even if a paper is otherwise accurate, frequent misspellings do much to lower the reader's opinion of it. Take particular care to spell and use correctly any technical terms or names that have been used in the course: *myosis, mercantile, assize, neurosis, imagery, Lamarck, Malthus, Schopenhauer.* Instructors are understandably disturbed if they think you have paid scant attention to terms you have heard in class and read in the text numerous times. Careful proofreading of the answers will help you eliminate any careless errors you may have made and will also give you a chance to fill in gaps in information.

## Examples of essay answers

Reproduced on the following pages are essay answers in biology, history, and American literature. Read each question carefully, decide what sort of answer is required, and compare the two student answers. Then read the criticisms that follow. The sentences in the answers are numbered to facilitate discussion.

**Question:** Define *dominant* as it is used in genetics.

**Answer A:**
(1) In genetics, dominant is the opposite of recessive. (2) Different characteristics are inherited by the individual by means of genes acquired from the male and female parents. (3) These genes are arranged, or carried, on chromosomes, and are paired, one from each parent. (4) A good deal is still unknown about the behavior of genes, although the science of genetics is making rapid progress. (5) Gregor Mendel, a monk, made discoveries in heredity by doing experiments with sweet peas. (6) He found that certain traits are stronger (dominant) and others are weaker (recessive). (7) Therefore, if two genes carry the same characteristic, one will be dominant over the other. (8) Examples of this are dark eyes, normal color vision, etc.

**Answer B:**
(1) The term *dominant* as used in genetics refers to that situation in which one gene in a pair takes precedence over another in determining a given characteristic in the individual. (2) For example, if a child inherits a gene for blue eyes from one parent and for brown eyes from the other, he will have brown eyes. (3) This is because the brown-eyed gene is *dominant;* the blue is *recessive.* (4) He still carries both genes and may transmit either to his offspring, but one has masked the effect of the other in his physical appearance. (5) Clear dominance does not occur in all pairings, however. (6) Sometimes *mixed dominance* occurs, as in the case of sweet peas, where a cross between a red and a white parent produces pink offspring. (7) Some cases of dominance are *sex-linked;* the gene for color blindness in humans, for instance, is dominant in the male and recessive in the female.

**Exam**

**27.5**

Writing
in and out
of
college
**430**

**Criticism:** Answer A contains irrelevant general information (sentences 2–5) and does not give a clear definition of *dominant*. You cannot explain the meaning of a word simply by naming its opposite (sentence 1). "Stronger" and "weaker" (sentence 6) are poor synonyms because they have such a variety of meanings. The answer also misleads by oversimplification: sentence 7 implies that complete dominance occurs in *all* pairings of genes. It is also not clear to what species of life the two examples in the last sentence (dark eyes and normal color vision) refer.

**Criticism:** Answer B is satisfactory. The term is clearly defined in the first sentence. Sentences 2–4 give an example of its use, distinguish it from its opposite, and add an important qualification. Sentences 5–7 note two important variants in the meaning of the term. There is no irrelevant material.

**Question:** Compare and contrast English and Spanish colonial methods in the New World.

**Answer A:**
(1) The Plymouth colony suffered many hardships in the early years of its existence. (2) This was also true of the Roanoke colony, but it eventually failed and did not survive. (3) The climate was more promising there, but it seemed as if the kind of people it included, like gentlemen unused to work, adventurers, and renegades, did not have the patience and religious fervor of the New England settlers. (4) The same was true of the Spanish colonies in Florida and elsewhere—the climate was good, but the men were selfish and had no direction. (5) The Spanish were more cruel toward the Indians than the English, and there was nothing constructive in their aims.

**Answer B:**
(1) The Spanish generally thought of the New World as a reservoir of riches to be tapped. (2) The great Spanish conquerors, like Cortez and Pizarro, were explorer-adventurers whose main aim was to subjugate the native population and wrench from them whatever riches and power they possessed. (3) The Spanish method was usually to impose a military dictatorship upon a restive populace; the domination depended on military force. (4) The English, on the other hand, thought of the New World colonies as a *permanent* extension of English civilization. (5) Their methods were not to immediately extract native riches, but to plant the seeds of English life in the new continent. (6) Unlike the Spaniards, the English generally emigrated in family units, placated rather than subdued the native inhabitants, invested labor and capital in the

**Criticism:** More than half the answer (sentences 1–3) contrasts *two English colonies* rather than *English and Spanish colonial methods.* Mention of climate in sentences 3 and 4 is also irrelevant to a question dealing with methods. "Selfish" and "had no direction" need further explanation, as do "cruel toward the Indians" and "nothing constructive."

New World soil, and awaited long-term fruits. (7) Settlement was their aim rather than exploitation.

**Criticism:** This answer is much more satisfactory than A. The basic differences in aim and the consequent differences in method are fairly well stated. The first section of the answer (sentences 1–3) describes Spanish methods; the second (sentences 4–7) presents the significant differences in English aim and method.

**Question:** Explain the significance of Walt Whitman's *Leaves of Grass* in the development of American literature.

**Answer A:**

(1) *Leaves of Grass,* by Walt Whitman, was published in 1851, more than a hundred years ago. (2) It was a long personal poem in free verse. (3) At first it did not get a very favorable reaction, although some critics liked it, but today it is widely praised. (4) It was important because

   1) free verse
   2) celebrated America
   3) democratic
   4) realism

(5) Carl Sandburg, in poems like "Chicago," (1920?) writes in the tradition established in *Leaves of Grass.* (6) Among Sandburg's contemporaries were Vachel Lindsay and William Vaughn Moody and Hart Crane. (7) *Leaves of Grass* brought new freedom to American poetry because it broke from many of the old traditions in poetry like that of Longfellow and Whittier. (8) Therefore, it is truly significant.

**Answer B:**

(1) Although Whitman's *Leaves of Grass* has many characteristics of nineteenth-century Romantic literature, it is an important landmark in American literature. (2) At a time when American poetry was rigidly conventional in meter and rhyme, Whitman boldly experimented with varying line lengths and free verse. (3) In subject matter, too, *Leaves of Grass* explored new frontiers. (4) A disciple of democracy and modern technology, Whitman made frequent reference to common trades and people, machinery and the less savory details of urban life: all considered "low" subjects unfit for poetry by such traditionalists as Longfellow and Whittier. (5) In his choice of such subjects and in the frankness with which he discussed human behavior, Whitman was preparing the way for the Realistic movement which was to emerge toward the close of the century. (6) Twentieth-century celebrants of industrial America like Sandburg and Hart Crane were poetic descendants of Whit-

**Exam**

**27.5**

Writing
in and out
of
college
**432**

**Criticism:** Sentences 1–3 and 6 do not specifically relate to the question. The heart of the answer seems to be sentence 4, but the unexplained list of headings conveys nothing. If these points are important, each should be developed in a separate sentence or two. Sentences 5 and 7 also seem to be relevant but are vague. *What* tradition did *Leaves of Grass* establish? *What* old traditions did it break? Was "Chicago" written in 1920 or not?

man; even today, poets like Allen Ginsberg are indebted to Whitman in style and attitude.

**Criticism:** In this essay the points merely listed in A are developed and made specific. The relation of the poem to both earlier and later poetic traditions is explained. All sentences are relevant and are well related to each other.

## Reports 27.6

The various kinds of reports you will be asked to prepare in school or on a job may require special forms of presentation, but the problems of gathering, organizing, and developing materials for reports are about the same as for expository papers. Usually the assignment of a report will define your subject for you and suggest the kind of resources you will need. For example, if a committee of the Student Congress wants to propose changes in the campus rules concerning dormitories, it may first ask a member of the committee to prepare a report on how the problem has been handled at other colleges and universities. Thus, the member's task is clearly defined: he or she must accumulate statements of policy regarding dormitories from the catalogs and guidebooks of other schools and then give an impartial account of his or her findings to the rest of the committee.

Usually the subject of a report will determine how you should approach your audience. Some reports, such as sales reports and progress reports, can appropriately include opinions, but most call for a straightforward presentation of factual information.

Rpt

27.6

## Class reports

The oral or written reports you may be asked to prepare for some of your classes are not drastically different from committee reports and other work you may do outside school. Ordinarily the purpose of a report is to bring before an audience (a class, a committee, one's employer) information that it might not receive otherwise. Class reports are often intended to acquaint class members with a book, an experiment, a field experience, or some other kind of information that is important to them but which they do not have time or opportunity to gather for themselves. In courses that you take in school, teachers will often tell you what they want in a report; reports required in work are often prepared according to plans determined by particular companies and employers. If you must prepare a report either in school or out, and if you've been given no specified form for the report, you may want to try one or the other of the general report schemes discussed below.

If the purpose of your report is to bring information to a class or to some other group, here is a fairly typical plan for a report:

1) An introduction explaining the topic and setting the limits to your report so that your audience will know what the report is about and can clearly understand that the report does *not* include related and associated matters

2) A brief note on the sources of your information

3) A chronological presentation of any background material; this should enable your audience to see what connection your report has to their work

4) A passage identifying the main point you wish to make, or the most important information, and any contributing points

5) A discussion of each minor point

6) A discussion of your major point

7) A conclusion discussing the pertinence of your report to the work your audience is engaged in

If the purpose of your report is not to bring information but to test some idea your class or group has been working on, or to discover the consequences of some work you have done, this is a workable plan for a report:

1) State the problem (the idea to be tested, the theory to be tried out, the consequences to be explored)

Rpt

27.6

Writing
in and out
of
college
434

2) State your expectations in attempting to solve the problem (what notions you had to start with about what you would discover, what theory you were working under)

3) Explain what material, equipment, or apparatus you used

4) Show what you did, the steps you took to work out the problem

5) Explain what happened; show the results of your work and any conclusions you draw from them

6) Offer any recommendations to the class or group for modifying or strengthening the ideas you were testing

## Laboratory reports

Laboratory reports present information only. Typically, they describe the specific methods used in research as well as the results obtained. Most science courses have a guide that prescribes the form of laboratory reports, as do most companies that depend on laboratory work.

## Briefings and critiques

Ordinarily a *briefing* is intended to prepare a group of people to do a particular piece of work; a *critique* is an evaluation of the work once it has been done. These types of reports are becoming increasingly important because of the trend in most institutions to involve more and more people in planning and decision-making. A briefing and a critique might typically follow these patterns:

**Briefing:**
A brief introductory account of the circumstances bringing you together (a program, a project, a piece of work to be done)

A brief account of the origin, nature, and goals of the program

A brief account of the various separate programs and goals that form the total program

An account of the goals of each specific part of the program

An account of how each of the specific programs integrates with the others

A presentation of the schedule that must be followed

A conclusion reiterating the importance of each separate program to the whole program

**Critique:**
An introduction discussing the success or failure of the program as a whole

An evaluation of each of the separate programs, with criticism of their accomplishments and suggestions for future programs

An evaluation of the whole program, with recommendations for change or shifted emphasis in the future

An evaluation of practical planning, schedules, deadlines, with recommendations for change if necessary

A summary of the achievements of the program

Rpt

**27.6**

In your college English courses you will often be asked to write about literature—to examine, interpret, and discuss fiction, poetry, drama. Literary analysis and interpretation is not radically different from the close reading and interpretive writing you might do in history, philosophy, and sociology courses or from your critical response to an editorial, magazine article, sermon, or letter to the editor. We read editorials, presumably, not just to discover the overt statements they make, but also to discover the writers' motivations, the choices and assumptions they have made in selecting and presenting their material, the values they have expressed and those they have implied through the connotative impact of their words. In much the same manner, we can examine a piece of literature critically and sort out our thoughts about it in order to understand it more fully.

Still, writing about literature is sometimes troublesome. You may sometimes find yourself thinking that "It's all a bunch of symbols and hidden meanings." You may sometimes feel that writing about literature requires a more specialized language and more advanced knowledge than you have. If an assignment calls for you to write an interpretive essay on a poem or story or play, and if you feel hopeless, or if you feel that "tearing a story or poem apart to analyze it spoils the story or poem," it may help if you remember some simple things.

First, a story or a poem or a play is someone's words, and they've been waiting, perhaps for generations, for you, an audience. Someone from out there in time and space is speaking to you. He may be hard to understand; he may say something you can't respond to easily; he may say something you can't accept. But you *can* understand, and the speaker who is sending his words to you deserves some of your time.

Second, curiosity may be a better guide to literary analysis than having a double handful of literary terms memorized. If, over a period of a couple of days you see four or five strange cars pull up for a visit at your neighbor's house, and you notice that they sometimes leave hurriedly after a short visit, and you accidentally notice that lights have been on late into the night, and if your neighbor hurries over to your house, hands

**Lit**

**27.7**

Writing
in and out
of
college
**436**

you the keys to his house, and calls back over his shoulder as he is trotting away, "Can you watch the house a couple of days, you know, bring in the mail and stuff—I'll talk to you when I get back," if all of that happens, your mind doesn't stand still. It starts racing around as you try to imagine for yourself what has happened. You recollect what you've seen, you remember things he's said in conversations earlier, you try to discern the meaning in these strange events. Often, in fact, you create a whole scenario in your mind—and it's often erroneous, as your neighbor tells you when he gets back. The point is that your mind races to understand, to imagine, to discern. There's no particular reason why your mind shouldn't be compelled by curiosity, too, when you look at a poem, for example. But you do have to learn to trust your curiosity, to be willing to ask questions: Why these words instead of others that would have served? Why doesn't the poem speak to me directly? Why do things occur in the order in which they occur? Exactly who is speaking to me? Am I meant to be the audience, or am I overhearing some speaker as he speaks to someone in the poem? Why this? And why that? In a conversation with a friend, you'd not hesitate to ask yourself what he really meant to say when he broke a sentence off in the middle—you'd think back to what he had said earlier, remember him as you've known him over the years, and try to piece together what he intended. If you trust your curiosity, you can begin to find your way into a poem, for only the poem will provide answers to questions about the poem.

Third, when your assignment is to write an analytical essay about a piece of writing, unless your instructor has given a very specific assignment, it's all right to seize an interesting point—a puzzling line, a peculiar phrase, a strange incident— and use it as a focal point for your essay. Unless your instructor has specifically called for a particular kind of discussion, you should feel under no obligation to talk about everything in a poem or a play or a story. If something in the work strikes you, set out to learn what you can about it, set out to figure it out.

In answering the questions that come up, or in discussing the points that interest you, use the poem or play or story that has been assigned, not your own experience. It's easy, sometimes, to treat the assigned work as a starting place for talking about similar experiences you've had, similar feelings you have enjoyed or suffered. The text of the work is the proper source of evidence and material. It's usually best, too, to avoid trying to paraphrase the assigned work, converting it to your own language. This may be something you need to do to aid in your own understanding, but don't think of paraphrasing as an end point. When you paraphrase a poem, for example, you're writing translation, not commentary. It's helpful to remember that most human things—including stories, poems, plays, yourself, and your acquaintances—are too complex to be reduced to a simple generalization or maxim or to a "moral of the story." A story or a play, for example, can be read in several ways (remember that different people see you in different ways, too); there's not likely to be a single "right" way to talk about a piece of literature.

## Some questions to start with

Some features of literature provide good questions that may help you get started in exploring a piece of writing. Attempting to answer any one of the questions below may get you sufficiently involved in the writing to be able to see more questions and to understand more of what is going on.

1) Does the *kind* of writing that you are studying give the author a perspective that he or she wouldn't have otherwise? Does it create limitations for the author, or does it offer special advantages? What can a writer do in a poem that can't be done in a short story? What can be done in a play that can't be done in a poem?

2) Who controls what we learn from the literary work? Who is telling the story? Who is speaking in the poem? Is the author speaking, or is it someone else? What difference does it make? Why does the author choose to tell the story, present the poem, or show the drama in that particular way? What distance is there between the author and us, or between the author and the speaker? Whose version of events are we reading?

3) What is the setting? Is it localized and shown in specific detail? If it isn't, why isn't it? What kind of environment do the characters live in? What effect does it have on them?

4) How do we learn about the characters? If a poem is at issue and no characters appear except the speaker, how do we

Lit

27.7

Writing
in and out
of
college
438

learn about him or her? Are the characters revealed by their words, by their actions, by both? What difference does it make? Are they identifiable as individuals, or do they seem to be representative types?

5) How does the author speak to us? What does the author reveal about himself by the way he speaks? If characters speak, do they have distinguishable styles? What do they reveal about themselves? What will the vocabulary tell us about the speaker or speakers? Does the style of the sentences tell anything about the speaker or about the work? What images and figures of speech occur? How do they determine the tone of the work?

6) Why is the work arranged as it is? What part of the structure gets primary attention? What part seems to get the least attention? How is the tempo of the work controlled? When does the author slow down the pace of the work? When is the pace speeded up?

## Some suggestions for writing and literary study

If you have plenty of time for your writing, and if your instructor is willing for you to support and possibly amplify your own critical commentary with material gathered in research, the following classification of types of literary study may help you to focus on a subject when you are planning a paper about a work of literature. This classification is based largely on a list of areas for literary research compiled by Professor B. Bernard Cohen in his *Writing About Literature.*

1) **Textual analysis.** One kind of literary criticism is devoted to a close examination of the text itself—preparation and publication, revisions, errors or misprintings, various editions, and so forth. Part of the meaning of Book III of *Gulliver's Travels* was clarified, for example, with the discovery—some 175 years after initial publication—of a short passage that had been printed in the first edition but had been deleted thereafter. It is unlikely that you will do highly specialized textual research for the papers you are assigned in undergraduate courses, but you can often find a subject in existing textual problems (such as the effect on the meaning of Keats' "Ode on a Grecian Urn" of the punctuation of the last two lines).

2) **Relationships among the author's works.** It is sometimes useful to examine the work in hand by considering it in the

light of the author's other works. For example, it may be possible to understand the manner of *Gulliver's Travels* better by considering it along with ''A Modest Proposal'' and some of Swift's other satires.

3) **Relevance to biography.** Some papers on literary subjects can profitably examine the particular circumstances in the author's life that helped give shape to the work.

4) **Study of the creative process.** If primary sources such as letters and diaries are available, it is possible sometimes to study a given work for what it reveals about the creative process. Why did Swift write the four books of *Gulliver's Travels* in an order other than that in which they are printed?

5) **Relation of the work to literary theory.** It is also possible to develop fruitful explorations of a work by examining it in the light of theories about art and literature current when the work was written.

6) **Impact of the times on the work.** Sometimes it is interesting to approach a work as an artifact, to determine how it records and reflects the ideas and events of its own time.

7) **Relationship of the work to literary tradition.** A work of literature can be studied in terms of the literary habits, assumptions, and techniques the author has inherited from other writers. You might examine *Gulliver's Travels,* for example, to see how Swift adopted, rejected, or refined the techniques of satire that were already in use.

8) **Relationship of the work to a particular subject area.** Sometimes you can find a worthwhile subject for a paper by looking at a literary work for what it reveals about a particular field of interest or idea. You could, for example, increase your understanding of *Gulliver's Travels* and write something of interest about it by focusing on what it says about English politics.

9) **Reception of the work.** You can often learn a great deal about a work by discovering how it was received in its own day or at any later time.

## Letters

Although letter-writing is not ordinarily taught in composition courses, it is one of the most important forms of written

Let

27.8

Writing
in and out
of
college
440

expression. In many situations, letters are the only means you have to make yourself heard. They deserve your best effort.

What you say in a letter and the way you say it will depend upon your purpose, the person you are writing to, and, above all, upon the way you customarily express yourself. Beyond that, you should be familiar with the conventions of correspondence, so that the form and appearance of your letters will make the intended impression. The form established for business letters is standard for most kinds of formal correspondence.

## Business letters

Neatness, clarity, and directness are the chief virtues of a business letter. It should include all relevant information (such as dates, prices, description of merchandise) and should be as brief as possible and still be clear. The tone should be courteous, even if you are complaining about an error.

The sample letter on page 443 illustrates the content and form of a typical business letter. Notice the position and punctuation of the heading, inside address, greeting (salutation), and close.

### Spacing and general appearance

Select stationery of appropriate size and good quality, with envelopes to match. Good stationery costs little more than an inferior grade, and it will make a much better impression on the person who receives your letter. For business letters the standard sheet is $8\frac{1}{2} \times 11$ inches, the same size as ordinary typing paper.

Typed letters are expected in business correspondence, and they are becoming increasingly popular for personal correspondence. In typing your letter, leave generous margins and center the body of the letter so that the page will look well balanced. Space paragraphs distinctly, using either block or indented form. Block paragraphs are set flush with the left margin of the letter; they are separated by a line space, as shown in the sample on page 443. For indented paragraphs, begin five spaces from the left-hand margin. Be consistent in form. If a letter runs to more than one page, use a separate sheet of paper for each page and number the pages at the top.

## The heading

A heading should be typed in the upper right-hand corner, giving the writer's complete address and the date. The standard form is the block pattern, with end punctuation omitted. The name of the city, the state, and the month are generally written out in full:

902 Luther Place
Duluth, Minnesota 55804
January 5, 1975

If you use a letterhead which includes the address, type the date below it, flush with the right-hand margin or centered, depending on the design of the letterhead.

## Inside address and greeting

The inside address of a business letter gives the full name and address of the person or firm to whom it is directed. It appears flush with the left-hand margin, at least one line below the last line of the heading. No punctuation is used at the ends of the lines. If you wish to mention the person's title or position in the firm, put the designation immediately below the name in the inside address:

Mrs. Carolyn McHenry
Personnel Director
Allen, Swift and Company
4863 Commercial Street
Dallas, Texas 75222

The greeting, or *salutation,* appears below the inside address, separated from it by a line of space. In business letters it is followed by a colon. If the letter is addressed to a particular individual in a firm, you may use either the name or an impersonal greeting:

Dear Mr. Keiser: [or Dear Sir:]   Dear Miss Jenkins: [or Dear Madam:]

Until recently it was customary to use the masculine form of address if the letter was addressed to the firm as a whole or to an individual whose name was unknown; this form is still widely used:

Gentlemen:   Dear Sirs:   Dear Sir:

Since the recipient is just as likely to be a woman, however, an acceptable salutation is simply the name of the company or, if appropriate, the title of the individual or department:

Dear Matthews Camera Company:   Dear Editor:

Let

27.8

Writing
in and out
of
college
442

1512 Moore Street
South Bend, Indiana 46556
September 11, 1974

Matthews Camera Company
5412 S. Kenwood Avenue
Chicago, Illinois 60615

Gentlemen:

The Odyssey Camera, Model 2-S, that I ordered from you
(Invoice No. 7343) came yesterday.

In examining it I found that the shutter is stuck fast and
will not open when I push the release. In addition, two of
the lens attachments are scratched and the third does not fit
the camera. I am returning the entire order with this letter
and hope that you will replace it promptly.

Can you tell me when the telephoto attachment for this model
will be available?

Yours very truly,

*Robert St Clair*

Robert St. Clair

## 27.8

### Close and signature
A conventional expression called the *complimentary close* is
used at the end of the letter. Only the first word of the close is
capitalized and a comma customarily follows. The general
tone of the letter will suggest how formal the close should be:

**Formal**
Yours truly,
Yours very truly,
Respectfully yours,

**Less formal**
Sincerely yours,
Sincerely,
Yours sincerely,

The close can be either flush with the left-hand margin or in the middle of the page.

The signature is always written in longhand below the close. For clarity, however, you should type your name below your signature. A woman may indicate her marital status in parentheses if she wishes, but this practice is dying out among businesswomen.

Addressing the envelope

Both the address of the person to whom you are writing and your own address should be clear and complete on the front of the envelope. A block style—with the left-hand margin even—is the standard form for both addresses.

No punctuation is used at the end of the lines in this form. A comma is used between the name of a city and the state if they are put on the same line, but not between the state and the ZIP code: Chicago, Illinois 60611.

```
Stanley Stoga
1421 College Avenue
Iowa City, Iowa 52240




                    Mrs. Carolyn McHenry
                    Personnel Director
                    Allen, Swift and Company
                    4863 Commercial Street
                    Dallas, Texas 75222
```

When you abbreviate street designations, use the standard forms *(St.* for *Street, Ave.* for *Avenue, Blvd.* for *Boulevard)*. For names of states, use only those abbreviations given in your dictionary *(Penn., Okla.)* or the ZIP code directory.

Use an envelope that matches your stationery and fold the letter to fit. With long business envelopes, a standard sheet (8½ × 11 inches) is folded horizontally into three sections. With short business envelopes, it is folded once across the middle and then twice in the other direction.

Let

27.8

Writing
in and out
of
college
444

## Letters of application

Among the more important—and most difficult—kinds of letters that you may have occasion to write are letters of application. When you apply by letter for a job, or perhaps for admission to a school, you are in effect trying to "sell yourself" through your writing. In such situations you may be torn between undue modesty and an understandable desire to present yourself in the most favorable light. The best thing to do is to express yourself simply and sincerely, to give all pertinent information, and to put your letter in attractive and suitable form. A sample letter of application is shown below.

The form of most letters of application—the heading, spacing, close, and so on—follows that of a typical business letter. To get the proper arrangement on the page, type an experimental draft of your letter. Before you mail the letter, be particularly careful to check for mechanical errors. A prospective employer will not be favorably impressed if you misspell his or her name or any common words.

```
                                   856 East Oceanside Drive
                                   Los Angeles, California 90016
                                   June 5, 1974



Dr. Hamilton Caine
Director of Research
Roan-Settering Foundation
780 West Augusta Boulevard
Los Angeles, California 90004


Dear Dr. Caine:


Your classified notice in the current Journal of Pathology
states that there is an opening for a bacteriologist on your
staff.  I would like to apply for the position.


I have a B.S. degree in bacteriology from Midwestern
University in Green Bay, Wisconsin, where I graduated in
1972.  I have also attended one summer session at the
University of Chicago, where I took a special seminar in
```

microbiology and statistical techniques. While a student at
Midwestern, I worked for two summers as a part-time
laboratory assistant in the Department of Bacteriology. I
also worked one summer for the late Dr. Joseph Roth at the
Froude Institute in Chicago, helping him prepare the
statistical tables for his recently published <u>Tropical
Diseases</u>. Since October 1972 I have been a bacteriologist
for the Los Angeles Board of Health. I am twenty-four years
old, single, and in good health.

A transcript of my academic work will be supplied on request
by the Registrar at Midwestern University. The following
persons have consented to furnish letters of reference:

> Dr. Donald Fenton, Chairman, Department of Bacteriology,
> Midwestern University, Green Bay, Wisconsin 54312

> Mr. Burton Powers, Froude Institute, 5116 S. Kimbark Avenue,
> Chicago, Illinois 60615

> Dr. George Komer, Los Angeles Board of Health, 212 Vine
> Street, Los Angeles, California 90017

If my qualifications are satisfactory, I would appreciate an
interview at your convenience. My phone number is 267-1927.

                    Yours sincerely,

                    *Mary Helfrich*

                    Mary Helfrich

Give all the information the prospective employer requires
(age, previous experience, education) and any other details
you believe might be useful: why you want the job, what special qualifications you possess, and so on. Be careful, however, that you do not include irrelevant material. A letter that
is brief and to the point will be better received than one that is
long-winded.

1734 Hilltop Road
Hartford, Connecticut 06118
May 16, 1967

Professor Robert Lawson
5142 S. University Avenue
Pittsburgh, Pennsylvania 15007

Dear Professor Lawson:

Since my graduation from the university two years ago I have
been working as a claims adjustor for the Equity Life
Insurance Company here in Hartford. I have found this job
very satisfying and have gained valuable experience from it,
but now I hope to obtain an even better position with a firm
in New Orleans: Williams, Le Sage, and Company. This is one
of the largest accounting firms in the South, and it offers
excellent opportunities for advancement.

The personnel office of Williams, Le Sage has asked me to
obtain several letters of recommendation from persons
familiar with my academic background. Since you were my
advisor and supervised the writing of my Honors paper, I
believe you are particularly well qualified to judge my
abilities. I would be very grateful if you would send a
brief assessment of my work and personal qualifications to
the following address:

Mr. Charles Smith
Personnel Director
Williams, Le Sage, and Company
912 Bourbon Street
New Orleans, Louisiana 70102

I hope to see you and thank you personally when I return to
the campus for the Alumni Weekend next month.

Sincerely,

*John Beasley*

John Beasley

Notice in the sample letter on page 445 that the writer begins by telling what job she is applying for. The body of the letter then lists the writer's previous experience and education, personal data, and references. In closing she suggests a personal interview and tells where she can be reached.

Always ask the permission of people you list as references. Give their complete addresses and correct titles (Professor, Dr., Mrs.). *Mr., Mrs., Ms.,* and *Dr.* are the only titles that are abbreviated. All others are written in full.

If you are asked to include documents (such as photographs, transcripts of academic records, or photostats), use a crushproof envelope. If you want the enclosures returned to you, include a self-addressed, stamped envelope.

Keep a carbon copy of your letter. If you don't get the job, study the letter and try to improve on it next time.

## Letters requesting recommendations

Some employers may ask you to supply letters of recommendation from former teachers or employers. Like application letters, requests for recommendations should be brief and courteous. Notice that in the sample letter on page 447 the writer begins by telling his former professor why he needs the recommendation. He then explains what kind of information the company requires and where the letter should be sent. He closes with an expression of personal gratitude. In writing such requests, be sure to remind the teacher or employer when you were his student or employee and where (which class or company department). It is difficult for a person to write a useful recommendation if he only vaguely remembers the writer.

## Letters to editors and public figures

People in a democratic society often wish to express their opinions to newspapers, magazines, or influential public figures. Such communications should be written in standard business letter form and should be brief and pointed. Even if you are expressing disagreement with some opinion or policy, try to be reasonable and courteous. Your letter is much more likely to have the desired effect if it relies on facts and logic than if it presents an impassioned subjective reaction. Formal greetings and closings are usual in these letters.

Consult the appropriate section of a dictionary or an eti-

Let

**27.8**

Writing
in and out
of
college
**448**

quette book for the proper forms of address for senators, cabinet members, and other high government officials.

## Personal correspondence

The types of correspondence discussed in the preceding sections present the major letter-writing problems for students. The form and manner of expression are crucial in making a favorable impression on a distant person or on an impersonal business organization. Other types of letters and notes, especially those written to friends, are easier to compose.

Familiar correspondence is like conversation between friends: the tone is cordial and relaxed, the form less rigid than in other types of letters. This does not mean, however, that letters written to friends should be sloppy; they should be neat and legible as well as interesting. Taking some pains with the appearance of a letter and with such matters as spelling and punctuation is a courtesy you owe the reader. Revising an occasional personal letter will perhaps raise the level of all your correspondence.

Whether you should type a personal letter or write it in longhand depends upon the purpose of the letter and the person to whom you are writing. Typing is appropriate for many kinds of personal correspondence, but handwriting is always better for invitations and replies and for letters that convey sentiment or sympathy.

No heading except the date is needed between regular correspondents, but it never hurts to include your address in the heading, particularly when you write someone infrequently. The envelope with your return address is often discarded long before your letter is answered.

The greeting between friends is usually *Dear Bob* or *Dear Ruth,* followed by a comma. If you are writing to an older person, someone you do not call by first name, either of these forms will serve (the colon is more formal):

Dear Miss Clark,     Dear Professor Brown:

The complimentary close ranges in warmth from *Love,* through *Yours* and *Sincerely,* to *Yours very truly* for persons whom you know only slightly.

Consult an etiquette book for the established forms used in issuing and replying to formal social invitations and announcements.

*For it may be laid down as a maxim that he who begins by presuming on his own sense has ended his studies as soon as he has commenced them.* — *Joshua Reynolds,* Discourses on Art

Anything you write *may* require some research. Unless your instructor expressly says not to use library materials (if, for example, the instructor particularly wants to see how you arrange your own thoughts without external assistance), the whole library, as well as other resources, is available to you whenever you write anything. One of the decisions you make in thinking out any paper is whether or not you know enough already to handle the subject, or whether or not the subject requires more than you already know. If you don't know enough, if the subject requires treatment that you can't give, then any assignment may become a research assignment.

Often, however, the planning and writing of a reference paper (also called a library paper, a research paper, or a term paper) is a separate and special part of freshman composition courses. The preparation of a reference paper has much in common with other writing assignments, but in addition it provides:

1) Practice in exploring the possibilities of a subject and limiting it so that it can be treated adequately in a paper longer than those you will customarily write; reference papers may often range from 1500 to 3000 words.

2) An introduction to the resources of the library and training in the most efficient ways of locating information.

3) Practice in using source material intelligently — choosing between what is useful and what is not, evaluating the ideas of others, organizing and interpreting the information.

4) Acquaintance with documentation and manuscript form typically expected in academic work and in reports and papers prepared for publication.

5) An opportunity to learn something new about a subject and to gain specialized, thorough knowledge of it. Because the reference paper is longer and more complex than most other compositions you may be asked to write, we discuss it here in successive steps: choosing a topic (§28.1), locating appropriate source materials (§28.2), preparing the working bibliography (§28.3), taking notes (§28.4), evaluating your

material (§28.5), planning the paper (§28.6), writing and revising the first draft (§28.7), documenting the paper (§28.8), and assembling the completed paper (§28.9). The actual task of preparing a reference paper, however, can seldom be divided into such neat categories. The steps overlap and certain operations must be repeated as work progresses. For example, as you get into your reading you may decide that your chosen topic needs to be modified; and as you write your paper you may discover gaps in your information that must be filled in by further reading. The best advice, perhaps, is to start on the assignment early and to take particular care in choosing and defining your topic, so that both your research and your writing will have a clear focus.

## Choosing a topic                                      28.1

One important prerequisite for writing a good reference paper is that you should have a genuine interest in the subject you are going to investigate. In some courses, the subject field may be limited by the instructor's general assignment (perhaps to various aspects of the United Nations, or to the history of a specific geographic area, or to an author or work of literature you have studied); but more often the choice of a subject will be left up to you.

In either instance, you should be reasonably certain that the specific topic you select will be one that you will like to read about, to think about, and then to write about. Since a reference paper may take as much as five or six weeks to prepare, it can easily become a chore—and be largely a waste of time—unless you feel that what you are doing is of some interest and importance. The suggestions in §18.1, Finding and exploring what you have to say, are as relevant to the reference paper as they are to other kinds of writing.

### Choosing a subject area

Before making a definite decision on your topic, consider your various interests in and out of school. These general subjects may suggest particular topics that you might want to investigate:

1) A subject related to one of the courses that you are now

taking or that you intend to take. For example, if you are going to major in business administration and you intend to take American economic history next year, you might investigate the beginning of child labor laws or early life insurance companies in the United States.

2) A subject related to your reading interests (biography, history, science fiction, detective stories) or one related to your favorite hobby or sport (music, dress design, mountain climbing, baseball).

3) A subject about which you now have an opinion but little actual information. Does capital punishment help prevent crime? Are children with high IQ's generally successful in later life? Do rapid readers retain more than slow readers?

4) A subject that has aroused your curiosity but that you have never had time or opportunity to investigate. Of what value are computers in education today? Do sun spots actually affect the weather? How has the popularity of television affected book sales?

It is easier to find a purpose and keep it before you if you select a topic that ties in with one of your current interests.

Limiting the topic

As soon as you know what general subject area you would like to concentrate on, find a specific topic within that area that can be treated adequately and profitably in a paper of the assigned length. Keep these considerations in mind when you are narrowing your topic:

1) **Length of the reference paper.** A freshman reference paper is not expected to be the last word on a topic; neither is it intended to be a disconnected listing of commonplace facts or a superficial summary of a complex topic. Limit your topic enough so that your treatment of it can be reasonably thorough. The danger of selecting a topic that is too narrow is far less than the danger of choosing one that is too broad and lacks focus. (See §18.1, page 231, Examining a situation for possible subjects.)

2) **Availability of source material.** Before you begin to read and take notes, find out whether the more important books and periodicals that you will need are available in your college library. Since half-a-dozen or more sources are usually required for a reference paper, you should be certain that enough material is available before you begin your research.

Ref

28.1

The
reference
paper
452

3) **Complexity of the source material.** For some subjects (chemical structures of synthetic rubber, for example), the available material may be too technical for a general reader to understand—and perhaps too complicated for you to interpret without a good deal of study.

If you have only a hazy notion about the approach you might take to the general subject you have selected, explore its possibilities by spending a few hours doing some preliminary background reading in one or more general or special encyclopedias, in some magazine articles, and perhaps in some newspaper articles, if the subject you have chosen is one of current interest and likely to be covered by the daily press.

Next, look through the library card catalog and the guides to periodical literature (§28.2) to see how the general subject you have selected may be broken down into smaller units. A broad subject like *aviation* might first be limited to *commercial aviation,* then to *the functions of the CAB,* and then still further to *recent safety measures suggested by the CAB.*

## Final definition of the topic

Before you begin to take notes, define your topic as precisely and clearly as possible. At this early stage in your planning, you are not expected to make a final statement of the central or controlling idea of your paper; but if you have decided to write on *rural electrification,* for example, you should certainly know whether you intend to discuss *the progress of rural electrification in the South* or *changes in farming methods brought about by electricity.* Unless you have a reasonably accurate idea of what the focus of your paper will be, your reading will be without direction and a great deal of the material you gather may later have to be discarded as useless. It is a good idea to check your topic with your instructor before you begin your research.

Avoid drastic last-minute changes in your topic unless it has proved completely unsuitable. A sudden switch, two or three weeks after the paper has been assigned, wastes precious time and usually indicates that the original topic was chosen without enough thought.

It is often advisable, however, to make minor changes in a topic. As you are gathering and evaluating your material, you may decide that you should narrow your topic further or shift its emphasis slightly, perhaps changing *the process of making oil paints* to *sources of pigments for oil paints.* Consult your instructor about any changes you would like to make in your topic before you continue extensive reading.

## Locating appropriate source materials        **28.2**

One purpose of the reference paper is to acquaint you with the resources of your college library so that you can locate the information you need quickly and efficiently. On most subjects, the material in the library is so extensive and so varied in form (books, periodicals, encyclopedias, newspapers, pamphlets) that to keep from being hopelessly lost you need to know something about the essential works in your subject, the methods used to index and catalog material, and the quickest way to obtain this information.

This section deals with library facilities and the various aids that will help you find the material for a reference paper. Librarians are always willing to help students with their research problems, but every student should also be willing to help the librarians, too, by showing some knowledge of the standard sources of reference.

### The library card catalog

The card catalog is an alphabetical card index of the items in the library. The cards, filed in drawers or trays, are located in the main reading room or other central spot. Most card catalogs, in addition to listing all books in the library, give the titles of periodicals (and indicate what copies the library has), encyclopedias, government publications, and other works.

Almost all books are listed in three places in the card catalog of most libraries, alphabetized by author, by subject, and by title. The cards issued by the Library of Congress, like those reproduced on page 457 for *The Great Films* by Bosley Crowther, are almost universally used for cataloging.

You can save yourself many hours of thumbing through books that are not relevant to your subject by learning to interpret and evaluate the information given in the card catalog. The subject card reproduced on page 457, for example, in-

Ref

**28.2**

The
reference
paper
**454**

cludes the following information (keyed to the circled numbers on the card):

1) **Subject.** The subject heading on the catalog card tells in general what the book is about. In this instance, the general subject is movie history. Also listed on the card (in item 7) are the other subject headings under which the book is cataloged.

2) **Call number.** The call number in the upper left-hand corner tells where the book is located in the library. In most libraries, borrowers obtain books by filling out a slip with the call number, author, title, and the borrower's name and address. If you have access to the stacks, the call number will enable you to locate the book you are looking for.

3) **Author's name.** If you are already familiar with the subject you are investigating, the author's name may tell you whether the book is likely to be authoritative.

4) **Title and facts of publication.** The date of publication is sometimes an important clue to the usefulness of a book. For example, if you are looking for more information on very contemporary films, you will not waste time examining this book.

5) **Number of pages, illustrations, height.** The number of pages in the book suggests how extensive its coverage is. This book is of medium length—258 pages of text. Notice, however, that it contains illustrations that may be useful. (The indication of height—29 cm.—is for librarians.)

6) **Special information.** The catalog card indicates that the book contains a bibliography that might prove helpful in directing you to other sources. None of the books listed, however, would be later than 1967, the year in which this particular book was published.

7) **Other subject headings.** The list of other subject headings under which the book is cataloged may provide a further clue to its content. The subject headings for this book show that it is concerned with the history of motion pictures but also has material about movie plots and themes.

8) **Facts for librarians.** The information at the bottom of the catalog card—such as the Library of Congress classification (PN1997.8.C7)—is generally for the use of librarians.

See §28.3, page 461, Preparing the working bibliography, to see what information from the library catalog card should be included on your own bibliography card.

## Trade bibliographies

The bibliographies published for booksellers and librarians should be consulted to locate books that are not listed in the card catalog of your library or to learn if a book is still in print. The most important trade bibliographies are:

*Books in Print.* New York, 1948–date. A listing by author and by title of books included in *Publisher's Trade List Annual* (New York, 1847–date), which lists—by publisher—all books currently in print.

*Cumulative Book Index.* New York, 1900–date. Gives complete publication data on all books published in the English language, listing them by author and by title. Published monthly, with cumulative volumes issued periodically.

*Paperbound Books in Print.* New York, 1955–date. Especially useful since some important books are available *only* in paperback. Published monthly, with cumulative volumes issued three times a year.

*Subject Guide to Books in Print.* New York, 1957–date. An invaluable index to the titles listed in *Books in Print*.

## Periodical indexes

A great deal of essential material, particularly on current topics, is available only in periodicals, which may range from popular magazines and newspapers to technical journals and learned publications. This material is cataloged in various guides and indexes, some of them published monthly, others annually. Knowing how to use periodical indexes will not only simplify the task of research but will also enable you to make your reference paper more authoritative and up-to-date.

*Readers' Guide*

The most generally useful of all periodical guides is the *Readers' Guide to Periodical Literature* (New York, 1900–date), which indexes the articles in more than 120 magazines of general interest. It is published monthly in paperbound volumes which are afterwards gathered in large cumulative volumes covering a year or more.

The entries in the *Readers' Guide* are listed alphabetically both by subject and by author. The abbreviations used in the listings—for the titles of periodicals, the month of publication, and various facts about the article itself—are explained on the first page of each volume. On page 458 is a reproduction and explanation of five consecutive main entries from a monthly issue.

Ref

28.2

The
reference
paper
456

**Subject card**

```
           1 MOVING-PICTURES - HIST.
  2 791.43
    C953g  Crowther, Bosley. 3
        4     The great films; fifty golden years of motion pictures.
              New York, Putnam ₁1967₎
        5     258 p.  illus.  29 cm.
        6     Bibliography : p. 253.


        7     1. Moving-pictures—Plots, themes, etc.  2. Moving-pictures—Hist.
              I. Title.

        8   PN1997.8.C7  1967          791.43'09          67—30265

            Library of Congress        ₁68r5₎
```

**Author card**

```
  791.43
  C953g  Crowther, Bosley.
              The great films; fifty golden years of motion pictures.
              New York, Putnam ₁1967₎
              258 p.  illus.  29 cm.
              Bibliography : p. 253.
```

**Title card**

```
              The great films; fifty golden years
  791.43                  of motion pictures.
  C953g  Crowther, Bosley.
              The great films; fifty golden years of motion pictures.
              New York, Putnam ₁1967₎
              258 p.  illus.  29 cm.
              Bibliography : p. 253.
```

## Other periodical indexes

In locating sources for a reference paper you may find it useful to refer to one of the specialized periodical indexes listed below. Most of them appear annually; the year after the title shows when publication began. The indexes are listed alphabetically.

*Applied Science and Technology Index.* New York, 1913–date. Subject index to periodicals on science, technology, and related subjects.

*Art Index.* New York, 1929–date. Author and subject index for fine-arts periodicals and museum bulletins.

*Bibliographic Index: A Cumulative Bibliography of Bibliographies.* New York, 1938–date.

Ref

28.2

Locating
appropriate
source
materials
457

## Sample entries from the *Readers' Guide*

(1) **FROZEN fish.** See Fish, Frozen.
(2) **FROZEN food.** See Food, Frozen
(3) **FRUIT culture**
    Tree fruits. G. L. Slate. il Horticulture 52:26 – 7+ Mr. '74
(4) **FRYE, John**
    Oil, super-ships & the oceans. il Oceans 7:48 – 55 Ja '74
(5) **FUEL**
    Converting garbage into energy. il Bus W p42+ Mr 30 '74
    Energy crisis; life in a Canadian wilderness. E. Kotzwinkle
      and W. Kotzwinkle. Mademoiselle 78:64+ Mr '74
    Fossil fuels. D. E. Thomsen. il Sci N 105:76 – 7 F 2 '74
    Garbage power. Time 103:26 Mr 18 '74
    Power from trash. W. C. Kasper. il Environment 16:34 – 8 Mr
      '74
    Pyrolysis; refuse as fuel. Archit Forum 140:16 Ja '74

Reprinted From *Readers' Guide to Periodical Literature*, Vol. 74, No. 6 (May 10, 1974). New York: H. W. Wilson Co., 1974, p. 114.

**Explanation:** Entries like (1) and (2) that are followed by *See* are cross-references to subjects listed elsewhere in the *Guide*.

Entry (3) is a *subject* entry. Only one article about "Fruit Culture" is listed: that's an *illustrated* (il) article titled "Tree fruits" by G. L. Slate in volume 52 of *Horticulture* (March 1974). It begins on pages 26 and 27 and is continued elsewhere in the issue. (The number before the colon refers to the volume of the periodical; the number after the colon refers to the page. If there is no volume number, only page numbers are given: p42+.)

Entry (4) is an *author* entry. John Frye is the author of the article titled "Oil, Super-ships, and the Oceans" in volume 7 of *Oceans* (January 1974), pages 48 – 55.

"Fuel" (5), a subject entry, is followed by a list of titles of articles on this subject found in various magazines issued during the period this particular *Readers' Guide* covers. These titles and the other information that follows are often useful in determining whether an article may be helpful or not in gathering material for a reference paper. A quick glance will show that most of the articles here are about converting garbage to fuel.

Ref

28.2

The
reference
paper
458

**Biography Index: A Cumulative Index to Biographical Material in Books and Magazines.** New York, 1946/47 – date.

**Book Review Digest.** New York, 1905 – date. Author, subject, and title index to published book reviews; gives extracts and exact references to sources.

**Business Periodicals Index.** New York, 1958 – date. Subject index to periodicals on all phases of business, including particular industries and trades.

**Catholic Periodical Index: A Guide to Catholic Magazines.** Scranton, Pa., 1930 – date.

**Dramatic Index.** Boston, 1909 – 1949. Index to articles and illustrations concerning the American and English theater.

**The Education Index.** New York, 1929 – 1964. Author and subject index for educational periodicals, books, and pamphlets.

**Poole's Index to Periodical Literature.** Boston, 1802 – 1881. Subject index to American and English periodicals, many of which are no longer published but are still important; supplements cover the years 1882 – 1906; precedes coverage of **Readers' Guide.**

**Public Affairs Information Service.** New York, 1915 – date. Subject index to books, periodicals, pamphlets, and other material on economics, government, and other public affairs.

**Social Sciences and Humanities Index.** New York, 1907 – date. Author and subject index to periodicals from various countries; devoted chiefly to the humanities and social sciences; formerly titled **International Index to Periodicals;** supplements **Readers' Guide.**

**United States Government Publications Monthly Catalog.** Washington, D.C., 1895 – date. Lists various publications of the government in all fields.

## Directory of periodicals

*Ulrich's International Periodical Directory* (14th ed., 1971 – 1972) answers the question "What periodicals are available in this field?" It classifies both American and foreign periodicals by subject area and also tells which periodical indexes cover them. At the start of volume I is a list of publications devoted primarily to abstracting articles in different fields. Volume II includes a list of periodicals that have begun publication since the last edition, as well as those no longer published. Editions of *Ulrich's* before 1967 (it was first published in 1932) do not include foreign periodicals.

## Newspaper index

*The New York Times Index* (New York, 1913 – date) is a monthly index to articles appearing in *The New York Times,* with annual volumes. This index will help you find articles of general interest in local papers as well as in the *Times,* because it gives the dates of events, speeches, and important documents that presumably would be covered in all papers of the same date.

### Pamphlet index

The *Vertical File Index: A Subject and Title Index to Selected Pamphlet Material* (New York, 1932/35–date) describes each pamphlet listed, tells how to purchase it, and lists the price.

### General encyclopedias

The following general encyclopedias are authoritative and include many bibliographies and cross-references. All are regularly revised; several are supplemented annually with yearbooks.

**Chambers's Encyclopaedia.** New rev. ed. 15 vols. New York: Oxford Univ. Press, 1967. Volume 15 contains a general index.

**Collier's Encyclopedia.** 24 vols. New York: Collier, 1965. Volume 24 contains a general index and bibliography. Supplemented annually.

**Columbia Encyclopedia.** New York: Columbia Univ. Press, 1963. A single-volume encyclopedia, but remarkably useful.

**Encyclopaedia Britannica.** Chicago: Encyclopaedia Britannica, Inc., 1972. 24 vols. Volume 24 contains a general index. Supplemented annually. An entirely new edition, in a new format, was published in 1974.

**Encyclopedia Americana.** New York: Encyclopedia Americana, 1963. Volume 30 contains a general index. Supplemented annually.

### Special reference works and encyclopedias

Many subject areas, from art to science, are covered by reference works that go into more detail than general encyclopedias, and their coverage is more specialized. You should be able to find most of these by browsing in the reference room of your library. The librarian will also be able to tell you what reference works exist for your area of interest.

### Yearbooks and annuals

The following annuals provide up-to-date facts and figures on a wide variety of subjects, particularly those of current interest.

**The Americana Annual: An Encyclopedia of Current Events.** New York: Americana Corporation, 1923–date. Annual supplement to the *Encyclopedia Americana* with a chronology of events of the preceding year.

**Britannica Book of the Year.** Chicago: Encyclopaedia Britannica, 1938–date. Annual supplement to the *Encyclopaedia Britannica*, with cumulative index.

**Ref**

**28.2**

The
reference
paper
**460**

*Collier's Year Book.* New York: Crowell-Collier, 1939–date. Annual supplement to *Collier's Encyclopedia.*

*Information Please Almanac.* New York: Simon & Schuster, 1947–date.

*Social Work Year Book.* New York: National Association of Social Workers, 1929–date. Biennially since 1929; social work and related fields.

*The Statesman's Year-Book: Statistical and Historical Annual of the States of the World, 1864–.* London: Macmillan, 1864–date. Covers historical and statistical events throughout the world.

*The World Almanac and Book of Facts.* New York: World-Telegram, 1868–date. This is one general reference that any student can afford to own, and one that anyone with a serious interest in current affairs can hardly afford to be without. The index is in the front of each volume.

*Yearbook of the United Nations.* Lake Success, N.Y.: United Nations, 1947–date. Activities of the United Nations.

## Guides to reference materials

Many other specialized reference works can be found by consulting the following guides:

Barton, Mary N., comp. *Reference Books: A Brief Guide for Students and Other Users of the Library.* 7th ed. Baltimore: Enoch Pratt Free Library, 1970.

Murphey, Robert W. *How and Where to Look It Up.* New York: McGraw-Hill, 1958.

*The Reader's Adviser: An Annotated Guide to the Best in Print in Literature, Biographies, Dictionaries, Encyclopedias, Bibles, Classics, Drama, Poetry, Fiction, Science, Philosophy, Travel, History.* Rev. and enl. by Hester R. Hoffman. 11th ed. New York: Bowker, 1968.

Shores, Louis. *Basic Reference Sources: An Introduction to Materials and Methods.* Chicago: American Library Association, 1954.

Walford, Arthur J., ed. *Guide to Reference Material.* London: Library Association, 1959. Supplement, 1963.

Winchell, Constance M. *Guide to Reference Books.* 8th ed. Chicago: American Library Association, 1967. Supplements, 1965–66 and 1967–68.

## Preparing the working bibliography    28.3

A working bibliography is a list—on note cards—of the books, magazine articles, and other published works that you intend to consult when gathering material for your reference paper. The number of references you should collect will depend on the nature of the assignment, but it is always best to begin with more than you will probably need. If your working bibliography includes only a bare minimum of sources, you will probably have to take time later to find more: a book you want from the library may already be out on loan; one article on your list may prove to be too technical; another may merely repeat material you have already collected.

Whether your initial bibliography contains many sources or relatively few, you will probably want to add others as you get into your research and find new avenues you want to explore.

Each entry in your working bibliography should be written on a separate card. Use either a 3 x 5-inch or 4 x 6-inch card or a slip of paper. Cards are sturdier and easier to work with than odd slips of paper. With only one reference on each, they can be rearranged quickly for alphabetizing; new ones can be inserted in the proper places and useless ones discarded. (You may want to use 3 x 5 cards for the working bibliography and 4 x 6 cards for taking notes, since the larger cards will obviously hold more data and will also be readily distinguishable from your bibliography cards.)

Bibliography cards for different types of references are illustrated on page 468. Each card should include all the facts you will need to identify the reference and obtain it from the library. It should also have all the information you will need in preparing the final bibliography. The punctuation suggested here is a standard form for bibliographies:

1) **Author's name,** with the last name first (followed by a period). If the book is edited, use the editor's name (followed by a comma), followed by *ed.* If the article or pamphlet is unsigned, write the title first on the card.

2) **Title** of the book (underlined and followed by a comma) or of the article (in quotation marks and followed by a comma).

3) **Facts of publication:**

   a) **For a book:** the place of publication (followed by a colon), the name of the publisher (followed by a comma), and the date (followed by a period). Former practice often left out the publisher's name, and usage is still divided. However, unless you are told otherwise, it's always safe to include it.

   b) **For a magazine article:** the name of the magazine (underlined and followed by a comma), the date of the issue (followed by a comma), and the pages covered by the article (preceded by *pp.* and followed by a period).

   d) **For a newspaper article:** the name of the newspaper

Ref

28.3

The
reference
paper
462

(underlined and followed by a comma), the date (followed by a comma), the page on which the story appeared (followed by a period). The column number may be added after the page number (separated from it by a comma).

4) **Library call number,** or the location of a reference work in the library. This information, placed in the upper left-hand corner, should be written just as it appears in the card catalog, so that you can relocate the reference if the need arises. See also §28.9, page 485, The final bibliography.

## Taking notes 28.4

Accurate and full notes are essential for writing a good reference paper. You can save time when taking notes if you approach the problem efficiently. Don't try to take down everything you read; instead, spend a little time looking over the book, the article, or the pamphlet to see if it contains the information you want. If you have given enough thought to formulating and narrowing your topic, you will have a pretty clear idea of what you are looking for.

When examining a book, look first at the index and the table of contents to see in what sections your subject is treated. See also if there are any tables, graphs, bibliographies, or further references that might be useful. Skim each chapter or article to find out what it covers. Then go over it again carefully, taking down the notes you will need.

Notes should be taken on either 3 x 5-inch or 4 x 6-inch cards so that you can later arrange the material according to the plan of your paper. It is usually a waste of effort to try to take notes in numbered outline form since you probably won't know the final plan of your paper until you have finished your research. What is important is to make each note card accurate, clearly written, and clearly labeled. Each note card should contain these essential parts, as illustrated by the sample cards shown on page 467:

1) The *heading* at the top of the card, showing what material it contains.

2) The *source* (just enough information, usually author and title, to identify it) and *page number,* accurately noted.

3) The *content,* facts or opinions (summarized in your own words or directly quoted) accurately recorded.

Notes that cannot be readily interpreted a week or a month after they have been written are obviously of little use; so too are incomplete or carelessly written notes. You can avoid a good deal of tedious, unnecessary work, including rereading and rechecking, by following these simple rules:

1) Use *one side* of each card only. Your material will then be easier to classify and arrange, and you won't run the risk of overlooking a statement on the back of a card.

2) Include only *one major point* or a few closely related facts from the same source on a single card. If the information is too extensive to write on one side of a card, use two or three cards and number them in sequence.

3) Get all the information accurately the first time you consult a source so that you won't have to make extra trips to the library.

4) Put all *direct quotations* (statements, including single sentences and phrases, that you copy word for word from any published source) in quotation marks. If you omit a word or words in a direct quotation use ellipsis periods (§14.3) to indicate the omission (. . .). If you are paraphrasing the source, state the idea in your own language. (See §28.8, page 476, Plagiarism.)

5) Write your notes legibly in ink (penciled notes may become blurred with frequent handling) so that you won't have to recopy them. When you use abbreviations, be sure that you will know later on what they mean.

It isn't necessary to write out all your notes in complete sentences; practical shortcuts such as the omission of *a, the, was,* and other such words are good for summarizing material. If the method you use for taking notes in lecture courses or on your textbooks has proved successful, use it also for your reference paper.

Accurate notes are one of the chief tools of scholarship. Early and careful practice in taking them is excellent training that may be useful in later college courses and in a great many positions after graduation.

## Evaluating your material 28.5

Since writing a reference paper is in part an exercise in critical judgment, it is important that you learn to evaluate the

Ref

28.5

The
reference
paper
464

sources you use. The statement "I found a book in the library that said . . ." is a confession of uncritical work. It is your responsibility to find and use the most informative books and the most authoritative material available to you.

## Facts to consider in evaluating

Freshmen engaged in writing their first reference papers on unfamiliar subjects are not expected to know offhand that a work by author A is wholly worthless or that author B is considered the foremost authority on the subject. They can, however, arrive at a fairly accurate estimate of their sources by considering these facts:

1) **Date of publication.** If your subject is one for which recent facts are important, see that the sources are up-to-date. The most recent edition of a book or an encyclopedia will generally be more useful and authoritative than an earlier one. (There are, of course, exceptions. Though the most recent edition of *Encyclopaedia Britannica,* for example, would obviously be most up-to-date, the earlier editions are more useful on many literary topics, since the treatments are fuller. Similarly, later editions of *Bartlett's Quotations* have dropped many of the quotes included in earlier editions.)

2) **Completeness.** With magazine articles, it is better to read the original article as it was printed in full instead of a condensation or reprint of it. Similarly, an article in a one-volume encyclopedia that you happen to have at home may not be as thorough or as reliable as one in the *Britannica* or other major reference work.

3) **Facts and opinions.** Distinguish carefully between an author's facts and opinions. Label the opinions "So-and-so thinks that. . . ." In general, pay more attention to *facts* (unless your paper is about various opinions), since you will need facts to support your own opinions.

4) **Objectivity of the source.** A book or an article based in large part upon an author's opinions or biases—particularly when the subject is controversial—should not be used as your sole authority on the matter. Read material on the other side of the question before reaching a conclusion.

When you are in doubt about the reliability of a source, a librarian or your instructor may be able to give you advice. Reviews in the more specialized journals review and evaluate books in their own fields. *Book Review Digest* (New York,

Ref

28.5

Evaluating
your
material
465

1905–date) may also prove helpful. Taking the time to read reviews of books may help you judge their reliability. And, of course, after you have worked a while on your subject, you will be in a better position to evaluate the material yourself.

### Primary and secondary sources

A *primary* source is an original document or a first record of any fact or event. A *secondary* source is another writer's discussion of such material. For example, the Constitution of the United States is a primary source; an article or a book written *about* the Constitution is a secondary source. A scientist's report of his experiments with penicillin therapy in the *Journal of the American Medical Association* is a primary source; a newspaper or magazine comment on these results is a secondary source.

While many undergraduate reference papers must rely heavily on secondary references, you should use primary sources whenever they are available so that you can get as close to the facts as possible and form your own conclusions. In preparing a biographical study, for instance, the actual letters, diaries, and other writings of a person provide excellent material and are often more helpful than the comments someone else has written on them. With other subjects, you may be able to use lecture notes taken in one of your courses, or you can perhaps get first-hand information through personal interviews with persons who are authorities on the matter—college professors, city officials, or other informed people in the field of your investigation.

## Planning the paper                                28.6

The central or controlling purpose of a reference paper should be clear in your mind long before you have finished investigating all your resources. You know, for instance, whether you are trying to reach a conclusion about two opposing viewpoints or whether you are trying to explain an event or situation. When you have gathered a sufficient amount of material to put your topic in focus, it is time to formulate a thesis sentence (§18.1, page 239) that will state your controlling purpose and to outline the order in which you will develop your material.

Ref

28.6

The
reference
paper
466

# Sample note cards

**Direct quote**

Origins of Parliament       Maurois

<u>Hist</u>. <u>of</u> <u>Eng.</u>, 146

"The convoking of the different 'Estates' of a Kingdom (military, priestly and plebian), in order to obtain their consent to taxation, was not peculiar to England in the fourteenth century."

**Summarized material**

Incidence of neurosis among the poor      Harrington

<u>Other</u> <u>Amer.</u>, 119

Though there is a myth that the richer you are the more neurotic you are likely to be, the truth is just the opposite: poor people suffer from mental illness more often than people in any other social class.

**Statistical data**

Enrollment in institutions of higher education (1000's)     <u>Stat</u>. <u>Abstract</u> (1973)   104

| | 1940 | 1950 | 1960 | 1970 | 1971 |
|---|---|---|---|---|---|
| Total | 1708 | 1851 | 2008 | 2525 | 2556 |
| Public | 603 | 641 | 701 | 1060 | 1089 |
| Private | 1105 | 1210 | 1307 | 1465 | 1467 |

Ref

28.6

Planning
the
paper
467

# Sample bibliography cards

**For a book by one author**

> 785.09
> E 94
>
> Ewen, David. *Orchestral Music: Its Story Told Through the Lives and Works of Its Foremost Composers.* New York: Franklin Watts, Inc., 1973.

**For a book, edited**

> 301.451
> L 616
>
> Lerner, Gerda, ed. *Black Women in White America: A Documentary History.* New York: Random House, Pantheon Books, 1972.

**For a signed article in an encyclopedia**

> Reference room shelf 12
>
> Heiberger, Philip. "Paint," *Encyclopedia Britannica* (1972), XVII, 66-70 d.

**For a journal article**

> Periodical desk
>
> Pearsall, Robert Brainard. "The Presiding Tropes of Emily Brontë," *College English*, 27 (January 1966), 266-273.

**For a magazine article**

> 051
> For
> v.90
>
> McQuade, Walter. "Management Problems Enter the Picture at Art Museums," *Fortune*, July 1974, pp. 100-103, 169, 173.

**For an unsigned newspaper article**

> Periodical desk
>
> "Excerpts from Watergate — related evidence," *Chicago Sun-Times*, July 12, 1974, p. 8, Col. 1.

## Examining and arranging your notes

First read through all your notes to refresh your memory and determine the general order in which you will arrange your material. Then arrange the notes in piles, grouping together all the notes on a particular aspect of your subject. The headings at the top of each card will be useful in helping you sort and arrange your material. At this stage you should note any gaps in your material that will have to be filled in with further reading before you start your first draft.

If any of the notes you have taken no longer seem relevant to your purpose in writing, put them aside in a tentative discard pile. Almost anyone engaged in research finds that a good deal of carefully recorded material has to be discarded. Don't succumb to the temptation to include material that has no bearing on your thesis simply because it is interesting or because you worked hard to find it.

## Making a preliminary outline

When you have arranged your note cards to your satisfaction, state the central idea of your paper in a thesis sentence (not in two or more sentences nor in the form of a question). Then make a rough outline showing the order in which you intend to present your material. Each point in the outline should contribute in some way to the development of your central idea or thesis. Often your instructor will want to see your working outline before you go much further with the work. To crystallize your plan and to make it possible for your instructor to examine it and make suggestions, you should follow standard outline form. At this stage a topic outline is generally sufficient; if necessary, you can later expand the entries into complete sentences. (See §18.3, Organizing your material, for a discussion of outlining and outline form.)

Neither your preliminary outline nor your thesis sentence needs to be considered as final. It is better, in fact, to make a reasonably flexible outline so that you can make whatever changes seem desirable as you write and revise your first draft.

## Writing and revising the first draft 28.7

A reference paper should represent your writing at its best—in terms of organization, sentence structure, wording, and emphasis. The most convincing proof that you have actually learned something new from your research is the way you have evaluated, organized, and expressed your material. Instructions concerning the proper form of footnotes (§28.8) and bibliography (§28.9) should be followed to the letter. The paper should be as neat as you can possibly make it, with each part in its proper order and all errors in spelling and punctuation carefully corrected.

## Writing the first draft

Make certain that you are thoroughly familiar with your material before you begin to write. You should have the information on your note cards so well in mind that you can write rapidly and with confidence once you start. For this reason, it is a good idea to review your notes once more just before you begin writing.

This draft should be written in the same way you would write the first draft of any other important assignment (as discussed in §19, Writing the first draft), but with ample room left for documentation. You can leave spaces between the lines or at the bottom of the page to insert the necessary footnotes. Some writers put the documentation in the text of the first draft:

The theory reserved the most desirable characteristics for northern people. Those of the south were pictured as jealous, superstitious, cowardly, lascivious, cruel, and inhuman.[3] Because of this belief, Shakespeare's choice of

_____

[3]Philip Butcher, "Othello's Racial Identity," Shakespeare Quarterly, 3 (July 1952), 246.

_____

Othello as the victim of Iago's plot makes it especially convincing to the audience.

In the first draft, the footnotes may be put all together on a separate page or handled in any other way that will be convenient when you make the final copy.

If a passage seems to need more facts or further documentation, don't interrupt your writing to do the necessary additional research. Put a question mark or some other notation in the margin, continue with your writing, and look up the material after you have finished the first draft.

Ref

28.7

The
reference
paper
470

Most reference papers are written in a rather formal, impersonal style. Usually there's no need to refer to yourself at all, but if you do, the reference should be brief. (It's also better to say "I" rather than use "the writer" or other third-person references.) Remember, however, that impersonal writing does not have to be flat or lifeless. The information itself will provide the interest if you express it clearly and directly.

## Revising the first draft

Revising a reference paper means more than merely putting the footnotes in proper form and order. To do a thorough job—one that will satisfy you as well as your readers—you should examine your paper from these viewpoints:

1) **The material or content.** See if the main parts in your paper relate directly to the central idea. Omit any sentences or passages that are repetitious or irrelevant and, wherever necessary, make your points clearer by additional illustration, either from your own knowledge or from one of your sources. Examine closely every direct quotation (particularly the longer ones) to see whether you might better put the statement in your own words. Check each technical or unfamiliar term: Is the meaning clear from the context or should you define it?

2) **The structure and the expression.** First look at the introduction of your paper to see if it actually gets the subject started quickly or is just an unnecessary preamble. Then consider the transitions between paragraphs, watching for any abrupt shifts in thought or lack of relationship between the main divisions of the paper. Finally, read the conclusion: Is it as definite and emphatic as the facts will permit? After checking the structure, go over the paper carefully to correct all the errors you can find in wording, punctuation, and spelling (pay particular attention to the spelling of proper names and technical terms).

3) **The outline and thesis sentence.** The outline should be an accurate table of contents for your reference paper in its final form. Make certain that it is stated in the way your instructor has requested (either in topics or complete sentences), and that you have followed the conventional numbering system. Generally the first outline, made before the first draft is written, contains too many divisions or misleading and overlapping headings; the central idea (thesis sentence) is also likely

**Ref**

**28.7**

Writing
and revising
the
first draft
**471**

to be vague or inexact. Both should be revised at this point for greater accuracy, following the form described on pages 255–257.

4) **The documentation.** When revising your first draft, you should ask yourself whether you have used too many or too few footnotes. A full page without any references may need further documentation; on the other hand, a great many footnotes on each page may indicate that some of the material could better be combined or rephrased to eliminate unnecessary references. When you are satisfied that your material is properly documented, check the form of each footnote in detail to make certain that it is complete, accurate, and consecutively numbered. Standard footnote form is described in the following section. Be sure to follow any special directions that your instructor may give you regarding the use of abbreviations, punctuation, and similar matters of footnote style.

## Documenting the paper                                    28.8

Any paper based on the writing of others should acknowledge each and every source from which an idea or statement is taken. In a reference paper the acknowledgments are made by footnotes—notes at the bottom of the page (numbered to correspond to numbers in the text) that show exactly where the information was obtained. The method of documentation recommended by most English instructors is described on pages 478–485 and illustrated in the student paper beginning on page 487. (Some style guides for research writing recommend putting all footnotes in proper sequence and numbering them in the usual way at the end of the paper, following the last page of the text and preceding the bibliography. This style should not be followed, however, unless your instructor specifically approves it.)

### Where footnotes are needed

When drawing on the work of another writer or researcher, you owe him or her the courtesy of giving credit where credit is due. You also owe your *readers* the courtesy of providing the sources of your information so that they can judge them for themselves. Failure to document borrowed information is at best carelessness; at worst, it is plagiarism, which means offering material written by someone else as your own work (see page 476). Footnotes are essential in two situations:

1) **After direct quotations.** Each statement taken word for word from a printed source should have a reference number at the end of the quotation and be properly identified in a footnote. The only exceptions to this rule are well-known expressions, such as familiar Biblical quotations ("Blessed are the poor"), famous lines from literature ("Something is rotten in the state of Denmark"), and proverbs ("A bird in the hand is worth two in the bush").

2) **After all important statements of fact or opinion taken from written sources and expressed in your own words.** These include figures, dates, scientific data, descriptions of events and situations about which you have no firsthand knowledge (what happened at a session of the United Nations, how coffee is cultivated in Brazil, the role of Madagascar in World War II, and so on), and all opinions and interpretations that are not actually your own (such as one writer's reasons for the popularity of baseball in the United States, or an opinion on foreign policy from a newspaper editorial).

In some publications, footnotes are also used for comments or additional information that the writer does not wish to include in the text. In freshman reference papers, however, this practice should be kept to a minimum; if a statement is worth making, it usually belongs in the text.

Footnotes are *not* needed for statements that would pass without question. These include obvious facts ("Certain chemicals cannot be used in the preservation of foods in the United States."), matters of common knowledge ("Hiroshima was devastated by an atomic bomb in August 1945."), general statements and expressions of the writer's own opinion ("The medical and biological sciences have made unbelievable progress in the last twenty years.").

The following sections discuss some things to consider in integrating footnoted material into the text of your paper.

## Using direct quotations
In incorporating material from sources into your reference paper, you will often have to decide whether to quote directly or to restate the material in your own words. In general, direct quotations are preferable only in these situations:

Ref

28.8

Documenting
the
paper
473

1) **Interpretations of literary works.** When a statement or opinion in your paper is based on a passage in a poem, essay, short story, novel, or play, quote from the passage so that the reader can see the basis for your interpretation:

The closing passages of *Moby Dick* also suggest that the whale represents some omnipotent force hostile to man. Ishmael says that Moby Dick rushed at the ship with a "predestinating head," and that "retribution, swift vengeance, eternal malice were in his aspect . . . in spite of all mortal man could do."[1]

When you are writing a paper that requires frequent references to a literary work, however, you need to footnote the edition of the text you are using only once, the first time you use a quotation. Thereafter, you may identify quotations by giving (immediately after the quotation, in parentheses) the page numbers for fiction; the line numbers for poetry; the act and scene for drama (followed by the line numbers if the play is in verse):

Man, who once stood at the center of the universe, confident that he was the end of Creation and could claim kinship with the angels, is now—to use the playwright's favorite figure—shrouded in a "mist" that isolates him from God and shuts off all his questioning about the problems of ultimate order. As Webster says of the Cardinal in *The Duchess of Malfi*, Man

> which stood'st like a huge pyramid
> Begun upon a large and ample base,
> Shalt end in a little point, a kind of nothing. (V.v.96–98)

2) **Important statements of information, opinion, or policy.** Whenever the *exact* wording of a statement is crucial in its interpretation, it should be quoted in full:

President Kennedy told Khrushchev that Russia could not expect to spread Communism abroad without opposition: "What your government believes is its own business; what it does in the world is the world's business."[2]

3) **Distinctive phrasing.** If your source states some idea or opinion in a particularly forceful or original way that would be weakened by paraphrasing, quote the exact words:

Russell does not believe that our age lacks great ideas because religion has declined: "We are suffering not from the decay of theological beliefs but from the loss of solitude."[13]

A quotation should be smoothly integrated into the text of your paper. Even though its source is given in a footnote, it should be preceded by some brief introductory remark like "a leading educator recently said that . . ."; "as Edmund Wilson points out . . ."; "an editorial in the *Chicago Tribune* argued that. . . ." If you inject a quotation without explanation, the reader is forced to interrupt his reading by looking for the footnote.

See §14.1, page 180, Quotation marks around quoted material, for a discussion of ways to set up long and short quotations from both prose and verse.

## Paraphrasing

Although a reference paper relies heavily on the writings of others, it should not consist simply of a long string of word-for-word quotations from sources. Like any other paper, it should represent your own characteristic style. Except in the situations described in the preceding section, information from a source should ordinarily be *paraphrased* — restated or summarized in your own words. Otherwise your paper will have a jumbled, patchwork effect that may distract or confuse the reader. Compare the two following passages for effectiveness:

**Too many direct quotations:** Authorities disagree about the dating of these pyramids. Professor Sheldon Muncie says, "The preponderance of evidence collected by investigators in recent years points to a date no earlier than 1300 A.D. for the construction of the lowest level."[1] Professor William Price basically agrees with him: "Bricks of this type were not used in the surrounding areas until the late fourteenth century."[2] But Robert McCall found that "The radiocarbon readings are completely out of line with the standard textbook dates; the original substructure is at least 700 years older than Muncie's earliest estimate."[3]

**Paraphrase:** Authorities disagree about the dating of the pyramids. Professors Sheldon Muncie and William Price concluded, on the basis of the type of brick used and other evidence, that they were begun no earlier than the fourteenth century.[1] But Robert McCall's radiocarbon readings indicate a date earlier than 600 A.D.[2]

The best way to write a smooth paraphrase is to absorb the content of the source passage and then, without looking at it, to write its information down in your own words. When you have finished, you should check it for accuracy and any unconscious borrowing of phrases and sentences. Remember that even though the words are your own, the information or ideas are not; you will still have to use a footnote to identify the source.

## Plagiarism

Most college writers know that copying another's work word for word without giving the author credit is considered plagiarism. But they often assume that this practice is frowned on only when long passages are involved — whole pages or paragraphs. Consequently, they feel free to copy phrases and sentences without using quotation marks and footnotes. Actually, any uncredited use of another's information, ideas, or wording is plagiarism. Under the mistaken notion that they are paraphrasing, students often reproduce sources almost exactly, changing only a word here and there. An honest paraphrase, however, is one in which the *ideas* of the source are stated in the student's *own words*. The examples on the following pages show the difference between genuine paraphrase and plagiarism of source material:

**Original source** (from Alexis de Tocqueville, *Democracy in America,* **I,** 248–249): No political form has hitherto been discovered that is equally favorable to the prosperity and the development of all the classes into which society is divided. These classes continue to form, as it were, so many distinct communities in the same nation; and experience has shown that it is not less dangerous to place the fate of these classes exclusively in the hands of any one of them than it is to make one people the arbiter of the destiny of another. When the rich alone govern, the interest of the poor is always endangered; and when the poor make the laws, that of the rich incurs very serious risks. The advantage of democracy does not consist, therefore, as has sometimes been asserted, in favoring the prosperity of all, but simply in contributing to the well-being of the greatest number.

**Student version A:**

Hitherto no one has found a political form that favors equally the prosperity and development of all the different classes of society. Experience has shown that it is just as dangerous to place the fate of these classes in the hands of one class as to let one nation dictate the destiny of another. Government by the rich endangers the poor; and the poor make laws that often harm the interests of the rich. Therefore, the advantage of democracy does not consist in raising general prosperity, but simply in adding to the well-being of the majority.

**[Plagiarism.** By omitting any reference to De Tocqueville, the writer implies that these ideas are his or her own. In organization the para-

graph follows the source very closely—same order of ideas, same number and structure of sentences. Many of the words and phrases are lifted bodily from the source without quotation marks to indicate that they are not the writer's. In other cases, word order has been simply rearranged and synonyms substituted *(found* for *discovered, nation* for *one people, adding* for *contributing, majority* for *greatest number).*]

**Student version B:**

> De Tocqueville says that no form of government in history has been uniformly beneficial to all classes of society. He maintains that both the rich and the poor, when in control of the government, pass laws favorable to their class and repressive toward the other. According to him, the virtue of a democracy is that it benefits the majority, not that it benefits the whole.[1]

[**Paraphrase.** The writer admits, both in the text and in a footnote, that the ideas in the paragraph are De Tocqueville's. He states them in his own words and does not slavishly follow the source. Quotation marks are unnecessary, since none of the phrases are De Tocqueville's.]

**Original source** (from Lionel Trilling, "F. Scott Fitzgerald," *The Liberal Imagination,* p. 42): Thus, *The Great Gatsby* has its interest as a record of contemporary manners, but this might only have served to date it, did not Fitzgerald take the given moment of history as something more than a mere circumstance, did he not, in the manner of the great French novelists of the nineteenth century, seize the given moment as a moral fact. . . . For Gatsby, divided between power and dream, comes inevitably to stand for America itself.

**Student version A:**

> Of course the one thing that makes The Great Gatsby interesting is its picture of the life of the twenties, but if it were only this it would by now be out of date. Instead, like the great French novelists, Fitzgerald made the particular moment a moral symbol. Gatsby, the main character, divided between power and dream, represents the American dilemma.

[**Plagiarism.** This version does not reproduce the source as closely as version A of the De Tocqueville passage; it more subtly plagiarizes the original. Again, the writer gives no indication that the ideas expressed are not his own. The wording, except for "divided between power and dream," is largely original. The comparison between Fitzgerald and the great French novelists is not original, and implies a critical breadth suspiciously beyond the range of most undergraduate writers.]

**Ref**

**28.8**

Documenting
the
paper
**477**

**Student version B:**

As Lionel Trilling points out, The Great Gatsby is much
more than a record of the manners of the twenties. In
miniature, Gatsby represents America, "divided between power
and dream."[1]

[**Paraphrase.** The writer credits Trilling as the originator of the ideas
he presents. He also puts quotation marks around the one phrase he
uses verbatim.]

## Numbering and Spacing of footnotes

In the text of the paper, the footnote number is placed *at the
end of the quotation or statement* for which the source is being given; it is never placed before the borrowed material.
The number is raised slightly above the line and is placed
outside the end punctuation of the statement to which it refers: ". . . nearly 400,000 in 1953."[13]

Footnotes are generally numbered consecutively throughout
the paper in Arabic numerals beginning with 1. If the last footnote on the first page is numbered 3, the first footnote on the
second page will be numbered 4, and so on. It is impossible
to say how many footnotes should appear in a paper of a giv-
en length because the number varies with the type of subject
and the kind of sources used; however, the typical student
reference paper contains from two to four footnotes on a
page. Studying some footnoted articles or books will help you
see how the system works.

In typed manuscript, footnotes are single spaced (but separated from each other by an extra line of space) and the first
line of each is indented as for a paragraph. It is a good idea to
separate footnotes from the text with a short line extending
about one inch from the left margin, as shown in the sample
paper on pages 487–495.

## Footnote form

Generally, each footnote should contain at least four essential
facts (the information a reader would need to locate the
source): the author's name, the title of the work, the facts of
publication (publisher, place, and date), and the specific page
or pages of the source used.

Practices in footnote form vary, chiefly in punctuation and
kinds of abbreviations. This section follows the form recom-

Ref

**28.8**

The
reference
paper
478

mended by the second edition of the *Style Sheet* of the Modern Language Association (MLA), the form most often used in academic writing. Alternative systems are frequently used in scientific papers (see p. 484). Follow carefully any changes your instructor may want you to make in the form described here.

Footnotes for books

The *first time* you refer to a book in a footnote, put the information in this order, including as much as is relevant in each case:

1) The author's name, first name or initials first: Austin Beard; I. A. Richards

2) When appropriate (as in footnote 5 on page 480), the title of the chapter or section of the book, in quotation marks: "The Conversion of the Anglo-Saxons"

3) The title of the book, underlined (to indicate italics): *A History of England*

4) When appropriate (as in sample footnotes 4 and 6), the name of the editor, compiler, or translator (first name or initials first), preceded by *ed., comp.,* or *trans.:* trans. Hamish Miles

   *Exception:* If the editor's or translator's name is more relevant to your citation than the author's, put that name at the beginning of the footnote, followed by *ed.* or *trans.* The author's name then comes *after* the title: Samuel Butler, trans. *The Iliad,* by Homer

5) When appropriate, the edition number (if other than the first edition) or the series name and number: 3rd ed.; Univ. of Washington Pubs. in Lang. and Lit., XVI

6) The place of publication, the publisher, and the date of publication, in parentheses: (Chicago: University of Chicago Press, 1971)

7) When appropriate (as in sample footnote 3), the volume number, in Roman numerals. But if the volumes were published in different years, the volume number *precedes* the publishing information: Ronald Smith, *Autobiography,* I (New York: Rinehart, 1913), 12

8) The page reference, using the abbreviations *p.* for *page* and *pp.* for *pages.* But if the footnote includes the volume number, the abbreviation *p.* or *pp.* is omitted: I, 80; I (New York: Rinehart, 1913), 12

If part of a reference is included in the text of the paper, it need not be repeated in the footnote. If the author's name is in the text, the footnote begins with the title; if both author and title are in the text, only the publication data and the page reference need be in the footnote. This is sometimes called a *split note.*

Sample footnotes—first reference to a book

Study the sample footnotes given below, noting the order of information and the punctuation: a comma between the author's name and the title; no comma between the title and the opening parenthesis; a colon between the place of publication and the publisher; a comma between the publisher and the date; a comma after the closing parenthesis; a period at the end of the footnote.

[1]Walter Gellhorn, *American Rights: The Constitution in Action* (New York: Macmillan, 1960), p. 178. [one author]

[2]Giles W. Gray and Claude M. Wise, *The Bases of Speech,* 3rd ed. (New York: Harper & Row, 1959), p. 322. [two authors; a revised edition]

[3]Walter Blair and others, *The Literature of the United States,* 3rd ed. (Glenview, Ill.: Scott, Foresman, 1966), I, 80. [more than three authors; a two-volume work, both volumes published in the same year; the Latin abbreviation *et al.* may be used instead of *and others*]

[4]*Letters of Noah Webster,* ed. Harry R. Warfel (New York: Library Publishers, 1954), p. 352. [an edited book]

[5]Harry Levin, "Literature as an Institution," *Literary Opinion in America.* ed. Morton Dauwen Zabel (New York: Harper & Row, 1951), pp. 658–659. [a signed article in an edited book of selections written by various authors]

[6]Paul Valéry, *Monsieur Teste,* trans. Jackson Mathews (New York: Alfred A. Knopf, 1947), p. 47. [a translated book]

[7]*A Manual of Style,* 12th ed. (Chicago: Univ. of Chicago Press, 1969), p. 37. [a book for which no author is given]

[8]David Fowler, *Piers the Plowman,* Univ. of Washington Pubs. in Lang. and Lit., XVI (Seattle, 1961), p. 23. [a book in a series; because the series number is considered part of the title, the abbreviation *p.* is kept before the page reference]

Subsequent references to a book

For subsequent references to the same work that do not immediately follow the original reference, a short form should be used: the author's last name only (if not more than one book by the same writer is being cited) and the page number, thus:

⁹Gellhorn, p. 150.

If two sources by the same author have previously been cited, the short form must also include the title, to make clear which work the note refers to. A shortened form of the title may be used:

¹⁰Gellhorn, *American Rights,* p. 150.

If the book has no author, the title should be used:

¹¹*A Manual of Style,* p. 92.

See page 483 for the use of *ibid.* in footnotes.

Footnotes for magazine and journal articles

The first time you footnote a magazine article, give (1) the author's name, (2) the title of the article, in quotation marks, (3) the name of the magazine, underlined to indicate italics, (4) the date of the publication, and (5) the page or pages. The volume number is used in footnoting an article from a scholarly journal and may also be included for a magazine.

¹²John Pearce, "Kentucky's Quiet Revolution," *Harper's Magazine,* January 1961, p. 45.

When a volume number is used, it is expressed in Arabic numbers and precedes the date (which is then in parentheses). The abbreviation *p.* or *pp.* is omitted if the volume is given:

¹³Ernest W. Kinne, "Reading Improvement for Adults," *College English,* 15 (January 1954), 224–227.

If the author's name is not given, begin the footnote with the title:

¹⁴"The New Old Heidelberg," *Time,* June 9, 1961, p. 49.

Sometimes an issue number (or name of the issue) is needed. It follows the volume number:

¹⁵William Thomson, "Hindemith's Contribution to Music Theory," *Journal of Music Theory,* 9, Spring (1965), 53–55.

Subsequent references to a magazine or journal article may be shortened in the same way as those for books.

Footnotes for encyclopedia articles

These are handled in much the same manner as references to books and magazine articles, except that the volume number, which follows the publication information, is in Roman numerals. When the author's name is given, put it first in the footnote:

Ref

28.8

Documenting the paper

**481**

[16]Donald Culross Peattie, "Trees of North America," *The Encyclopedia Americana* (New York: Encyclopedia Americana, Inc., 1962), XXVII, 36.

If the article is unsigned, begin with the title:

[17]"Rivet" *Encyclopaedia Britannica* (Chicago: Encyclopaedia Britannica, Inc., 1972), XIX, 364.

Notice that the abbreviation *p.* or *pp.* is omitted.

Footnotes for newspaper articles

Unless the article is signed, the reference to a news story consists of the name of the paper, underlined; the date; and the page. The headline is usually omitted, since it may change from edition to edition:

[18]*Chicago Tribune,* June 13, 1974, p. 28.

If the newspaper has sections that are paged separately, the section number should be included. The column number may also be given:

[19]*Chicago Tribune,* Dec. 10, 1974, Sec. 2, p. 4, col. 3.

If the section of the paper has a title, that title should be indicated:

[20]Sanche de Gramont, "Jerusalem: Experiment in Coexistence," *The New York Times Magazine,* July 30, 1967, p. 14.

Footnotes for pamphlets, documents, unpublished material

The form is similar to that for a book, but the footnote may include added identification taken from the title page of the source:

[21]Ella B. Ratcliffe, *Accredited Higher Institutions 1944,* U.S. Office of Education Bulletin 1944, No. 3 (Washington, D.C.: GPO, 1954), pp. 87–88.

[22]Wallace Joseph Smith, "The Fur Trade in Colonial Pennsylvania," Diss. Univ. of Washington 1950, p. 19. [titles of unpublished works—theses and dissertations—are usually enclosed in quotation marks]

As with a book, the citation begins with the title when the author's name is not given:

[23]*Higher Education for American Democracy,* Report of the President's Commission on Higher Education, I (Washington, D.C.: GPO, 1947), 26.

Footnotes for biblical citations

Unless the quotation is very familiar ("Thou shalt not steal"), citations from the Bible should be identified by book, chapter, and verse:

[24]Matthew 6:26–30.

Often the identification is given in parentheses immediately following the quotation instead of in a footnote. Notice that the name of the book is neither underlined nor placed in quotation marks. A colon separates chapter and verse.

## Footnotes for material at second hand
When the material used is taken at second hand from another work, give both the original source and the source from which it was taken:

[25]Ronald Bryden, "Pseudo-Event," *New Statesman,* Oct. 4, 1963, p. 460, in *The Deputy Reader: Studies in Moral Responsibility*, ed. D. B. Schmidt and E. R. Schmidt (Glenview: Scott, Foresman, 1965), p. 78.

## Use of *ibid.* in footnotes
As used in a footnote, the abbreviation *ibid.* (for the Latin *ibidem,* "in the same place") means that the reference is to the same book or article as the preceding footnote. It can be used only to refer to the work listed in the footnote *immediately* preceding:

[26]Margaret Mead, *Blackberry Winter* (New York: Wm. Morrow, 1972), pp. 86–87.
[27]*Ibid.,* p. 93.

When it stands first in a footnote—as it almost always does—*ibid.* is capitalized; because it is an abbreviation, it is always followed by a period. *Ibid.* is not usually italicized, but usage varies; follow the recommendation of your instructor.

The use of *ibid.,* and of Latin abbreviations in general, is decreasing in academic writing. Usually it is just as simple to use a shortened reference to author and title (as illustrated on page 481) as it is to use *ibid.* As a convenience to the reader, a short form of the footnote should always be used instead of *ibid.* for the first footnote on a new page.

## Other abbreviations in footnotes
Standard abbreviations such as those for states *(Menasha, Wis.; Norwood, Mass.)* are commonly used in footnotes (but *New York* rather than *N.Y.* in reference to the city). The following abbreviations may also be used to save space. Follow the recommendation of your instructor about whether to underline those from Latin.

**Ref**

**28.8**

Documenting
the
paper
483

| anon. | anonymous |
| ca. or c. *(circa)* | about a given date *(ca.* 1490) |
| ch., chs. | chapter, chapters |
| col., cols. | column, columns |
| ed. | edited by or edition (2nd ed.) |
| et al. *(et alii)* | and others (used with four or more authors); you may also simply write "and others" |
| e.g. *(exempli gratia)* | for example (preceded and followed by a comma) |
| ibid. *(ibidem)* | in the same place (explained on page 000) |
| i.e. *(id est)* | that is (preceded and followed by a comma) |
| l., ll. | line, lines (in typewritten copy it is better to write these out, to avoid confusion with the figures 1 and 11) |
| MS., MSS. | manuscript, manuscripts |
| n.d. | no date of publication given |
| n.p. | no place of publication given |
| p., pp. | page, pages (the word *page* is never written out in footnotes) |
| rev. | revised edition or revised by |
| sic | thus (placed in brackets after an error in quoted material to show that you are aware of the error; seldom used by contemporary writers) |
| trans. or tr. | translated by |
| vol., vols. | volume, volumes |

## Alternative forms for footnotes

Research papers in the sciences often use systems of reference to sources quite different from the system just described, which is one generally used in the humanities and social sciences. The references have the same purpose—giving the author, title, and facts of publication of articles and books used, to acknowledge the source of materials and to make it possible for a reader to go directly to a source for further information. The details of form vary considerably among the different scientific and technical fields and often among the books and journals within a field. If you are writing a paper for a course in the sciences, you will need to follow your instructor's specification of which system to use or study the form of a particular journal and follow its practice. For more complex systems and variations in footnotes for scientific

Ref

28.8

The
reference
paper
484

fields, see the special guides listed in the sample bibliography, page 486. Whatever system you follow, do not shift from one system to another in your paper: consistency in form is essential in the use of footnotes.

Any description of footnotes makes their use seem much harder than it really is. If you have good notes with the exact sources of the facts clearly recorded, it is relatively simple to keep track of the necessary sources in the first draft and to place them in the final paper in the proper form.

## Assembling the completed paper · 28.9

In preparing the final copy of your research paper, refer to the suggestions given in §20.2, Manuscript form. You will also find it useful to study the sample student paper on pages 487–495. Proofread your final copy carefully before turning it in. A well-researched paper can be seriously marred by careless errors and inconsistencies.

### The final bibliography
The finished reference paper concludes with a bibliography of the sources used in the paper. This is an alphabetic list of all books, magazine articles, or other publications that have been documented in the footnotes. Occasionally it may also include references that you have explored in depth but have not cited directly in your paper. The principal purpose of a bibliography is to help the reader identify the sources you have used.

Your bibliography cards (§28.3) should contain all the information you need to compile the final bibliography. The form for a bibliography (which differs somewhat from footnote form) is illustrated on page 486. Follow these general guidelines:

1) All entries are listed in alphabetical order, by the author's *last name* or, if the author is unknown, by the first *significant* word of the title (disregarding *A* or *The*). When two or more works by the same author are listed, a line of dashes, followed by a period, may be used instead of the author's name for all but the first work.

2) It isn't necessary to give the page numbers you cited in a

book or the number of pages the book contains. You should, however, list the inclusive pages for articles in periodicals or newspapers.

3) Do not separate the list according to kinds of publications. Since the bibliography for most student papers is short, all sources should appear in the same list.

4) Do not number the entries.

Punctuation varies in different bibliography styles, mainly in the use of commas, colons, and parentheses. The form shown here illustrates one style that can be followed without difficulty. Be sure to note carefully any different practices your instructor may want you to follow.

The sample bibliography that follows lists books, articles, and pamphlets on various aspects of writing and documenting research papers:

Bleifuss, William W. "Introducing the Research Paper Through Literature." *College English,* 14 (April 1953), 405–406. [article in a scholarly journal]

Campbell, William G. *Form and Style in Thesis Writing.* Boston: Houghton Mifflin, 1954. [book; one author]

Cooper, Charles W., and Edmund J. Robins. *The Term Paper.* Stanford, Calif.: Stanford Univ. Press, 1934. [two authors; notice that only the first author is listed last name first]

*Handbook for Authors of Papers in the Journals of the American Chemical Society.* Washington, D.C.: American Chemical Society, 1967. [author unknown]

Hilbish, Florence M. A. *The Research Paper.* New York: Bookman Associates, 1952.

Lester, James D. *Writing Research Papers: A Complete Guide.* Glenview, Ill.: Scott, Foresman, 1971.

*A Manual of Style.* 12th ed. Chicago: Univ. of Chicago Press, 1969. [a revised edition]

*Publication Manual of the American Psychological Association.* Rev. ed. Washington, D.C.: American Psychological Association, 1967.

Seeber, Edward D. *A Style Manual for Authors.* Bloomington, Ind.: Indiana Univ. Press, 1965.

——————. *A Style Manual for Students.* Bloomington, Ind.: Indiana Univ. Press, 1964. [second work listed for the same author]

*Style Manual for Biological Journals.* Washington, D.C.: American Institute of Biological Sciences, 1960.

Sypherd, W. O., Alvin M. Fountain, and V. E. Gibbens. *Manual of Technical Writing.* Glenview: Scott, Foresman, 1957. [three authors; for four or more authors, give the name of the first author only, followed by *and others* or *et al.*]

## Final order of contents

The reference paper, usually submitted in a manila folder, should contain all the parts in the order your instructor has assigned. Typically, the completed paper has the following units. Make sure that you include any other material (such as your first outline or first draft) that your instructor asks for.

1) **Title page.** The title of the paper should be centered; your name, the date, the course number, and any other information your instructor requests should be put in the lower right-hand corner, unless your instructor gives you different instructions.

2) **Outline.** Some instructors will expect you to turn in your final outline (topic or sentence outline) and the thesis sentence. The revised outline should correspond to the organization of the final paper.

3) **Text of the paper.** The final copy of the paper, complete with footnotes, charts, and diagrams wherever needed. The numbering of the text usually begins on the second page, with Arabic numerals centered at the top or at the top right-hand corner.

4) **Bibliography.** The final bibliography should follow the last page of the text, starting on a separate page.

This extended explanation may suggest to you that writing a reference paper is an impossible task to accomplish in a mere five or six weeks of work. It isn't. Done carefully, with due attention to each of the stages outlined in this section, it may be accomplished with no more effort than you would put forth for your other courses. And if your reference paper represents your best work, you will find the assignment a satisfying one and good training for later college work.

The following pages present a sample student paper, complete with outline, text, and bibliography. See pages 495–497 for a key to the symbols in the margin of the text.

**Ref**

**28.9**

F. Scott Fitzgerald: Spokesman of the Jazz Age

[A] Thesis sentence: As an honest commentary on his own life and on the era in which he lived, F. Scott Fitzgerald's work represents a valuable contribution to American literature.

I. Fitzgerald grew up with a desire for wealth but also with a poor person's distrust of the rich.

    A. His family was proud of its background but had little money.

    B. He was educated in expensive schools, where he felt at a disadvantage among his rich classmates.

    C. His early feelings about wealth are seen in "The Diamond as Big as the Ritz" and "Winter Dreams."

II. World War I brought optimism, then disillusionment.

    A. Fitzgerald enlisted in 1917 and, while stationed in Alabama, met and became engaged to the beautiful, socially prominent, and spoiled Zelda Sayre.

    B. His hopes for marriage and for a writing career were both temporarily dashed after the war.

III. Fitzgerald's writing and life during the twenties made him a symbol of the Jazz Age.

    A. Publication of This Side of Paradise (1920), a novel of the postwar generation, made him famous overnight.

    B. He married Zelda and plunged into an irresponsible, pleasure-seeking life, first in New York and later in Europe, where the couple's continued extravagances forced him to resort to commercialized writing.

    C. While in Europe he also wrote his best novel, The Great Gatsby, whose hero reflects Fitzgerald's conflicting feelings toward his own life.

IV. The end of the twenties brought a tragic decline in Fitzgerald's personal life and in his literary career.

    A. Zelda had a mental collapse from which she never fully recovered.

    B. Fitzgerald's writing became discredited along with the values of the twenties, and he began a progressive physical and mental decline.

    C. Fitzgerald's disillusionment during this period

Ref

28.9

The
reference
paper
488

is reflected in "Babylon Revisited."

V. Though thoroughly discredited at the time of his
death in 1940, Fitzgerald made a lasting
contribution to American literature.

   A. His works were lyrical presentations of the
ideals of the Jazz Age.

   B. He honestly portrayed a way of life that was
his personal ruin.

C

F. Scott Fitzgerald: Spokesman of the Jazz Age

In the closing lines of This Side of Paradise, the
novel that made him famous overnight, F. Scott Fitzgerald
described his generation as one that had "grown up to
find all gods dead, all wars fought, all faiths in men

D

shaken."[1] With the war over, America was settling back to
Harding "normalcy" with reckless abandon. Money was

E

plentiful, and material pleasures were wantonly pursued.
This was the era of the flapper and the Charleston, of
the raccoon coat and the speakeasy, an era when playing
the stock market was a kind of national Bingo. More than
any other writer, Fitzgerald became the literary
spokesman of the Jazz Age. And, because he embodied so
many of its characteristics himself, his writings were a
chronicle of his personal life as well.

Francis Scott Key Fitzgerald was born in St. Paul,
Minnesota, on September 24, 1896, the only son of Edward
and Mollie McQuillan Fitzgerald. The father was a weak,
pleasant man who had little success in business, and the
family was for the most part supported by a small

F

inheritance of Scott's mother.[2] The Fitzgeralds were
descendants of socially prominent Maryland families; the
McQuillans were among St. Paul's first settlers, and
Scott was brought up to feel he was of aristocratic

---

[1]This Side of Paradise (New York: Charles Scribner's
Sons, 1920), p. 304.

[2]Andrew Turnbull, Scott Fitzgerald (New York: Charles
Scribner's Sons, 1962), p. 18. Unless otherwise noted,
all biographical data on Scott in this paper are from
this source.

stock, regardless of the family's rather straitened circumstances. He attended Newman School, a prestigious Catholic prep school in the East, where he was painfully conscious of being "a poor boy in a rich boys' school."[3] Although he tried hard to win praise, his aggressiveness and occasional unwillingness to conform made him unpopular. As was to be true of him throughout life, he was drawn to the rich at the same time he distrusted them. He once wrote: "I have never been able to forgive the rich for being rich, and it has colored my entire life and works."[4] A story written in 1922, "The Diamond as Big as the Ritz," expresses these early feelings in fantasy form: a young man, spending the holidays with a wealthy schoolmate, learns that the mountain on which the estate is built covers the largest diamond in the world and that he will never be permitted to return to the outside world to betray this fact. And when eventually the secret is revealed, Scott gives a scathing portrayal of a wealthy, sinister tycoon, so corrupt he tries to bribe God in order to keep his secret covered.[5]

Since early childhood, Scott had planned to attend Princeton, traditionally a social, rich boys' school. He twice failed the entrance exams (despite his cheating on his first attempt), and had to talk his way into the school before the Admissions Committee. Once there, he again strove to become accepted, to become part of the world of the rich. Too small for football, he directed his efforts in other directions, and acquired a moderate campus renown by writing musicals for the theatrical Triangle Club. Failing grades and illness forced him to drop out of Princeton in the middle of his junior year, and when he returned the next fall, he found that by dropping out he had lost the Triangle presidency and wasn't even an officer. His interest in school

---------------

[3]Scott Fitzgerald, p. 150.

[4]Ibid.

[5]Babylon Revisited and Other Stories (New York: Charles Scribner's Sons, 1960), pp. 75–113.

I  diminished with this social blow.[6]

When the war came in 1917, he was one of the first to enlist as an officer in the army.  Perhaps, like Dexter Green in the 1922 story "Winter Dreams," Scott "was one of those young thousands who greeted the war with a certain amount of relief, welcoming the liberation from webs of tangled emotion."[7]  While stationed outside Montgomery, Alabama, he met and became engaged to Zelda Sayre, the daughter of an Alabama judge.  Zelda, the quintessential Fitzgerald heroine, was beautiful, restlessly intelligent, and incredibly spoiled.[8]

In 1918, just as Fitzgerald's unit was to sail overseas, the Armistice was signed, and there was no more war.  To Scott's everlasting disappointment and regret, he had missed it.  Discharged in 1919, he optimistically set out for New York to become a famous writer, but had to settle for a ninety-dollar-a-month job in advertising.  Zelda, after some wavering, broke their engagement, and Scott, distraught, went back to St. Paul to work on a novel he had written at Princeton.

The publication in March 1920 of _This Side of Paradise_, a novel about the pleasure-seeking postwar generation, brought Fitzgerald immediate literary and financial success.  Suddenly, popular magazines were clamoring for the short stories they had previously rejected, and money seemed to pour in.  In April, Zelda, having reconsidered Scott's proposal, came to New York to marry him.  At once the couple plunged into the giddy, irresponsible whirl of café society, as if determined to become living symbols of the Jazz Age:

---

[6]F. Scott Fitzgerald, "Pasting It Together," _The Fitzgerald Reader_, ed. Arthur Mizener (New York: Charles Scribner's Sons, 1963), p. 412.

[7]_Babylon Revisited and Other Stories_, p. 133.

[8]Nancy Milford, _Zelda: A Biography_ (New York: Harper & Row, 1970), pp. 7-8.  Unless otherwise noted, all biographical data on Zelda in this paper are from this source.

**Ref**

**28.9**

Sample paper
**491**

They rode down Fifth Avenue on the tops of taxis because it was hot or dove into the fountain at Union Square or tried to undress at the Scandals, or, in sheer delight at the splendor of New York, jumped, dead sober, into the Pulitzer fountain in front of the Plaza. Fitzgerald got in fights with waiters and Zelda danced on people's dinner tables.[9]

Neither Scott nor Zelda knew anything of household or money management. During the early twenties, Scott's annual income ranged between $20,000 and $30,000, but practically the entire amount was squandered, leaving Scott with his old feelings of financial insecurity. His letters to his editor, Maxwell Perkins, reveal a pattern of constant requests for more money.[10] Finally, in 1924, he and Zelda and their daughter, Scottie, moved to Europe, where expenses were lower. But Paris and the Riviera were as drunk with spending as America, and Fitzgerald was forced to interrupt work on his novels—which he considered his real work—to turn out what he called "trash": commercialized writing to pay off a mounting pile of bills. Now that he was on the money merry-go-round, he found it impossible to get off.

During his stay in Europe, Fitzgerald also wrote what is generally considered his finest work, The Great Gatsby. The hero of this novel, a tragic victim of romantic illusions, in many ways resembles Fitzgerald. Born James Gatz in North Dakota, he seeks association with the rich, apes their manners, and creates the glittering Jay Gatsby from "his Platonic conception of himself."[11] Stationed in the South during the war, he falls in love with Daisy, a wealthy, irresponsible belle, but his poverty stands between them, and Daisy marries Tom Buchanan, a rich profligate. Gatsby is unwilling to

------------

[9]Arthur Mizener, The Far Side of Paradise: A Biography (Boston: Houghton Mifflin Co., 1951), p. 22.

[10]John Kuehl and Jackson R. Bryer, eds., Dear Scott/Dear Max (New York: Charles Scribner's Sons, 1971), pp. 32 passim.

[11]The Great Gatsby (New York: Charles Scribner's Sons, 1953), p. 29.

give up his dream; grown rich through bootlegging and convinced that money can buy anything, he lavishes a fortune in winning Daisy back. But in the end he is destroyed by the "vast carelessness" of the rich and his false dream of "the orgiastic future."[12] As Lionel Trilling points out, Gatsby, "divided between power and dream," represents not only the anomaly in Fitzgerald's character, but in the American character as well.[13]

As the dream world of the twenties abruptly ended with the stock-market crash of 1929, Fitzgerald's own life entered a tragic decline. His life with Zelda had been a stormy one, bounded by heavy drinking, jealousies, and manic behavior. In 1930 Zelda suffered the first of several severe mental breakdowns. Sanitarium and psychiatrist costs added to Scott's worries. His already heavy drinking increased, and his writing output dropped considerably. His income fell to less than half of what it had been in the late twenties as his expenses rose. In addition, both critics and the public, now in the depths of the Depression, turned angrily on the ideals of the orgiastic twenties and everything associated with them. Still in his early thirties, Scott found himself an overnight has-been, as he had once been an overnight success.

The pathos of his life at this period is reflected in one of his own favorite works, "Babylon Revisited," in which the central character, a reformed alcoholic, seeks to regain the custody of his daughter. Returning to Paris after the crash, he finds the gay crowds of the twenties gone, except for a few dissipated cronies. He sees in retrospect the illusory life of his past, where "the snow of twenty-nine wasn't real snow. If you didn't want it to be snow, you just paid some money."[14]

---------

[12]Ibid., pp. 180, 182.

[13]Lionel Trilling, "F. Scott Fitzgerald," _The Liberal Imagination_ (Magnolia, Mass.: Peter Smith, Inc., 1950), p. 251.

[14]_Babylon Revisited and Other Stories_, p. 229.

In 1934, Zelda suffered another breakdown; from then on she spent most of her life in mental hospitals or with her mother. Scott, a year later, suffered his pathetic "crack-up," a complete mental and physical collapse. As he recovered, he realized that he owed his agent and his publisher thousands of dollars, and that he would have to borrow money from friends to send Scottie to school.[15] He spent the rest of his life working to extricate himself from debt by trying to write scripts for movies. When he died in 1940, the obituaries made it clear that most people regarded him as a relic from a discredited age, the leader, as Westbrook Pegler put it, of a "cult of juvenile crying drunks."[16]

But time has eroded this harsh view of Fitzgerald and his works. As his biographer, Andrew Turnbull, notes: "Through his tales ran a lyric beat, a fox-trot, a melody. Fitzgerald was a born romancer and illusionist, whose ever-beautiful, ever-witty people did not exist outside his pages although later they seemed to typify the age."[17] Because Fitzgerald was so deeply committed to the ideals of the twenties, their ruin became his personal ruin; because he portrayed them honestly and unsentimentally, he left a valuable contribution to American literature.

**Ref**

**28.9**

The
reference
paper
**494**

---

[15]Calvin Tomkins, "Living Well Is the Best Revenge," The New Yorker, July 28, 1962, p. 68.

[16]The New York World Tribune, December 26, 1940, in Mizener, Far Side of Paradise, p. xvii.

[17]Scott Fitzgerald, p. 117.

U   Allen, Frederick Lewis. <u>Only Yesterday</u>. New York:
     Harper & Row, 1957.
Fitzgerald, F. Scott. <u>Babylon Revisited and Other
     Stories</u>. New York: Charles Scribner's Sons, 1960.

V   ------------. <u>The Great Gatsby</u>. New York: Charles
     Scribner's Sons, 1953.
------------. "Pasting It Together," in <u>The Fitzgerald
     Reader</u>. Ed. Arthur Mizener. New York: Charles
     Scribner's Sons, 1963.
------------. <u>This Side of Paradise</u>. New York: Charles
     Scribner's Sons, 1920.
Kuehl, John, and Jackson R. Bryer, eds. <u>Dear Scott/Dear
     Max</u>. New York: Charles Scribner's Sons, 1971.
Milford, Nancy. <u>Zelda: A Biography</u>. New York: Harper
     & Row, 1970.
Mizener, Arthur. <u>The Far Side of Paradise: A Biography</u>.
     Boston: Houghton Mifflin Co., 1951.
Tomkins, Calvin. "Living Well Is the Best Revenge." <u>The
     New Yorker</u>, 28 July, 1962, 31-69.
Trilling, Lionel. "F. Scott Fitzgerald," in <u>The Liberal
     Imagination</u>. Magnolia, Mass.: Peter Smith, Inc.,
     1950.
Turnbull, Andrew. <u>Scott Fitzgerald</u>. New York: Charles
     Scribner's Sons, 1962.

## Key to symbols

A   The thesis sentence shows clearly the direction this paper will take. The careful formulation of a thesis statement helps a writer to keep the focus on a central idea and to avoid the temptation of introducing irrelevant material. (A consideration of Fitzgerald's literary technique, for example, would probably contribute nothing to the support of this writer's thesis.)

B   This sentence outline follows standard outline form and, like the thesis sentence, focuses on the development of a central idea.

C   Although the title of the paper has been given at the start of the outline, it should be repeated on the first page of the text.

**Ref**

**28.9**

**D** Direct quotation. Since the author's name is given in the text, it need not be repeated in the footnote. The title of the source, also mentioned in the text, might similarly be omitted, but its inclusion makes the note immediately clear.

**E** General information requiring no footnote.

**F** Biographical information from a specific source, requiring a footnote. The covering statement at the end of footnote 2 eliminates the need for further footnoting of simple biographical data.

**G** Summary of a short story. Since the author and title are given in the text, both may be omitted from the footnote. Thus, footnote 5 begins with the name of the collection in which the story can be found.

**H** This biographical information is covered by the comprehensive footnote on page 1; no footnote is required here.

**I** Biographical information from a source other than *Scott Fitzgerald* and therefore requiring a footnote.

Direct quotation from a newly cited short story, with title given in the text. Since footnotes 5 and 7 refer to the same collection of short stories by the same author, the writer doesn't need to document the source completely; the title of the book (or even a shortened form) is enough.

**K** Biographical information about Zelda Fitzgerald from a new source needs complete documentation.

**L** A long quotation set off by indention and single spacing, with no quotation marks.

**M** *Passim* means "here and there throughout the work." This is appropriate here because it refers to something that is obviously repeated in various letters.

**N** A direct quotation from a novel. It is necessary to include the novel's title in footnote 11 so that the source of the actual quotation will be absolutely clear; the author, however, is adequately identified in the context of the paper.

**O** Direct quotations from two different pages in the novel cited immediately above. The writer might have used a shortened reference instead of ibid.: *The Great Gatsby,* pp. 180, 182.

**P** Direct quotation and paraphrase of critical judgment. (A footnote would be necessary for the paraphrase even if the direct quotation had not been used.) Although the author's name is given in the text, it is repeated in the footnote to show that Trilling is author of the entire work *(The Liberal Imagination)* as well as the particular essay cited.

Q  Direct quotation from a short story, with author and title made clear in the text. A shortened note form is used because there have been previous references to the collection.

R  Direct quotation from a newspaper article quoted in a book. The original source of the quotation is given in full, but a shortened form is used for the secondary source, which has been previously cited (footnote 9).

S  Direct quotation, with the author's name but not the title given in the text.

T  This bibliography follows the style recommended in *The MLA Style Sheet,* Second Edition.

U  Source not cited in a footnote but used for background reading.

V  Several works by the same author, alphabetized by title (disregarding *The, A,* or *An*). A line, followed by a period, is substituted for the author's name for all but the first work.

Ref

28.9

# Index

This index lists words, phrases, and affixes discussed in the text as well as general topics. In looking up a particular point of usage (use of *shall* or *will*, agreement with *one of those who*, choice of *good* or *well*), look first under the individual word or phrase.

Page references in **boldface** refer to the most important discussions of a topic. The page numbers of appropriate exercises are listed in *italics* after the other references.

**A**

*A, an,* when to use, 95
*A while, awhile,* 198
Abbreviations, 151, 152, **217–221**; *ex. 224–225;* academic degrees, 217; addresses, 218, 444; appropriateness of, 217; capitalization of, 208, 221; dates, 218; explanation of, first time used, 219; in footnotes, 479–483, **483–484;** measurement, expressions of, 219; names of organizations, 151–152, 218; names of persons, 217–218; place names, 218–219, 444, 483; punctuation of, 151–152, **221,** 484; scientific and technical words, 219; titles, 217–218; trade names, 219
*-able, -ible,* spelling changes with, 199–201; words formed with, 201
*Able to,* for *can,* 128
Absolute modifiers, 74 (table), 77–78; *ex. 78*
Absolute use of the comparative degree, 142
Absolute words, comparison of, 143
Abstractions, capitalization of, 210
Abstract words, defined and illustrated, 90 (table), 316, **324–325;** effective and ineffective use of, **325–328;** *ex. 331*
Academic degrees, 164, 217
Accent, shown in dictionaries, 305
*Accept, except,* 198, 321
*Accordingly,* 43, 56

Accusative case. *See* Objective case *and* Objects.
Acknowledgment of borrowed material, 412–413, **472–485.** *See also* Bibliography *and* Footnotes.
Acronyms, 218
*Act,* as a linking verb, 36
Action, in narrative, 401, 423–428; verbs indicating, 115
Active voice, defined, 117 (table), 126; uses of, 126–127; of verbals, 74 (table)
*A.D., B.C.,* 220
*Adapt, adopt,* 321
Addresses, envelope form, 444; letter headings, 442; punctuation of, 164, 442–444; street numbers, 223, 444; ZIP codes, 444
Adjective clauses, 42, **61–62;** *ex. 69; and* or *but* misused before, 62; connectives used with, 61–62, 66; defined and illustrated, 61–62; misused as sentences, 53; restrictive and nonrestrictive, 158–159, 166–167. *See also* Subordination.
Adjectives, 38, 40 (table), **133–136, 141–145;** *ex. 146–148;* comparison of, **141–144,** 143–145; compound, hyphen with, **211–212;** coordinate, 66, 162–163; degrees of, 141–143; demonstrative, 136; in description, 421; forms of, compared to adverbs, 136, 141–142; functions of, 39, 40 (table), 133–136; modified by other elements, 39, 134; position of, 38, 134–136; predicate adjectives, 36, **135–136;** proper, capitalized,

two words or phrases, omission of comma with, 166; misused before *who* or *which,* 62; repetition of, in a series, 363; semicolon in place of, 169–170

*And which, and who,* 62

Anglicized words, 188

Announcements, formal, 449

Annuals and yearbooks, 460–461

Answers, omission of verb in, 46

Answers for essay examinations, 427–433

*-ant, -ent,* 201

Antecedent, agreement of pronoun with, 103–106; *ex. 112–114;* clear reference of pronoun to, 99–103; *ex. 112–114*

Anticipating subjects (expletives), 37, 85–86

Antonyms, 310, 323; *ex. 313*

*Any, anybody, anyone,* agreement with, 104–105; masculine or feminine pronoun used to refer to, 102–103; possessive form of, 109

*Anyone else,* possessive form of, 109

Apologetic quotation marks, 183, 338

Apology, avoidance of, in beginnings and endings, 274, 277

Apostrophe, 214–215; in contractions, 214–215; in dates, 215; for letters dropped in representing speech, 215; misused with possessive pronouns, **108–109,** 215; for plurals of letters and figures, 215; for possessive of nouns, **93–94,** 214–215; for possessive of some indefinite pronouns, 109

*Apparatus,* plural forms, 91

*Appear,* as linking verb, 36, 135

*Appendix,* plural forms, 91

Application letters, 444–448

Applied science, reference works in, 457

Appositional sentence, 47

Appositives, defined, 39; gerunds and gerund phrases as, 74; noun clauses as, 64; punctuation of, 159–160

Arabic numerals, 224; for footnotes, 479–481; for numbering manuscript, 287, 487; for outline subheads, 254. *See also* Numbers.

Archaic words, 202, 309, 340

*Are, aren't, ain't,* 122

*Argue, arguing, argument,* 199

Argumentation, 388–389, **413–420;** argument from analogy, 416; argument from authority, 416; argument from consequence, 416; argument from nature, 415; fallacies in logic, 418–420; finding an arguable proposition, 414; testing the argument, 418–420; use of details, 388–389; use of evidence, 414–415

*Argumentum ad hominem,* 419–420

*Arise,* principal parts of, 120

Arrangement of material. *See* Development of ideas *and* Outlining.

*Arrive, arrival,* 199

Art, reference sources in, 457

Articles *(a, an, the),* capitalization of, in titles, 286–287; choice of *a* or *an,* 95; disregarded in alphabetizing, 458, 497; use of *the* to introduce a gerund phrase, 73

*As,* adverb clauses introduced by, 63, 66–67; inexactness of, 66–67; or *like* to introduce comparisons, 145; similes introduced by, 346

*As . . . as,* construction of double comparisons with, 145

*As, as if, as though,* to introduce clauses of comparison, 145

*As long as,* introducing adverb clauses, 63

*As well as,* agreement with subjects joined by, 82

Asides, parenthetical, 176–177

choice of personal pronoun,
109–112; defined and
classified, 98, 101 (table);
demonstrative, 101 (table),
102; indefinite, 101 (table),
104–106, 109; intensive, 110;
interrogative, 101 (table);
masculine/feminine, 103;
number of, **103–106;**
paragraph continuity through
use of, 398; personal, 101
(table), 102, **103–104,
106–112;** possessive, 101
(table), 108–109, 215;
reference of, **99–103;**
reflexive, 110; relative, 42,
101 (table). 102, 108, 109;
repetition of, for continuity,
398; shift in person or number
of, 112; subject or object
form, 72, 106–107
Pronunciation, dictionary as a
guide to, 305, 308; *ex. 312;*
divided usage in, 305, 308; of
homonyms, 193, 197–198,
321; spelling in relation to,
193, 196–198
Proofreading, 193, 205, 287–288
Proper adjectives, 207–211
Proper nouns, 90 (table);
abbreviations for, 217–218;
capitalization of, 207–211;
prefixes with, 213; as subjects
of gerund phrases, 72
*Prosecute, persecute,* 321
*Prove,* as linking verb, 135;
principal parts of, 121
*Provided that,* introducing
adverb clauses, 63
*Public,* agreement with, 83–84
*Public Affairs Information
Service,* 459
Publication, form of manuscripts
for, 288
Publisher, citation of, in
bibliography, 486; in
footnotes, 479
Punctuation, **150–189;** *ex. 167–
168, 189–191;* abbreviations,
151, 221, 484; addresses and
letter headings, 165, 442–444;
ambiguity corrected by, 163;
bibliographies, 462–463, 485–

486; close or open, 15;
comma faults and fragmentary
sentences corrected by, 52,
55–57; *ex. 59–60;* emphasis
shown by, 159–160, 175–176,
187–188, 379; footnotes, 479–
482. *See also individual marks
listed under* Conventions of
writing.
Purpose, adverb clauses of, 67
Purpose in writing, 231–232.
*See also* Prewriting *and*
Thesis statement.

**Q**

Qualifiers. *See* Modifiers
Qualifying statement, as an
ending to avoid, 277,
378–379
Quantity, agreement of verb with
expressions of, 83
*Quarrel,* forms of, 201
Question marks, 152–153;
position of, with quotes, 184
Questions, 45; agreement of
verb with compound subjects
in, 81; courteous, punctuation
of, 151; direct vs. indirect,
151–152; interrogative
pronouns, 101 (table); inverted
word order of, 37–38;
punctuation of, 152–153; for
sentence variety, 373; *shall*
and *will* in, 125
*Quick, quickly,* 137
*Quiet, quite,* 198
Quotation marks, **179–184;** *ex.
189–191;* apologetic, 183, 338;
double or single, **179,** 181–
182; for emphasis, 380–381;
or italics, for titles, **182, 187,**
287; or italics, for words used
as words, **183,** 187; other
punctuation marks with,
**184–185**
Quotations, acknowledgment of,
473; capitalization of, 206;
comma or colon before, 165,
173; dialog, form and
punctuation of, 180; direct
and indirect, 180, 473–474;
ellipses for omissions in, 186,
464; errors in, marked by *sic,*

**523**

125; idiomatic use of, 123–124, **128–129;** irregular (strong), 117 (table), **119–121** (listed); linking, **36,** 117 (table), 121–122; modifiers of, 38–40, 62–63, 133; mood of, 117 (table), 127–128; number of, 80–86, 117 (table); objects of, 35–36; omission of, 46; position of, 35, **37;** principal parts of, 117 (table), 120–121; regular (weak), 117 (table), 118 (table); *shall* and *will,* 124–125; subjects of, 34–35, 80–86; subjunctive mood of, 117 (table), 127–128; tenses of, **115–119,** 118 (table); terms describing, 117 (table); transitive and intransitive, defined, 117 (table); voice of, 117 (table), **126–127.** *See also* Verbals.

Verse. *See* Poetry.

*Vertebra,* plural forms, 92

*Vertical File Index,* to locate pamphlets, 460

*Viz.,* 188

Vocabulary, methods for increasing, 195, **323–324;** *ex. 331. See also* Diction *and* Dictionaries.
commas with, 161

Vogue words, 339–340

Voice, active and passive, of infinitives, participles, and gerunds, 74; of verbs, 117 (table), **126–127**

Vocative (direct address),

Volume number, in bibliography, 462–463, 486; in footnotes, 479–481

Vowels, changed in irregular verbs (table), 120–121; changed in plurals of special nouns, 89. *See also* Spelling.

*Vs.,* 188

**W**

*Wake,* principal parts of, 121

*Want, want to, want that,* 129

*Was, were,* Standard usage of, 121

**528**   *We, I,* appropriate use of, 110–111

*We, us,* 106–107

Weak connectives. *See* Conjunctive adverbs.

Weak verbs. *See* Regular verbs.

*Wear,* principal parts of, 121

*Webster's Third New International Dictionary,* 302, 308

Weight, expressions of, 219

*Well,* as adjective or adverb, 135; irregular comparison of, 142; as predicate adjective, 135; as weak exclamation, 161

*What,* introducing noun clauses, 63

*Whatever,* introducing noun clauses, 63

*When,* 53–54, 56–57; as exact connective 66–67; introducing adjective clauses, 62; introducing adverb clauses, 63; introducing noun clauses, 63

*Where,* introducing adjective clauses, 62; introducing adverb clauses, 63; introducing noun clauses, 63

*Whether,* introducing noun clauses, 63, 64

*Which,* 42; *and* or *but* misused before, 62; introducing adjective clauses, 53–54, 61; introducing nonrestrictive clauses, 102, 158–159; possessive of, 109; reference of, compared to *who* and *that,* 102

*While,* as exact connective, 66–67; for *at the same time that,* 362; introducing adverb clauses, 53–54, 63, 66–67

*Who, and* or *but* misused before, 62; introducing adjective clauses, 61; introducing nonrestrictive clauses, 102, 158–159; introducing noun clauses, 63; object form of, 108; possessive of, 108–109; reference of, to persons, 102

*Who, whom,* 108

*Who's, whose, of which,* 109

*Why,* introducing adjective clauses, 62; introducing noun

## Correction chart

This list of correction symbols and abbreviations covers the most common errors in writing. The number following the explanation refers to the section to be consulted for information regarding revision.

| | |
|---|---|
| **Ab** | improper abbreviation 17.1 |
| **Abst** | too abstract 22.4 |
| **Adj** | incorrect form of adjective 9 |
| **Adv** | incorrect form of adverb 9, 9.4 |
| **Amb** | ambiguous |
| **Awk** | awkward expression |
| **Big W** | big word or stilted language 23.1 |
| **Cap** | use capital letter 16.1 |
| **Case** | wrong case form of pronoun 7.3 |
| **CF** | comma fault 2.2 |
| **Coh** | lacks coherence (continuity) between paragraphs 19.3 within paragraphs 26.3 |
| **Comp** | mistake in comparison of adjective or adverb 9.7, 9.8 |
| **Dead** | deadwood 24.4 |
| **Dic** | error in diction 22, 23 connotation 22.1 poor figure of speech 23.4 slanted 22.2 stilted 23.1 too abstract 22.4 too informal 23.2 trite 23.3 wrong word 22.3 |
| **Div** | word division 20.2 |
| **DM** | dangling modifier 4.4 |
| **Ec** | economy of expression 24 |
| **Emph** | sentence emphasis 25.4 |

| | |
|---|---|
| **Frag** | fragmentary sentence 2.1 |
| **FS** | fused sentence 2.3 |
| **Gr** | error in grammar 1 |
| **Hyph** | error in use of hyphen 16.2 |
| **Id** | unidiomatic expression 8.5 unidiomatic comparison 9.8 |
| **Inf** | expression too informal 23.2 |
| **Ital** | add italics (underline) 14.4 |
| **lc** | use lower case letter 16.1 |
| **Mix** | mixed construction 2.4 |
| **MM** | misrelated modifier verbal phrase 4.3 adverbial modifier 9.5 |
| **Mng** | meaning not clear |
| **MS** | error in manuscript form 20.2 |
| **No cap** | no capital letter 16.1 |
| **Num** | Use of figures or words for numbers 17.2 |
| **Org** | faulty organization 18.3 |
| **Par, ¶** | paragraph 26 |
| **¶ con** | paragraph continuity 26.3 |
| **¶ dev** | paragraph development 26.1 |
| **Paral** | elements should be parallel in form 25.3 |
| **Parens** | use of parentheses 13.2 |
| **Pass** | ineffective use of passive voice 8.3 |
| **Pl** | incorrect plural form 16.1 |

| | | | |
|---|---|---|---|
| **Pron** | error in pronoun form 7 | **Rest** | error in punctuation of restrictive or nonrestrictive modifier 11.3 |
| **Pron agr** | error in pronoun and antecedent agreement 7.2 | | |
| **Punc** | error in punctuation | **Shift** | shift (inconsistency) in pronoun form 7.5 |
| **No punc** | punctuation should be omitted | | |
| . | period 10.1 | | in tense of verb 8.1 |
| ! | exclamation mark 10.3 | **SL** | sentence length 24.2 |
| ? | question mark 10.2 | **Sp** | spelling error 15 |
| , | comma 11 | **St** | stilted word or expression 23.1 |
| | with coordinate clauses 11.1 | | |
| | after introductory element 11.2 | **Sub** | faulty subordination 3.4, 25.2 |
| | with nonrestrictive modifiers 11.3 | **Subj.-Verb** | |
| | with interrupting elements 11.4 | **Agr** | error in subject-verb agreement 5 |
| | in a list or series 11.5 | **T** | error in use of tense 8.1 |
| | for clarity 11.6 | **Tr** | order should be transposed |
| | conventional use 11.7 | **Trans** | needs better transition 19.3 |
| **No,** | omit comma 11.8 | **Trite** | trite expression 23.3 |
| ; | semicolon 12.1 | | |
| : | colon 12.2 | **Var** | sentence variety 25.1 |
| /—/ | dash 13.1 | | |
| (/) | parentheses 13.2 | **Vb** | error in verb form 8 |
| " | quotation marks 14.1 | **Wdy** | wordy 24.3 |
| [/] | brackets 14.2 | **WW** | wrong word 22.3 |
| /. . ./ | ellipses 14.3 | / / | elements should be parallel in form |
| /=/ | hyphen 16.2 | ⌒ | close up space |
| , | apostrophe 16.3 | # | separate with space |
| | for possessive of nouns 6.2 | ʌ | omission |
| | with possessive pronouns 7.3 | x | careless error |
| **Ref** | reference of pronoun unclear 7.1 | ↙ | good |
| **Rep** | careless repetition 24.5 | | |